Women Artists and

Designers in Europe Since 1800

An Annotated Bibliography

Women Artists and Designers in Europe Since 1800

An Annotated Bibliography

PENNY McCRACKEN

G.K. Hall & Co.
An Imprint of Simon & Schuster Macmillan
New York

Prentice Hall International
London   Mexico City   New Delhi   Singapore   Sydney   Toronto

G.K. Hall Library Reference
An Imprint of Simon & Schuster Macmillan
1633 Broadway
New York, NY 10019

Library of Congress Catalog Card Number: 97–39199

Printed in the United States of America

Printing Number
10 9 8 7 6 5 4 3 2 1

Library of Congress Cataloging-in-Publication Data

McCracken, Penny.
    Women artists and designers in Europe since 1800 : an annotated bibliography / Penny McCracken.
        p.   cm.
    Includes bibliographical references and indexes.
    ISBN 0–8161–0596–0 (v. 1 : alk. paper). — ISBN 0–7838–0087–8 (v. 2 : alk. paper)
    1. Women artists—Europe—Bibliography—Catalogs. 2. Women designers—Europe—Bibliography—Catalogs. I. Title.
Z7963.A75M33 1997
[N6757]
016.704′042—dc21   97–39199
                                                                                      CIP

This paper meets the requirements of ANSI/NISO Z.39.48–1992 (Permanence of Paper).

Contents

Preface

The aim of this bibliography is to provide information about published sources on some of the women artists and designers who have worked in Europe between 1800 and the present day. It represents the beginning of a process which it is hoped will enable and encourage others to undertake further research, particularly in those parts of the European continent that are relatively under-represented here. For the purposes of this study, Europe extends from Ireland in the west to Russia in the east and from Finland to Portugal and Greece. Inevitably it has proved impossible to gain access to certain areas of literature, and insufficient numbers of women are represented in some specialisms as well as those from certain countries. The inequalities are acknowledged and the author hopes that readers will contact her to offer additional material. This is the first bibliography to bring together publications in so many European languages and practitioners in so many specialisms in art and design.

Specialist media initially identified were Ceramics, Glass, Textiles, Design (to include interiors, wallpaper and metalwork) for volume one, with Graphic Art (to include book illustration and printmaking), Painting, Photography, Video and Performance Art, Mixed media and Photography in volume 2. In the course of the research, fashion, bookbinding and garden design emerged as sufficiently interesting to warrant additional sections. The stained glass and garden design sections are small and deserve further research. A surprising number of designers worked across several, sometimes many, specialisms.

It proved impossible to access most of the material by searching under the heading of women artists or designers. Establishing criteria for the inclusion of publications and individuals evolved during the preparation of the first volume. Ideally only those reference publications and catalogues of which over 25 per cent of the contents related to women practitioners would have been included; in practice this was unrealistic as there were too few. Due to the preponderance of women in textiles, for example, this method would also have increased the imbalance between the different specialist media. Instead books and catalogues on all the specialisms were searched for women practitioners and this method allowed a parity of approach for all European countries. Where ten or fewer women were mentioned in a publication, all their names are usually listed in the annotations. The intention again was to promote knowledge of female practitioners. The publications and individuals included are obviously not exhaustive. It is impossible to ensure acquaintance with all publications. One of the inevitable consequences of producing this kind of reference work is the observation that *x* has beeen omitted or that publication *y* is not included. It should be remembered that however thorough one's search, it can only be as good as the information sources; there is also the unpredictable element of luck. Many further years of work would be required to access articles from periodicals past and present across the continent. Work of this kind nevertheless uncovers many more women artists and designers than are commonly known and, even if each occurs in only one publication which I have found, the possibility of further research is made easier.

The bibliography is divided into three main sections: general, those on the specialist media and those on individual practitioners. The general section includes publications which deal with several specialisms or, more rarely, with both art and design. In design, several specialist media frequently appear together in exhibitions. In postwar art, and particularly since the 1970s, the range of techniques and materials used by artists has expanded greatly. As a result a number of recent exhibitions include artists who may be working in many different media including, for example, photography, video, installation, performance and mixed media. Such exhibitions and other publications covering similar fields have been included in the General section. Exhibitions that are confined to two fine art specialisms, most frequently painting and sculpture, have been retained under the first named practice since this often represents the majority of works discussed.

It emerged that there are relatively few publications which cover both art and design. Notable exceptions include the series of catalogues of exhibitions in Paris, which examine the range of artistic production during a particular period in a capital city, among them Moscow, Paris and Berlin. Similarly the series edited by Anne Bony that examines art and design activities organised by decade endeavours to convey a broad picture of the cultural production of a particular period. The General section is also that in which publications on multidisciplinary design movements or groups, most notably the Wiener Werkstätte and the Arts and Crafts movement, have been placed. Individual practitioners of these groups who worked across several specialisms can be found primarily in the Interior Design section.

The sections on the specialist media deal in volume 1 with design media: bookbinding, ceramics, fashion, garden design, glass and stained glass, textiles, and an interior design section which includes the smaller areas of metalwork (excluding publications that only deal with jewelry or silversmithing) wallpaper and furniture design. Industrial design, landscape design and architecture have not been included. Although the years from 1800 were examined, in the design fields it is only in the later nineteenth century that individual designers begin to be identified and more regularly documented. This does not occur consistently either across the design media or geographically. Under the system of ceramic production in Scandinavian countries, for example, the individual designers remained almost anonymous under the name of the factory until the 1950s; conversely some individuals have now emerged from detailed research on the ceramic production of the

Wiener Werkstätte at the beginning of the century. In textile design the identity of individuals appears with any frequency only in the twentieth century. The extent to which women were active in the design media also varies. Not surprisingly they are always in the majority in textile design but a significant number were active in ceramics from the later nineteenth century in several countries.

Volume 2 deals with those specialisms that are in the field of fine art: graphics, mixed media, painting, performance and video, photography and sculpture. Documentation of individuals is well established in fine art by 1800. Individuals who were active for at least the first ten years of the nineteenth century have been included. This is only one of the differences between the literature of art and design. The history of art is a long-established discipline even if its methods, approaches and ideologies have changed fundamentally since 1970. It therefore has well-established reference publications documenting practitioners. Few such reference tools exist in design. Information concerning designers is less accessible and instead the documentation in catalogues has to be utilised. International reference publications in design, the equivalent of Bénézit, for example, do not exist and information about certain countries is difficult to obtain.

Problems inevitably occur as to how an individual should be categorised when they work across specialisms. Where there could be doubt, there are cross references but the short description of the type of work produced by each individual will indicate the sections under which they may be found. A painter who also makes installations will be in the section where her main contribution is judged to lie. In design there were groups of women, those for example associated with the Arts and Crafts Movement, the Glasgow School of Art around 1900 and the Wiener Werkstätte, whose design abilities observed few boundaries. They produced work in five or even more specialist media. In most cases these women have been placed in the Interior Design section, which also includes metalwork, wallpaper design and furniture. Elsewhere, in the case of a designer who works in both glass and ceramics, she will be in the section indicated by the majority of the publications or her main area of activity where this is known. The reader who is uncertain where to find an individual may consult the indices at the end of volume 2.

The debate concerning definitions of art and design could not be addressed in such a book as this. Nevertheless there will undoubtedly be criticism of the designation of glass or textile designers, for example, as designers rather than as artists. This in itself indicates that the status of the two is not seen as equal even today. For reasons of prior classification, almost all workers in ceramics, glass and textiles are referred to in this publication as designers. It is intended as an objective method of enabling readers to locate individuals. No other significance should be attached to the use of these terms. It is in these specialisms that most claim could be made for the title artist for some individuals. There are ceramics designers who sometimes produce sculptural works or figurines and there are also sculptors who work in clay. In such cases the context in which the person worked and exhibited was considered and where this was predominantly with designers, they were so designated. Sonia Delaunay is therefore with the textile designers but this is not to deny her activities as a painter. As far as possible, all the media in which women worked have been indicated in the short description under the name.

Within the textile field there has been considerable debate carried out through a number of the publications included here for much textile work to be considered as art. Mildred Constantine and Jack Lenor Larsen argued the case for this in *The Art Fabric.* Other factors, such as the status of art versus craft and the effect of the traditional association of women with textiles also have to be considered. Parker and Pollock, in *Old Mistresses: Women Art and Ideology,* demonstrated the contradictory claims of artists, designers and critics when dealing with certain types of work in textiles. The case study of Stephanie Bergman showed that the vocabulary of criticism had inbuilt biases about the hierarchy of art and craft. This issue is also dealt with by several writiers in Katy Deepwell's *New Feminist Art Criticism.* The context in which the textile artist/designer operates has been one factor in determining in which section they were placed, provided there was sufficient evidence, but there will undoubtedly be those who disagree with my judgment, and when looking for women working in these areas, readers should consult both volumes.

In considering the range of literature that has been consulted for this publication, it is evident that the levels of review and debate within the design world remain very different from those in art. There are a small number of publications which deal with critical issues rather than simply aesthetic and technical considerations. In Britain the development of the social and critical histories of art has a few parallels in publications in the history of design and this approach is found infrequently in mainland Europe. In France the decorative arts are highly esteemed and are better documented in their historical contexts. The Musée des Arts Décoratifs in Paris has played an invaluable role in the promotion of the history of design. Germany and Austria also have well-established design museums that exhibit both contemporary and historical works. In Scandinavia the emphasis is primarily on design since 1950, and the historical aspects are less well researched. Overall the sociocritical approach appears only rarely. The large majority of reviews of design exhibitions remain on the aesthetic and technical level and do not seek to engage with theoretical issues.

The definitions and parameters of the individual specialist sections should be further clarified, particularly in relation to design. The Bookbinding section includes those who designed, or designed and made, bindings. Individual women are known from the 1870s and many were active from 1910. There was a Guild of Women Bookbinders in Britain that held regular exhibitions of members' work. In France there were a number of outstanding women binders active from the 1920s, including Rose Adler, Germaine de Coster and Hélène Dumas, and there have been many exhibitions of bindings which include their work and that of other French women. Unfortunately in many other countries the literature is often not sufficiently specific about individuals.

The Ceramics section includes both studio pottery and the design of items for industrial manufacture. There are also a number of ceramic decorators who have made a significant contribution to the medium. In some cases it was difficult to decide whether some of the studio potters might also be classified as sculptors, and the description of the designer's activity will refer to both practices. Where they are producing only sculpture, they appear under that section. Only in a few cases do we know who the designers were in major porcelain factories, whether state or private, before the 1920s. Recent work on Sèvres, Staffordshire and Berlin porcelain, for example, has not only published the names of individuals involved but also shown that many women were involved in production from the earliest days in these factories, although further work needs to be done on their precise roles and status. Much work has been done over the last twenty years on the productions of the Wiener Werkstätte and, as a result, much more is known about the activities of the individual designers. Most of them were able to design for a range of media and many designers were women. Scandinavian factories employed relatively small numbers of designers, who might remain with the firm for many years. Their work would only be exhibited under the name of the factory. Nevertheless with the strong tradition in both ceramics and glass in those countries, there were regular exhibitions which gave prominence to the designers. The Glass section similarly includes studio glass and design for industrial production. There is a small number of glass engravers included. As with ceramics, the advent of studio glass led to a focus on the individual rather than the company. Given the strong tradition of Italian glass, there are few identifiable women designers.

The fashion designers included are predominantly French and Italian and active in the twentieth century. Where women designed both textiles and fashion, they tend to be included in the latter category. A few examples of nineteenth-century designers were found, including the Russian Nadejda Lamanova. In some instances, such as that of Jessie Newbery in Glasgow, they also designed textiles.

A distinction has been drawn between garden designers, who are included in this volume, and landscape designers, who are not. This rather fine line is similar to that which has also been drawn between interior designers and architects. In garden design, it has proved difficult to find women other than in the United Kingdom. Nevertheless, given the current interest in this area and the prolific publications of some of the designers, it is a useful selection to include. As in other areas, the author would be pleased to receive any information from mainland European countries.

The Textiles section includes women who designed individual items such as rugs, tapestries and hangings, women who designed fabrics for manufacture for fashion or furnishings, and embroiderers. The development of modern tapestry dates from the early 1960s with the establishment of the Lausanne Tapestry Biennale. This became the showcase for innovative ways of using thread and other materials to produce new effects. Magdalena Abakanowicz was among the early exhibitors but her later work has meant that she is catalogued in sculpture. In other countries, such as Latvia, a strong indigenous textile tradition remained largely untouched by ideological pressures under Soviet rule. Unlike the fine arts, textile designers were able to develop new techniques and imagery; figurative work (often derived from folklore) co-exists with abstract, tactile works.

The section on Interior Design, Furniture, Lighting and Metalwork, has as its rationale the production of objects for domestic settings. Industrial design and design for offices have been excluded, although there are many women active in these fields, especially in Italy and Germany. It was judged that the field is closer to architecture, which has also been omitted. There have been many women active in production of a range of objects for domestic settings from the nineteenth century. In the Arts and Crafts movement in Britain and Ireland, women were engaged in metalwork, enamelling, and designs for mirrors and screens. Similarly the Werkbund and the Wiener Werkstätte in Austria encouraged designs for many decorative domestic objects. In France Eileen Gray and Charlotte Perriand were highly successful designers of interiors and furniture in the modernist style.

The question of nationality has proved more than usually difficult. During the preparation of this work boundaries in Europe underwent major changes. Germany reunited; Czechslovakia became the Czech Republic and Slovakia; the USSR dissolved into the Russian Federation and Yugoslavia underwent the trauma of civil war and the destruction of its national library. I have dealt with these in a pragmatic way. Where artists were born in one country and moved to live in another, both have been given where they are known. The United Kingdom has been separated into its constituent parts and English therefore refers only to that one part of the U.K. Artists from the former Czechoslovakia have all been referred to as Czech since their birth predated the division. Those who were active before the creation of Czechoslovakia may be categorised as Austrian or Czech depending on their place of birth if this was known. A similar problem was experienced with the former Soviet Union. There was also a problem of access to information on activities in the more distant parts of the Russian Federation. Where artists and designers came to Moscow or St. Petersburg, they were more likely to feature in documents but in a few cases their city of origin was not found. From Yugoslavia and Romania information was almost impossible to obtain, although a small number of women are included where they have an international reputation and sources from outside their country could be traced. A determined search of Spanish literature yielded few women artists or designers, the reasons for which are difficult to determine. Material on Greece was also very difficult to find. The author regrets the unevenness in coverage between countries. It is something I have tried to overcome, not always successfully.

In dealing with women in a work such as this, there is the additional problem of their married names. Customs vary across Europe. The U.K. has only relatively recently developed the custom in which women retain their own names after marriage, and the practice observed in much of the rest of Europe of using both names to create a double-barrelled name has not been common here. Up to 1970, the vast majority of British women ceased to use their own names on marriage, a fact which makes tracing their careers more difficult. Where women married more than once, the problem is compounded. In Germany, central European countries and Scandinavia, both names are commonly used although, confusingly, the order may vary. In France, women changed their names in the nineteenth and early twentieth centuries but after the mid-twentieth century they either use both or keep their own name in a professional capacity; this is rarer in Italy. In individual entries, the name by which the artist or designer is best known will dictate the alphabetical listing. Née has been used to indicate the name(s) a woman was given at birth. Where a deliberate pseudonym was used, this too is shown. In addition, other names, the order of surnames or their combination have been listed, since this information can be crucial in tracing an individual through different publications. Some slight variations of spellings have also been included as further alternative names where these have been found in publications.

The General and Specialist sections are subdivided into reference publications, where relevant ones exist, and nonreference in alphabetical order by the authors' names. Where there is no author, the title is inserted into the alphabetical sequence. In many publications, especially catalogues, biographies of varying lengths were included. In the notes on these publications these have been categorised in order to indicate to the reader the amount of information included. A "brief biographical outline" denotes a minimal level of information, as was unfortunately common practice in catalogues until the 1970s, and later in Eastern Europe; a "biographical outline"' denotes a chronology giving dates, place of training and perhaps date of first exhibition. More detailed still are biographical accounts. Under each specialism, relevant individuals are listed and cross-references included.

Reference publications for the General section were problematic for both art and design. The design reference books tend to include technical information. In fashion, for example, reference books may contain definitions of styles, materials, garments and, in addition to fashion designers, include fashion journalists, photographers and agencies. As we have noted, the history of design literature does not possess the wealth of biographical and other reference books of fine art; this very wealth of art reference material creates its own difficulties. Many of the standard reference books on the artists of particular countries have not been included precisely because they are the obvious sources to consult and partly on practical grounds in order to avoid the exclusion of more relevant and informative but less familiar material. They have, however, been included where relatively little other material on a country was easily available and where they were found to be a particularly good source on women. After the reference books, the General section follows an alphabetical sequence. The Specialist sections follow a similar pattern, with reference books first where they exist, followed by all other publications, each in an alphabetical sequence.

Within the individual entries, there are various sections, although relatively few practitioners have entries under all. The sections are organised in the following ways. Where there is discrepancy in the dates in published sources or where the precise date of birth is assigned to a period of several years, the figures have been separated as in, for example, 1896/8. Recent dates of death are extremely difficult to find and there are many cases where the designer/artist must be deceased but no precise evidence has been located. Again the author would welcome information. The short description of the type of work done, together with the geographical information, provides an instant indicator to the reader. Following this are publications by the artist or designer. Under the heading Main Sources are publications devoted to or containing relatively detailed information on the individual. The existence of monographs is relatively rare except in the case of the better known designers and artists. Indeed among designers, monographs are almost entirely a phenomenon of the fashion world. Much of the information here will be in the form of exhibitions or reviews, but there are also individuals for whom there are no such entries. Only exhibitions for which the catalogues have been consulted are listed, but the annotations will indicate which publications, if any, contain a full list of exhibitions. The exhibition catalogues consulted are listed in chronological order and the titles demonstrate whether they were solo or group shows. Solo shows are almost entirely limited to artists until the advent of studio pottery and glass. The final section, headed Other Sources, includes books in which the individual is mentioned, although the amount of information varies. Some reference books are included here. Some women, designers in particular, may have entries only in this section. Such individuals have been deliberately included in the hope that further research may be undertaken once they have been identified. Where sources in individual entries are also in the General or relevant specialist section, the full bibliographic details are not given in the individual's entry, nor are the notes repeated. Some publications on specialist areas may only discuss one or two women artists. In such cases the publications appear only under the individuals concerned.

This has been a truly exciting project to be engaged on. There is a sense of excavating women practitioners, particularly designers, from obscurity so that further research may be carried out and students will be able readily to gain access to information on such women. It has been fascinating to find evidence from so many countries of the activities of women in art and design. Bringing together in one work over two thousand women practitioners and publications in over fifteen languages will add to the evidence of women's achievements and hopefully promote future work across the European continent.

Acknowledgments

Many people have contributed in various ways towards this project. A key group of people who were, albeit in many cases unwittingly, central to the gathering of the data were librarians. Most significant have been the librarians at my present institution, the University of Lincolnshire and Humberside, and at my previous one, the University of Sunderland, where Rose Pearson and then Tricia Dodsworth patiently helped with my many Inter-library loans in several languages. The National Art Library staff, who suffered most of my attentions, were unfailingly helpful over the years, as were staff at the British Library, the Royal Horticultural Society's Lindley Library, the Courtauld Institute, the Crafts Council, the Bibliothèque Nationale, the Bibliothèque d'Art et d'Archéologie at the Universités de Paris, the Bibliothèque Marguérite Durand, the library of the Musée d'Orsay and the Bibliothèque Forney in Paris.

I am grateful to both universities for their support in a number of ways and to my colleagues for their patience when I was engaged on this work. Paola Chiarmonte encouraged the beginning of this project. Many scholars and curators were generous with their help, in particular Moira Vincentelli; Rosemary Fitzgibbon; Virginia Bodman; Jack Dawson; Gudrun Schubert; Pat Phippard; the Comitato Biennale Donna in Ferrara and their energetic co-ordinator Liviana Zagagnoni. I would also like to thank the following: Amanda Farr; Peter Frank, Director of the Design Centre Stuttgart; the Ateneumin Taidemuseo, Helsinki; Crane Kalman Gallery; staff at the Academy of Art in Riga; Joao Castel-Branco Pereira, Director of the Museu Nacional do Azulejo, Lisbon; Gwen Hardie; Margaret Hunter; the London Transport Museum; Alexander Moffat; Agniewska Morawinska; Elisa Oliver; Nicholas Penny; Anne Rivière; Stichting Vrouwen in de Beeldende Kunst, Amsterdam; the Museo Civico, Treviso; Lea Vergine; Maureen Wayman; Whitford and Hughes Gallery; Ann Wichstrøm; the Women's Art Library, London.

I would like to express my grateful thanks to friends who allowed me to stay with them, or even to use their house in their absence: Jean-Pierre and Annie Barbier, whose hospitality in Paris I shall never be able to repay, Etta and Arnoldo Toni, Raffaela and Angelo Lucchesi. There were also people who helped with some of the translation work: Pirjo Walton and her Norwegian friend, Justin and Enid McCracken, Pat Rowley, Brian Birch and Karen King. David Parker of Leeds University spent time showing me the software and Stephen Shipley was endlessly patient with the problems of converting the material from one programme to another for the final editing process.

Finally I would like to thank my son, Alastair, and daughter, Ashley, for their patience and forbearance during the project and particularly during the final stages of the manuscript. It is to them that I dedicate this book.

General

1   ALLEMANDI, UMBERTO. *Dizionario degli artisti italiani del XX secolo.* 2 vols. Turin: Giulio Bolaffi Editore, 1979, 1: 418pp.; 2: 347pp., illus.

     Text in Italian. Each artist included in this dictionary is given a biographical account and bibliographical notes. There is a tendency to include only older, better established artists. The dominant media are painting and sculpture, with some assemblage artists also included. The second volume is entirely devoted to illustrations.

2   BACHMANN, DONNA, and SHERRY PILAND. *Women Artists: An Historical, Contemporary and Feminist Bibliography.* Metuchen, N.J.: Scarecrow Press, 1978, 323pp., illus.

     Consists of an initial general section of publications, subdivided by type, on either women artists or artists in general. This is then followed by sections organised by century from the fifteenth to twentieth centuries in which individual women have entries. There is a bias towards American women and only the now better known Europeans are included. On those who are included it provides detailed references. For the later edition see below under Piland, S.

3   BENEZIT, EMMANUEL. *Dictionnaire Critique et Documentaire des Peintres, Sculpteurs, Dessinateurs et Graveurs de tous les temps et de tous les pays.* 8 vols. New edition. Paris: Librairie Grund, 1960.

     Text in French. This standard reference work is invaluable for tracing even obscure women artists from across Europe.

4   CAMPOY, ANTONIO. *Diccionario critico del arte español contemporaneo.* Madrid: Ibérico Europea de Ediciones, 1973, 490pp., illus.

     Text in Spanish. The main focus of the dictionary is on twentieth-century artists and in particular those active in the 1960s and 1970s. Others are included and the earliest artist was born about 1860. The length of the entries varies considerably. About 10 per cent are women.

5   CLEMENT, CLARA ERSKINE. *Women in the Fine Arts from the Seventh Century B.C. to the Twentieth Century A.D.* Boston: Houghton Mifflin, 1904. Rev. ed. New York: Hacker Art Books, 1974.
     Dictionary of women painters and sculptors active in Europe and America. Entries vary in length and some use Ellett's earlier text (q.v.) as the main source of information.

6   CLEMENT, CLARA, and LAURENCE HUTTON. *Artists of the Nineteenth Century and Their Works.* 2 vols. London: Trubner, 1879, vol. 1: 386pp., vol. 2: 373pp.
     Includes large numbers of artists, although entries are often succinct. It is a useful source for women active in the nineteenth century.

7   DAHLANDER, A. (ED.). *Svenskt konstnärslexikon.* 5 vols. Mälmo: Allhems Förlag, vol. 1: 1952, 334pp.; vol. 2: 1953, 360pp.; vol. 3: 1957, 612pp.; vol. 4: 1961, 598pp.; vol. 5 1967, 838pp.
     Text in Swedish. A biographical dictionary of Swedish artists from the eighteenth century in which women are well represented, even in the earlier period.

8   DAY, MICHAEL. *Modern Art in Church: A Gazetteer of Twentieth Century Works of Art in English and Welsh Churches. Royal College of Art Papers no. 12.* London: Royal College of Art, 1982, 30pp., illus.
     Lists works of art in several media, including mosaic and stained glass, in churches in England and Wales. The first list is by town and the second by artist or designer.

9   *Design and Applied Arts Index.* Burwash: Design Documentation, first appeared 1987.
     A reference service covering individuals and topics in design, which here includes design management, design education and industrial design. Brief abstracts are provided where titles are not self-explanatory. Published twice yearly, it appears in a cumulated edition every three years.

10   DE BREFFNY, BRIAN (general editor). *Ireland: A Cultural Encyclopaedia.* London: Thames and Hudson, 1983, 256pp., illus.
     An alphabetical listing of individuals and institutions concerned with a wide range of cultural activities contributed by a number of writers. Many of the entries on women artists and designers have been contributed by Ciarán MacGonigal and a useful number of women are included. Each entry contains an short biography, a summary of their achievements and, where available, published monographs. In addition to those listed under their own

names, others may also be referred to in the entries on institutions or particular media.

11   *Design français, 1960–1990: trois décennies.* Paris: APCI, Editions Georges Pompidou: Centre Pompidou, 1988, 295pp., illus.

In the five preliminary essays, various aspects of art and design over thirty years are discussed. There follows an alphabetical listing of designers, with an emphasis on industrial design, each with a biographical outline and a selection of works illustrated. Eight women are included.

12   *Dictionnaire biographique illustré des artistes en Belgique depuis 1830.* Brussels: Arto, 1987, 416pp., illus.

Includes a useful number of women active in Belgium in the nineteenth and twentieth centuries. Each entry has biographical information.

13   DORMER, PETER (ED.). *Illustrated Dictionary of Twentieth Century Designers: Key Personalities in Design and Applied Arts.* London: Headline, 1992, 255pp., illus.

An alphabetical listing of 400 international designers and companies. For individuals a short biographical outline is given, together with a summary of their contribution to a particular sphere. A broad definition of design is adopted which makes the book particularly useful.

14   DUNFORD, PENNY. *Biographical Dictionary of Women Artists in Europe and America since 1850.* Hemel Hempstead: Harvester Wheatsheaf and Philadelphia: University of Pennsylvania Press, 1990, 340pp., illus.

Includes 730 biographies of women artists, predominantly painters, sculptors and graphic artists, working in Europe and America. The entries show how each artist managed their career and how they took advantage of available opportunities. Each entry also has a bibliography and, where appropriate, a list of public collections.

15   DUROZOI, GERARD (ED.). *Dictionnaire de l'art moderne contemporain.* Paris: Hazan, 1992, 676pp., illus.

An international dictionary of twentieth-century artists. Although women are included, they are the mainstream, more familiar names. Each entry consists of about twenty-six lines of biography plus some bibliographical references to recent monographs or catalogues.

16   EHRESMAN, D. L. *Applied and Decorative Arts: A Bibliographic Guide to Basic Reference Works, Histories and Handbooks.* Littleton, Colorado: Libraries Unlimited Inc., 1977, 232pp.

Consists of nineteen sections, some of only three pages, of bibliography on different types of decorative arts. Of particular interest are the first general section, together with those on ceramics, glass, textiles, metalwork, leather and bookbinding, and jewellery.

17   *Encyclopédie des Arts Décoratifs et Industriels Modernes au XXème siecle.* 12 volumes. Reprint of 1925 edition. New York and London: Garland, 1977, illus.

Text in French. Published to accompany the 1925 Exposition Internationale des Arts Décoratifs. After a history of the evolution of the decorative arts, the following volumes are largely organised by media. Particularly relevant here are Volumes 4–5 on furniture, metalwork, lighting, glass and furnishings; Volume 6 on textiles; Volume 7 on all aspects of the book and Volume 9 on fashion and accessories.

18   GABET, CHARLES. *Dictionnaire des artistes de l'école française au XIXe siécle. Peinture, sculpture, architecture, gravure, dessin, lithographie et composition musicale.* Paris: Verge, 1831, 709pp.

Contains biographies of artists living in France between 1800 and 1830. For the early nineteenth century there is a surprising number of women included.

19   HATTON, BETH (ED.). *Index to Craft Journals 1984–88.* 3 vols. Sydney: Crafts Council of Australia, 1990, 1:200pp.; 2:290pp.; 3:244pp.

A comprehensive international guide to seventy craft journals published in Europe, North America and Australia. Volume 1 lists articles by author, Volume 2 under subject hedings and volume 3 under personal subjects. A previous publication covering 1979–83 included fifty journals.

20   HATTON, BETH (ED.). *Index to Craft Journals 1989–90.* Sydney: Crafts Council of Australia, 1992, 302pp.

Abstracts of over seventy craft journals published in Europe, N. America and Australia. Covering a shorter period of time than previous publications in this series, all three indices are included in the one volume.

21   HAVLICE, PATRICIA. *Index to Artistic Biography.* 2 vols. Metuchen, New Jersey: Scarecrow Press, 1973, 1362pp.

Indexes biographical information of artists taken from sixty-four reference works in ten languages. These are primarily standard dictionaries of artists and collective biographies but exclude Thieme-Becker and Bénézit. It is useful only for the most general of enquiries. A supplement in the same format published in 1981 covers seventy more titles published between 1926 and 1980.

22   *Images of Finnish design, 1960–1990. Published on the Occasion of the 80th Anniversary of the Finnish Association of Designers (Ornamo).* Espoo: Kustannusosakeyhtiö Tietopuu, 1991, 276pp., illus.

This catalogue is organised by decade. Within each, details are given of individuals active at that time together with an illustration of their work. Media covered include glass, ceramics, industrial design, fashion, jewellery, furniture and interior design. The length of each entry varies. Overall an excellent source for women.

23   JAGGER, JANETTE, and ROGER TOWE. *Designers' International Index.*
3 vols. London, Melbourne, Munich and New York: Design International,
1991, vol. 1: A–K, 746pp.; vol. 2: L–Z, 752pp.; vol. 3: (Index) 479pp.

An earlier version, which excluded architecture but included photography, appeared on microfiche as Design International. An excellent source for
women although no biographical information is given. Publications are listed
under the names of designers in the first two volumes while in the third
designers are listed by country (either of birth or where they chiefly work)
and by medium.

24   JERVIS, SIMON. *The Penguin Dictionary of Design and Designers.*
London: Allen Lane Penguin Books Ltd., 1984, 533pp., illus.

Includes individuals, movements, institutions and styles chiefly from the
eighteenth century, but there are few women. For example, Anni Albers is
not mentioned even in the entry for Josef Albers.

25   JULIER, GUY. *Encyclopaedia of Twentieth Century Design and Designers.*
London: Thames and Hudson, 1993, 216pp., illus.

Includes individual designers, styles, companies and political and ideological ideas which have influenced design. Better known women designers
are featured.

26   *Lexikon der zeitgenössichen Schweizer Künstler. Dictionnaire des artistes
suisses contemporains. Dizionario di artisti svizzeri contemporanei.*
Stuttgart: Verlag Huner, 1981, 538pp.

Text in German, French and Italian. This book includes Swiss painters,
sculptors, graphic artists and photographers born after 1900. The language of
each entry is determined by that used by the artist. There is an outline biography, an indication of the type of work produced, lists of prizes won, and
exhibitions. Entries are brief and there are indices by place of residence and
medium. A reasonable number of women are included.

27   MARTIN, JULES. *Nos peintres, sculpteurs, graveurs et dessinateurs.
Portraits et biographies suivis d'une notice sur les Salons Français depuis
1673, les Sociétés des Beaux-Arts, la propriété artistique etc.* Paris, 1897.

Text in French. Provides information about women artists active in the
late nineteenth century in France.

28   MILNER, JOHN. *A Dictionary of Russian and Soviet Artists, 1420–1970.*
Woodbridge: Antique Collectors Club, 1993, 483pp., illus.

Contains many women among the hundreds of artists included, since
all artists who exhibited at least once in certain venues are included. The
entries vary in length and detail but normally contain a list of collections
and an individual bibliography in addition to the short biographical
account.

29 MITCHELL, PETER. *European Flower Painters.* London: Adam and Charles Black, 1972, 272pp., illus.

A biographical dictionary that includes artists from the seventeenth to the twentieth centuries from many European countries. The biographies vary in length. There is a general bibliography.

30 MOE, LOUISA, and VICKI HILL. *Female Artists Past and Present.* 2nd edition. Berkeley: Women's History Research Center Inc., 1974, 158pp.

A combination of directory, bibliography and exhibition listing. It reflects the tremendous enthusiasm of the early 1970s in disseminating information about the activities of women in art and design. The emphasis is on contemporary women in America, although both historical and European women are included.

31 No entry 31.

32 NAYLOR, COLIN (ED.). *Contemporary Designers* 2nd edition. *Contemporary Arts Series.* Chicago and London: St. James Press, 1990, 641pp.

A biographical dictionary of over 600 designers who were either currently active or who had died between 1970 and 1990 and were still well known. Individual entries consist of the following categories: outline biography, list of major exhibitions, list of better known works, publications by and on the designer and a short critical essay assessing their work. The scope is international and includes design forms from architecture to fashion. Many women are included.

33 PETTYS, CHRIS. *An International Dictionary of Women Artists Born before 1900.* Boston: G.K. Hall, 1985, 851pp., illus.

One of the earliest serious reference books on women artists. The author consulted many of the standard reference texts (e.g., Bénézit, Thieme-Becker and Edouard-Joseph) and lists of nineteenth-century exhibiting venues in order to establish this invaluable listing of over 21,000 women artists born before 1900. Entries are brief biographical outlines together with an indicative bibliography.

34 PILAND, SHERRY. *Women Artists: An Historical, Contemporary and Feminist Bibliography.* 2nd edition. Metuchen, N.J. and London: Scarecrow Press, 1994, 454pp., illus.

An updated edition of the 1978 publication (q.v. vol. 2). The same artists are included with the addition of more recent material. The approach seems to favour depth of coverage over the number of artists. There are more Americans than Europeans and there is a tendency to include only better known figures.

35   PILE, JOHN. *Dictionary of Twentieth Century Design.* New York: Roundtable Press, 1990, 312pp., illus.

Covers styles, design journals, institutions, firms, critics and techniques in addition to individuals. Geographically it covers Europe and the United States. There is a tendency toward commercial and industrial design. Fashion is included but glass and ceramics occupy a minor place.

36   PRATHER-MOSES, ALICE. *International Directory of Women Workers in the Decorative Arts: A Historical Survey from the Distant Past to the Early Decades of the Twentieth Century.* Metuchen, N.J.: Scarecrow Press, 1981, 200pp.

An introductory essay and a discussion of the sources consulted precede the biographies of individual women. The majority of entries are for American women but, given the shortage of publications of women in design, this is an extremely useful source. The biographies vary in length according to the information available. At the end there are lists of the women involved in different specialisms subdivided in the case of ceramics, for example, into particular potteries.

37   RAFOLS, JOSE. *Diccionario biográfico de artistas de Cataluña desde la época romana hasta nuestros dias.* 3 vols. Barcelona: Editorial Millá, 1951–1954; vol. 1: 535pp, vol. 2: 520pp., vol. 3: 625 pp. A revised edition was published in 1980 under the title *Diccionario de artistas de Cataluña, Valencia y Baleares.*

Text in Catalan. This dictionary covers many specialist media and some Spanish women artists are included. Since their names are normally difficult to find, this publication is a useful starting point. The final part of Volume 3 contains several indices, including lists of artists by date and medium.

38   THIEME, ULRICH, and FELIX BECKER. *Allgemeines Lexikon der bildenden Künstler von der Antike bis zur Gegenwart.* 37 vols. New edition of first edition pulished 1907–1950. Leipzig: Seemann Verlag, 1978.

Text in German. Includes painters, graphic artists (engravers, printmakers) and sculptors from across Europe. Includes a fair proportion of women artists, many of whom are not cited elsewhere. Entries consist of a brief biographical outline and abbreviated references to a few key items of relevant literature.

39   VOLLMER, HANS. *Allgemeines Lexikon der Bildenden Künstler des XX Jahrhunderts.* 6 vols. Leipzig: Seemann Verlag, 1953–1962.

Text in German. The volumes are designed to update the material in Thieme-Becker and follow the same format. A useful number of women are included.

NONREFERENCE SOURCES

40   *16 Plus.* Copenhagen: Dansk Kunstindustrimuseet, 1981, n.p., illus.
Text in Danish. An exhibition of sixteen designers working in a variety of media together with two invited graphic designers. Eight of the exhibitors are women: Inge Alifrangis, Bodil Bødtker-Noess, Vibeke Klint and Kim Naver are all weavers, Hanne Backhaus is a textile printer, Alice Mogensen and Pia Hedegaard are fashion designers, while Ursula Munch is a ceramicist.

41   *20th Century Craftsmanship.* Bath: Holburne of Menstrie Museum, 1972, 63pp., illus.
An exhibition of work from the Crafts Study Centre Trust in Bath. The catalogue is little more than a list of exhibits. Women are well represented in textiles, by four out of twelve ceramicists and in small numbers elsewhere.

42   *25 Ausstellung der Gesellschaft schweizerische Malerinnen, Bilhauerinnen und Kunstgewerblerinnen.* Bern: Kunstmuseum, 1964, n.p.
Text in German. A listing of the exhibits of the Swiss Society of women painters, sculptors and designers. The majority of exhibits are paintings (108 out of 160). There is no information about the artists other than the name. This seems to be one of an irregular series of exhibitions held by this society.

43   *6e exposition Club international féminin: peinture, sculpture, tapisséries.* Paris: Club International Féminin, 1961, 20pp.
Text in French. A catalogue of one of a series of annual exhibitions held by this association for women artists. It consists only of a list of artists and titles of works arranged according to country of origin.

44   *Anni trenta: arte e cultura in Italia.* Milan: Comune di Milano and Mazzotta Editore, 1982, 658pp., illus.
Text in Italian. An ambitious overview of cultural events in Italy in the 1930s seen in the context of social and political events. Despite the wide range of art and design media which are discussed—painting, sculpture, graphics, design, and photography—only a small number of women are included and the majority of those are painters: Carla Badiali, Benedetta, Gigia Corona, Bice Lazzari, Antonietta Raphael and Regina (qq.v. vol. 2).

45   ANSCOMBE, ISABELLE. *A Woman's Touch: Women in Design from 1860 to the Present Day.* London: Virago and New York: Penguin, 1984, 261pp., illus.
One of the earliest surveys of women designers in Europe and America. Beginning with the Arts and Crafts Movement it covers the Macdonald sis-

ters, early interior designers, early Russian modernists, the Wiener Werkstätte, the Bauhaus, designers in Paris between the wars and the rise of studio pottery and craft textiles.

46 *Art nouveau belgique*. Brussels: Palais des Beaux-Arts, 1980, 481pp., illus.

Text in French. This wide-ranging exhibition catalogue includes several general essays with additional ones on specific media which cover both fine art and design. Despite this extensive coverage, only five women are included: Anna Boch, Hélène de Rudder (q.v.), Louise Danse, Gabrielle Montald and Juliette Wytsman (q.v.).

47 *Art tchèque contemporain: gravure, céramique, verre*. Freiburg [Switzerland]: Musée d'Art et d'Histoire, 1973, 80pp., illus.

Text in German and French. After a short introductory essay there are entries on each artist which include a short biography. There are thirteen women included—six engravers and seven working in ceramics or glass.

48 *Artiste, artisan*. Paris: Musée des Arts Décoratifs, 1977, 195pp., illus.

Discusses various aspects of the art/craft debate in the preliminary essays by different writers. Included in the exhibition are at least twelve women working either in textiles, ceramics, or glass and whose work could be seen as either fine art or craft. Little information is given on individuals.

49 ASCHERSON, NEAL. *Shocks to the System: Social and Political Issues in Recent British Art from the Arts Council Collection*. London: Royal Festival Hall, 1991, 75pp., illus.

After the introductory essay there is an alphabetical listing of the thirty-seven artists who feature in the exhibition. Of these eleven are women. Each entry provides a succinct biography and an indication of the aims of the work shown in this exhibition. The exhibition included work in many media executed between 1976 and 1990 with the majority of pieces dating from the 1980s and dealing with a range of social and political debates informed by theoretical analysis.

50 ATTFIELD, JUDY, and PAT KIRKHAM (EDS.). *A View from the Interior: Feminism, Women and Design*. London: Women's Press, 1989, 246pp., illus.

A collection of essays on women's activities in various areas of design in Britain, mainly in the twentieth century. The three sections are Images of Difference, Women as Designers and Women in Design Production. There is an appendix on the archive material of women designers housed at the Archive of Art and Design in London.

51   BANGERT, ALBRECHT, and KARL ARMER. *Design: les années 80.* Paris: Editions du Chêne, 1990, 240pp., many illus.

Text in French. Surveys products of the 1980s in chapters on furniture, lighting, table arts, textiles and industrial design. Biographies of the designers, who are mainly European, are also given. There are sixteen European women included.

52   BAYER, PATRICIA. *Art Déco: The Book.* London: Quarto Publishing, 1988, n.p. mostly illus. French edition: Paris: Florilège, 1989.

A broad survey of manifestations of the Art Déco style in Europe in a wide variety of art and design media. It is most useful for its illustrations and works by a number of women are included

53   BEAULIEU, GERMAINE ET AL. *La femme artiste: d'Elizabeth Vigée-Lebrun à Rosa Bonheur.* Lacoste: Musée Despiau-Wlerick et Dubalen Mont-de Marsan, 1981, 128pp. illus.

Text in French. After an introduction on the position of women artists from the sixteenth century onwards, there are individual entries of about one page in length on women painters, photographers and sculptors in France in the later eighteenth and nineteenth centuries. Included are twenty-three painters, two photographers and ten sculptors. As not all are now familiar, this is a useful source for nineteenth-century French women artists.

54   BEER, EILEENE HARRISON. *Scandinavian Design. Objects of a Lifestyle.* New York: Farrar, Straus and Giroux in collaboration with the New York American-Scandinavian Society, 1975, 214pp., illus.

An overview of the subject by chapters on different fields of design. Within each chapter there are further subdivisions by country. Most women are to be found in the chapters on textiles and ceramics.

55   BETTERTON, ROSEMARY. *An Intimate Distance: Women, Artists and the Body.* London: Routledge, 1996, 240pp., illus.

A series of critical and scholarly essays which address the question of how women artists have dealt with the female body. Case studies are taken from the early twentieth century (Kollwitz, Modersohn-Becker and the suffrage movment) and also from more recent artists who use a variety of media to deal with issues such as food and its phobias, AIDS and its socio-political repercussions. The analysis involves a theoretical approach to a study of culture. Most of the works discussed are by women.

56   BIRJUKOVA, N. J. and V. A. SUSLOV. *Prikladnoe iskusstvo konca XIX—nacala XX veka katalog vystavki* [The decorative arts in the late 19th and early 20th centuries]. Leningrad [St. Petersburg]: Hermitage Museum, 1974.

Text in Russian. An introductory essay describes the decorative arts in Russia up to the nineteenth century, bringing in references to developments in other countries such as William Morris and Jugendstil. The largest part of the book is a catalogue with the names of artists given in Russian and transcriptions provided for those who are not Russian. Outline biographies are included. Areas covered include ceramics, fabric design, furniture, glass and fashion. Some women are included.

57   BOCHNAK, ADAM, and BUCZKOWSKI, KAZIMERZ. *Decorative art in Poland.* Warsaw: Arkady, 1972, 331pp., illus.

There are only 80 pages of text, most of which is devoted to the periods before 1850. Despite the brevity of the text on the years since 1850, a relatively large number of women are mentioned, particularly those working this century in textiles and ceramics.

58   BONY, ANNE (ED.). *Les années 10.* 2 vols. Les années. Paris: Editions du Regard, 1991, 1027 pp., illus.

59   BONY, ANNE (ED.). *Les années 20.* 2 vols. Les années. Paris: Editions du Regard, 1989, 1275pp., many illus.

60   BONY, ANNE (ED.). *Les années 30.* 2 vols. Les années. Paris: Editions du Regard, 1987, 1380pp., illus.

61   BONY, ANNE (ED.). *Les années 40.* 2 vols. Les années. Paris: Editions du Regard, 1985, 811 pp., illus.

62   BONY, ANNE (ED.). *Les années 50.* 2 vols. Les années. Paris: Editions du Regard, 1982, 571pp., many illus.

63   BONY, ANNE (ED.). *Les années 60.* 2 vols. Les années. Paris: Editions du Regard, 1983, 765pp., many illus.

Text in French. This series constitutes a survey of mainly French cultural history during the decade in question. In addition to the fine and decorative arts there are chapters on film, music, fashion and architecture. There is little detailed information on any individuals but women are most frequently mentioned in the chapters on fashion and design.

64   BOORMAN, GOTTFRIED. "Ex-DDR Spezial. Sachsen-Anhalt (11) und Burg Giebichenstein." *Kunst und Handwerk* 91, no. 1 (1991): 33–38.

Text in German. One of a series of articles that examines the work of young craftspeople from the former East Germany. They include Gabriele Putz, Christina Brade and Astrid Lucke.

65   BOSSAGLIA, ROSSANA. *Il "Déco" italiano: fisionomia dello stile 1925 in Italia.* Milan: Rizzoli, 1975, 87pp., illus.

Text in Italian. Published to accompany an exhibition. Essays on the Italian version of Art Deco are followed by individual catalogue entries, each of which is illustrated. Biographical notes on the artists are provided but only five women are mentioned: Emma Bonazzi (metalwork, graphics and glass), Adelina Zandrino (graphics), Rosa Giolli Menni (textiles) Luisa Lovarini (furniture) and Angoletta Bruno.

66   BRUNHAMMER, YVONNE, ET AL. *Art Nouveau: Belgium, France.* Chicago: Institute of the Arts, Rice University, and the Art Insitute, 1976, 512pp., illus.

An overview essay of the movement is followed by catalogue entries in section by medium. Biographies of artists are included. A few women are included.

67   BRUNHAMMER, YVONNE, ET AL. *Les années 1929–1958: UAM* [Union des Artistes Modernes]. Paris: Musée des Arts Décoratifs, 1988, 268pp., illus.

Text in French. An essay by Brunhammer on these thirty decisive years is followed by the manifestos of the UAM of 1934 and 1949. The dictionary of the UAM consistes of short articles about aspects of the group followed by an alphabetical listing of artists and designers whose work was included in this exhibition. Six of the sixty-six are women: Rose Adler, Sonia Delaunay, who was a founder member, Eileen Gray, Hélène Henry, Jan Martel and Charlotte Perriand. Others are mentioned in different parts of the text.

68   BURKHAUSER, JUDE, and ELIZABETH BIRD. *Glasgow Girls: Women in the Art School, 1880–1920.* Glasgow: Mackintosh Gallery, Glasgow School of Art, 1988, 35pp, illus.

Catalogue which is a precursor to the later exhibition by Burkhauser with a similar title (q.v.). Divided into two sections on Art and Design, many documentary photographs are illustrated. The essays represent an earlier stage of the research evident in the later publication.

69   BURKHAUSER, JUDE (ED.). *Glasgow Girls: Women in Art and Design, 1880–1920.* Edinburgh: Canongate, 1990, 264pp., 329 illus.

A detailed study of the women artists and designers who studied and taught at the Glasgow School of Art. Many of the works of these women were exhibited internationally and widely discussed in periodicals of the time. This is the first publication to draw together the women of the Glasgow School.

70   CALLEN, ANTHEA. *Angel in the Studio: Women in the Arts and Crafts Movement, 1870–1914.* London: Architectural Press, 1979, 232pp., illus.

A thorough analysis of the role played by women of different classes within the Arts and Crafts movement and includes a study of design education for women in the later nineteenth century in Britain. It looks not only at the main figures but at other women involved at various levels with the design and production of products from Morris and Co. and the sociohistoric context in which they operated.

71 CALVERT, GILL, JILL MORGAN, and MOUSE KATZ (EDS.). *Pandora's Box*. Bristol: Arnolfini Gallery, 1984, 120pp., illus.

This exhibition arose out of an earlier exhibition, *Women's Images of Men* (1980), and shares some of its organisers. Women artists were invited to submit works on the theme of Pandora's Box and offer varied reworkings of this myth. Each of the thirty-two women has written a statement about her reactions to the myth and the generation of the work exhibited. No biographical information is given.

72 *Centenary Exhibition to Celebrate the Founding of the Glasgow Society of Lady Artists in 1882*. Glasgow: Collins Gallery, 1982, 40pp., illus.

Gives a history of the Society up to its dissolution in 1971 and reconstitution as the Glasgow Society of Women Artists four years later. The alphabetical catalogue includes artists and designers of textiles, embroidery, metalwork and ceramics.

73 *Česká secesse umení 1900 (L'Art Nouveau au Bohème)*. Brno: Moravská Gallery, 1966, 324 pp., illus.

Text in Czech with a summary of the introduction in French. The exhibits cover a range of media and four women are included: the painter Zendka Braunerová, ceramicist M. K. Krivanková, Anna Boudová-Suchardová, who worked in ceramics and other media, and Marie Louisa Kirschenerová, who worked in several design areas, including glass.

74 CEYSSON, B., ET AL. *Vingt-cinq ans d'art en France, 1960–85*. Paris: Larousse and Jacques Legrand s.a., 1986, 355pp., illus.

Text in French. There are ten essays on different aspects of the art of this period. Organised on an approximately chronological basis, some have a thematic emphasis while others concentrate on stylistic or media-specific developments. At the end a list of the artists included is given with monographs and exhibitions catalogues. The artists originate from a number of countries but all worked in France. More than thirty women are included.

75 CHADWICK, WHITNEY. *Women, Art and Society*. London: Thames and Hudson, 1990, 384pp., illus.

A concise survey of women's contribution to the visual arts since the Middle Ages. Bibliographies are included for many individuals.

76 CHAPON, FRANÇOIS. *Le peintre et le livre: l'âge d'or du livre illustré en France 1870–1970*. Paris: Flammarion, 1987, 319pp., illus.

Text in French. An introductory essay deals with the links between painters, illustrators and bookbinders before the period dealt with in detail in the subsequent nine chapters. Two further chapters then examine links between poets and painters. Eight women are included: Rose Adler, Geneviève Asse, Edith Boissons, Sonia Delaunay, Maryse Lafont, Marie Laurencin, Brigitte Simon and Maria Vieira da Silva.

77 *Cinquantenaire de l'Exposition de 1925.* Paris: Musée des Arts Décoratifs, 1976, 165pp., illus.

This exhibition was held to mark the fiftieth anniversary of the Exposition Internationale des Arts Décoratifs and includes artists and designers who took part in the original exhibition. Under the separate media, artists are listed alphabetically. There are 9 women out of 190 exhibitors. Brief biographies are provided.

78 COLLINS, JUDITH. *The Omega Workshops.* London: Secker and Warburg Ltd., 1983, 310pp., illus.

A critical chronological account of the Omega Workshops from its foundation in 1913. Several of the women artists involved are included with most information about Vanessa Bell and Winifred Gill.

79 COLLINS, JUDITH. *Writing on the Wall.* London: Tate Gallery, 1993, n.p., illus.

A brochure accompanying an exhibition of work by women artists from the permanent collection chosen by twenty women writers. The Tate Gallery holds works by 228 women from the seventeenth century to the present day.

80 *Constructivism in Poland 1923–36: BLOK, Praesens, a.r.* Essen and Rijksmuseum Kröller-Müller, Otterlo: Museum Folkwang, 1973, 208pp., illus.

Foreword and Introduction in English, Dutch and German. A study of the activities of the Polish avant-garde through the study of the three journals in the exhibition title. Organised in conjunction with the Museum Stuki in Lodz, a number of documents are included together with biographical notes of the artists. Maria Puciatycka, Teresa Zarnower, Katarina Kobro and Maria Nicz-Borowiak are discussed.

81 COTTELL, FRAN, and MARIAN SCHOETTLE. *Conceptual Clothing.* Birmingham: Ikon Gallery, 1986, 44pp., illus.

Two critical essays precede entries on thirty-two artists who have used clothing as subject matter. The majority are women and the techniques and materials are varied. For each there is an outline biography, list of exhibitions and a short statement.

82 COURTHION, PIERRE. *L'art indépendant. Panorama international de 1900 à nos jours.* Paris: Editions Albin Michel, 1958.

Text in French. A chronological survey following the principal modernist movements, each with subsections the majority of which deal with individual male artists. The author knew many of the artists personally, resulting in anecdotal detail. The main emphasis is on painting, with one section each given to sculpture, architecture and ceramics. A number of women, not all familiar names, are briefly mentioned: Maria Blanchard, Vieira da Silva, Natalie Dumitresco, Marie Raymond, Jeanne Coppel, Magdaleine Vessereau, Geneviève Sarrade, Sonia Delaunay (q.v.), Suzanne Duchamp, Maria Jarema, Marie Laurencin, Sophie Taeuber-Arp and Suzanne Valadon (qq.v., vol. 2).

83   COUTOT, MAURICE. *La création chez la femme: communication faite à la séance du 16 mars 1983 à l'Académie des Beaux-Arts.* Paris: Institut de France, 1983, 14pp.

In comparison with women holding responsible jobs in society generally, the author addresses the question of why there are still apparently so few women achieving renown in the four areas with which the Académie is concerned: painting, sculpture, architecture and music. After using short biographical details on some nineteenth-century women artists in France, he concludes that engaging in art causes women to abandon what he sees as their primary function of procreation.

84   CRAWFORD, ALAN (ED.). *By Hammer and Hand: The Arts and Crafts Movement in Birmingham.* Birmingham: City Museum and Art Gallery, 1984, 169pp., illus.

After an introduction to the Arts and Crafts in Birmingham, there are sections on activities in the different media, including wallpainting, ceramics, metalwork, stained-glass, book illustration and binding. There is also a Gazetteer. Apart from the better known figures such as Kate and Myra Bunce (qq.v. vol. 2), about thirty other women are mentioned.

85   CUMMING, ELIZABETH, and BILLCLIFFE, ROGER. *Glasgow 1900: Art and Design.* Amsterdam; Zwolle, Waanders Publishers: Van Gogh Museum, 1992, 160pp., illus.

Text in English. After an essay on the links between art and industry there are sections on the Glasgow School of Painters and the Glasgow Style. Each of these includes biographical notes on the artists and designers included in the exhibition, of which a considerable number were women. All the women prominent in the Glasgow movement are found here.

86   CUMMING, ELIZABETH, and WENDY KAPLAN. *The Arts and Crafts movement.* London: Thames and Hudson, 1991, 216pp., 167 illus.

Discusses the architecture and design associated with the Arts and Crafts movement in Britain, Ireland, mainland Europe and the United States. There are a number of references to women, including some from the Guild of Women Bookbinders: Elizabeth McColl, Florence and Edith de Rheims, Constance Karslake and other designers such as Mary Newill, Edith Dawson, Phoebe Traquair, Jessie Newbery, Margaret and Frances Macdonald, Evelyn Gleeson and Sarah Purser (qq.v.).

87   *Dansk Kunsthåndvoerkere: Danish Arts and Crafts.* Copenhagen: Danske
      Kunstindustrimuseet, 1976, n.p., illus.

      In 1976 a large organisation of Danish Arts and Crafts was dissolved and
      replaced by the Danish Arts and Crafts Association. This operates more on a
      regional basis with seven local groups. This was the first national exhibition
      when the works of all seven were brought together. Under each group a few
      works are illustrated but a list of members is given so that interested patrons
      may contact them. Many women belonged to this association.

88   DAY, MICHAEL. *Modern Art in English Churches.* London: Mowbray,
      1984, 91pp., illus.

      A survey of works executed for churches from the Gothic Revival award.
      The author examines the patrons of these works and includes a gazetteer to
      find them. Women executed paintings, sculpture, textiles and stained glass.

89   DEEPWELL, KATY. *Ten Decades: Careers of Ten Women Artists Born
      1897–1906.* Norwich: Norwich Gallery, Norfolk Institute of Art and Design,
      1992, n.p., illus.

      A scholarly and comprehensive essay analyses the art practice of ten
      British women over the decades of their careers and within the social and
      political contexts of the time. It considers, inter alia, educational and employ-
      ment opportunities, travel and study abroad and the impact of World War II.
      Under the individuals there are chronologies, lists of exhibitions, public col-
      lections and publications.

90   DEEPWELL, KATY (ED.). *New Feminist Art Criticism.* Manchester:
      Manchester University Press, 1995, 201pp., illus.

      A collection of some twenty essays by women on varied aspects of the
      contemporary art world. Practitioners, theorists, critics and curators all con-
      tribute to the much needed area of women's critical dialogue in a published
      form. Several essays discuss questions around textile art as well as other
      forms of current art practice. Theory, strategy and practice are all demon-
      strated in this publication.

91   DENT-COAD, EMMA. *Spanish Design and Architecture.* London: Studio
      Vista, 1990, 208pp., illus.

      Contains chapters on architecture, interior design, fashion, graphic
      design, furniture and product design. In the fashion section three women are
      included: Sybilla, Sara Navarra and Roser Marce (qq.v.), and a commercial
      graphic designer, Pati Nuñez is mentioned.

92   DORMER, PETER, TANYA HARROD, ROSEMARY HILL, and BAR-
      LEY ROSCOE. *Arts and Crafts to Avant-Garde. Essays on the Crafts from
      1880 to the Present.* London: South Bank Centre, 1992, 34pp., illus.

      Consists of four critical essays on aspects of the crafts in Britain over the
      past century. The essays eschew the survey approach in favour of the analyt-

ical, making this one of the small number of issue-based discussions of the decorative arts. Several women are mentioned, particularly in the essay on textiles.

93   DROSTE, MAGDALENA. *Bauhaus: 1919–1933*. Berlin: Bauhaus Archiv Museum für Gestaltung and Benedict Taschen Verlag GmbH and Co KG, 1990, 256pp., illus.
      Text in German. Some information about women at the Bauhaus. Amongst the artists' biographies at the end of the book are those on Marianne Brandt, Gunta Stölzl and Lilly Reich.

94   DUFRESNE, JEAN-LUC (ED.). *Femmes créatrices des années vingt.* Granville, Manche: Musée Richard Anacréon, 1988, 80pp., illus.
      Text in French. An exhibition of works by women artists and designers who were either French or working in France during the 1920s. There are also sections on women who achieved fame in other fields such as sport, literature, music and science. The treatment of individuals and the different media is rather unbalanced and use is made of personal reminiscences where they were available. There is a detailed section on fashion. Nearly 400 women from all fields are included in the biographies at the end of the catalogue. In all it provides a vivid picture of the scale of women's contribution to French culture of the 1920s.

95   DUNCAN, ALASTAIR, and GEORGES DE BARTHA. *Art Nouveau and Art Deco Bookbinding, 1880–1940*. London: Thames and Hudson, 1989, 200pp., illus.
      After a general introduction to the subject, there is an alphabetical section of fifty bookbinders, of whom eight are women. A brief biography is given, together with illustrations of their work. Following this sequence there is another which gives fuller biographies and bibliographies for each of the fifty, together with additional bookbinders. More women feature in these additions.

96   DUNTHORNE, KATHERINE. *Artists Exhibited in Wales, 1945–1974*. Cardiff: Welsh Arts Council, 1976, 344pp., illus.
      Alphabetical listing of artists who exhibited in Wales during the period stated. A number of women, from Wales and elsewhere, are included.

97   EIDELBERG, MARTIN (ED.). *Design 1935–1965: What Modern Was. Selections from the Liliane and David M. Stewart Collection.* New York: Abrams Inc. in association with Le Musée des Arts Décoratifs, Montreal, 1991, 424pp., illus.
      After three substantial essays there are seven short introductory sections to successive styles. Some individuals appear in more than one section. There is detailed information on the each work exhibited although there are more American than European designers. Approximately ten women are included.

98   ELINOR, GILLIAN, ET AL. *Women and Craft.* London: Virago, 1987, 190pp., illus.
      An anthology of essays, interviews and artist/designer statements which critically consider the role of women in the crafts and the crafts in relation to fine art in Britain.

99   ELLIOTT, MAUD HOWE. *Art and Handicraft in the Women's Building of the World's Columbian Exposition, Chicago, 1893.* Paris and New York: Boussod and Valadon and Co., 1893, 287pp., illus.
      The Women's Building was a distinguishing feature of the World's Columbian Exposition of 1893 and this book describes the contents of the Women's Building in which many European women, including Queen Victoria, exhibited. It is useful to determine how many women were able to exhibit internationally in the late nineteenth century.

100   EVERS, ULRIKA. *Deutsche Künstlerinnen des 20. Jahrhunderts: Malerei— Bildhauerei—Tapisserie.* Hamburg: Ludwig Schultheis Verlag, 1983, 398pp., many illus.
      Provides separate information on 280 German women artists of the twentieth century. The entry for each artist has four parts: a brief biographical outline, a longer discussion of the work, a list of works in public collections and a bibliography. There is one illustration for the majority of artists. There is a particular emphasis on those born after 1940. Overall an extremely informative source.

101   EXPORT, VALIE, and SILVIA EIBLMAYR. *Kunst mit Eigen-Sinn: Aktuelle Kunst von Frauen. Texte und Dokumentation.* Vienna: Museum moderner Kunst and Museum des 20 Jahrhunderts in association with Locker Verlag, 1985, 301pp., illus.
      Text in German. Several critical essays on issues concerning women's art practice are followed by illustrations, some accompanied by text, of the works of artists in the exhibition. An international selection of women representing many areas of art practice are included. Short outline biographies are included.

102   *First Forum of Women Designers 13 to 15 March 92: Documentation.* Stuttgart: Design Center, 1992, 150pp., illus.
      Text in German and English. Held to review the position of women designers in Germany after the debates generated by the Women in Design exhibition held in the Design Center Stuttgart in 1989. It reprints the discussion papers, some of which were given by designers. Apart from the Director of the Design Center, all the speakers are women.

103   *Forme nuove in Italia.* Rome: Bestetti, 1962, 173pp., illus.
      Text in Italian, French, English and German. After a brief introduction there are sections containing photographs of contemporary designs by medi-

um, including glass, ceramics, textiles, metalwork and lighting. Five women are included: Caterina Biondi and Rosanna Bianchi for ceramics; Franca Helg Poggi for furniture; Fede Chieti in textiles and Anna Monti for lighting.

104   FROST, ABIGAIL. "Women in the Crafts." *Crafts* 62 (1983): 13–16.
      This brief survey looks at the situation up to 1939.

105   GARNIER, PHILIPPE. *The contemporary decorative arts from 1940 to the present day.* Oxford: Phaidon, 1980, 224pp., illus.
      Separate chapters are devoted to furniture, metalwork, ceramics, jewellery, glass, textiles, fashion, industrial design, graphic design, film and photography in Europe and America. Provides an overview to the subject in which quite a number of women designers are included.

106   No entry 106.

107   "Glasgow International Exhibition." *Studio* 23 (1901): 165–73; 237–46.
      Lengthy reviews of this major exhibition mention the work of nearly twenty women designers working in a range of different media.

108   GRASSI, ALFONSO, and ANTY PANSERA. *Atalante del design italiano 1940–1980.* Milan: Fabbri Editori, 1980, 320pp., mainly illus.
      Text in Italian. After chapters devoted to a chronological survey of each decade, there are sections looking at changes in design in different areas such as transport and communications. One hundred biographical outlines of designers of three generations are included, of whom only three are women: Anna Castelli Ferrieri, Laura Griziotti and Carla Venosta.

109   GRESTY, HILARY, and JEREMY LEWISON. *Constructivism in Poland, 1923 to 1936.* Cambridge: Kettle's Yard, in association with the Muzeum Stuki, Łodz, 88pp., illus.
      An introduction and three essays on the subject are followed by a series of documents from the movement and biographies of the artists which include five women: Katarzina Kobro, Maria Nicz-Borowiak, Helena Syrkus, Franciszka Themersen and Teresa Zarnower.

110   GWINNER, S. V. "Die GEDOK und das Kunsthandwerk. Frauen-hobby oder gegenein verzerrtes Image." *Kunst und Handwerk* 91, no. 4 (1991): 31–34, illus.
      Text in German. An exhibition review in which all the work featured is by women: Barbara Holtmeyer, Ulrica Scriba, Hiltrud Schaefer, Barbara Schulte-Hengesbach, Ingelborg Zeuker and the author.

111   HALD, ARTHUR, and SVEN SKAWONIUS. *Contemporary Swedish design: A survey in pictures.* Translation of *Nyttokonst. En bildrevoy med*

kommentar. 1951. Stockholm: Nordisk Rotogravyr, 1951, 179pp., many illus.

A general reader's book aimed at non-Swedes explaining life and culture in Sweden. The large number of illustrations include objects by quite a number of women. This book is useful for identifying names and the types of work but there is little substantial information.

112 HARROD, TANYA. "What are Exhibitions in the late 1980s Telling Us about the Crafts?" *Crafts* 86 (1987): 54–55.

Review of the exhibition *2D/3D: Art and Craft Made and Designed for the late Twentieth Century* (q.v.).

113 HÅRD AF SEGERSTAD, ULF. *Modern Finnish Design.* London: Weidenfeld and Nicolson, 1968, 63pp., illus.

Consists of a survey of Finnish design from the late nineteenth century. Illustrations exemplify the developments in the different media. Of the seventy-six designers whose works are mentioned and/or illustrated, almost half are women.

114 HIESINGER, KATHRYN. *Design since 1945.* New York: Rizzoli and Philadelphia: Museum of Art, 1983, 252pp., illus.

An initial series of essays analyses the social, political and economic contexts of design while a second series concentrates on individual media. The scope is international. There are outline biographies of designers and an extensive bibliography. Includes a considerable number of women.

115 HIESINGER, KATHRYN (ED.). *Art Nouveau in Munich: Masters of Jugendstil from the Stadtmuseum, Munich and other collections.* Munich: Prestel in association with the Philadelphia Museum of Art, 1988, 180pp., illus.

An essay on the origins and development of Art Nouveau is followed by a listing of the artists included in the exhibition together with detailed comments on the works which are in graphics and several areas of design. Only two women are included: Margarete von Brauchitsch and Gertraud von Schnellenbühel.

116 HIESINGER, KATHRYN, and GEORGE MARCUS III. *Landmarks of Twentieth Century Design: An Illustrated Handbook.* New York and London: Abbeville Press, 1993.

A chronological survey of design history since 1895. Each chapter covers a period, such as Art Nouveau, with an essay followed by a series of key works which are annotated and contextualised. Over twenty women are included.

117 HILDEBRANDT, HANS. *Die Frau als Kunstlerin, mit Abbildungen nach Frauenarbeiten bildender Kunst von den frühesten Zeiten bis zur Gegenwart.* Berlin: Rudolf Mosse Buchverlag, 1928, 188pp., 337 illus.

Text in German. Comprehensive chronological survey of a large number of women artists and designers. Although the information given on each is not lengthy, the number of women included and the range of illustrations make this a useful source. In addition to fine artists, ceramics and textile designers are also included.

118 HIMID, LUBAINA. *The Thin Black Line.* London: Institute of Contemporary Art, 1985, n.p. [8pp], illus.

An exhibition of eleven women artists of colour, working in a different media specialisms, curated by one of them. The information on each varies but there is ususally a chronology and a statement by the artist.

119 HOFMANN, WERNER (ED.). *Eva und die Zukunft: das Bild der Frau seit der Französichen Revolution.* Hamburg in association with Prestel, Munich: Kunsthalle, 1986, 463pp., illus.

Text in German. Examines images of women in art by theme, such as Mother and Madonna, femmes fatales, partners, lesbians. Three scholarly essays examine different aspects of the topic, including the sociohistorical context. Some 20 per cent of the artists are women. Short biographies of the artists are included

120 HOGBEN, C. *British Art and Design 1900–1960: A Collection in the Making.* London: Victoria and Albert Museum, 1983, 240pp., illus.

The introductory essay surveys design in Britain from the turn of the century. The exhibition is based on items purchased for the museum collection and there is an illustration and annotation for each item. Some thirteen female designers are included.

121 HORNE, RICHARD. "The Female School of Design in the Capital of the World." *Household Words* 51 (15 March 1851): 577–81.

The author describes a visit made to the School of Design. The tone is slightly facetious but shows evident dismay at the dreadful conditions in the School through lack of Government support and admiration for the work produced by the students.

122 HOUSTON, JOHN (ED.). *Craft Classics Since the 1940s: An Anthology of Belief and Comment.* London: Crafts Council, 1988, 133pp., illus.

A collection of texts from 1939 to the 1980s, several of which attempt a theoretical analysis. The emphasis is mainly on ceramics. The three women contributors include Dora Billington and Ethel Mairet (qq.v.).

123 INGELMAN, INGRID. *Kvinuliga konstnarer i Sverige en undersokning av Elevervid Konstakademin Inskrivna, 1864–1924. Ars suetica 6.* Uppsala: Almqvist & Wiksell, 1982, 140pp. illus.

Swedish text with English summary. A study of the position and activities of women artists during the sixty years after the opening of a women's section in the Swedish Academy of Art. This was a result of a surplus of women in the population and the resulting need to find employment for them. The author analyses the social backgrounds, media, subjects, exhibition patterns and prizes of women artists and compares them to those of men. She concludes that the twentieth-century women were more professionally active than the earlier group and received relatively more prizes than contemporary men. She ends the book with eighteen case studies.

124 "International Exhibition of Modern Decorative Art at Turin." *Studio* 26 (1902): whole issue.

Review of the many different types of decorative art from European countries. Work by many women is mentioned and illustrated.

125 *Kaléidoscope: foire aux créateurs: 50e Salon de la Société des artistes décorateurs.* Paris, 1980, 22pp., illus.

Text in French. Newsletter to members of the Society in which a press cutting of the above title is reprinted from *L'Officiel de l'ameublement,* no. 335, November 1979 together with other reviews. The fair took place in September and October of that year. Four women are mentioned by the reviews: Sophie Morgaine, Michèle Moreau, Catherine Noll and Yvette Herzberg.

126 KALLIR, JANE. *Viennese Design and the Wiener Werkstätte.* New York: Braziller in association with the Galérie St. Etienne, 1986, 152pp., illus.

A short history of the Wiener Werkstätte is followed by more detailed sections on individual design media, which here include graphics and fashion. Most of the chief female designers are included.

127 KARLSEN, ARNE and ANKER TIEDEMANN. *Made in Denmark: A Picture Book about Modern Danish Arts and Crafts.* Copenhagen: Jul. Gjellerup, 1960, 175pp., illus.

Discussion of the nature of the artist-craftsperson in modern design. Examples discussed include a number of women in the chapters on ceramics (Nathalie Krebs, Eva Stoehr-Nielson, Edith Sonne Bruun, Kirsten Weeke) and textiles (Vibeke Klint, Gerda Henning, Dorte Raaschon, Lis Ahlman). The work of others is illustrated.

128 KLEIN, DAN, and MARGARET BISHOP. *Decorative Arts 1880–1980. Christies Pictorial Archives.* Oxford: Phaidon in association with Christies, 1988, 263pp., illus.

A heavily illustrated chronological survey of design in Europe from the Arts and Crafts Movement. The text is aimed at collectors. A small number of women are included.

129   KOOS, JUDITH. *Style 1900*. Budapest: Kepzomuweszeti Alap Kiadoval-lalata, 1979, 396pp., illus.

   Text in Hungarian. A country-by-country survey of European design in 1900 with a more detailed section on Hungary. A small number of women are included.

130   KRICHBAUM, J., and R. ZONDERGELD. *Künstlerinnen: von der Antike bis zur Gegenwart.* Cologne: Dumont, 1979, 324pp. illus.

   Text in German. A biographical dictionary of women artists, chiefly European, from the earliest examples to the 1970s. Entries vary in length but aim to provide a useful summary of the information then available. There are references to key texts in some entries.

131   *Künstlerinnen des 20 Jahrhunderts.* Wiesbaden: Museum. Published by Verlag Weber & Weidermeyer GmbH, Kassel, 1990, 399pp., illus.

   Text in German. A very useful text containing five essays on the practice of groups of women artists and individuals from the early twentieth century to the present day. Examples are "Women artists of the Russian Revolution" and "Women artists in the 1970s and 1980s." This is followed by individual alphabetical entries for the fifty-eight women artists included in the exhibition. Each entry consists of at least one page on the work of the artist and an illustration. Also included are extensive biographies with bibliographies and lists of exhibitions.

132   *Künstlerinnen international, 1877–1977.* Berlin: Schloss Charlottenberg, 1977, 375pp., illus.

   Catalogue of one of the earliest large exhibitions in Europe of women artists. It helped to establish the existence of artists active after 1877. Most of those included are European.

133   LANGER, CASSANDRA. *Feminist Art Criticism: An Annotated Bibliography.* Reference Publications in Art History. New York: G.K. Hall, 1993, 290pp.

   Divided into four main categories, this book collects reference publications, books, exhibitions catalogues and articles and chapters. Within the book category are also diaries, letters and autobiographies, dissertations, biographies and critiques. American publications and artists are understandably more throughly covered than European, perhaps because only English-language publications have been included. In the author's terms criticism includes history and this book includes a very different type of material from that of Deepwell's similarly titled publication (q.v.).

134   *La part des femmes dans l'art contemporain.* Vitry-sur-Seine: Centre d'animation culturelle, 1984, 46pp., illus.

One hundred seven women artists, the majority of whom are represented by one work, are included in this catalogue. With a few exceptions, such as Stepanova, Toyen and Richier, the work shown dates from the previous decade. The artists are from many European countries or from other countries and based in Europe. The publication is also useful for providing some less familiar names.

135   LAMAČ, MIROSLAV. *Contemporary Art in Czechoslovakia.* Prague: Orbis, 1958, 140pp., illus.

After an introductory section, three chapters deal respectively with landscape painting, sculpture and the graphic arts. In all three, women are included: two painters, Mária Medvecká and Vilma Vrbová, and one graphic artist, Ludmila Jirinková.

136   LEITGEB, HILDEGARD, ELIZABETH SCHMUTTERMEIER, and ANGELA VOLKER. *Wiener Werkstätte: atelier viennois, 1903–32.* Brussels: Galérie CGER, 1987, 263pp., illus.

Text in French. Catalogue of an exhibition held on the anniversary of the publication of a booklet by Mathilde Flögl of the Wiener Werkstätte. She initiated the idea and edited the publication which was bound by Vally Wieselthier and Gudrun Baudisch. It mentioned five women graphic designers. This catalogue contains an overview of the workshop before separate sections dealing with different media and projects. Eight women feature in the text of the fashion and fabrics sections: Lotte Frömel-Fochler, Maria Likarz, Mathilde Flögl, Fritzi Löw, Hilda Jesser (qq.v.), Gertrude Weinberger, Mitzi Friedmann and Leopoldine Hirsch. Several of these and a small number of others have work in ceramics and glass included.

137   *Les Années 25.* Paris: Musée des Arts Décoratifs, 1966.

Text in French. A partial reconstruction of the 1925 Exposition Internationale des Arts Décoratifs from objects which are in the Museum's collections. Only five women are included: Sophie Taeuber-Arp (here represented by stained glass), Blanche Klotz (furntiture and textile design), Hélène Henry (textile design), Mlle de Glehn (ceramics) and Suzanne Lalique (textile design and china painting) (qq.v.).

138   *Les femmes artistes d'Europe exposent au Musée du Jeu de Paume.* Paris: Musée des Ecoles Etrangères [Musée du Jeu de Paume], 1937, 64pp.

Organised by a committee of women which included Laure Albin Guillot (q.v. vol. 2), the President of the Union Féminine des Carrières Libérales et Commerciales, there was a retrospective section for women artists of the past in addition to a contemporary one. In all, fifteen European countries were represented. The majority of artists were invited to take part, while others submitted their work to a jury. The catalogue provides names and details of the works but no illustrations.

139   LEWIS, FRANK. *British designers: Their work.* Leigh-on-Sea: Frank Lewis, 1941, n.p., 25pp. of pl.

Little text is present, and of the twenty-three designers mentioned and illustrated five are women: Meriel Tower, Jessie Sturgeon, Margaret Long, Joan Joseph and Sylvia Haig. All except the last are referred to as belonging to a professional design association.

140   *Lexikon der Frau.* 2 vols. Zurich: Encyclios Verlag AG, vol. 1: 1953, 1447pp.; vol. 2: 1954, 1695pp.

Text in German. Contains entries for women active in a wide variety of fields, including art, and provides a useful initial source. It also contains entires under things connected with women in medical, psychological and social fields.

141   LINDKVIST, LENNART (ED.). *Design in Sweden.* Stockholm: Swedish Institute, 1972, 144pp., illus.

After an overview of the situation for design in Sweden between 1917 and 1970, there are chapters on glass, ceramics, silver, textiles, furniture, industrial design, the design schools and employment situation for designers. In most, the work of the principal designers is described and many of these are women.

142   LUTTEMAN, HELENA. *Svenskt silver i dag; contemporary Swedish silver; modernes Schwedisches Silber.* Copenhagen: Kunstindustrimuseet, 1976, n.p., illus.

Text in Swedish, English and German. A short essay is followed by information on each of the thirty-one artists represented in the exhibition, of which a good proportion are women.

143   MØLLER, VIGGO STEN. *Recent and Contemporary Arts and Crafts in Denmark.* New York: Danish Information Office, 1947, 4pp.

After a summary indicating the strength of the Danish design tradition, the author introduces the leading figures in different media. The women included here are Cathinka Olsen, working at the porcelain factory of Bing and Grøndahl, Nathalie Krebs for stoneware and Marie Gudme Leth, Helga Foght, Ruth Hill and Bodil Oxenvad all for printed textiles.

144   MATHEY, FRANÇOIS. *Au bonheur des formes: design français 1945–1992.* Paris: Editions du Regard, 1992, 395pp., illus.

Text in French. Seven extensive essays on French design, including industrial design. Chapters on interiors, furniture and furnishings (including textiles) contain references to some women designers but the emphasis is not on individuals. Notable is the involvement of artists in French design.

145 MAZENOD, LUCIENNE (ED.). *Les femmes célèbres.* Vol. 1, *L'immortelle: les femmes de lettres,* 1960, 479pp.; vol. 2, *Femmes de science, intrépides et sportives, les femmes terribles et les grandes artistes,* 1961, 477pp. Paris: Lucien Mazenod Editions d'Art.

Text in French. Of nearly 1,000 pages on famous women only 10 are devoted to women artists from the sixteenth century. Seven women are allotted a page while others have an entry of 12 to 15 lines.

146 MÄKI, OILI. *Taide ja Työ: Finnish designers of today.* Helsinki: Werner Söderström Osakeyhtiö, 1954, 175pp., mainly illus.

Text in Finnish and English. Concerns twenty-four designers active in the immediate postwar period and is divided into three media: textiles, ceramics, glass. An introduction recounts the history of Finnish Design, from the founding by painter Fanny Churberg (q.v. vol. 2) of the Friends of Finnish Handicraft in 1879. The majority of designers included are women, indicating the role women played in Scandinavian design generally and making this a very useful source.

147 McQUISTON, LIZ. *Women in Design: A Contemporary View.* London: Trefoil Publications, 1988, 144pp., many illus.

Profiles of forty-three women, mainly from Europe and the United States, who are engaged in various kinds of design. Maintains that women involved in craft and decorative art activities have received more attention than those in design areas more closely related to industry and production. The emphasis here is on women involved in fields such as furniture design, product design, architecture, animation, television and computer graphics, graphic design, advertising and textile design.

148 MILLARD, JOHN, and TONY KNIPE. *2D/3D: Art and Craft Made and Designed for the Twentieth Century.* Sunderland: Northern Centre for Contemporary Art, 1987, 72pp., illus.

A wide-ranging set of short essays about objects on the boundary of art and craft as well as some performance art by women dealing with the domestic environment. A considerable number of women were included in the exhibition, not all of whom are discussed in the essays.

149 MILLER, FRED. "Women Workers in the Art Crafts." *Art Journal* (1896): 116–18.

Description of work executed by six women in the Arts and Crafts style, with the greatest detail being given about the stained glass designer Mary Lowndes, whom the author visited. The others are Mary Nevill, Esther Moore, Miss Birkenruth, M. Reeks and M. Hussey, the last three being bookbinders.

150 *Moderne Hollandsk Tekstilkunst og Glas.* Copenhagen: Dansk Kunstindustrimuseet, 1979, pp., illus.

Text in Danish with an English summary of the introduction. A small travelling exhibition in two sections which includes the works of seven textile designers and fourteen glass designers. There are six women designers in each section. A paragraph of information is provided about each.

151   *Moscow Women Artists.* Moscow: International Women's Congress, 1975, 277pp., illus.

Text in Russian and English. The introduction explains that this exhibition was organised to coincide with the World Congress of Women held in International Women's Year. The works, in a variety of media by artists from several countries in the former U.S.S.R., were on the themes of peace, the motherland and the achievements of society. The catalogue section is organised by medium—painting, sculpture, graphic and poster art, stage design and applied art—and gives the name of the artist in cyrillic and a romanised version, together with a brief biographical outline. The majority of works are recent. This catalogue provides a source of names for women working in a socialist realist style in this period.

152   *Mothers.* Birmingham: Ikon Gallery, 1990, 38pp., illus.

Organised around the experience of motherhood, as mother or daughter, for 15 artists. A theoretical context is set in an essay by Hilary Robinson while two of the artists—Jo Spence and Cate Elwes—also provide written commentaries. Each artist includes a statement about her work.

153   MUNDT, BARBARA. *Nostalgie warum? Kunsthandwerkliche Techniken im Stilwandel vom Historismus zur Moderne.* Berlin: Kunstgewerbemuseum, S.M.P.K., 1982, 115pp., illus.

Text in German. The exhibition looks at design in four media: glass, porcelain, ceramics and metal from about the 1930s and there are separate chapters and catalogue entries for each. A small number of women are mentioned in each section: glass: Benny Motzfeld (Norway) (q.v.); porcelain: Elizabeth Scatter, Ursula Sax and Christine Atmer de Reig; ceramics: Rosemunde Navac, Ingeborg Zenker, Elizabeth Alkins and Hannah Barlow (q.v.), both of Royal Doulton in Britain, Hilda Storr-Britz (q.v.), Magarete Schott, Wendelin Stahl, Gerda Comitz, Elise Harney and Elisabeth Pluquet-Ulrich; metal: Kate Ruchenbrodt and Marinne Schliwinski.

154   MUNDT, BARBARA, SUSANNE NETZER, and INES HETTLER. *Interieur + Design in Deutschland, 1945–1960.* Berlin: Kunstgewerbemuseum in association with Dietrich Reimer Verlag, 1994, 254pp., illus.

Text in German. Essays on interior design in Germany since 1945 and on the development of certain media, including glass, ceramics and furniture, precede the catalogue itself. The work of twenty-eight women is included.

155   MUYSERS, CAROLA (ED.). *Profession ohne tradition: 125 Jahre der Berliner Künstlerinnen.* Berlin: Kupfergraben: Berlinische Galerie, 1992, 619pp., illus.

Text in German. A comprehensive catalogue dealing with the Berlin Association of Women Artists from its founding in 1867 to 1992. There are thirty-seven essays in three sections: Profession ohne Tradition; Auftrage—kunstmarkt—Elgensinn; 125 Jahre Konflikte—Strategien—Erfolge. This is then followed by a chronology of the Association and the catalogue of exhibits. The emphasis of the text is on issues and analysis rather than on biography. The text has copious footnotes.

156   *National Museum of Women in the Arts.* New York: Harry N. Abrams Inc., 1987, 253pp., illus.

Catalogue of the permanent collection of the museum on its opening. The collection derived from that of Wilhelmina Holliday, founder of the museum. European artists of the later nineteenth and first half of the twentieth century are well represented and there is a useful introduction to each artist.

157   NEUE GESELLSCHAFT FÜR BILDENDE KUNST. *Das Verborgene Museum: Dokumentation der Kunst von Frauen in Berliner öffentlichen Sammlungen.* Berlin: Edition Hentrich, 1988, 364pp., illus.

Text in German. A detailed study of the lives and works of European women artists from the sixteenth to the twentieth centuries whose works are in the permanent collections of the Berlin Museums. Six critical essays analyse women's art production in its social context. Biographical essays on each of the women follow, except for the more recent artists, when an illustration is accompanied by a short biographical outline.

158   NEUWIRTH, WALTRAUD. *Vienna Workshops: Avant-garde, Art Déco Industrial Design.* Vienna: Selbstverlag W. Neuwirth with Austrian Museum of Applied Art, 1984, 240pp., illus.

Text in German and English. Ten women, chiefly active in the fields of glass and ceramics, are included in this study.

159   NICOLA, K.-G. "Österreichischer Staatspreis '91. Art Austria: Auf der Suche nach Vision." *Kunst und Handwerk* 91, no. 5 (1991): 35–38.

Text in German. Several women, including the ceramicists Maria Baumgartner, Judith Rataitz and Lisa Waltl, are included in this article on recent award-winners.

160   OEDEKOVEN-GERISCHER, ANGELA (ED.). *Frauen im Design: Berufsbilder under Lebenswege seit 1900. Women in design: careers and life histories since 1900.* 2 vols. Stuttgart: Design Center, 1989, vol. 1: 349pp., many illus.; vol. 2: 377pp., many illus.

Text in German and English. An invaluable publication on women designers, for it includes not only detailed information about the women whose work was exhibited but also a variety of essays and interviews relating to the debates about women and design. The earliest section deals with women involved in Art Nouveau, not all of whom are German but all of whom worked or exhibited in that country. There is a section on contemporary designers from other countries at the end of volume 2. The media include industrial products in addition to ceramics, furniture, interiors, glass and textiles.

161 *Paris-Berlin, 1900–33: rapports et contrastes France-Allemagne.* Paris: Centre nationale d'art et de culture Georges Pompidou, 1978, 576pp., many illus.

Text in French. Detailed survey of Franco-German visual culture and cultural history. Separate chapters are devoted to different media. A relatively small number of women are mentioned and none is treated in depth.

162 *Paris-Moscou, 1900–1930.* Paris: Centre nationale d'art et de culture Georges Pompidou, 1979, 583pp., many illus.

Text in French. Aims at an overview of Franco-Russian visual culture and cultural history. There are ten sections dealing with different media: fine art, design, architecture, propaganda art, posters, theatre and ballet, literature, music, film and photography. Twenty-five women are mentioned but not dealt with in detail.

163 *Paris-Paris: créations en France 1937–1957.* Paris: Musée Nationale d'Art Moderne, 1981, 527pp., many illus.

Text in French. An exhibition looking at the artistic activities in Paris over two decades. Many individuals are mentioned but there is little detailed information.

164 PARKER, ROSZIKA, and GRISELDA POLLOCK. *Old Mistresses: Women, Art and Ideology.* London: Routledge & Kegan Paul, 1981, 184pp., illus.

A seminal work in the study of women's involvement in art and craft. The first text to analyse why women appeared to have had a minor role in the art world, comparing it to the crafts and also analysing the dominant imagery of high art and the radical work by contemporary women such as Mary Kelly.

165 PARKER, ROSZIKA, and GRISELDA POLLOCK (EDS.). *Framing Feminism: Art and the Women's Movement, 1970–1985.* London and New York: Pandora, 1987, 345pp., illus.

Two substantial chapters chart the history of the women's art movement in Britain and analyse women's position within modernism. The second part of the book consists of an anthology of texts dealing with debates within the women's art movement under the headings Images and Signs, Institutions, Exhibitions and Strategies of Feminism.

166   *Partners.* London: Annely Juda Fine Art, 1993, n.p., illus.

An exhibition of sixteen artist couples, of whom twenty-eight individuals were active in Europe although the extent and impact of their collaboration is not investigated. This exhibition prefigures the book *Significant Others* by Whitney and De Courtivron (q.v.). Sonia Delaunay, Goncharova, Taueber-Arp, Hoch, Popova, Stepanova and Kobro feature from the early period, Hepworth and Mary Martin from the middle period, while there are five contemporary couples from England also included. Short biographies are given.

167   PEACOCK, NETTA. "The new movement in Russian decorative art." *Studio* (1901): 268–276.

Helen Polenoff (died 1899) was the first to revive the decorative arts in Russia through the use of folk art. In Moscow there arose a group of artists who turned to decorative art indigenous to Russia for their designs for furniture, embroidery and carved wooden objects. Amongst them were Marie jacounch-icoff and Nathalie Davidoff. Princess Ternichev also followed these ideas.

168   PILE, JOHN. *Dictionary of 20th Century Design.* New York: Roundtable Press, 1990.

Includes styles, individuals, firms, critics, insitutions of different kinds, journals, technical terms and techniques. Architects and some photographers are also included. Although the scope is wide, some women are included. There is no bibliography.

169   PIRHOFER, GOTTFRIED, and GMEINER, ASTRID. *Der Österreichischer Werkbund: Alternative zur klassischen Moderne in Architektur, Raum-und Produktgestaltung.* Salzburg: Residenz Verlag, 1985, 258 pp., illus.

Text in German. Deals with the Austrian Werkbund and its relationship to those in Germany, Hungary and Czechoslovakia. Examines how it continued during the war years and searched for an identity afterwards. For women the most useful section is the extensive listing of all those who were either members of the Werkbund or participated in the exhibitions. There are seventy-two women included from this relatively unfamiliar area. Each has an outline bibliography together with the dates of involvement as far as any of this information is known.

170   *Polish Art: Graphic Art, Textiles.* London: Victoria and Albert Museum, 1975, 52pp., illus.

After a section on old folk woodcuts there are sections on contemporary graphic art and textiles, both of which contain the works of several women from different generations.

171   PUVIANI, FLAVIO. *Dizionario dei pittori, scultori e incisori.* Ferrara: Casa Editrice Alba, 1974, 407pp., illus.

Text in Italian. Each artist is given a brief biography and a paragraph of critical comment. The majority of artists were born in the 1920s and 1930s and there is a useful number of women included.

172 QUENIOUX, GASTON. *Les arts décoratifs modernes*. Paris: Librairie Larousse, 1925.

Text in French. An introductory overview of design is followed by chapters on various media in which some fifteen women feature although the approach means that there is no detailed discussion of individuals.

173 ROGALIER, JEAN. "La Participation de la France à la Triennale de Milan." *L'Art Ménager,* September 1936, 512–513, illus.

Text in French. Review of French exhibits at the Sixth Triennale (Exposition des Arts Décoratifs et Industriels Modernes et de l'Architecture) at Milan. Six women are mentioned.

174 RUNDE, SABINA, HELGA HILSCHENZ-MLYNEK, and STEFAN SOLTER. *Zeitgenöschisches deutsches Kunsthandwerk: 5 Triennale 1990–1: Möbel, Schmuck und Gerät, Keramik, Textil, Buchkunst und Paper in Funktion, Glas*. Munich: Prestel Verlag; Museum of Frankfurt-am-Main, 1990.

Text in German. After two short introductory sections there are sections on each of the media represented. Each contains an alphabetical listing of the contemporary designers who took part in this exhibition. Many women are included. Each entry consists of a comprehensive biography and a list of exhibitions and collections, together with information on the exhibits in the Triennale.

175 SAUER, MARINA. *L'entrée des femmes à l'Ecole des Beaux-Arts, 1880–1903*. Paris: ENSBA, 1991, 89pp., illus.

Text in French. A study of the campaign, led by sculptor Hélène Bertaux (q.v. vol. 2) while President of the Union des Femmes Paintres et Sculpteurs, for the entry of women to the most prestigious academy for the training of artists in France. Comparisons are made with women's art education in Germany and England.

176 *Scandinavian Modern Design, 1880–1980*. New York and Harry Abrams Inc.: Cooper-Hewitt Museum, 1982, 286pp., illus.

Contains nine essays, of which five form a chronological evaluation from Art Nouveau to 1980. There is also a chapter on contemporary debates on national identity. A list of designers provides a biographical outline for each of the many women included.

177 No entry 177.

178 SCHWEIGER, WERNER. *Wiener Werkstätte: Kunst und Handwerk, 1903–32*. Vienna: Christian Brandstaetetter Verlad & Edition, 1982.

Text in German. A comprehensive examination of the productions of the Werkstätte in a variety of media: glass, ceramics, textiles, fashion, jewellery, theatrical costumes and interior design. There is a chronological account and brief biographies of 214 artists and designers, of whom 86 are women making this a useful source for the period.

179 SEDDON, JILL, and SUZETTE WORDEN (EDS.). *Women Designing. Redefining Design in Britain between the Wars.* Brighton: University of Brighton, 1994, 140pp., illus.

A collection of essays on women designers active in the 1920s and 1930s. The essays are in three main sections: Women and art and design education, Women, industry and institutions while the last, Women designing, is devoted to studies of individuals. They worked in many different media including textile design, graphics and interiors.

180 SHIMIZU, FUMIO, and MATTEO THUN. *Descendants of Leonardo da Vinci: The Italian design.* Tokyo: Graphic Publishing, 1989, 346pp., illus.

Text in English and Japanese. Three essays analyse the development of Italian design in the twentieth century, particularly since 1945. Short biographies are given of the four generations of designers whose work is included. A total of fifteen women are included, either in entries for design groups and studios or featured as individuals.

181 SMYTH, CHERYL. *Damn Fine Art by New Lesbian Artists.* London: Cassell, 1996, 154pp., illus.

Presents work by lesbian artists, mostly from America and England with a small minority from mainland Europe, divided by subject matter or approach. Within each category artists are discussed individually on the basis of their own statements. An introductory essay and section to each chapter present the issues as seen by the author.

182 *Société des femmes artistes modernes—France.* Paris: FAM, annual exhibitions 1900–45.

This series of exhibitions by contemporary women artists provides the names of many artists working in France together with a few from other European countries. There are no illustrations or information other than the list of names so their primary use is as a starting point for further research.

183 STAVENOW, ÅKE, and ÅKE HILLDT. *Design in Sweden.* Stockholm: Gothia, 1961, 268pp., illus.

An introductory essay on Swedish design in the twentieth century is followed by surveys on each of the main media. A section on the designer at work looks at education in the crafts and design while the third section on the artist/craftsperson includes several women. The work of others is illustrated. All designers are discussed in the context of their work rather than with any focus on individuals.

184 "Studio Talk." *Studio* 21 (1901): 265–268.

Discusses the success of Mount Street School in Liverpool in the recent National Competition and at the Paris International Exposition of 1900. The article also reviews an exhibition of student work from this school then open in Liverpool. More than fifteen women are mentioned, with metalwork being a particularly strong field.

185 SUTER, MARGRIT, and DOROTHEA CHRIST (EDS.). *Schweizer Künstlerinnen heute/Artistes suisses aujourd'hui.* Zurich: Helmhaus, in association with publ. Basel, Schwabe und Co., 1984, 152pp., illus.

Text in German and French. An exhibition organised by the Société Suisse des Femmes Peintres, Sculpteurs et Décoratrices. The catalogue gives the history of the organisation and lists the presidents since its inception. One of the editors, Dorothea Christ, was then the president. The work of sixty-one women artists is organised in four sections—painting, sculpture, graphics, textiles—and brief biographical outlines are given. A photograph of each artist and one illustration of their work is included.

186 SYDHOFF, BEATE. *Sweden Comes to New York: An Exhibition of Six Women Artists.* New York: A.I.R. Gallery, 1981, n.p., illus.

A brief statement only is provided on each of the exhibitors: Grete Billgren, Barbro Backstrom, Kristina Elander, Marie-Louise de Geer Bergenstrahle, Ann-Charlotte Johannsson and Lenke Rothman.

187 *Szot Ösztöndíjasok Kiállitása.* Budapest: Magyar Nemzeti Galéria, 1986, n.p., illus.

Text in Hungarian. Consists of a alphabetical list of exhibitors with a brief biography for each. There are nine women exhibitors in painting, sculpture and textiles.

188 TANNOCK, MICHAEL. *Portuguese Twentieth Century Artists: A Biographical Dictionary.* Chichester: Phillimore & Co. Ltd., 1978, 192pp, 381 illus.

Quite a number of women are included in this dictionary, particularly those among more recent artists. A summary of their biography and artistic activities is given, providing a starting point for further research.

189 *The Craftsman's Art.* London: Victoria and Albert Museum, 1973, 104pp., illus.

Six selectors, two of whom were women, chose the contents of the exhibition. Preliminary essays deal with the changing concept of the artist/designer/craftsperson. Many women are included in the exhibition, especially in the sections on ceramics and textiles.

190   *The Lunning Prize.* Stockholm: Nationalmuseum, 1986, 215pp., illus.
        An exhibition of work by winners of the Lunning prize for design in
        Scandinavia. The prize was awarded to two designers each year from 1951 to
        1970 and the introductory essay suggests that this played a key role in the evo-
        lution of Scandinavian design. Winners worked in many media. For each there
        is a critical essay and details of the exhibits. Fifteen women are included.

191   *The Maker's Eye.* London: Crafts Council, 1981, 120pp., illus.
        An exhibition of works from the Crafts Council's permanent collection
        selected by designers who include Alison Britton, Mary Farmer (qq.v.) and
        Connie Stephenson. Profiles of the selectors and their work is followed by
        brief information about the items selected. The work of many women is
        included.

192   *Thirties: British Art and Design before the War.* London: Hayward Gallery,
        1979, 320 pp., illus.
        After an introductory essay and a chronology of events in the decade,
        there are essays on developments in the different media in the period. The
        aim is to locate the cultural artefacts within their social, political and eco-
        nomic context. This is followed by the catalogue, which is also organised by
        medium, after which are short biographies of the artists and designers. There
        is a useful bibliography. Thirty-six women are included.

193   TIMMERS, MARGARET. *The Way We Live Now: Designs for Interiors
        1950 to the Present Day.* London: Victoria and Albert Museum, 1978, 39pp.,
        illus.
        Essays on interior design, including wallpapers and furnishing textiles,
        are organised by decade. A considerable number of women are included
        although there is little information about individuals.

194   *Tout droit au but: neuf femmes constructivistes: Christa van Santen, Lou
        Loeber, Els de Groot, Karin Daan, Sonja Vincent, Ria van Eyk, Yvonne
        Kracht, Truus Wilmink, Neeltje Korteweg.* Paris: Institut néerlandais, 1976,
        12pp, illus.
        Text in French. The artists are introduced in the first two pages of the cat-
        alogue. A range of media are included and several of the artists also work
        across a number of media.

195   TRAFFELET, URSULA (ED.). *Das Leben zur Kunst machen: Arbeiten auf
        Papier von Frauen der russischen Avantgarde, Stoffe und Porzellan aus der
        jungen Sowjetunion.* Zurich: Helmhaus, 1989, 150pp., illus.
        Text in German. Consists of a collection of essays by different writers on
        the fields in the exhibition: works on paper, ceramics and textiles produced
        by women between 1917 and 1930. There are short biographies at the end of
        the text.

196 TUROWSKI, ANDRZEJ. *Konstruktywizm polski próba rekonstrukcji nurtu (1921–34).* Wroclaw: Zaklad im Ossolinskich-Wyddawnictwo PAN, 1981, 360pp., 373 illus.

Text in Polish with an English summary. Five chapters provide a historical and analytical discussion of the contructivist movement in Poland. The main female protagonists are included: Katarina Kobro, Maria Nicz-Borowiak and Teresa Zarnower.

197 *Un âge d'or des Arts Décoratifs, 1814–1848.* Paris: Grand Palais, 1991, 560pp., illus.

Text in French. Contains information on a small number of women but for a period at which few women are identified: Princess Marie d'Orléans, (q.v.), Mlle Dubuquoy-Lalouette and Marie-Victoire Jaquotot are all included in the biographical section as well as the main text.

198 *Utopia.* Bonn: Frauen Museum, 1984, 196pp., mainly illus.

Text in German. Catalogue of an exhibition by mainly German women artists on the theme of Utopia to which individuals and groups contributed. They also prepared the catalogue entries, which are more works of art than sources of information.

199 VACHON, MARIUS. *La femme dans l'art: les protectrices des arts, les femmes artistes.* Paris: J. Rouan et Cie., 1893, 617pp., 400 illus.

Text in French. Most of this book is devoted to images of women but there are chapters of women collectors and patrons from the eighteenth century. One chapter examines women artists in Europe from the sixteenth century, including the early women members of the Academy. The nineteenth century chapter has three parts, of which only the shortest looks at women artists of the author's own time.

200 VALLANCE, AYMER. "British Decorative Art in 1899 and the Arts and Crafts Exhibition." *Studio* 18 (1900): 179–94, 247–72.

Reviews the state of the decorative arts at the end of the nineteenth century and an Arts and Crafts exhibition. Mary Newill (q.v.)(stained glass), Mrs Gaskin (q.v.) (metalwork), Adele Hay (metalwork), Nelia Casella (metalwork and enamelling) and Ellen M. Rope (q.v. vol. 2) (plaster reliefs) are among the women mentioned.

201 VAN RAAY, STEFAN. *Imitation and Inspiration: Japanese Influence on Dutch Art.* Art Unlimited Books, 1992, 180pp., illus.

Discusses artists and designers who have been influenced by Japanese culture. Women included are Maria Blaisse, Maryan Geluk, Madelon Hookaas and Johnny Rolf.

202 VERGINE, LEA. *L'altra metà dell'avanguardia, 1910–40.* Milan: Mazzotta Editore 1980. French edition: *L'autre moitié de l'avant-garde, 1910–40.* Paris: Des Femmes, 1982, 313pp., illus.

Includes over 100 women who were involved in the avant-garde groups in Europe. Organised around movements, it begins with the Blue Rider and ends with Surrealism. A large section on abstract art allows the inclusion of those not directly connected to a movement. An invaluable text with useful discussion of the work of many women.

203 VERONESI, GIULIA. *Into the Twenties: Style and Design 1909–1929.* Florence: Valecchi Editore, 1966. English translation: London: Thames and Hudson, 1968, 371pp., 10 pl., 246 illus.

Seeks to map the history of design in Europe from Art Nouveau to 1930 as two principal strands: continuity from earlier traditions and revolt from those traditions. Chapters are devoted to Germany, Paris and Italy before World War I, design during the war, the postwar period in Paris, Germany, England, America and Italy, the International Exhibition of the Decorative Arts in 1925 and its aftermath. A glossary and brief biographies of the main participants ends the book. A small number of women are included.

204 WELLER, SIMONA. *Il complesso di Michelangelo: ricerca sul contributo dato dalla donna all'arte italiana del novecento.* Pollenza-Macerata: La Nuova Foglio [*sic*] Editrice, 1976, 261pp., illus.

Text in Italian. Consists of several discrete sections. The first essay by Cesare Vivaldi discusses the problems for women artists and the reasons behind what he sees as their minor role in the world of art. This is followed by a philosphical argument by Weller, herself an artist, concerning her thesis for the book that women suffer from an inferiority complex (the complex of Michelangelo) in respect to what they can achieve. The other sections of the book set out to demonstrate the achievements of Italian women artists of this century, particularly in the postwar period. Reproduced are interviews with a number of artists or their responses to her request for an interview, an analysis of the responses to the questionnaire which Weller distributed and statements by other artists. The final section consists of a biographical dictionary of women artists in Italy in the twentieth century.

205 WHITEFORD, FRANK (ED.). *The Bauhaus: Masters and Students by Themselves.* London: Conran Octopus, 1992, 328pp., illus.

An anthology of texts, which are grouped chronologically, from teachers and students at the Bauhaus. A small number of these, especially those concerning the Weaving Workshop, are by women: Gunta Stölzl, Anni Albers, Helene Nonne Schmidt, Otti Berger, Ellen Auerbach, Marianne Brandt and Lucia Moholy-Nagy.

206 WICHSTRØM, ANNE. *Rooms with a View: Women's Art in Norway, 1880–1990*. Oslo: Royal Ministry of Foreign Affairs, 1989, 53pp., illus.

A useful essay on the sociopolitical context of the activities of women artists in Norway from the mid-nineteenth century precedes the catalogue sections. Four chronological divisions into generations include artists and designers. Numerically the last two generations from 1940 to 1970 and 1970 to 1990 are larger. Each artist is represented by one illustration and a short page of biographical information and stylistic discussion.

207 WIRTH, GÜNTHER. *Verbotene Kunst: verfolgte Künstler im deutschen Sudwesten 1933–45*. Stuttgart: Hatje, 1987, 351pp., illus.

Text in German. A series of chapters on the situation in Germany for artists who were banned from practising by the Nazi authorities, including restrictions on students and information on those who emigrated. Biographies of the artists are given. Three women occur: Maria Caspar-Filser, Alice Haatburger and Gretel Haas-Gerber.

208 WOHL, H. *Portuguese art since 1910*. London: Royal Academy of Art, 1978.

Four women are featured in this exhibition: Paula Rego, Aña Hatherly, Vieira da Silva (qq.v. vol. 2) and Menez.

209 WOOD, ESTHER. "The National Competition at South Kensington, 1899." *Studio* 17 (1899): 250–266.

This review mentions the work of at least ten women designers in stained glass, metalwork and tapestry.

210 WOOD, ESTHER. "Home Arts and Industries Exhibition at the Albert Hall." *Studio* 20 (1900): 78–83.

Review of annual exhibition in which work by amateur and professional designers was included.

211 WOOD, ESTHER. "Home Arts and Industries Exhibition at the Albert Hall." *Studio* 23 (1901): 106–109.

Review of annual design exhibition to which mainly amateur women artists contributed.

212 WOOD, ESTHER. "National Competition of Schools of Art." *Studio* 26 (1902): 286–281.

Despite the title, this is a review of decorative art produced by students. Eighteen works by women are illustrated and other women designers active in a range of media are mentioned in the text. The strongest fields were textiles and ceramics.

213   WOOD, ESTHER. "The National Competition, 1901." *Studio* 23 (1901): 257–268.

Almost twenty women designers are included in this review. The work ranges from a plaster relief panel to wallpaper design, embroidered screens, bookbinding and designs for furniture and stained glass.

214   ZAHLE, ERIC (ED.). *Scandinavian domestic design.* London: Methuen, 1963, 300pp., 418 illus.

After an introduction on Scandinavian design between 1930 and 1960, there are four chapters, one on each of Denmark, Finland, Sweden and Norway. There are lengthy explanatory captions for the illustrations in the section devoted to them. Finally there is an extensive listing of designers with short biographies for each. There are many women in all fields.

215   ZILLIACUS, BENEDICT. *Decorative Arts in Finland.* Porvoossa: Werner Söderström Osakeyhtiön Kirjapainossa, 1963, 20pp., illus.

A short survey of the state of modern design in glass, ceramics, textiles including tapestry and metalwork. Twenty-two women are included.

Bookbinding

REFERENCE

216   BRENNI, VITO. *Bookbinding: A Guide to the Literature.* Westport, Connecticut and London: Greenwood Press, 1982, 199pp.
       A useful bibliography on the arts of bookbinding, bookplates, bookjackets and various technical process. The chapter on the history of bookbinding generally and then by country is the most useful.

217   RAMSDEN, CHARLES. *French bookbinders 1789–1848.* London: Lund Humphries, 1950, 228pp., illus.
       After an essay on the development of bookbinding over the period covered by this study, the largest part of the book consists of a biographical dictionary of binders. Ramsden has listed all the names he encountered on his research even when there was little other information. This provides names of women on whom further research may be carried out.

OTHER SOURCES

218   BYRNE, JOHN. "Designer Bookbinders." *Crafts* 34 (1978): 50–51.
       Exhibition review which specifically mentioned Elizabeth Greenhill, Denise Lubett and Sally Lou Smith (qq.v.).

219   CUMMING, ELIZABETH, and WENDY KAPLAN. *The Arts and Crafts movement.* London: Thames and Hudson, 1991, 216pp., 167 illus.
       Discusses the architecture and design associated with the Arts and Crafts movement in Britain, Ireland, mainland Europe and the United States. There are a number of references to women, including some from the Guild of Women Bookbinders: Elizabeth McColl, Florence and Edith de Rheims, Constance Karslake and other designers such as Mary Newill, Edith Dawson, Phoebe Traquair, Jessie Newbery, Margaret and Frances Macdonald, Evelyn Gleeson and Sarah Purser (qq.v.).

220   *Designer Bookbinders 1974.* London: Crafts Council, 1974, 46pp., illus.
           A short introduction about the organisation Designer Bookbinders is fol-
lowed by an alphabetical arrangement of the seventeen exhibitors. These are
all members who are only admitted on the basis of the quality of their work.
Four of the exhibitors are women: Elizabeth Greenhill, Denise Lubett, Faith
Shannon and Sally Lou Smith.

221   DEVAUCHELLE, ROGER. *La reliure en France de ses origines à nos
jours.* 3 vols. Paris: Rousseau-Girard, vol. 1 [up to 1700]: 1959, 209pp.,
illus.; vol. 2 [1700–1850]: 1960, 259pp., illus.; vol. 3 [from 1851]: 1961,
287pp., illus.
           Text in French. Chronological account of the development of French
bookbinding, including technical aspects, collectors, styles and individual
binders. Only volume 3 provides any information about women binders and
is a useful source for the less well researched nineteenth century.

222   DEVAUX, YVES. *Dix siècles de reliure.* Paris: Editions Pygmalion, 1977,
398pp., illus.
           Text in French. A historical account of bookbinding in France. The last
two chapters cover the nineteenth and twentieth centuries respectively. In the
final chapter the following women are mentioned: Rose Adler, Germaine de
Coster, Thérèse Moncey and Monique Mathieu. The book ends with a list of
the artists, craftspeople and collectors who are referred to only briefly in the
text.

223   DUBOIS D'ENGHIEN, H. *La reliure en Belgique au dix-neuvième siècle.*
Brussels: Alexandre Leclerq et Paul van der Perre, 1954, 255pp., illus.
           Text in French. A historical essay is followed by a dictionary of binders,
cover-printers and some printing businesses. Many of these are only known
by their initials but at this early period there are a number of women included. A large proportion of these are widows, suggesting not simply that they
took over their husband's business at his death but also that they had participated in it beforehand so that they were familiar with its operation.

224   DUNCAN, ALASTAIR, and GEORGES DE BARTHA. *Art Nouveau and
Art Deco Bookbinding, 1880–1940.* London: Thames and Hudson, 1989,
200pp., illus.
           After an introduction to the subject, there is an alphabetical section of
fifty bookbinders, of whom eight are women. A brief biography is given,
together with illustrations of their work. Following this sequence there is
another which gives fuller biographies and bibliographies for each of the
fifty, together with additional bookbinders. More women feature in these
additions.

225   *Exposition de la Société de la Reliure Originale accompagnée d'une présen-*
tation des reliures ayant appartenu à Jean Grolier. Paris: Bibliothèque
Nationale, 1959, 150pp., 42 illus.

     Text in French. Catalogue of 438 bookbindings, of which 290 are by con-
temporary bookbinders, either members of the Society or invited designers.
Rose Adler, Germaine de Coster and Hélène Dumas are represented as
Society members while Madeleine Gras and Claude Stahly are among the
second category. Biographies are given before the information about the individual exhibits for each person.

226   FARNOUX-REYNAUD, LUCIEN. "La reliure d'art: triomphe du gout
français." *Mobilier et Décoration* (February 1938): 58–78.

     Text in French. A short article with many illustrations concerning French
bookbinding in the 1920s and 1930s. Works by Rose Adler, Antoinette
Cerrutti, Hélène Cauchetier, Artita Garcia, Cécile Grandgeorges, Marguérite
Fray and N. Gras are illustrated although they are only listed in the text.

227   FLEMING, JOHN, and PRISCILLA JUVELIS (ED.). *The Book Beautiful*
and the Binding as Art. 2 vols. Boston, Mass.: Nimrod Press, vol. 1: 1983,
n.p., illus.; vol. 2: 1985, n.p. illus.

     Volume 1 is a limited edition (750 copies) of catalogue of 219 items for
sale, the majority of which are French, each with a detailed description. The
works of seven women, some known better as artists, are included: Adler,
Gras, Marot-Rodde. Vieira da Silva, Lydis, Laurencin and Clouzot. Volume
2 follows the same format and amongst the fifty-seven items are works by
Adler, Laurencin, Lydis and Richier.

228   GARRIGOU, MARCEL. *Cent ans de reliures d'art, 1880–1980.* Toulouse:
Bibliothèque Municipale, 1981, 125pp., illus.

     Text in French. Using mainly sources available in the region, part of the
aim of the exhibition was to show where original bookbindings are held by
municipal libraries in France. Arranged chronologically, women binders
appear from the second section, 1920–1960. Some nineteen women are
included altogether although there is limited information on each. There are
appendices on the holdings of original bindings by municipal libraries.

229   GARVEY, ELEANOR, ET AL. *The Turn of a Century, 1885–1910: Art*
Nouveau Jugendstil Books. Cambridge, Mass.: Dept. of Printing and Graphic
Arts, Harvard University, 1970, 124pp., illus.

     Describes various aspects of book production in western Europe. The
number of women included is not large. The emphasis is mainly on illustration, whether the production of designs or their execution through wood
engraving or other techniques, but there is also some information about bookbinding. The Austrian Bertha Czega is mentioned in this repect; illustrators
included are Jessie King, Frances and Margaret Macdonald, the Belgians

Juliette Wytsman and Marie Danse, Suzanne Lepère of France and Elena Luksch Makovsky from Vienna.

230 GARVEY, ELEANOR, and PETER WICK. *The Arts of the French Book, 1900–1965.* Dallas: South Methodist University Press, 1967, 119pp., illus.

Looks at book design, illustration and bookbinding in France at a period when there were many outstanding practitioners. A number of women are mentioned.

231 GRIESBACH, ELSIE. "The Art of the French Bookbinder." *Columbia Library Columns* 4, no. 1 (November 1954): 19–27.

A survey of bookbinding in France from the sixteenth through the twentieth centuries. A few women are listed in the brief section on the twentieth century.

232 HOLME, CHARLES. *The art of the book: A review of some recent European and American work in typography, page decoration and binding.* London: The Studio, 1914, 276pp., mainly illus.

After a chapter on British typography, there are seven more devoted to the art of the book in seven countries, six of which are European. In each case there is a small proportion of text and the names of women occur mainly in the illustrations. Six British women bookbinders are included (Norah Hewitt, Katharine Adams, Sybil Pye, Sarah Prideaux, Alice Pattinson, Mary Robinson), four Austrians (Marianne Hitschmann-Steinberger, Miss Frimberger, Bertha Bindtner, Dora Cross) and two Swedes (Countess Eva Sparre and Greta Morssing).

233 *La Reliure originale française. Bookbindings by contemporary French binders.* New York: New York Museum of Contemporary Crafts, 1964, 52pp., illus.

Describes 142 books by contemporary French binders who include four women: Jacqueline Antona, Monique Mathieu, Germaine de Coster and Hélène Dumas.

234 *La Reliure originale.* Paris: Bibliothèque Nationale, 1953, 94pp., illus.

Text in French. Looks at French bookbinding from the early nineteenth century. The later period is represented by members of the Société de la Reliure Originale. Rose Adler, Germaine de Coaster and Hélène Dumas are the only women included.

235 LEWIS, ROY. *Fine Bookbinding in the Twentieth Century.* London and Newton Abbott: David and Charles, 1984, 151pp., 33pls., 89 illus.

Adopts a largely chronological approach, with the final chapter about collecting designer bookbindings. Of the earlier generation Sarah Prideaux, Sybil Pye and Katherine Adams are included. More recent designers discussed are Faith Shannon, Dee Odell-Foster, Angela Jones, Sally Lou Smith and the Belgian Jacqueline Liekens.

236   *Modern British bookbinders: An exhibition of modern British bookbinding by members of Designer Bookbinders.* New York: Designer Bookbinders; London: Pierpont Morgan Library, 1971, 63pp.

Consists mainly of an alphabetical list of the fourteen exhibitors, all of whom are members of the Designer Bookbinders, with short biographies and details of bindings exhibited. There are three women: Deborah Evetts, Elizabeth Greenhill and Faith Shannon.

237   *Modern bookbindings and their designers.* London: The Studio, 1899, 82pp., illus.

Chapters on individual countries provide an overview of late-nineteenth-century bookbinding activity. Seventeen women are included in the two chapters on Britain (written by Esther Wood), four for France (Mmes Waldeck-Rousseau, Antoinette Vallgren, Thaulow and Jeanne Rollince) and four from Scandinavia (Countess Eva Sparre from Finland, the Swedes Miss Gisberg and Gisela Henckel, and Maria Hansen of Norway). Some of those mentioned are designers in several media rather than bookbinders specifically.

238   *Modern bookbindings: Their design and decoration.* London: Constable, 1906, 131pp., illus.

The chapter on Britain mentions the following as active in different regions of England: Miss Talbot, Alice Shepherd, Misses Power, Adams, Paget, Philpott, Nathan, Pattinson, Stebbing and Elizabeth McColl. In Scotland Jessie M. King, Jane Hamilton, Alice Gardner, Agnes Watson and Miss McLure are referred to. The chapter on France includes no women.

239   NIXON, HOWARD. *Five centuries of English bookbinding.* London: Scolar Press, 1978, 241pp., illus.

One hundred examples from the period 1483–c. 1928 are illustrated and commented on. Each entry contains information, where available, about the history of the individual item, the binder, the book and its owner. The earliest woman binder mentioned is Jane Steel, working from 1717. Sarah Prideaux, Katherine Adams and several women from the Guild of Women Bookbinders—Constance Karslake, Edith and Florence de Rheims and Miss Edwards—are included.

240   NIXON, HOWARD. *Broxbourne Library: Styles and designs of book binding from the 12th to the 20th centuries.* London: for the Broxbourne Library by Maggs Brothers,, 1956, n.p., illus.

Of the 119 bindings in the Broxbourne library collection, 22 are from after 1800. Two of these are anonymous and of the remainder four are by women: Elizabeth McColl, Katharine Adams, Madeleine Kohn and Sybil Pye.

241 NIXON, HOWARD, and MIRJAM FOOT. *The History of decorated bookbinding in England.* Oxford: Clarendon Press, 1992, 124pp., 11 pl., 128 illus.

Based on the Lyell lectures given by Nixon in 1979, the book was prepared for publication after his death in 1983 by Mirjam Foot. The nineteenth century is reached in the sixth and final chapter. Women first appear towards the end of the century and are designated amateur, possibly because they treated the work as a craft in the manner of William Morris. Sarah Prideaux and her two pupils, Katherine Adams and Elizabeth McColl (qq.v.), are followed by members of the Guild of Women Binders: Constance Karslake, Edith and Florence de Rheims and Miss Edwards. Sybil Pye and Elsa Taterka are cited among the twentieth-century examples.

242 PABST, MICHAEL. *Wiener Grafik um 1900.* Munich: Verlag Silke Schreiber, 1984, 348pp., many illus.

Text in German. A detailed analysis of graphic art in Vienna at the turn of the century, which includes journals, bookbinding, printmaking, posters and book illustration. The final section consists of biographies of the artists and designers. There are seven women: Bertha Czegka, Nora Exner von Zumbusch, Marianne Frimburger, Broncia Koller, Minka Podhajska, Mileva Roller and Maria von Uchatius.

243 *Reliures du XXe siècle, de Marius Michel à Paul Bonet.* Brussels; organised by the Société de bibliophiles et iconophiles de Belgique: Bibliothèque Royale de Belgique, 1957, 84pp., illus.

Text in French. Following a brief introduction the text is arranged by individual artist, with a brief biography and information about the items exhibited. Some less familiar names, such as Berthe van Regemorter and Margot Nyst, are included with the better known Jeanne Legrand, Rose Adler, Geneviève de Léotard, Madeleine Gras, Louise Levêque and Thérèse Moncey.

244 *Un demi-siècle de reliures d'art contemporain en France et dans le monde.* Paris: Bibliothèque Forney, 1984, 307pp., illus.

Text in French. An excellent source for the many European women involved in bookbinding. The first section deals with the years 1920–1970, while the second, and larger, covers contemporary activity. The final section includes the work of bookbinders from European countries other than France: Belgium, Britain, Germany and Switzerland.

245 UZANNE, OCTAVE. *L'art dans la décoration extérieure des livres en France et à l'étranger; les couvertures illustrées, les cartonnages d'éditeurs, la reliure d'art.* Paris: L.H. May et la Société Française des éditions d'art, 1898, 275pp., illus.

Text in French. Essentially a survey, the book is divided into four sections: illustrated covers, commercial bindings, contemporary masters and artists decorations for bindings. A number of works by women are illustrated but often with the absence of any mention in the text. Chapter 1 illustrates works by Mlle Bertrand and Mlle A. Poidevin in this way but Kate Greenaway is commented on; Chapter 3 includes Mme J.-M. Belville, Mme M. Jacquinot, Irene Nichols, Sarah Prideaux, Eva Sparre and Elizabeth McColl. Women providing artist bindings are listed, as Eva Sparre, Amalia Wallgren and Mme Waldeck-Rousseau.

246 WOOD, ESTHER. "The National Competition, 1901." *Studio* 23 (1901): 257–268.
    Almost twenty women designers are included in this review. The work ranges from a plaster relief panel to wallpaper design, embroidered screens, bookbinding and designs for furniture and stained glass.

INDIVIDUALS

247 ADAMS, KATHARINE (Alt. WEBB) (1862–1952)
    English bookbinder who was a pupil of Sarah Prideaux (q.v.) in the 1890s.

Exhibitions

Hobson, G. *English Bindings in the Library of J. R. Abbey. An Exhibition of the Modern English and French Bindings from the Collection of Major J. R. Abbey.* No. 128. London: Arts Council, 1949.

Other Sources

Modern Bookbindings and their Designers. The Studio, Winter no. 1899–1900.
    Nixon, Howard. *Broxbourne Library: Styles and Designs of Bookbinding from the 12th to the 20th Centuries.* London: Maggs Brothers for the Broxbourne Library, 1956.
    ———. *Five Centuries of English Bookbinding.* London: Scolar Press, 1978.
    Nixon, Howard, and Mirjam Foot. *The History of Decorated Bookbinding in England.* Oxford: Clarendon Press, 1992.

248 ADLER, ROSE (1890–1959)
    French bookbinder who was made a Chevalier de la Légion d'Honneur in 1951.

Main Sources

Rose Adler: Reliures. Paris: Charles Moreau, 1931, 50pl.
Chapon, Francois. "Rose Adler." *Jardin des Arts* 77 (April 1961): 53–55.
Cheronnet, Louis. "Rose Adler." *Art et Décoration* 57 (1930): 119–128.
"Un maître de la reliure d'art: Rose Adler." *Art et Décoration* 73 (May 1959): 46–47.

Exhibitions

La Reliure Originale. Paris: Bibliothèque Nationale, 1953, 94pp., illus. Exhibition organised by the Société de la Reliure Originale.
Reliures du XXe siècle, de Marius Michel à Paul Bonet. Brussels: Bibliothèque Royale de Belgique, 1957. Short biography followed by information on her exhibits.
Exposition de la Société de la Reliure Originale. Paris: Bibliothèque Nationale, 1959.
Barré-Despond, Arlette. *Les Années UAM, 1929–1958.* Paris: Musée des Arts Décoratifs, 1988.
Cinquantenaire de l'Exposition de 1925. Paris: Musée des Arts Décoratifs, 1976. Contains a brief biography.
Dufresne, Jean-Luc, and Olivier Messac, eds. *Femmes créatrices des années vingt.* Granville: Musée Richard Anacréon, 1988. Gives an outline biography.

Other Sources

Brenni, Vito. *Bookbinding: A Guide to the Literature.* Westport, Connecticut and London: Greenwood Press, 1982.
Dally, P. "Les techniques modernes de la reliure." *Art et Décoration* 51 (1927): 15–24.
Byars, Mel. *The Design Encyclopedia.* London: Lawrence King, 1994.
Devauchelle, Roger. *La reliure en France de ses origines à nos jours.* Paris: Rousseau-Girard, vol. 3, 1961.
Duncan, Alastair, and Georges De Bartha. *La reliure en France: Art Nouveau et Art Déco, 1880–1940.* Paris: Les Editions de l'Amateur, 1989.

249 ANTONA, JACQUELINE
French bookbinder.

Exhibitions

La reliure originale française. Bookbindings by Contemporary French Binders. New York: Museum of Contemporary Crafts, 1964.

Other Sources

Brenni, Vito. *Bookbinding: A Guide to the Literature.* Westport, Connecticut and London: Greenwood Press, 1982.

250 BERNARD, MARGUERITE
French bookbinder.

Other Sources

Brenni, Vito. *Bookbinding: A Guide to the Literature.* Westport, Connecticut and London: Greenwood Press, 1982.
Dally, P. "Les techniques modernes de la reliure." *Art et Décoration* 51 (1927): 15–24, illus.

251 BILLOW, EVA (Alt. Comtesse de SPARRE) (1870–?)
Swedish bookbinder.

Main Sources

Ellsworth, C. "Hand Bookbinding in Sweden." *Craft Horizons* 13 (January–February 1953): 13–15, illus.

Other Sources

Brenni, Vito. *Bookbinding: A Guide to the Literature.* Westport, Connecticut and London: Greenwood Press, 1982.
Modern Bookbindings and their Designers. The Studio, Winter no. 1899–1900. Referred to here as Finnish.

252 BONVOISIN, JACQUELINE (active from 1936)
French bookbinder.

Other Sources

Devauchelle, Roger. *La reliure en France de ses origines à nos jours.* Paris: Rousseau-Girard, vol. 3, 1961.

253 BORJESON, INGEBORG
Swedish bookbinder.

Main Sources

Ellsworth, C. "Hand Bookbinding in Sweden." *Craft Horizons* 13 (January–February 1953): 13–15, illus.

254 CERRUTTI, ANTOINETTE (c. 1905–)
French bookbinder active from c. 1931 who won many prizes.

Main Sources

Colas, Henri. "Les Reliures d'Antoinette Cerutti" [*sic*]. *Mobilier et Décoration,* January 1938, 31–37.

Other Sources

Byars, Mel. *The Design Encylopedia.* London: Lawrence King, 1994.

Devauchelle, Roger. *La reliure en France de ses origines à nos jours.* Paris: Rousseau-Girard, vol. 3, 1961.

Duncan, Alastair, and Georges de Bartha. *Art Nouveau and Art Déco Bookbinding, 1880–1940.* London: Thames and Hudson, 1989.

255　COBDEN-SANDERSON, ANNIE
English bookbinder who worked in and financed her husband's Doves Press.

Other Sources

Callen, Anthea. *Angel in the Studio: Women in the Arts and Crafts Movement 1870–1914.* London: Architectural Press, 1979.

256　DANIEL, EMILY.
English bookbinder, printer of special editions and illuminator who worked in her husband's Daniel Press.

Other Sources

Callen, Anthea. *Angel in the Studio: Women in the Arts and Crafts Movement 1870–1914.* London: Architectural Press, 1979.

257　DE COSTER, GERMAINE (1895–)
French bookbinder and designer who collaborated closely with Hélène Dumas (q.v.) and who together were known for their sumptuous bindings.

Main Sources

Kulche, August. "Germaine de Coster, Hélène Dumas." *Art et Métiers du Livre* 161 (May–June 1990): 2–9.

Thornton, Lynne. "Contemporary Crafts in France." *Connoisseur* 206 (1981): 229–233.

Exhibitions

La reliure originale. Paris: Bibliothèque Nationale, 1953, 94pp., illus. Exhibition organised by the Société de la Reliure Originale.

Exposition de la Société de la Reliure Originale. Paris: Bibliothèque Nationale, 1959.

Germaine de Coster, Hélène Dumas. Ascona: Galleria del bel libro, 1968, 20pp., illus.

Relieurs contemporains. Paris: Bibliothèque Nationale, 1979.

Other Sources

Brenni, Vito. *Bookbinding: A Guide to the Literature.* Westport, Connecticut and London: Greenwood Press, 1982.

Byars, Mel. *The Design Encyclopedia.* London: Lawrence King, 1994.

Devauchelle, Roger. *La reliure en France de ses origines à nos jours.* Paris: Rousseau-Girard, vol. 3, 1961.

Duncan Alastair, and Georges de Bartha. *Art Nouveau and Art Déco Bookbinding.* London: Thames and Hudson, 1989.

Thornton, Lynne. "Contemporary Crafts in France." *Connoisseur* 206 (March 1981): 229–233.

258 DE FELICE, MARGUÉRITE (c. 1874–)
French bookbinder.

Other Sources

Brunhammer, Yvonne, and Suzanne Tise. *Les artistes décorateurs, 1900–42.* Paris: Flammarion, 1990.

Byars, Mel. *The Design Encyclopedia.* London: Lawrence King, 1994.

Duncan Alastair, and Georges de Bartha. *Art Nouveau and Art Déco Bookbinding, 1880–1940.* London: Thames and Hudson, 1989.

259 DE LÉOTARD, GENEVIVE.
French bookbinder active from c. 1925.

Exhibitions

Reliures du XXe siècle, de Marius Michel à Paul Bonet. Brussels: Bibliothèque Royale de Belgique, 1957. Short biography followed by information on her exhibits.

Other Sources

Brenni, Vito. *Bookbinding: A Guide to the Literature.* Westport, Connecticut and London: Greenwood Press, 1982.

Byars, Mel. *The Design Encyclopedia.* London: Lawrence King, 1994.

Dally, P. "Les techniques de la reliure moderne." *Art et Décoration* 51 (1927): 15–24.

Devauchelle, Roger. *La reliure en France de ses origines à nos jours.* Paris: Rousseau-Girard, vol. 3, 1961.

Duncan, Alastair, and Georges de Bartha. *La reliure en France: art nouveau et art déco, 1880–1940.* Paris: Les Editions de l'Amateur, 1989.

260   DE RHEIMS, EDITH and FLORENCE
English bookbinders who were members of the Guild of Women Bookbinders.

Other Sources

Cumming, Elizabeth, and Wendy Kaplan. *The Arts and Crafts Movement.* London: Thames and Hudson, 1991.

Nixon, Howard. *Five Centuries of English Bookbinding.* London: Scolar Press, 1978.

Nixon, Howard, and Mirjam Foot. *The History of Decorated Bookbinding in England.* Oxford: Clarendon Press, 1992.

261   DUMAS, HÉLNE
French bookbinder who collaborated with Germaine de Coster (q.v.) and who together were known for their sumptuous bindings.

Main Sources

Kulche, August. "Germaine de Coster, Hélène Dumas." *Art et Métiers du Livre* 161 (May–June 1990): 2–9.

Exhibitions

La reliure originale. Paris: Bibliothèque Nationale, 1953, 94pp., illus. Exhibition organised by the Société de la Reliure Originale.

Exposition de la Société de la Reliure Originale. Paris: Bibliothèque Nationale, 1959.

La reliure originale française. Bookbindings by Contemporary French Binders. New York: Museum of Contemporary Crafts, 1964.

Germaine de Coster, Hélène Dumas. Ascona: Galleria del bel libro, 1968, 20pp., illus.

Relieurs contemporains. Paris: Bibliothèque Nationale, 1979.

Other Sources

Brenni, Vito. *Bookbinding: A Guide to the Literature.* Westport, Connecticut and London: Greenwood Press, 1982.

Byars, Mel. *The Design Encyclopedia.* London: Lawrence King, 1994.

Duncan, Alastair, and Georges de Bartha. *Art Nouveau and Art Déco Bookbinding.* London: Thames and Hudson. 1989.

Thornton, Lynne. "Contemporary Crafts in France." *Connoisseur* 206 (March 1981): 229–233.

262   GERARD, LILIANE (1946–)
Belgian bookbinder.

Other Sources

Brenni, Vito. *Bookbinding: A Guide to the Literature*. Westport, Connecticut and London: Greenwood Press, 1982.

263 GERMAIN, LOUISE DENISE (1870–1936)
French bookbinder.

Main Sources

Vernier, E. "Louise Germain." *L'Art décoratif* (1910): 237–242.

Other Sources

Brenni, Vito. *Bookbinding: A Guide to the Literature*. Westport, Connecticut and London: Greenwood Press, 1982.
Byars, Mel. *The Design Encyclopedia*. London: Lawrence King, 1994.
Duncan, Alastair, and Georges de Bartha. *La reliure en France: art nouveau et art déco, 1880–1940*. Paris: Les Editions de l'Amateur, 1989.

264 GISBERG, MISS
Swedish designer of bookbindings active in the nineteenth century.

Other Sources

Modern Bookbindings and their Designers. The Studio, Winter no. 1899–1900.

265 GOY, ANNE.
Swiss-born bookbinder who works in Belgium.

Main Sources

Fulacher, Pascal. "Anne Goy: la reliure design." *Arts et Métiers du Livre* 179 (1993): 30–31.

266 GRAS, MADELEINE (1891–1958)
French bookbinder.

Exhibitions

Reliures du XXe siècle, de Marius Michel à Paul Bonet. Brussels: Bibliothèque Royale de Belgique, 1957. Short biography followed by information on her exhibits.
Exposition de la Société de la Reliure Originale. Paris: Bibliothèque Nationale, 1959.

Other Sources

Brenni, Vito. *Bookbinding: A Guide to the Literature.* Westport, Connecticut and London: Greenwood Press, 1982.

Byars, Mel. *The Design Encyclopedia.* London: Lawrence King, 1994.

Dally, P. "Les techniques modernes de la reliure." *Art et Décoration* 51 (1927): 15–24.

Devauchelle, Roger. *La reliure en France de ses origines à nos jours.* Paris: Rousseau-Girard, vol. 3, 1961.

Duncan, Alastair, and Georges de Bartha. *La reliure en France: art nouveau et art déco, 1880–1940.* Paris: Les Editions de l'Amateur, 1989.

Garvey, Eleanor, and Peter Wick. *The Arts of the French Book, 1900–1965.* Dallas: South Methodist University Press, 1967.

267 GREENHILL, ELIZABETH (1907–)
French bookbinder working in England.

Main Sources

Harrop, D. "Elizabeth Greenhill." *Book Collector* 28 (summer 1979): 199–209, illus. There is a bibliography at the end of this article.

Exhibitions

Modern British Bookbinders: An Exhibition of Modern British Bookbinding by Members of Designer Bookbinders. London, 1971.

Other Sources

Brenni, Vito. *Bookbinding: A Guide to the Literature.* Westport, Connecticut and London: Greenwood Press, 1982.

268 GRUEL, MADAME
French bookbinder of the nineteenth century whose husband, Pierre-Paul, was an active binder between 1832 and 1848.

Exhibitions

The Crystal Palace Exhibition illustrated catalogue. London, 1851. An unabridged replication of the *Art Journal* Special Issue, with a new introduction by Jonathan Gloag. New York: Dover, 1970.

Other Sources

Brenni, Vito. *Bookbinding: A Guide to the Literature.* Westport, Connecticut and London: Greenwood Press, 1982.

269 HANSEN, MARIA
Nowegian designer of bookbindings active in the nineteenth century.

Other Sources

Modern Bookbindings and their Designers. The Studio, Winter no. 1899–1900.

270 HENKEL, GISELA
Swedish bookbinder.

Other Sources

Modern Bookbindings and their Designers. The Studio, Winter no. 1899–1900.

271 HORSTSCHULZE, MARY (1945–)
German bookbinder.

Other Sources

Brenni, Vito. *Bookbinding: A Guide to the Literature.* Westport, Connecticut and London: Greenwood Press, 1982.

272 JAMES, ANGELA (1948–)
English bookbinder.

Other Sources

Brenni, Vito. *Bookbinding: A Guide to the Literature.* Westport, Connecticut and London: Greenwood Press, 1982.

273 KANZLER-SEEHASE, LEONORE (1930–)
German designer of bookbindings.

Exhibitions

Mundt, Barbara, Suzanne Netzer, and Innes Hettler. *Interieur + Design in Deutschland, 1945=60.* Berlin: Kunstgewerbemuseum and Dietrich Reimer Verlag, 1994.

274 KARSLAKE, CONSTANCE
English bookbinder who was a member of the Guild of Women Bookbinders.

Other Sources

Modern Bookbindings and their Designers. The Studio, Winter no. 1899–1900. Contains little on individual designers.
Cumming, Elizabeth, and Wendy Kaplan. *The Arts and Crafts Movement.* London: Thames and Hudson, 1991.

Nixon, Howard. *Five Centuries of English Bookbinding.* London: Scolar Press, 1978.

Nixon, Howard, and Mirjam Foot. *The History of Decorated Bookbinding in England.* Oxford: Clarendon Press, 1992.

275 KING, JESSIE MARION (1875–1949)
Scottish illustrator, designer of graphics, bookbindings, woven and print-ed textiles, wallpaper and ceramics.

See volume 2: Graphic Art.

276 KINGSFORD, FLORENCE.
English bookbinder and illustrator who worked for the Ashendene and Essex House Presses.

Other Sources

Callen, Anthea. *Angel in the Studio: Women in the Arts and Crafts Movement 1870–1914.* London: Architectural Press, 1979.

277 KOHN, MADELEINE (1892–1940)
English bookbinder who worked in London and Paris.

Exhibitions

Hobson, G. *English Bindings in the Library of J. R. Abbey. An Exhibition of the Modern English and French Bindings from the Collection of Major J. R. Abbey.* London: Arts Council, 1949. No. 130.

Hogben, C. *British Art and Design 1900–1960: A Collection in the Making.* London: Victoria and Albert Museum, 1983.

Other Sources

Brenni, Vito. *Bookbinding: A Guide to the Literature.* Westport, Connecticut and London: Greenwood Press, 1982.

Nixon, Howard. *Broxbourne Library: Styles and Designs of Bookbinding from the 12th to the 20th Centuries.* London: Maggs Brothers for the Broxbourne Library, 1956.

278 KRYGER-LARSEN, BIRGIT
Danish bookbinder.

Main Sources

"Renaissance in Danish Bookbinding." *Bookbinding and Book Production* 55 (February 1952): 42–43.

279   LANGRAND, JEANNE (c. 1893–)
      French bookbinder and gilder.

Exhibitions

Reliures du XXe siècle, de Marius Michel à Paul Bonet. Brussels: Bibliothèque Royale de Belgique, 1957. Short biography followed by information on her exhibits.

Other Sources

Byars, Mel. *The Design Encyclopedia.* London: Lawrence King, 1994.

Dally, P. "Les techniques de la reliure moderne." *Art et Décoration* 51 (1927): 15–24.

Devauchelle, Roger. *La reliure en France de ses origines à nos jours.* Paris: Rousseau-Girard, vol. 3, 1961.

Duncan, Alastair, and Georges de Bartha. *Art Nouveau and Art Déco Bookbinding.* London: Thames and Hudson, 1989.

280   LEONARD, CHRISTINE (1949–)
      Belgian bookbinder.

Other Sources

Brenni, Vito. *Bookbinding: A Guide to the Literature.* Westport, Connecticut and London: Greenwood Press, 1982.

281   LEROUX, ALICE
      French bookbinder.

Main Sources

Karlikow, Abe. "Bookbindings by Alice and Georges Leroux." *Craft Horizons* 22 (March 1962): 32–35.

Other Sources

Brenni, Vito. *Bookbinding: A Guide to the Literature.* Westport, Connecticut and London: Greenwood Press, 1982.

282   LEVÊQUE, LOUISE
      French bookbinder active from c. 1933.

Exhibitions

Reliures du XXe siècle, de Marius Michel à Paul Bonet. Brussels: Bibliothèque Royale de Belgique, 1957. Short biography followed by information on her exhibits.

Other Sources

Devauchelle, Roger. *La reliure en France de ses origines à nos jours.* Paris: Rousseau-Girard, vol. 3, 1961.

283 LUBETT, DENISE (1922–)
French bookbinder who worked in Paris and London.

Other Sources

Brenni, Vito. *Bookbinding: A Guide to the Literature.* Westport, Connecticut and London: Greenwood Press, 1982.

284 McCOLL, ELIZABETH (1863–1951)
Scottish bookbinder.

Other Sources

Brenni, Vito. *Bookbinding: A Guide to the Literature.* Westport, Connecticut and London: Greenwood Press, 1982.
Cumming, Elizabeth, and Wendy Kaplan. *The Arts and Crafts Movement.* London: Thames and Hudson, 1991.
Modern Bookbindings and their Designers. The Studio, Winter no. 1899–1900.
Nixon, Howard. *Broxbourne Library: Styles and Designs of Bookbinding from the 12th to the 20th Centuries.* London: Maggs Brothers for the Broxbourne Library, 1956.
———. *Five Centuries of English Bookbinding.* London: Scolar Press, 1978.
Nixon, Howard, and Mirjam Foot. *The History of Decorated Bookbinding in England.* Oxford: Clarendon Press, 1992.

285 MAROT-RODDE, MME (–1935)
French bookbinder.

Other Sources

Byars, Mel. *The Design Encyclopedia.* London: Lawrence King, 1994.
Devauchelle, Roger. *La reliure en France de ses origines à nos jours.* Paris: Rousseau Girard, vol. 3, 1961.
Duncan, Alastair, and Georges de Bartha. *La reliure en France: art nouveau et art déco, 1880–1940.* Paris: Les Editions de l'Amateur, 1989.

286 MATHIEU, MONIQUE
French bookbinder.

Publications

"Note sur l'art du relieur" followed by a catalogue of her bindings executed between 1961 and 1973. *Bulletin du Bibliophile* (1973): 128–146, 271–296.

Main Sources

De Gaigneron, A. "Cet art discret; la reliure." *Connaissance des Arts* 305 (July 1977): 62–69, illus.

Exhibitions

La reliure française originale. Bookbindings by contemporary French Binders. New York: Museum of Contemporary Crafts, 1964.
Monique Mathieu, Georges Leroux, Jean de Gonet. Paris: Bibliothèque Nationale, 1978, 123pp., illus.

Other Sources

Brenni, Vito. *Bookbinding: A Guide to the Literature.* Westport, Connecticut and London: Greenwood Press, 1982.

287 McCULLY, MADELEINE (1944–)
Irish bookbinder.

Other Sources

Brenni, Vito. *Bookbinding: A Guide to the Literature.* Westport, Connecticut and London: Greenwood Press, 1982.

288 MONCEY, THÉRSE (active from 1946)
French bookbinder.

Exhibitions

Reliures du XXe siècle, de Marius Michel à Paul Bonet. Brussels: Bibliothèque Royale de Belgique, 1957. Short biography followed by information on her exhibits.

Other Sources

Brenni, Vito. *Bookbinding: A Guide to the Literature.* Westport, Connecticut and London: Greenwood Press, 1982.
Devauchelle, Roger. *La reliure en France de ses origines à nos jours.* Paris: Rousseau-Girard, vol. 3, 1961.
Duncan, Alastair, and Georges de Bartha. *La reliure en France: art nouveau et art déco, 1880–1940.* Paris: Les Editions de l'Amateur, 1989.

289 MORSSING, GRETA
     Swedish bookbinder.

Other Sources

Brenni, Vito. *Bookbinding: A Guide to the Literature.* Westport, Connecticut and London: Greenwood Press, 1982.

290 MUNCH, RUTH (1939–)
     Swiss bookbinder.

Other Sources

Brenni, Vito. *Bookbinding: A Guide to the Literature.* Westport, Connecticut and London: Greenwood Press, 1982.

291 O'CONNOR, GEMMA (1940–)
     Irish bookbinder.

Other Sources

Brenni, Vito. *Bookbinding: A Guide to the Literature.* Westport, Connecticut and London: Greenwood Press, 1982.

292 PEYFUSS, MARIETTA (1868–?)
     Austrian bookbinder and designer of textiles.

Other Sources

Pirhofer, G., and A. Gmeiner. *Der Österreichische Werkbund.* Vienna: 1985.

293 PINARD, LOUISE (née DURVAND)
     French bookbinder.

Other Sources

Duncan, Alastair, and Georges de Bartha. *La reliure française: art nouveau et art déco.* Paris: Les Editions de l'Amateur, 1989.

294 POWER, ANNIE (Alt. LOOSELEY)
     English bookbinder who ran the Essex House Bindery at Charles Ashbee's Guild of Handicraft, at which Florence Kingsford (q.v.) also worked, from 1903.

Other Sources

Callen, Anthea. *Angel in the Studio: Women in the Arts and Crafts Movement 1870–1914.* London: Architectural Press, 1979.

295 PRIDEAUX, SARAH T (1853–1933)
English bookbinder.

Publications

"Some Scottish Bookbindings of the Last Century." *Magazine of Art* 18 (January 1895): 110–114.
"French Binders of Today." *Scribners Magazine* 19 (March 1896): 361–370.
"Modern French Binding" and "Modern English Binding." In *Modern Bookbindings: Their Design and Decoration.* London: Constable, 1906.
"Colour photography in England." *Printing Art* 10 (January 1908): 305–312.
"Aquatint Engraving." In *The History of Book Illustration.* London: Duckworth, 1909, 234pp.

Main Sources

A Catalogue of Books Bound by S. T. Prideaux Between 1890–1900, With 26 Illustrations. London: S. T. Prideaux and K. Adams, 1900, 20pp., illus.

Other Sources

Brenni, Vito. *Bookbinding: A Guide to the Literature.* Westport, Connecticut and London: Greenwood Press, 1982.
Holme, Charles. *The Art of the Book.* London: The Studio, 1914.
Modern Bookbindings and their Designers. The Studio, Winter no. 1899–1900.
Nixon, Howard. *Broxbourne Library: Styles and Designs of Bookbinding from the 12th to the 20th Centuries.* London: Maggs Brothers for the Broxbourne Library, 1956.
————. *Five Centuries of English Bookbinding.* London: Scolar Press, 1978.
Nixon, Howard, and Mirjam Foot. *The History of Decorated Bookbinding in England.* Oxford: Clarendon Press, 1992.

296 PYE, SYBIL (1879–1958)
English bookbinder.

Main Sources

Moore, Sturge. "Miss Sybil Pye's Bookbindings." *Apollo* (October 1925): 222–226, illus.

Exhibitions

Hobson, G. *English Bindings in the Library of J. R. Abbey. An Exhibition of the Modern English and French Bindings from the Collection of Major J. R. Abbey.* London: Arts Council, 1949. Sybil Pye's work is no 125.

Other Sources

Brenni, Vito. *Bookbinding: A Guide to the Literature.* Westport, Connecticut and London: Greenwood Press, 1982.

Holme, Charles. *The Art of the Book.* London: The Studio, 1914.

Nixon, Howard. *Broxbourne Library: Styles and Designs of Bookbinding from the 12th to the 20th Centuries.* London: Maggs Brothers for the Broxbourne Library, 1956.

————. *Five Centuries of English Bookbinding.* London: Scolar Press, 1978.

Nixon, Howard, and Mirjam Foot. *The History of Decorated Bookbinding in England.* Oxford: Clarendon Press, 1992.

297 REYNOLDS, MARY

American-born bookbinder who worked in Paris for over thirty years.

Main Sources

Lada-Mocarski, Polly, and Mary Lyon. "Bookbinding: The Art of Mary Reynolds." *Craft Horizons* 21 (1961): 11–13.

298 ROLLINCE, JEANNE

French bookbinder.

Other Sources

Modern Bookbindings and their Designers. The Studio, Winter no. 1899–1900.

299 SCHRÖDER, GERMAINE (1889–1983)

French bookbinder.

Main Sources

Dally, P. "Les techniques modernes de la reliure." *Art et Décoration* 51 (1927): 15–24, illus.

Other Sources

Brenni, Vito. *Bookbinding: A Guide to the Literature.* Westport, Connecticut and London: Greenwood Press, 1982.

Byars, Mel. *The Design Encyclopedia.* London: Lawrence King, 1994.

Duncan, Alastair, and Georges de Bartha. *Art Nouveau and Art Deco Bookbinding, 1880–1940.* London: Thames and Hudson, 1989.

300 SHANNON, FAITH (1938–)

English bookbinder.

Main Sources

Cashin, Geraldine. "Book Now: Fine Bookbindings by the Fellows of the Designer Bookbinders, Midland Group, Nottingham." *Crafts* 39 (1979): 55–56.
Taylor, Michael. "Judged by Cover." *Crafts* 67 (1984): 14–20.

Exhibitions

Modern British Bookbinders: An Exhibition of Modern British Bookbinding by Members of Designer Bookbinders. London, 1971.

Other Sources

Brenni, Vito. *Bookbinding: A Guide to the Literature.* Westport, Connecticut and London: Greenwood Press, 1982.

301 SMITH, SALLY LOU (1925–)
American-born bookbinder working in London.

Other Sources

Brenni, Vito. *Bookbinding: A Guide to the Literature.* Westport, Connecticut and London: Greenwood Press, 1982.

302 THIERSCH, FRIEDA (1889–1947)
German bookbinder.

Main Sources

Krinitz, Fritz. *Frieda Thiersch und ihre Handbuchbinderei.* Stuttgart, 1968, 72pp., illus.

Other Sources

Brenni, Vito. *Bookbinding: A Guide to the Literature.* Westport, Connecticut and London: Greenwood Press, 1982.

303 TRAQUAIR, PHOEBE ANNA (1852–1936) (née MOSS)
Irish-born painter and designer in the Arts and Crafts movement who worked in Scotland; she produced metalwork, decorated furniture, jewellery, bookbindings and enamels.

See Interior Design section.

304 VALLGREN, ANTOINETTE
French bookbinder active in the nineteenth century.

Other Sources

Brenni, Vito. *Bookbinding: A Guide to the Literature.* Westport, Connecticut and London: Greenwood Press, 1982.
Modern Bookbindings and their Designers. The Studio, Winter no. 1899–1900.

305 VAN REGEMORTER, BERTHE
Belgian designer of bookbindings who worked independently from c. 1911 and won an important prize in 1913.

Exhibitions

Reliures du XXe siècle, de Marius Michel à Paul Bonet. Brussels: Bibliothèque Royale de Belgique, 1957. Short biography followed by information on her exhibits.

306 VINDING, KIRSTEN
Bookbinder working in France.

Main Sources

De Gaigneron, A. "Cet art discret, la reliure." *Connaissance des Arts* 305 (July 1977): 62–69.

Other Sources

Brenni, Vito. *Bookbinding: A Guide to the Literature.* Westport, Connecticut and London: Greenwood Press, 1982.

307 WALDECK-ROUSSEAU, MME.
French designer of bookbindings active in the nineteenth century.

Other Sources

Modern Bookbindings and their Designers. The Studio, Winter no. 1899–1900.

308 WEILL, LUCIE (1901–after 1978)
French bookbinder and illustrator.

Other Sources

Brenni, Vito. *Bookbinding: A Guide to the Literature.* Westport, Connecticut and London: Greenwood Press, 1982.
Byars, Mel. *The Design Encyclopedia.* London: Lawrence King, 1994.
Devauchelle, Roger. *La reliure en France de ses origines à nos jours.* Paris: Rousseau-Girard, vol. 3, 1961.

Duncan, Alastair, and Georges de Bartha. *Art Nouveau and Art Déco Bookbinding, 1880–1940.* London: Thames and Hudson, 1989.

309 WIRZ, VERENA (1945–)
French bookbinder.

Other Sources

Brenni, Vito. *Bookbinding: A Guide to the Literature.* Westport, Connecticut and London: Greenwood Press, 1982.

310 WOLF-LEFRANC, MADELEINE
French bookbinder active from c. 1924.

Other Sources

Devauchelle, Roger. *La reliure en France de ses origines à nos jours.* Paris: Rousseau-Girard, vol. 3, 1961.

311 WYTSMAN, JULIETTE.
Belgian bookbinder and designer.

Exhibitions

Art Nouveau Belgique. Brussels: Palais des Beaux-Arts, 1980.

Other Sources

Garvey, Eleanor, et al. *The Turn of a Century, 1885–1910: Art Nouveau Jugendstill Books.* Cambridge, Mass.: Dept. of Printing and Graphic Arts, Harvard University, 1970.

Ceramics

312   BERGESEN, VICTORIA. *Encyclopaedia of British Art Pottery, 1870–1920.*
London: Barrie & Jenkins, 1991, 304pp., illus.
An alphabetical arrangement of firms, exhibition societies, potteries,
organisations and individuals producing art pottery. The number of entries
for women is relatively small, but those that are included are usefully informative.

313   CARTER, PAT. *Dictionary of British Studio Potters.* London: Scolar Press,
1990, 187pp., illus.
One hundred seventy-seven studio potters are each given a page with one
photograph of their work, a paragraph on the development of their work over
the course of their career and a selected list of exhibitions and collections in
which their work may be found. Many women are included.

314   *Guide des céramistes. 700 potiers et sculpteurs en France.* Paris: Editions La
Revue de la Céramique et du Verre, 1993, 334pp., illus.
Text in French. A directory of ceramicists and sculptors in clay working
in France, organised by geographical region. Each ceramicist is given half a
page of text and one or two photographs. The information includes their
training, contact address and a statement by the designer about their work.
Many women are included.

315   REILLY, ROBIN, and GEORGE SAVAGE. *The Dictionary of Wedgwood.*
Woodbridge: Antique Collectors Club, 1980 414pp., illus.
Although the majority of entries are for technical or other aspects,
designers and decorators for Wedgwood are also included. It is a useful
source, particularly for less well known women who worked for the firm
from the eighteenth century onward.

OTHER PUBLICATIONS

316   *1 + 9 céramistes: 1 + 9 keramisten.* Brussels in association with the Musées
Royaux: Parc du Cinquantenaire, 1977, 26pp., illus.
     Text in French and Flemish. Of the ten designers included, seven are
women.

317   *15 Schweizer Keramiker: Ausstellung der Nationen; 15 Céramistes Suisses:
Exposition des Nations; 15 Ceramisti Svizzeri: Mostra delle Nazioni.* Faenza:
Palazzo delle Esposizioni, 1984, n.p., illus.
     Text in German, French and Italian. A short introduction is followed by a
page on each exhibitor, most of whom produce ceramic sculpture. Eight of
the participants are women: Margreth Daepp, Pierette Favarger, Elizabeth
Langsch, Renée Mangeat-Duc, Ruth Monnier, Sabine Nadler, Setsuko
Nagasawa and Petra Weiss.

318   *Actuelle keramiek en textielkunst uit antwerpen.* Het Sterckshof: Provinciaal
Museum voor Kunstambrachten, 1974, n.p., illus.
     Text in Flemish. After short introductory essays there is very brief infor-
mation on the artists and the exhibits. Several women are included in both
sections, although the proportion is greater in that on textiles.

319   ADES, DAWN. "The Shock of the Old." *Crafts* 71 (1984): 30–35.
     Review of an exhibition of early Soviet ceramics and textiles at the
Museum of Modern Art, Oxford.

320   ALESSON, JEAN. *Les femmes artistes au Salon de 1878 et à l'Exposition
Universelle.* Paris: Gazette des femmes, 1878, 31pp.
     Text in French. After providing a list of women artists exhibiting at the
Salon between 1874 and 1878, the author takes each medium/genre in turn
and summarises the numbers of women in each, the subject and gives some
critical evaluation. In 1878, 762 women exhibited. Overall this provides
access to names that are little known today and can therefore act as a platform
for further research. There is little space given to artists at the Exposition
Universelle.

321   "Arrêtons-nous à Dieulefit." *Connaissances des céramiques,* no. 16 (1976):
58–61.
     Text in French. Describes the work produced in a community of cerami-
cists in Haute Provence, which includes Nicole Elmer, Jeanne Grandpierre
and Nanou Lachieze-Rey.

322   ATKINS, NIGEL. "New French Ceramics." *Ceramic Review* 77 (1982):
26–27.
     Review of an exhibition which mentions several women.

323   ATTERBURY, PAUL. "Pots under the Hammer." *Ceramic Review* 78 (1982): 4–47.

Discusses recently auctioned contemporary ceramics, which includes pots by Rie and Fritsch (qq.v.).

324   BARRY, VAL. "Porcelain: Craftsmen Potter's Shop." *Ceramic Review* 22 (1973).

Review of an exhibition of the works of twenty-six ceramicists, including Mary Rogers, Kathleen Pleydell-Bouverie, Sally Dawson and Joan Hepworth.

325   BECKER, INGEBORG, and DIETER HOGERMANN. *Berliner Porzellan vom Jugendstil zum Funktionalismus, 1889–1939.* Berlin: Bröhan Museum, n.d. [1987?], 215pp., illus.

Text in German. A series of essays by several writers on aspects of the development of porcelain produced by the KPM factory is followed by an annotated catalogue. Seven women are mentioned, but little biographical information is given about any of the designers: Marguerite Friedländer, Trude Petri, who was the decorator of Friedlander's designs, Marianne Höst, Effie Hegermann-Lindencrone, Gertrude Kant, Nicola Moufang and Agnes Sorma.

326   BEEH, WOLFGANG, and CARL BENNO HELLER. *Keramik '88: Ton in Ton.* Darmstadt: Hessisches Landesmuseum, 1988, 58pp. plus illus.

Text in German. Ceramics from eight countries are represented. The catalogue is organised by country, with biographical outlines, a paragraph about each designer's work and a contact address. Women are included for each country.

327   BENNETT, IAN. *British 20th Century Studio Ceramics.* London: Christopher Wood Gallery, 1980, 104pp., illus.

An essay, in part anecdotal, looks at the changing status of studio ceramics and at the contributions of those represented in this exhibition. Lengthy biographical accounts for each are included.

328   BIRKS, TONY. "Contemporary French Studio Ceramics." *Ceramic Review* 74 (1982): 8–9.

Review of an exhibition at the Musée des Arts Décoratifs in Paris.

329   BRITTON, ALISON. "Le cru et le cuit: manifeste de la nouvelle céramique anglaise." *La Revue de la Céramique et du Verre* 86 (January–February 1996): 18–22.

Review of the exhibition "The Raw and the Cooked," in which the work of Pamela Leung, Elizabeth Fritsch and Jill Crowley is featured.

330 BRUNHAMMER, YVONNE, and MARIE-LAURE PERRIN. *Céramique française contemporain: sources et courants.* Paris: Musée des Arts Décoratifs, 1981, 100pp., illus.

Text in French. A comprehensive treatment of the subject organised partly by geographical region and partly by the type of work produced (e.g., Japonism and ceramic sculpture). The nature of ceramic practice in France resulted in many individuals working in artist communities in the provinces because of the greater freedom this permitted them. Many women are included. Brief biographical outlines are given.

331 BRUNHAMMER, YVONNE, and SUZANNE TISE. *Les artistes décorateurs, 1900–1942.* Paris: Flammarion, 1990, 285pp., mainly illus.

Text in French. This book is primarily useful for the list of all those who exhibited in the Salons or Pavilions of the Société des Artistes Décorateurs. A large number of women are included, although only twenty-one are included in the text, which is organised chronologically. Nevertheless, this provides a useful source of names to pursue elsewhere.

332 BUCKLEY, CHERYL. *Potters and Paintresses. Women Designers in the Pottery Industry, 1870–1955.* London: Women's Press, 1990, 184pp., illus.

An analytical study of the circumstances which enabled women to work as designers within the pottery industry in Britain over a period of some eighty years. Many previously unknown women designers are discussed. The author places the discussion within the debates about the methodology of design history as a discipline.

333 CAROLA-PERROTTI, ANGELA. *Ceramiche del Museo Artistico Industriale di Napoli, 1920–50.* Naples: Museo Artistico Industriale, 1985, 127pp., illus.

Text in Italian. After essays discussing the museum, its history and its collection, there is a catalogue of its collection of ceramics from the three decades. Only Diana Franco and Launa Rosario from the end of this period are mentioned.

334 CATLEUGH, JOHN. "Ceramics for children at Cheyne." *Ceramic Review* 63 (1980): 26–27.

An exhibition review in which the work of several women is included.

335 *Ceramic Forms: Recent work by Seven British Potters between 1973 and 1974.* London: Crafts Council, 1974, 35pp., illus.

Four women—Glenys Barton, Jacquie Poncelet, Elizabeth Fritsch and Jill Crowley (qq.v.)—are featured in this catalogue.

336   *Céramique Suisse '93. 17e Biennale de l'Association des Céramistes Suisses.*
       Geneva: Musée Adriana, 1993, 119pp., many illus.
       Main text in German and French, one essay in Spanish and French. The
       first alphabetical sequence gives information and illustrations of the exhibits,
       whereas the second gives biographical information. Of the thirty-four
       exhibitors, nineteen are women.

337   *Ceramische Hoogtepunten Nederland Pottenkijker, 1959–1969.* Rotterdam:
       Museum Boymans-van Beuningen, 1969, 224pp., illus.
       Text in Dutch. A lengthy essay discusses the works of individuals in the
       exhibition. About twelve women are included.

338   *Céramique et Tapissérie contemporaines en Belgique.* Brussels. Published
       Ghent: Snoek-Ducaju & Zoon: Musées Royaux d'Art et d'Histoire, 1978,
       n.p., illus.
       Text in French and Flemish. The exhibition catalogue is organised into
       sections on sculptural ceramics, everyday and decorative ceramics and tapes-
       try. After several short introductory essays there is very brief information
       about the designers and the exhibits. Women are well represented.

339   *Céramiques des maîtres de la peinture contemporaine.* Lausanne: Musée des
       Arts Décoratifs, 1953, n.p., illus.
       The exhibition concerned painters who also made ceramics at some point
       in their career and collaborated with a ceramicist or factory. Five women are
       included: Suzanne Ramié, Yolaine and Geneviève Bauby, Ginette Renaux
       and Géa Augsbourg. Little information is given about them.

340   CHAVANCE, RENE. *La céramique et la verrerie. L'art français depuis
       vingt ans.* Paris: Les Editions Rieder, 1928, 127pp., illus.
       Text in French. Divided into two sections, each deals in turn with devel-
       opments from c.1900 to 1925 in ceramics and glass. More women are men-
       tioned in connection with the former, particularly in connection with the
       production at Sèvres. Little information about individuals is given.

341   CLARK, JIMMY. "East European Ceramics." *Ceramic Monthly* 40, no. 8
       (October 1992): 33–42.
       Report on a survey exhibition, held in Philadelphia, of ceramics from
       most of the countries of Eastern Europe.

342   "Clay in Revolution." *Ceramic Review* 90 (1984): 26–27.
       Review of the exhibition *Art in Production: Soviet Textiles, Fashion and
       Ceramics 1917–35* at the Museum of Modern Art, Oxford and the Crafts
       Council, London. Particular attention is paid to the ceramics.

343   DIGBY, GEORGE WINGFIELD. *The Work of the Modern Potter in
       England.* London: John Murray, 1952, 110pp., 64 illus.

The first four chapters discuss the rise of hand-thrown pottery and the increase in its status, together with technical spects. The fifth chapter gives biographical accounts of twenty potters, of whom seven are women.

344 DORMER, PETER, ET AL. *Fast Forward: New Directions in British Ceramics.* London: Institute of Contemporary Art, 1985, 44pp., illus.

A series of critical essays looks at aspects of British ceramics in the 1980s. Several of the principal figures are women, including Poncelet, Fritsch and Britton (qq.v.).

345 DORMER, PETER. *The new ceramics: Trends and traditions.* London: Thames and Hudson, 1986, 208pp., 234 illus. of which 86 in colour.

Consists of three main sections: the new role of the potter; pottery form; the painted pot. This is followed by short biographies of the main European and American ceramicists, of which twenty-eight are women, from countries in western Europe. In addition there are lists of galleries and museums exhibiting contemporary ceramics and of the chief exhibitions of this work since 1976.

346 ELLIOTT, DAVID, and VALERY DUDAKOV. *100 years of Russia art, 1889–1989, from private collections in the USSR.* London: Lund Humphries, with the Barbican Art Gallery, London and the Museum of Modern Art, Oxford, 1989, 152pp., illus.

A number of the better known Russian women artists and designers are included in this survey of a century of Russian art: the ceramics sculptor Danko, and the ceramic designer Shchekotikina-Pototskaya are included as well as Ermolaeva, Exter, Khodasevich, Popova, Serebriakova, Stepanova and Udaltsova. Short biographies of artists/designers are included.

347 *Europäische Keramik der Gegenwart. Zweite Internationale Ausstellung im Keramion.* Frechen: Keramion—Museum für keramische Kunst, 1986, 332pp., mainly illus.

Text in German and English. After a brief introduction highlighting developments in European ceramics over the previous ten years, there are two alphabetical lists of the seventy-seven ceramicists from twenty countries of whom thirty-two are women. Twenty-six German designers are included, but the organisers note that a number of those invited to exhibit, particularly younger artists from England, did not do so. In the first list one colour illustration for each exhibitor is featured. In the second there is an outline biography with black and white illustrations.

348 *Europäischer Keramik des Jugendstils. Art Nouveau Modern Style.* Dusseldorf: Hetjens-Museum, 1974, 232pp., illus.

Text in German. Consists of sections devoted to each country. These begin with short introductory essays followed by an alphabetical listing of designers, each of which has a brief biographical outline, a bibliography and a longer entry on the exhibited works. Women are included in the sections on France, Great Britain, Scandinavia and Hungary.

349 *Expo Barcelone.* Barcelona: Museu de Ceramica, Published by the Ajuntamento de Barcelona, 1985, 71pp., illus.

Text in Catalan/Spanish. Catalogue of an exhibition featuring several women: Rosa Amorós, Maria Bonfill, Magda Martí-Coll and Madola (qq.v.). There is a section on each artists which contains information on their work, a biography, bibliography and illustrations.

350 FARÉ, MICHEL. *La céramique contemporain.* Paris: Compagnie des Arts Photoméchaniques, 1954, 104pp., 100 illus.

Discusses the precursors, young contemporary ceramicists and the ceramics of painters and sculptors. A useful source for women, many of whom are mentioned.

351 GAILLARD, KARIN. *Céramique néerlandaise contemporaine. Contemporary Dutch Ceramics. Niederlandische Keramik der Gegenwart.* Roanne: Musée Joseph Dechelette, 1988, 48pp., illus.

Text in French, English and German. Of the fifteen exhibitors, eight are women: Evelyn van Baarda, Babs Haenen, Susanne Hahn, Vilma Henkelman, Netty van den Heuvel, Irene Vonck, Pauline Wiertz and Christian Wisse (qq.v.). A biographical outline is followed by about 200 words of analysis of the individual's work, highlighting characteristics and developments.

352 HAMACHER, BÄRBEL (ED.). *Expressive Keramik der Wiener Werkstätte, 1917–1930.* Munich: Bayerische Vereinsbank, 1992, 142pp., illus.

Text in German. One of the two main essays deals with the work of the eleven women ceramics designers featured in the exhibition. In addition the catalogue entries are detailed and include the literature on each object and outline biographies on the designers. Each of these contains a chronology, a list of membership, exhibitions and a bibliography.

353 HIORT, ESBJØRN. *Modern Danish Ceramics.* New York: Museum Books Inc.; London: A. Zwemmer Ltd.; Stuttgart: Verlag Hatje; Teufen: Arthur Niggli und Willy Verkauf; Copenhagen: Jul. Gjellerups Forlag, 1955, 131pp., illus.

Text in English, French, German and Danish. An essay sets Danish ceramics in their context and explains the importance and characteristics of each designer who is featured. Eight women are included: Nathalie Krebs and her collaboration with Eva Staehr-Nielson, Gudrun Meedom, Gertrude Grøndhal Vasegaard, Anne-Lise Linnemann-Schmidt, Lillemor Clement, Inger Folmer Larsen and Lisbeth Munch Petersen.

354   HOUSTON, JOHN (ED.). *Craft Classics Since the 1940s: An Anthology of Belief and Comment.* London: Crafts Council, 1988, 133pp., illus.

A collection of texts from 1939 to the 1980s, several of which attempt a theoretical analysis. The emphasis is mainly on ceramics. The three women contributors include Dora Billington and Ethel Mairet (qq.v.).

355   HOUSTON, JOHN. *The Abstract Vessel. Ceramics in Studio: Forms of Expression and Decoration by Nine Artist Potters.* London: Bellew with the Oriel Gallery and the Welsh Arts Council, 1991, 64pp., illus.

Discusses the nature of pots and vessels, including nonfunctional ones, in contemporary ceramics. Five women—Alison Britton, Elizabeth Fritsch, Carol McNicoll, Jacqui Poncelet (qq.v.) and Betty Woodman are included. There are useful biographies at the end of the text.

356   "International Ceramic Symposium Bechyne." *Ceramic Review* 63 (1980): 25.

Report of a symposium on ceramics held in Czechoslovakia. The works of three women are illustrated: Elisienda Sala of Spain, Leena Liljestrom of Finland and Katalin Orban of Hungary.

357   *International Ceramics 1972.* London: Victoria and Albert Museum, 1972, 122pp., illus.

One of a series of exhibitions initiated at intervals by the International Academy of Ceramics, which encourages exhibits from all over the world. Thirty-eight countries are represented but neither the former USSR nor China chose to exhibit. Apart from the former, all European countries are represented. Designers' works are listed alphabetically within another alphabetical listing of countries. Women are included by the majority of European countries.

358   JARCHOW, MARGARETE. *Berliner Porzellan im 20 Jahrhundert. Berlin Porcelain in the 20th Century.* Berlin: Dietrich Reimer Verlag, 1988, 342pp., illus.

Text in German and English. Examines the social, political and economic conditions of production for the chief factory, the Königliche Porzellan Manufaktur, which was founded by Frederick the Great in 1763. It includes lists and biographies, often very brief, of the designers employed by the factory, of which a number were women.

359   KAPFERER, SIMONE. "Les artistes céramistes et verrriers au Salon des Artistes Décorateurs." *Les Arts du Feu* 2 (June 1938): 62–64.

Text in French. Review of this annual exhibition includes mention and illustrations of the work of several women ceramicists: Laure Albin-Guillot, Tyra Lundgren, Suzanne Alexandre, Marjolaine Guidette Carbonel, Mme. Dem, Cécile Baillot-Jourdain and Mme. Luc-Lanel.

360   *Keramik i rum* [Ceramics in space]. Copenhagen: Danske Kunstindustrimuseum, 1981, 31pp., illus.

Text in Danish, Swedish and Norwegian with summaries in English and German in a supplement. Contains essays of two thousand to three thousand words on each of the three ceramic sculptors: Francesca Lindh, Karen Park and Ulla Viotti.

361   KIM, JACQUES. "Les maîtres du feu au Salon d'Automne." *Les Arts du Feu* 6 (December 1938): 180–181.

Text in French. Brief room by room summary of cermic exhibits ranging from sculpture to tea services. Women mentioned are Mme. Masésente, Tyra Lundgren, Guidette Carbonnel and Josette Hébert Cöffin.

362   KIM, JACQUES. "Les arts du feu au Salon des Artistes Décorateurs." *Les Arts du Feu* 11 (May 1939): 147–151.

Text in French. Review of this annual exhibition includes a brief mention of several women.

363   KLINGE, EKKART. *Deutsche Keramik Heute.* Dusseldorf: Verlagsanstalt Handwerk, 1984, 212pp., illus.

Text in German. A brief essay is followed by an alphabetical arrangement of designers for whom a brief biographical outline is given. Thirty women are included.

364   KLINGE, EKKART. *Tschechesche Keramik.* Dusseldorf: Hetjens-Museum, 1991, 59pp., illus.

Text in German. Four of the eight exhibitors are women. For each a detailed list of exhibitions is given together with a short bibiography . Those included are Zdena Fibichová, Hana Purkrábková, Helena Samohelová and Jindra Viková. The works of all are primarily sculptural.

365   *Les grès contemporains en France.* Sèvres: Musée National de Céramique, 1963, 30pp.

Text in French. Consists of little more than a list of exhibits together with a biographical outline. Seventeen women are included, several working in partnership with their husbands.

366   LEWENSTEIN, EILEEN, and EMMANUEL COOPER (EDS.). *New Ceramics.* London: Studio Vista, 1974, 223pp., illus.

A series of essays on contemporary ceramics in different parts of the world although the main emphasis is on Europe. The introductory essay gives a historical background and traces the emergence of the studio potter. The essays on individual countries or groups of countries expand on these issues where relevant and indicate the main types of work being produced and the key individuals involved.

367 LEWENSTEIN, EILEEN. "Impressions of Life—Imre Schammel and Hungarian Ceramics." *Ceramic Review* 81 (1983): 22–25.

   Short discussion of potters in Hungary, including Margit Kovács (q.v.), Katalin Tovolgyi, Maria Orosz and Maria Gezler.

368 LOBANOV-ROSTOVSKY, NINA. *Revolutionary Ceramics: Soviet Porcelain 1917–1927.* London: Studio Vista, 1970, 160pp., illus.

   Discusses the subject under six headings: agit pieces, symbolic and commemorative pieces, figurines, traditional themes, Russian folklore and the avant-garde. Includes biographies of all thirty-nine artists, of whom fifteen are women, together with a chronology and information about artists' signatures, monograms and factory marks.

369 MARGETTS, MARLINA. "Métamorphose: la Culture Céramique." *La Revue de la Céramique et du Verre* 86 (January–February 1996): 23–25.

   Text in French. An analytical article which explores theoretical perspectives of sculptors and ceramicists. Women in both categories are included in the discussion.

370 MARGRIE, VICTOR. "British Ceramics." *Ceramic Review* 71 (1981): 22–24.

   Reprint of the introduction to a catalogue of an exhibition held at Knokke-Heist Scharpoord in Belgium and organised by the British Council, in which the work of several women is featured.

371 *Meister der Deutschen Keramik 1900 bis 1950.* Cologne: Kunstgewerbemuseum der Stadt, 1978, 329pp., illus.

   Text in German. An extensive catalogue on the development of German ceramics in the first half of this century. Individuals, workshops and factories are included. There are many exhibits for each individual as well as an outline biography and a short discussion of the evolution of their work and the exhibits included. Seven women are featured: Elfriede Balzar-Kopp, Hedwig Bollhagen, Ida Erdös, Margarete Friedländer, Clara von Ruckteschell-Trüeb, Elisabeth Dörr and Luise Harkort.

372 "Modern German Ceramics." *Ceramic Review* 52 (1978): 4–5.

   Review of exhibition held at the Craftsman Potters' Association. The work of several women is included.

373 *Mostra della ceramica italiana 1920–1940.* Turin: Palazzo Nervi, 1982, 221pp., illus.

   Text in Italian. The catalogue is organised into eight geographical areas from north to south, each further subdivided according to the individuals or firms active there. Three women are mentioned but only in Turin: Elena

Scavini, Princess Bona Sancipriano (as designer) and Clelia Bertetti, who ran a ceramics studio from 1931 to 1942, at which time she turned to sculpture.

374   *Neue Formen der Keramik aus der Niederlanden.* Darmstadt: Hessichen Landesmuseum, 1967, 215pp., illus.

Text in German and Dutch. An introductory essay is followed by an alphabetical catalogue which includes outline biographies, exhibition and collection lists in addition to details of the works exhibited in this exhibition. The first section includes artists whose work might be classified as sculpture while the second deals with designers in the tradition of Delft porcelain. Some fifteen women are included.

375   NEUWIRTH, WALTRAUD. *Die Keramik der Wiener Werkstätte.* Vienna: W. Neuwirth, 1981, 352pp., illus.

Introductory essays in German and English. Discusses the ceramics production in the later period of the Wiener Werkstätte, 1920–1931. The book focusses on the discovery of catalogues of original designs for one-off ceramics and reproduces pages from these on the left pages of the publication while on the right he lists and identifies works and artists. Many women were involved but their names and biographies are largely unknown today.

376   NIBLETT, KATHY. *Dynamic Design: The British Pottery Industry, 1940–1990.* Stoke-on-Trent: City Museum and Art Gallery, 1990, 158pp., 74 illus.

The introductory essay, which gives short histories of the principal pottery firms, is followed by the catalogue, which includes biographies of designers in the industry. A substantial number of women are included.

377   NIKIFOROVA, L. *Russian porcelain in the Hermitage Collection.* Leningrad: Aurora Art Publishers, 1973, 160pp., illus.

Introductory essay in English and Russian. Consisting mainly of illustrations, this book covers porcelain production and decoration in St. Petersburg. More informative about works produced before 1920 than later, it includes little from after 1940. There are no references to women in the prerevolutionary period and minimal information about those included for the later period, of which there are six: A. Shchekotikhina-Pototskaya, N. Danko, Z. Kobyletskaya, Y. Yakovleva, A. Leporskaya and L. Lebedinskaya (qq.v.).

378   *Nine Potters: Bernard Leach, Katherine Pleydell-Bouverie, Michael Cardew, Hans Coper, Lucie Rie, Elizabeth Fritsch, Ewen Henderson, Elizabeth Raeburn, Claudi Casanovas.* London: Fischer Fine Art, 1986, 40pp., mainly illus.

After a brief overview, an outline biography is provided for each exhibitor. Most space is given to works by Rie and Coper.

379   *Oeuvres des céramistes modernes: 1890–1930.* Sèvres and Imprimérie Lapina, Paris: Musée Céramique, 1931, 20pp., illus.

    Text in French. A short essay by René Chavance surveys the changes in ceramics in the period covered and the achievements of those exhibiting. Ten women are included: Marguérite Briansan, Berthe Cazin, Jeanne Lecoeur, Marjolaine Luc-Lanel, Mmes. Quentel, Moreau-Nélaton, Galtier-Boisière, Bachelet, Jacqueline Marval, better known as a painter, and Maryvonne Méheut.

380   OPIE, JENNIFER. *Scandinavia: Ceramics and Glass in the Twentieth Century.* London: Victoria and Albert Museum, 1989, 183pp., illus.

    Based on the collection in the Victoria and Albert Museum, London, the book provides an analysis of the ceramics and glass produced in each of the four Scandinavian countries. For each country there is also a list of key exhibitions. Following this are biographies of the artists and designers whose work features in the collection, amongst whom are many women.

381   PATAKY-BRESTYNSKY, ILONA. *Modern Hungarian Ceramics.* Translated by L. Halápy. Budapest: Corvina, 1961.

    Six women are included in this survey of Hungarian ceramics: the pioneer Margit Kovács, who helped to raise the level of ceramics between the wars, Ilona Kiss-Roóz, who was one of her pupils, Livia Gorka, Hedwig Majoros, Katalin G. Staindl (qq.v.) and Mme Garányi.

382   PELICHET, EDGAR, ET AL. *La céramique art deco.* Lausanne: Les Editions du Grand-Pont, 1988, 199pp., illus.

    A lavishly illustrated book, most of which consists of an alphabetical listing of artists, ateliers and factories. Coverage is international and many women are included.

383   PETROVA, SYLVA. "Le verre et la céramique contemporains des collections du Musée des Arts Décoratifs de Prague." *Revue du Verre* 42, no. 7 (1987): 14–19, mainly illus.

    Text in French. A short account of the formation of the contemporary collection is followed by some illustrations of individual works. Women whose works are illustrated are Edita Devinská, Dagmar Hendrychová, Grethe Meyer (Denmark), Marta Taberyová, Dana Zanecniková, and Jirina Zertová (qq.v.).

384   PINTARIC, JARANKA. "4th World Triennial of Small Ceramics." *Ceramics: Art and Perception* 19 (March 1995): 86–90.

    Review of exhibition, held in Zagreb, Croatia in 1993, in which most of the women designers mentioned are from Eastern Europe.

385   PREAUD, TAMARA. *Sèvres: des origines à nos jours.* Fribourg: Office du Livre and Paris: Société du Livre, 1978, 390pp., illus.

Text in French. The definitive history of the factory and production of Sèvres porcelain, it mentions women as designers only in the twentieth century. At the end of the book there is an exhaustive list of all the workers found in the archives, including commissioned artists, from the eighteenth century. From this it appears that women were involved in a variety of processes from the earliest days.

386   RAWSON, PHILIP. "Eight Ceramicists." *Crafts Magazine* 68 (1984): 42–43.

Review on an exhibition which featured the work of Nisbet, Lowndes and Constantinidis (qq.v.).

387   "Recent Work by 3 Potters in East Germany." *Ceramic Review* 84 (1983): 36.
Review of an exhibition of work by women potters.

388   RICE, PAUL, and CHRISTOPHER GOWING. *British Studio Ceramics in the Twentieth Century.* London: Barrie and Jenkins, 1989, 254pp., many illus.

A thorough historical account of the subject in which the works of forty-nine women are included. There is a list of potters with a brief biographical outline for each.

389   RIDDICK, SARAH, and R. GREEN, (EDS.). *Pioneer studio pottery: The Milner-White collection.* London: Lund Humphries in association with York City Art Gallery, 1990, 136pp., illus.

Milner-White was the Archdeacon of York from 1941 to 1963. During the last fifteen years of his life, he augmented his originally small collection of works with more than 170 examples of modern stoneware pottery. He donated these to York City Art Gallery and it is these which form the subject of this catalogue. After an essay on Milner-White and the formation of the collection, the designers are listed in alphabetical order. Biographical information together with details of the individual works in the collection are provided. Women ceramicists represented are Katherine Pleydell-Bouverie, Norah Braden, May Davis, the Dane Agnete (Anita) Hoy, Nathalie Krebs, Edith Pincombe, Margaret Rey, Frances Richards and Nell Vyse.

390   *Rosenthal: Hundert Jahre Porzellan.* Hanover: Kestner Museum, 1982, 285pp., illus.

Text in German. A comprehensive history of the porcelain factory from its foundation in 1879 is followed by a list of its designers in that period. For each there is a short biographical account and a list of the main sources of information.

391   ROSE, MURIEL. *Artist potters in England.* London: Faber and Faber, 1970, 64pp. and 117pp. of illustrations.

In a chronological survery of the field eight women are included: Denise Wren, Kathleen Pleydell-Bouverie, Janet Leach, Norah Braden, Lucie Rie, Helen Pincombe, Ruth Duckworth and Eileen Lewenstein (qq.v.). There is also a reference to the French potter Berthe Cazin.

392   ROTHSCHILD, HENRY. "Collecting—a Personal View." *Ceramic Review* 80 (1983): 26–29.

Includes references to the work of several British and German women ceramicists whose work he collected.

393   *Russisches und sowjetisches Porzellan im Umbruch, 1895–1935, aus Leningrader Museen und Schloss Peterhoff dem Museum für Angewandte Kunst, Köln und dem Badischen Landesmuseum, Karlsruhe.* Cologne: Museum für Angewandte Kunst, n.d., 187pp., illus.

Text in German. Essays on Russian and Soviet ceramics from 1744 to the twentieth century are followed by an illustrated catalogue and biographies of the designers included. Many women are mentioned, including the Danko sisters and Eva Zeisel (qq.v.).

394   SAVE, COLETTE. "Les artisans du Bérri." *L'Estampille: art et artisanat* 35 (September 1972): 29–39.

Text in French. Describes the work of a number of male and female designers who work in an area of France to the north of Bourges, often in small villages. The best known of these is La Borne.

395   SINZ, DAGMAR. "Welche Zukunft hat die Vergangen heit. Email in Limoges." *Kunst und Handwerk* 92, no. 2 (1992): 21–25, illus.

Text in German. Several women are included in this exhibition review of enamels and ceramics.

396   *Sovietski Farfor 1920–1930* [Soviet Porcelain 1920–1930]. Moscow: Sovietskii Khudozhnik, 1975, 345pp. illus.

Text in Russian. Introductory essays on late-nineteenth century-and early-twentieth-century porcelain, together with illustrations, precede the chapter on the 1920s. Each of the many exhibits is listed.

397   STORR-BRITZ, HILDEGARD. "German Ceramics '79." *Ceramic Review* 60 (1979): 9.

Describes the biennial ceramics competition and resulting travelling exhibition held at Hohr-Grenzhausen, near Koblenz.

398   STORR-BRITZ, HILDEGARD. *International Keramik der Gegenwart.* Cologne: Du Mont, 1980, 244pp., mainly illus.

Text in English and German. The illustrations are grouped by type of work, such as representational and abstract objects, sculptures, reliefs, architectural ceramics. After a glossary the ceramicists whose work is represented in the illustrations are listed. There are a considerable number of women but no information is provided.

399   TE DUITS, THIMO. *Moderne Keramiek in Nederland. Modern Ceramics in the Netherlands.* The Hague: SDU uitgevrerij, 1990, 163pp., illus.

Text in Dutch and English. Introductory essays give a history of the development of modern ceramics from the early 1960s, an overview of the ceramics courses in Dutch academies and other training organisations. The alphabetical catalogue gives an outline biography and selected exhibitions for each person in addition to a paragraph outlining the development of her/his work. Women are well represented.

400   TERRIER, MAX. "Tendances nouvelles de la céramique française." *Art et Industrie* 45 (November): 37–42.

Text in French. Overview of several exhibitions of contemporary ceramics noting the different styles and influences. Considerable numbers of women are mentioned.

401   *Une passion pour la céramique. Collection Fina Gomez: 30 ans de céramique contemporaine.* Paris: Musée des Arts Décoratifs in association with Union des Arts, 1991, 147pp., illus.

An exhibition of part of the collection of contemporary ceramics owned by Fina Gomez. Over one-third of the sixty-two ceramicists represented are women from Europe and the U.S. On each there is half a page of biographical information followed by colour illustrations. The introductory essays concern Gomez and the formation of the collection. A bibliography on each exhibitor is included.

402   VARGA, PÉTER. *A VII Országos Kerámia Biennále. VII National Biennale of Ceramics.* Pécs: Pécsi Galeria, 1982, n.p., illus.

Text in Hungarian. One of a series of exhibitions of contemporary ceramics in Hungary. Over seventy designers are included, of which almost a half are women. For each only an outline biography is given.

403   VINCENTELLI, MOIRA. *Aberystwyth: Y Casgliad Cerameg; the Ceramics Collection.* Aberystwyth: School of Art Press, 1993, 28pp., illus.

Text in Welsh and English. A history of the ceramics collection at University College, Aberystwyth, in which many women designers are included. These include several of the designers of small, figurative sculptures from the 1920s as well as women producing studio pottery from the 1980s.

404   VINCENTELLI, MOIRA. *Early Studio Ceramics in the Collection of the University College of Wales, Aberystwyth.* Aberystwyth: School of Art Press, 1986, n.p., illus.
      After a brief introductory essay about the University Collection, there is a catalogue of the early works. A number of women are included and their entries are preceded by a short biographical outline.

405   WALGRAVE, JAN. *Ars Ceramica: Céramique contemporaine en Belgique. Contemporary Ceramics in Belgium. Hedendaagse keramiek en Belgie.* Liège: Mardaga, 1992, 208pp., illus.
      Text in French, English and Flemish. After an introductory essay on the development of contemporary ceramics in Belgium in which the author contends that the great variety is a new phenomenon, there are seven sections each devoted to a different type of work. They vary from Following Tradition to figurative and abstract sculpture. Twenty-one women are included.

406   WARDROPPER, IAN, ET AL. *News From a Radiant Future. Soviet Porcelain from the Collection of Craig H. and Kay A. Tuber.* Chicago: Art Institute of Chicago, 1992, 92pp., illus.
      Five essays examine aspects of propaganda in relation to the production of Soviet porcelain, the relationship of porcelain and the October Revolution and on collecting Soviet porcelain. There are biographies of ten of the State Porcelain Factory designers, of whom five are women: Liubov Gaush, Alisa Golenkina, Zinaida Kobyletskaia, Elizaveta Rozendorf and Aleksandra Shchekotikhina-Pototskaia.

407   WATSON, OLIVER. *British Studio Pottery.* Oxford: Phaidon in association with the Victoria and Albert Museum and Christie's Ltd., 1990, 288pp., 120 color plates, illus.
      A thorough essay documents the studio pottery movement in Britain from the early 1920s. The catalogue which follows is based on items in the collection of the Victoria and Albert Museum. For each artist/designer there is biographical information and a bibliography. Since seventy-two women are included this is an invaluable source.

408   *Waves of Influence: cinco séculos do azulejjo português.* Staten Island, New York: Snug Harbor Cultural Center, 1995, 94pp., illus.
      Text in Portuguese and English. After a survey of the history of the ceramic tile in Portugal, the exhibition focusses on the revival of the tradition in the twentieth century, partly through designers who have worked on pro-

jects for the Lisbon metro stations and partly through painters who have adapted their work to the format. About eight women are included.

409   WEBER, KLAUS (ED.). *Keramik und Bauhaus.* Berlin: Bauhaus-Archiv, 1989, 286pp, illus.
Text in German. A scholarly publication on the subject containing thoroughly researched essays on a variety of aspects of ceramics at the Bauhaus. These precede the catalogue section. Nine women are included: Gertrud Coja, Lydia Driesch-Foucar, Marguerite Friedländer-Wildenhain, Thoma Graefin-Grote, Margarete Heymann-Marks, Else Mögelin, Eva Oberdieck-Deutschbein, Renate Riedel and Ingrid Triller.

410   WERNER, PETRA, and WILHELM SIEMEN (EDS.). *Die Zwanziger Jahre: deutsches Porzellan zwischen Inflation und Depression: die Zeit der Art Deco.* Hohenberg an der Eger: Museum für Deutschen Porzellan Industrie, 1992, 263pp., illus.
Text in German. Essays on Germany in the 1920s and the porcelain industry are followed by a lengthy consideration of the subject matter of the works exhibited within their cultural context. These include Pierrots, dancers, images of sport. Finally tableware production is considered. The section containing information on forty-four designers and decorators includes only two women: Helma Bøhm and Dorothea Charol.

411   No entry 411.

412   *Zeitgenössische Keramik aus Belgien, Luxemburg, den Niederland und Nordrhein-Westfalen. Kunst im Keramion, no. 31.* Frechen: Keramion—Museum für Zeitgenössischen Karamische Kunst, 1990, 83pp., illus.
Text in German. After short introductions on each of the countries represented, the works are introduced in an overall alphabetical sequence of makers. An outline biography and list of collections is provided for each. Women are well represented.

INDIVIDUALS

413   AERNI-LANGSCH, ELIZABETH
Swiss designer of ceramics, including reliefs.

Other Sources

Lewenstein, Eileen, and Emmanuel Cooper. *New Ceramics.* London: Studio Vista, 1974.

414   ALBRECHT, JULIA (1948–)
      Hungarian ceramics designer.

Exhibitions

Varga, Péter. *A VII Országos Kerámia Biennale Pécs* [VII National Ceramics Biennale]. Pécs: Pécsi Galéria, 1982.

415   ALÓS, ANGELINA (1917–)
      Spanish designer of ceramics.

Exhibitions

Angelina Alós 1933–1984. Exposició-Homenatge. Barcelona: Museu de Ceramica, n.d. [c. 1984], n.p., illus. Text in Catalan. Retrospective exhibition of works made over the half-century of her career.

416   AMBRUS, ÉVA (1941–)
      Hungarian ceramics designer.

Exhibitions

Varga, Péter. *A VII Országos Kerámia Biennale Pécs* [VII National Ceramics Biennale]. Pécs: Pécsi Galéria, 1982.

417   AMOROS, ROSA (1945–)
      Spanish designer of ceramics.

Exhibitions

Exposition Barcelone. Barcelona: Museu de Ceramica, 1985.

418   ANDREASSEN, KRISTIN (1959–)
      Norwegian ceramics designer.

Exhibitions

Opie, Jennifer. *Scandinavia: Ceramics and Glass in the Twentieth Century.* London: Victoria and Albert Museum, 1989.

419   ASSHOFF, INGEBORG (1919–)
      German ceramicist.

Exhibitions

Klinge, Ekkart. *Deutsche Keramik Haute.* Dusseldorf: Verlagsanstalt Handwerk, 1984.

Europäische Keramik de Gegenwart: zweiter Internationale Ausstellung in Keramion. Frechen: Museum für zeitgenössische keramische Kunst, 1986.

Other Sources

Lewenstein, Eileen, and Emmanuel Cooper. *New Ceramics.* London: Studio Vista, 1974.

420   BAARSPUL, ADRIANA (1940–)
Dutch designer of ceramics.

Exhibitions

International Ceramics. London: Victoria and Albert Museum, 1972.

421   BACHELET, MME
French designer of ceramics.

Exhibitions

Oeuvres des Céramistes Modernes, 1890–1930. Sèvres: Musée Céramique in association with Imprimérie Lapina, Paris, 1931.

422   BAILLOT-JOURDAIN, CÉCILE
French designer of ceramics.

Exhibitions

Les grès contemporains en France. Sèvres: Musée Nationale de Céramique, 1963.

Other Sources

Kapferer, Simone. "Les artistes céramistes et verriers au Salon des Artistes Décorateurs." *Les Arts du Feu* 2 (June 1938): 62–64.

423   BALZAR-KOPP, ELFRIEDE (1904–)
German designer of ceramics.

Exhibitions

Meister der Deutschen Keramik 1900–1950. Cologne: Kunstgewerbemuseum, 1978.

424 BAPTENDIER, GENEVIVE (1947–)
French ceramicist who collaborates with Laurence Molinard.

Exhibitions

Brunhammer, Yvonne, and Marie-Laure Perrin. *Céramique française contemporaine: sources et courants.* Paris: Musée des Arts Décoratifs, 1981.

425 BARLOW, FLORENCE ELIZABETH (?–1909)
English decorator of ceramics and painter; sister of Hannah.

Other Sources

Bergesen, Victoria. *Encyclopaedia of British Art Pottery, 1870–1920.* London: Barrie & Jenkins, 1991.

426 BARLOW, HANNAH BOLTON (1851–1916)
English decorator of ceramics, particularly at Doulton's; also a painter and sculptor. Sister of Florence.

Main Sources

Goodman, Barbara. "Breaking the mould." *Ceramic Review* 93 (1985): 38–39.
Rose, P. *Hannah Barlow: A Pioneer Doulton Artist.* London: Richard Dennis, 1985.

Exhibitions

Mundt, Barbara. *Nostalgie warum? Kunsthandwerkliche techniken im Stilwandel vom Historismus zur Moderne.* Berlin: Kunstgewerbemuseum, S.M.P.K., 1982.

Other Sources

Bergesen, Victoria. *Encyclopaedia of British Art Pottery, 1870–1920.* London: Barrie & Jenkins, 1991.
Buckley, Cheryl. *Potters and Paintresses: Women Designers in the Pottery Industry, 1870–1955.* London: Women's Press, 1990.
Parry, Linda. *Textiles of the Arts and Crafts Movement.* London: Thames and Hudson, 1988.

427 BARRES, ANNE (1938–)
French ceramicist who produces relief panels whose textures resemble textiles.

Exhibitions

Brunhammer, Yvonne, and Marie-Laure Perrin. *Céramique française contemporaine: sources et courants.* Paris: Musée des Arts Décoratifs, 1981.

428 BARRETT-DANES, RUTH (née LONG) (1940–)
English ceramicist who works with Alan Barrett-Danes.

Main Sources

Birks, Tony. "Alan Barrett-Danes: Narrative Potter." *Ceramic Review* 36 (1975): 4–6.
Cook, Malcolm. "Ruth Barrett-Danes—Ambiguities of Identity.*"* *Ceramics Review* 113 (1988).
Raine, Craig. "Ruth and Alan Barrett-Danes: Ceramic sculpture." *Crafts* 30 (1978): 48.

Other Sources

Watson, Oliver. *British Studio Pottery.* Oxford: Phaidon, 1990.

429 BARTON, GLENYS (1944–)
English ceramicist and sculptor.

Publications

"A Search for Order." *Ceramic Review* 34 (1975): 4–6.

Main Sources

"Glenys Barton." *Ceramic Review* 69 (1981): 27.
Adamceski, F. "Outside Tradition." *Crafts* 2 (1973): 20–23.
Barry, Val. "Glenys Barton." *Ceramic Review* 31 (1975): 17.
Bayley, Stephen. "Glenys Barton at Wedgwood." *Crafts* 27 (1977): 46–47.
Birks, Tony. "Towards Ceramic Sculpture." *Ceramic Review* 29 (1974): 19.
Catleugh, John. "Bone China by Jacqueline Poncelet and Glenys Barton." *Ceramic Review* 22 (1973): 15.
Cooper, Emmanuel. "Glenys Barton: Sculptures and reliefs." *Ceramic Review* 85 (1984): 10–11.
Fritsch, Elizabeth. "Glenys Barton." *Crafts* 12 (1975).

Exhibitions

International Ceramics. London: Victoria and Albert Museum, 1972.
Bennett, Ian. *British 20th Century Studio Ceramics.* London: Christopher Wood Gallery, 1980.
Watson, Oliver. *British Studio Pottery.* Oxford: Phaidon, 1990.

Other Sources

Lewestein, Eileen, and Emmanuel Cooper. *New Ceramics.* London: Studio Vista, 1974.

430 BARTOSOV, LISBETH (1943–)
Swiss-born designer of ceramics who worked in the Czech Republic.

Exhibitions

Art tchèque contemporain: gravure, céramique, verre. Freiburg: Musée d'Art et d'Histoire, 1973.

431 BASQUE, LORRAINE (1949–)
Canadian-born ceramicist who works in the Netherlands.

Exhibitions

Duits, Thimo Te. *Keramiek '90. Moderne Keramiek in Nederland.* The Hague: SDU Uitgevrerij, 1990.

432 BAUDISCH, GUDRUN (Alt. BAUDISCH-WITTKE or WITTKE-BAUDISCH (1906–1982)
Austrian ceramicist and sculptor who worked for the Wiener Werkstätte in the early part of her career.

Main Sources

Wutzel, Otto. *Gudrun Baudisch: Keramik von der Wiener Werkstätte bis zur Keramik Hallstadt.* Linz, 1980

Exhibitions

Gudrun Baudisch: Keramik. Linz: Oberösterreichen Landesmuseum, 1967.
Kallir, Jane. *Viennese Design and the Wiener Werkstätte.* New York: Braziller in association with the Galérie St. Etienne, 1986.
Leitgeb, Hildegard, Elizabeth Schmuttermeier, and Angela Völker. *Wiener Werkstätte: atelier viennois, 1903–1932.* Brussels: Galérie CGER, 1987.
Hamacher, Bärbel, ed. *Expressive Keramik der Wiener Werkstätte, 1917–1930.* Munich: Bayerische Vereinsbank, 1992. Contains a bibliography.

Other Sources

Byars, Mel. *The Design Encyclopedia.* London: Lawrence King, 1994.
Pirhofer, G., and A. Gmeiner. *Der Österreichische Werkbund.* Vienna: 1985.

Neuwirth, Waltraud. *Die Keramik der Wiener Werkstätte.* Vienna: W. Neuwirth, 1981.

Schweiger, W. *Wiener Werkstätte: Kunst und Handwerk, 1903–32.* Vienna: Christian Brandstätter Verlag, 1982.

433 BAUMFALK, GISELA (1938–)
German ceramics designer.

Exhibitions

Beeh, Wolfgang, and Carl Benno Heller. *Keramik '88: Ton in Ton.* Darmstadt: Hessiches Landesmuseum, 1988.

434 BAUMGARTNER, MARIA (1952–)
Austrian ceramicist.

Exhibitions

Europäische Keramik de Gegenwart: zweiter Internationale Ausstellung in Keramion. Frechen: Museum für zeitgenössische keramische Kunst, 1986.

435 BÄRTSCHI, EVA (1958–)
Swiss ceramics designer.

Exhibitions

Céramique Suisse '93: 17e Biennale des Céramistes Suisses. Geneva: Musée Adriana, 1993.

436 BEARDMORE, FREDA (1910–)
English designer of ceramic decoration; sister of Hilda.

Other Sources

Buckley, Cheryl. *Potters and Paintresses: Women Designers in the Pottery Industry, 1870–1955.* London: Women's Press, 1990.

437 BEARDMORE, HILDA
English designer of ceramics; sister of Freda.

Other Sources

Buckley, Cheryl. *Potters and Paintresses: Women Designers in the Pottery Industry, 1870–1955.* London: Women's Press, 1990.

438 BELLENOT, JÖELLE (1959–)
Swiss ceramics designer.

Exhibitions

Céramique Suisse '93: 17e Biennale des Céramistes Suisses. Geneva: Musée Adriana, 1993.

439 BELL-HUGHES, BEVERLEY
English ceramicist who grew up in the village where Denise and Rosemary Wren (qq.v.) were working and was initially influenced by them.

Main Sources

Fournier, Robert. "Handbuilt ceramics: Denise and Rosemary Wren, Terry and Beverley Bell-Hughes." *Ceramic Review* 10 (1971).

Exhibitions

Tyler, Sheila. *Beverley Bell-Hughes.* Ceramic Series, no. 26. Aberystwyth: Arts Centre.

440 BENGTSON, HERTHA (1917–)
Swedish designer of ceramics.

Exhibitions

Rosenthal: Hundert Jahre Porzellan. Hanover: Kestner-Museum, 1982.
Opie, Jennifer. *Scandinavia: Ceramics and Glass in the Twentieth Century.* London: Victoria and Albert Museum, 1989.
Mundt, Barbara, Suzanne Netzer, and Innes Hettler. *Interieur + Design in Deutschland, 1945=60.* Berlin: Kunstgewerbemuseum and Dietrich Reimer Verlag, 1994.

441 BENNICKE, KAREN (1943–)
Danish ceramicist.

Other Sources

Dormer, Peter. *The New Ceramics: Trends and Traditions.* London: Thames and Hudson, 1986.

442 BERCLAZ-BOTELHO, ANNICK (1962–)
Swiss ceramics designer.

Exhibitions

Céramique Suisse '93: 17e Biennale des Céramistes Suisses. Geneva: Musée Adriana, 1993.

443 BERGNE, SUZANNE (1943–)
German-born ceramicist who worked in several countries before settling in England in 1988.

Publications

"Colour and Light." *Ceramic Review* 86 (1984): 6–8.

Exhibitions

Watson, Oliver. *British Studio Pottery.* Oxford: Phaidon, 1990.

444 BERNHARDT-RAUSSER, LISBETH (1940–)
Swiss ceramicist.

Exhibitions

Céramique Suisse '93: 17e Biennale des Céramistes Suisses. Geneva: Musée Adriana, 1993.

445 BERTRAND, DOMINIQUE (1949–)
French ceramicist who has worked jointly with her husband, Paul, since 1976.

Exhibitions

Brunhammer, Yvonne, and Marie-Laure Perrin. *Céramique française contemporaine: sources et courants.* Paris: Musée des Arts Décoratifs, 1981.

446 BILLINGTON, DORA (1890–1968)
English ceramicist.

Publications

The Art of the Potter. London, 1937. (Reprinted 1953 and 1955.)
"The Younger English Potters." *The Studio,* March 1953.
"The New Look in British Pottery." *The Studio,* January 1955.
The Technique of Pottery, London, 1962.

Exhibitions

Watson, Oliver. *British Studio Pottery.* Oxford: Phaidon, 1990.

Other Sources

Buckley, Cheryl. *Potters and Paintresses: Women Designers in the Pottery Industry, 1870–1955.* London: Women's Press, 1990.

447   BIZETTE, FRANÇOISE
      French designer of ceramics.

Other Sources

Faré, Michel. *La céramique contemporaine.* Paris: Compagnie des Arts Photoméchaniques, 1954.

448   BJORQUIST, KARIN (1927–)
      Swedish designer of ceramics who won the Lunning Prize.

Exhibitions

McFadden, David. *Scandinavian Modern Design, 1880–1980.* New York: Harry Abrams in association with the Cooper-Hewitt Museum, 1982.
The Lunning Prize. Stockholm: Nationalmuseum, 1986.
Mundt, Barbara, Suzanne Netzer, and Innes Hettler. *Interieur + Design in Deutschland, 1945=60.* Berlin: Kunstgewerbemuseum and Dietrich Reimer Verlag, 1994.

Other Sources

Byars, Mel. *The Design Encyclopedia.* London: Lawrence King, 1994.
Naylor, Colin, ed. *Contemporary Designers.* 2nd edition. Chicago and London: St. James Press, 1990. Contains a bibliography.

449   BLIN, CATHERINE (1932–)
      French ceramicist.

Exhibitions

Brunhammer, Yvonne, and Marie-Laure Perrin. *Céramique française contemporaine: sources et courants.* Paris: Musée des Arts Décoratifs, 1981.

450   BOBERG, ANNA KATARINA (1864–1935)
      Swedish designer of ceramics, textiles and glass.

Exhibitions

McFadden, David. *Scandinavian Modern Design, 1880–1980.* New York: Harry Abrams and the Cooper-Hewitt Museum, 1982.

Other Sources

Byars, Mel. *The Design Encyclopedia.* London: Lawrence King, 1994.

451   BOFILL, MARIA (1937–)
      Spanish ceramics designer.

Main Sources

Sanchez-Pacheco, Trinidad. "Deux barcelonaises à Paris." Translated by Jacqueline Jacquet. *La Revue de la Céramique et du Verre* 31 (November/December 1986): 36–37.

Exhibitions

Exposition Barcelone. Barcelona: Museu de Ceramica, 1985.
Collection Fina Gomez: 30 ans de céramique contemporaine. Paris: Musée des Arts Décoratifs, 1991.

452   BOGINO, CLAIRE (1949–)
        French ceramicist.

Exhibitions

Brunhammer, Yvonne, and Marie-Laure Perrin. *Céramique française contemporaine: sources et courants.* Paris: Musée des Arts Décoratifs, 1981.

453   BOIJE, LENA (1944–)
        Swedish designer of ceramics, graphics, textiles and wallpaper.

Exhibitions

Opie, Jennifer. *Scandinavia: Ceramics and Glass in the Twentieth Century.* London: Victoria and Albert Museum, 1989.

454   BOLLHAGEN, HEDWIG (1907–?)
        German designer of ceramics.

Exhibitions

Meister der Deutschen Keramik 1900–1950. Cologne: Kunstgewerbemuseum, 1978.
Mundt, Barbara, Suzanne Netzer, and Innes Hettler. *Interieur + Design in Deutschland, 1945=60.* Berlin: Kunstgewerbemuseum and Dietrich Reimer Verlag, 1994.

455   BORZA, TERÉZ (1953–)
        Hungarian ceramics designer.

Exhibitions

Varga, Péter. *A VII Országos Kerámia Biennale Pécs* [VII National Ceramics Biennale]. Pécs: Pécsi Galéria, 1982.

456 BOUCRAUT, MARIE-MADELEINE (1939–)
     French ceramicist.

Exhibitions

Brunhammer, Yvonne, and Marie-Laure Perrin. *Céramique française contemporaine: sources et courants.* Paris: Musée des Arts Décoratifs, 1981.

457 BOUDOV-SUCHARDOV, ANNA (1870–1940)
     Czech designer of ceramics.

Exhibitions

Českái secesse umen 1900 [Art Nouveau in Bohemia]. Brno: Moravska Gallery, 1966. She is one of the few women included.

458 BRADEN, NORAH (née D. K. NORAH BRADEN) (1901–)
     English designer of ceramics.

Main Sources

Rose, Muriel. *Artist Potters in England.* London: Faber and Faber, 1970.

Exhibitions

Thirties: British Art and Design before the War. London: Arts Council of Great Britain at the Hayward Gallery, 1979.
     Bennett, Ian. *British 20th Century Studio Ceramics.* London: Christopher Wood Gallery, 1980.
     Watson, Oliver. *British Studio Pottery.* Oxford: Phaidon, 1990.

Other Sources

Byars, Mel. *The Design Encyclopedia.* London: Lawrence King, 1994.

459 BREDON, MARIANNE VAN DEN (1954–)
     Dutch ceramicist.

Exhibitions

Duits, Thimo Te. *Keramiek '90. Moderne Keramiek in Nederland.* The Hague: SDU Uitgevrerij, 1990.

460 BRENNAN, HELEN (1942–)
     Irish designer of ceramics.

Exhibitions

International Ceramics. London: Victoria and Albert Museum, 1972.

461 BRENNER NÜNHST, REGINA (1954–)
    Swiss ceramics designer.

Exhibitions

Céramique Suisse '93: 17e Biennale des Céramistes Suisses. Geneva: Musée Adriana, 1993.

462 BRESSEM-WIEGAND, JUTTA (1953–)
    German ceramics designer.

Exhibitions

Beeh, Wolfgang, and Carl Benno Heller. *Keramik '88: Ton in Ton.* Darmstadt: Hessiches Landesmuseum, 1988.

463 BRIANSON, MARGUÉRITE
    French designer of ceramics.

Exhibitions

Oeuvres des Céramistes Modernes, 1890–1930. Sèvres: Musée Céramique in association with Imprimérie Lapina, Paris, 1931.

464 BRITTON, ALISON (1948–)
    English ceramicist.

Publications

"Sèvres with Krazy Kat." *Crafts* 61 (1983): 18–23.
"Hans Coper 1920–1981." *American Craft,* April/May 1984.
"The Modern Pot." In *Fast Forward: New Directions in British Ceramics,* 11–14. London: Institute of Contemporary Art, 1985, illus.
"The Touch of Dreams." *Crafts* 78 (1986): 55–56. Review of exhibition Joan Miró: Ceramics and Bronzes, 1949–80.
"Pots by Sara Radstone." *Crafts* 82 (1986): 54.
"The Critic's Eye." *Crafts Magazine* 98 (1989): 19.
"Le cru et le cuit: manifeste de la nouvelle céramique anglaise." *La Revue de la Céramique et du Verre* 86 (January–February 1996): 18–22.

Main Sources

Coleman, Marigold. "Public and Private." *Crafts* 21 (1976): 27–30.

Dormer, Peter, and David Cripps. *Alison Britton in Studio. A view by Peter Dormer and David Cripps.* London: Bellew, 1985, 96pp., illus. Critical essays by Dormer and photographs of her work by Cripps.

Fritsch, Elizabeth. "Juggling with Pots." *Crafts* 41 (1979): 26–31.

Harrod, Tanya. *Alison Britton: Ceramics in Studio.* London: Bellew in collaboration with Aberystwyth Arts Centre, 1990, 64pp., illus. Bibliography.

Harrod, Tanya, and Peter Dormer. "Alison Britton—New Work." *Crafts* 90 (1988): 39.

Russel Taylor, J. "Playing with Clay." *Ceramic Review* 60 (1979): 6–8.

Exhibitions

Fast Forward: New Directions in British Ceramics. London: Institute of Contemporary Art, 1985.

Bennett, Ian. *British 20th Century Studio Ceramics.* London: Christopher Wood Gallery, 1980.

Houston, John. *The Abstract Vessel. Ceramics in Studio: Forms of Expression and Decoration by Nine Artist Potters.* London: Bellew with the Oriel Gallery and the Welsh Arts Council, 1991.

Watson, Oliver. *British Studio Pottery.* Oxford: Phaidon, 1990.

Other Sources

Dormer, Peter. *The New Ceramics: Trends and Traditions.* London: Thames and Hudson, 1986.

465   BROWN, CHRISTIE (1946–)
Â Â Â Â Â English ceramic sculptor.

Exhibitions

Watson, Oliver. *British Studio Pottery.* Oxford: Phaidon, 1990.

466   BROWN, SANDY (1946–)
Â Â Â Â Â English ceramics designer.

Publications

"The Sensuous Pots of Takeshi Yasuda." *Ceramic Review* 93 (1985): 30–33.

"A Potter in Japan." *Ceramic Review* 96 (1985): 10–12.

"A Theatre of Colour." *Ceramic Review* 99 (1986).

Exhibitions

Briers, David. *Sandy Brown.* Ceramic Series no. 16. Aberystwyth: Aberystwyth Arts Centre, n.d., 4pp., illus.

Sandy Brown: The Complete Picture. Welshpool: Oriel Gallery and Welsh Arts Council, 1987.

Watson, Oliver. *British Studio Pottery.* Oxford: Phaidon, 1990.

467   BRÜGGEMANN-BRECHWOLDT, ANTJE (Alt. BRÜGGERMANN) (1941–)
German ceramics designer.

Exhibitions

Klinge, Ekkart. *Deutsche Keramik Heute.* Dusseldorf: Verlagsanstalt Handwerk, 1984.

Europäische Keramik de Gegenwart:zweiter Internationale Ausstellung in Keramion. Frechen: Museum für zeitgenössische keramische Kunst, 1986.

Beeh, Wolfgang, and Carl Benno Heller. *Keramik '88: Ton in Ton.* Darmstadt: Hessiches Landesmuseum, 1988.

Other Sources

Dormer, Peter. *The New Ceramics: Trends and Traditions.* London: Thames and Hudson, 1986.

Lewenstein, Eileen, and Emmanuel Cooper. *New Ceramics.* London: Studio Vista, 1974.

468   BRYK, RUT (1916–)
Swedish designer of ceramics, textiles and graphics now best known for her abstract reliefs in glazed tiles.

Exhibitions

McFadden, David. *Scandinavian Modern Design, 1880–1980.* New York: Harry Abrams and the Cooper-Hewitt Museum, 1982.

Rosenthal: Hundert Jahre Porzellan. Hanover: Kestner-Museum, 1982.

Opie, Jennifer. *Scandinavia: Ceramics and Glass in the Twentieth Century.* London: Victoria and Albert Museum, 1989.

Other Sources

Byars, Mel. *The Design Encyclopedia.* London: Lawrence King, 1994.

Mäki, Oili. *Taide ja Työ: Finnish Designers of Today.* Helsinki: Werner Söderström Osakeyhtiö, 1954. Gives an outline biography.

Naylor, Colin, ed. *Contemporary Designers.* 2nd edition. Chicago and London: St. James Press, 1990. Contains a bibliography.

469   BUCHER, HERTHA (1898–1960)
Austrian designer who produced ceramics for the Wiener Werkstätte.

Exhibitions

Hamacher, Bärbel, ed. *Expressive Keramik der Wiener Werkstätte, 1917–1930.* Munich: Bayerische Vereinsbank, 1992. Contains a bibliography.

Other Sources

Pirhofer, G., and A. Gmeiner. *Der Österreichische Werkbund.* Vienna: 1985.

Neuwirth, Waltraud. *Die Keramik der Wiener Werkstätte.* Vienna: W. Neuwirth, 1981.

Schweiger, W. *Weiner Werkstätte: Kunst und Handwerk, 1903–32.* Vienna: Christian Brandstätter Verlag, 1982.

470 BÜLOW-HÜBE, TORUN VIVIANNA (1927–)
Swedish designer of metalwork, ceramics, glass and jewellery.

See Glass section.

471 BURNET, DEIDRE (1939–)
English ceramicist.

Main Sources

"CPA New Members." *Ceramic Review* 29 (1974).

"Deidre Burnet, Sheila Casson and Janice Tchalenko." *Crafts* 22 (1976): 45–46.

Catleugh, John. "Tessa Fuchs and Deidre Burnet: Ceramics." *Ceramic Review* 13 (1972): 18.

Exhibitions

Watson, Oliver. *British Studio Pottery.* Oxford: Phaidon, 1990.

472 BUTHOD-GARÇON, GISELE
French ceramicist working in raku.

Main Sources

J. P. R. "Réagir à l'imprévisible." *La Céramique Moderne* 330 (November 1989): 7.

473 BUTTERTON, MARY (Active at Lambeth Potteries c. 1874–1894)
English decorator of ceramics.

Other Sources

Bergesen, Victoria. *Encyclopaedia of British Art Pottery, 1870–1920.* London: Barrie & Jenkins, 1991.

474 CALM, LOTTE (née CHARLOTTE ALICE) (1897–after 1953)
Austrian designer of ceramics.

Exhibitions

Kallir, Jane. *Viennese Design and the Wiener Werkstätte.* New York: Braziller in association with the Galérie St. Etienne, 1986.
Hamacher, Bärbel, ed. *Expressive Keramik der Wiener Werkstätte, 1917–1930.* Munich: Bayerische Vereinsbank, 1992. Contains a bibliography.

Other Sources

Neuwirth, Waltraud. *Die Keramik der Wiener Werkstätte.* Vienna: W. Neuwirth, 1981.
Pirhofer, G., and A. Gmeiner. *Der Österreichische Werkbund.* Vienna: 1985.
Schweiger, W. Weiner *Werkstätte: Kunst und Handwerk, 1903–32.* Vienna: Christian Brandstätter Verlag, 1982.

475 CAMPAVIAS, ESTELLA (c. 1918–)
Turkish-born ceramicist and, from 1974, sculptor who lives in England.

Main Sources

Couteau, G., and P. *Estella Campavias.* Paris, 1981.

Exhibitions

Watson, Oliver. *British Studio Pottery.* Oxford: Phaidon, 1990.

476 CAMPI, ANTONIA (1921–)
Italian designer of ceramics and household objects.

Exhibitions

Hiesinger, Kathryn, and George Marcus III, eds. *Design since 1945.* Philadelphia: Philadelphia Museum of Art, 1983.

477 CARBONNEL, GUIDETTE (Alt. CARBONEL) (exhibited from c. 1932)
French designer of ceramics who trained first as a painter with Lhôte before turning to ceramics in 1932; she designed large fountains for the 1937 Exposition and reliefs for plates and vases at Sèvres.

Other Sources

Faré, Michel. *La céramique contemporaine.* Paris: Compagnie des Arts Photoméchaniques, 1954.

Kapferer, Simone. "Les artistes céramistes et verriers au Salon des Artistes Décorateurs." *Les Arts du Feu* 2 (June 1938): 62–64.

Kim, Jacques. "Les maîtres du Feu au Salon d'Automne." *Les Arts du Feu* 6 (December 1938): 180–181.

478 CARRASCO, FRANÇOISE
French ceramicist who makes small figure sculptures.

Exhibitions

Brunhammer, Yvonne, and Marie-Laure Perrin. *Céramique française contemporaine: sources et courants.* Paris: Musée des Arts Décoratifs, 1981.

479 CARTER, TRUDA (née SHARP; alt. GERTRUDE ADAMS) (1890–1958)
English designer of ceramics.

Exhibitions

Thirties: British Art and Design before the War. London: Arts Council of Great Britain at the Hayward Gallery, 1979.

480 CASS, BARBARA (Alt. WOLSTENCRAFT) (1921–)
German-born ceramicist who worked in England.

Exhibitions

Watson, Oliver. *British Studio Pottery.* Oxford: Phaidon, 1990.

481 CAZIN, BERTHE
French designer of ceramics who, for part of her career, worked at Sèvres.

Exhibitions

Oeuvres des Céramistes Modernes, 1890–1930. Sèvres: Musée Céramique in association with Imprimérie Lapina, Paris, 1931.

Other Sources

Rose, Muriel. *Artist Potters in England.* London: Faber and Faber 1970.

482 CHAMPY, CATHERINE (1945–)
French ceramicist.

Exhibitions

Brunhammer, Yvonne, and Marie-Laure Perrin. *Céramique française contemporaine: sources et courants.* Paris: Musée des Arts Décoratifs, 1981.

483 CHATZINIKOLI, MARY
    Greek ceramics designer.

Other Sources

Lewenstein, Eileen, and Emmanuel Cooper. *New Ceramics.* London: Studio Vista, 1974.

484 CHINELLATO, DANIELA
    Italian designer of ceramics.

Exhibitions

Bacci, N. *Il Design delle Donne.* Ravenna: Museo dell'Arredo Contemporaneo, 1991.

485 CHRISTENSEN, KARI (1938–)
    Norwegian ceramics designer.

Exhibitions

McFadden, David, ed. *Scandinavian Modern Design, 1880–1980.* New York: Harry Abrams and the Cooper-Hewitt Museum, 1982.

Other Sources

Byars, Mel. *The Design Encyclopedia.* London: Lawrence King, 1994.
Dormer, Peter. *The New Ceramics: Trends and Traditions.* London: Thames and Hudson, 1986.
Opie, Jennifer. *Scandinavia: Ceramics and Glass in the Twentieth Century.* London: Victoria and Albert Museum, 1989.

486 CHRISTENSEN, KARI (1938–)
    Norwegian ceramicist.

Exhibitions

Europäische Keramik de Gegenwart:zweiter Internationale Ausstellung in Keramion. Frechen: Museum für zeitgenössische keramische Kunst, 1986.

487 CLIFF, CLARICE (1899–1972)
    English ceramics designer.

Main Sources

Griffen, Leonard, Louis K. Meisel, and Susan Pear. *Clarice Cliff: The Bizarre Affair.* London: Thames and Hudson and New York: Harry Abrams, 1988, 80pp., illus. Consists of a biographical account, a catalogue of the—mainly women—decorators who worked for her and an alphabetical list of all her designs.

Wentworth-Shields, Peter, and Kay Johnson. *Clarice Cliff.* London: L'Odeon, 1976, 81pp., many illus. A chronological account in three chapters. The first examines the years up the the birth of her design Bizarre and her years at Foley China. Several famous women artists were involved by her in designing for China.

Exhibitions

Thirties: British Art and Design Before the War. London: Arts Council of Great Britain at the Hayward Gallery, 1979.

Other Sources

Buckley, Cheryl. *Potters and Paintresses: Women Designers in the Pottery Industry, 1870–1955.* London: Women's Press, 1990.

Byars, Mel. *The Design Encyclopedia.* London: Lawrence King, 1994.

488   CLINTON, MARGERY (1931–)
      English ceramicist.

Publications

"Elusive lustres." *Ceramic Review* 103 (1987).

Main Sources

"CPA New Members." *Ceramic Review* 41 (1976): 12.

Horsman, Kathleen. "Margery Clinton: Ceramics and Paintings." *Ceramic Review* 19 (1973): 16.

Exhibitions

Watson, Oliver. *British Studio Pottery.* Oxford: Phaidon, 1990.

Other Sources

489   COJA, GERTRUD (c. 1902–)
      German ceramicist who worked at the Bauhaus.

Exhibitions

Weber, Klaus, ed. *Keramik und Bauhaus.* Berlin: Bauhaus-Archiv, 1989.

Other Sources

490 COLAS, MARIE-THE (1929–)
French ceramicist who makes mural or relief panels assembled from a number of pieces.

Exhibitions

Brunhammer, Yvonne, and Marie-Laure Perrin. *Céramique française contemporaine: sources et courants.* Paris: Musée des Arts Décoratifs, 1981.

491 COLMEIRA, ELENA (1931–)
Spanish ceramics designer.

Exhibitions

International Ceramics. London: Victoria and Albert Museum, 1972.

Other Sources

Lewenstein, Eileen, and Emmanuel Cooper. *New Ceramics.* London: Studio Vista, 1974.

492 CONSTANTINIDIS, JOANNA (1927–)
English ceramics designer.

Main Sources

"Joanna Constantinidis." *Ceramic Review* 90 (1984): 35.
Dunning, R. "Joanna Constantinidis." *Ceramic Review* 21 (1973): 14.
Harrod, Tanya. "Joanna Constantinidis." *Crafts* 96 (1989): 57.
Ismay, W. "Joanna Constantinidis—Recent Work." *Ceramic Review* 42 (1976): 17.

Exhibitions

International Ceramics. London: Victoria and Albert Museum, 1972.
Watson, Oliver. *British Studio Pottery.* Oxford: Phaidon, 1990.

Other Sources

Lewenstein, Eileen, and Emmanuel Cooper. *New Ceramics.* London: Studio Vista, 1974.

493 CONSTANT, CHRISTINE
English designer of ceramics.

Exhibitions

Brown, Stephanie. *Christine Constant: Sculptural Ceramics.* Ceramics Series, no. 64. Aberystwyth: Aberystwyth Arts Centre, 1994, 6pp., illus.

494   COOPER, SUSIE (née SUSAN VERA COOPER) (1902–1995)
English ceramic designer, especially of tableware.

Main Sources

Battersby, Martin. "Elegance and utility: Ceramics by Susie Cooper, 1924–1978." *Crafts* 34 (1978): 50.

Buckley, Cheryl. "Pottery Women: A Comparative Study of Susan Vera Cooper and Millicent Jane Taplin." In *A View from the Interior: Feminism, Women and Design,* edited by Judy Attfield and Pat Kirkham, 71–89. London: Women's Press, 1989, 5 illus.

Marsh, Madeleine. "Susie Cooper: Kitchen Sink Classics." *The Guardian,* 31 July 1995, 9. Obituary.

Woodhouse, Adrian. *Elegance and Utility, 1924–1978. The Work of Susie Cooper R.D.I.* London, 1978.

———. *Susie Cooper.* Matlock: Trilby Books, 1992.

Youlds, Bryn. "Susie Cooper OBE, RDI." RSA Journal 143, no. 5463 (October 1995): 18. Obituary.

Exhibitions

Timmers, Margaret. *The Way We Live Now: Designs for Interiors 1950 to the Present Day.* London: Victoria and Albert Museum, 1978.

Thirties: British Art and Design before the War. London: Arts Council of Great Britain at the Hayward Gallery, 1979.

Hogben, C. *British Art and Design 1900–1960: A Collection in the Making.* London: Victoria and Albert Museum, 1983.

Eatwell, A. *Susie Cooper Productions.* London: Victoria and Albert Museum, 1987, 107pp., illus. Adopts a chronological approach with an essay for each section followed by exhibit details. Contains a bibliography.

Thirties: British Art and Design Before the War. London: Haywood Gallery, 1979.

Other Sources

Buckley, Cheryl. *Potters and Paintresses: Women Designers in the Pottery Industry, 1870–1955.* London: Women's Press, 1990.

Byars, Mel. *The Design Encyclopedia.* London: Lawrence King, 1994.

495   COPPO BARBERIS, LILIANA (1927–)
Italian designer of ceramics.

Other Sources

Byars, Mel. *The Design Encyclopedia.* London: Lawrence King, 1994

496   CORKE, DAPHNE
English ceramicist.

Exhibitions

Watson, Oliver. *British Studio Pottery.* Oxford: Phaidon, 1990.

497   COSIJN, LIES (1931–)
Indonesian-born ceramicist who works in the Netherlands.

Exhibitions

Neue Formen der Keramik aus der Niederlanden. Darmstadt: Hessischen Landesmuseum, 1967.
Ceramische Hoogtepunten Nederland Pottenkijker, 1959–1969. Rotterdam: Museum Boymans-van Beuningen, 1969.
Europäische Keramik de Gegenwart:zweiter Internationale Ausstellung in Keramion. Frechen: Museum für zeitgenössische keramische Kunst, 1986.

498   COVILLE, JACKY (1936–)
French ceramicist who first trained as an engineer.

Exhibitions

Brunhammer, Yvonne, and Marie-Laure Perrin. *Céramique française contemporaine: sources et courants.* Paris: Musée des Arts Décoratifs, 1981.

499   COWPER, JOAN
English designer of ceramic decoration.

Other Sources

Buckley, Cheryl. *Potters and Paintresses: Women Designers in the Pottery Industry, 1870–1955.* London: Women's Press, 1990.

500   CRAWLEY, MINNA L.
English decorator of ceramics who worked at Lambeth Pottteries from c. 1876 to 1885.

Other Sources

Bergesen, Victoria. *Encyclopaedia of British Art Pottery, 1870–1920.* London: Barrie & Jenkins, 1991.
Clayton, Ellen. *English Female Artists.* London: Tinsley, 1876.

501 CRIPPA, FLORA (1954–)
Italian designer of ceramics and interiors. Collaborates with Giulio Manzoni.

Other Sources

Shimuzu, Fumio, and Matteo Thun. *The Descendants of Leonardo da Vinci: The Italian design.* Tokyo: Graphic Publishing, 1987.

502 CROWLEY, JILL (1946–)
Irish-born ceramicist who works in England.

Main Sources

Coleing, Linda. "Weaving by Tadek Beutlich with Ceramics by Jill Crowley." *Crafts* 39 (1979): 51.
Harrod, Tanya. "Ceramic sculpture by Jill Crowley." *Crafts* 76 (1985): 50.
Reid, Christopher. "Jill Crowley." *Crafts* 55 (1982): 26–31.
Ross, Sheila. "Ceramics by Jill Crowley." *Crafts* 34 (1978): 50–51.

Exhibitions

Briers, David. *Jill Crowley.* Ceramic Series, no. 9. Aberystwyth: Aberystwyth Arts Centre, n.d. 4pp., illus.
Watson, Oliver. *British Studio Pottery.* Oxford: Phaidon, 1990.

Other Sources

Dormer, Peter. *The New Ceramics: Trends and Traditions.* London: Thames and Hudson, 1986.

503 CSKI-MARÓNYAK, ÉVA (1956–)
Hungarian ceramics designer.

Exhibitions

Varga, Péter. *A VII Országos Kerámia Biennale Pécs* [VII National Ceramics Biennale]. Pécs: Pécsi Galéria, 1982.

504 CSAVLEK, ETELKA (1947–)
Hungarian ceramics designer.

Exhibitions

Varga, Péter. *A VII Országos Kerámia Biennale Pécs* [VII National Ceramics Biennale]. Pécs: Pécsi Galéria, 1982.

505 CUPPENS, RI-JEANNE (1957–)
     Dutch ceramicist.

Exhibitions

Duits, Thimo Te. *Keramiek '90. Moderne Keramiek in Nederland.* The Hague: SDU Uitgevrerij, 1990.

506 DAEHLIN, LISBET (1922–)
     Danish-born ceramicist who worked in Norway.

Other Sources

Dormer, Peter. *The New Ceramics: Trends and Traditions.* London: Thames and Hudson, 1986.

507 DAEPP, MARGRETH (1959–)
     Swiss ceramics designer and sculptor.

Exhibitions

15 Schweizer Keramiker: Ausstellung der Nationen. Faenza: Palazzo delle Esposizioni, 1984.

508 DAILLER, MIREILLE (1939–)
     French ceramicist.

Exhibitions

Brunhammer, Yvonne, and Marie-Laure Perrin. *Céramique française contemporaine: sources et courants.* Paris: Musée des Arts Décoratifs, 1981.

509 DAMAS, MARTINE (1954–)
     French ceramics designer.

Exhibitions

Beeh, Wolfgang, and Carl Benno Heller. *Keramik '88: Ton in Ton.* Darmstadt: Hessiches Landesmuseum, 1988.

510 DANNEGGER, ASTRID (1940–)
     German designer of ceramics.

Exhibitions

International Ceramics. London: Victoria and Albert Museum, 1972.

511   DAVIES, PEGGY
      English designer of ceramic decoration.

Other Sources

Buckley, Cheryl. *Potters and Paintresses: Women Designers in the Pottery Industry, 1870–1955.* London: Women's Press, 1990.

512   DE GERMAY, BEATRICE (1946–)
      French ceramicist.

Exhibitions

Brunhammer, Yvonne, and Marie-Laure Perrin. *Céramique française contemporaine: sources et courants.* Paris: Musée des Arts Décoratifs, 1981.

Other Sources

Dormer, Peter. *The New Ceramics: Trends and Traditions.* London: Thames and Hudson, 1986.

513   DE LERMA—VAN DER DOES DE WILLEBOIS, SOPHIE JOHANNA
      MARIA (1891–1961)
      Dutch designer of ceramics.

Exhibitions

Neue Formen der Keramik aus der Niederlanden. Darmstadt: Hessischen Landesmuseum, 1967.
Ceramische Hoogtepunten Nederland Pottenkijker, 1959–1969. Rotterdam: Museum Boymans-van Beuningen, 1969.

514   DE LOURDES CASTRO, MARIA
      Portuguese designer of ceramics.

Exhibitions

International Ceramics. London: Victoria and Albert Museum, 1972.

Other Sources

Lewenstein, Eileen, and Emmanuel Cooper. *New Ceramics.* London: Studio Vista, 1974.

515   DE SOUSA, CECÍLIA (1937–)
      Portuguese ceramicist and sculptor.

Exhibitions

Cecilia de Sousa. Lisbon: Museu Nacional do Azulejo, 1990, n.p., illus. In Portuguese and English. Short introduction and a biographical summary.

Cecilia de Sousa: Cerâmica. Lisbon: Museu Nacional do Azulejo, 1991, 10pp., illus. In Portuguese and English. A short introduction is followed by extended biographical notes.

Waves of Influence: cinco séculos do azulejo português. Staten Island, New York: Snug Harbour Cultural Center, 1995.

516   DE TREY, MARIANNE (1913–)
       English ceramicist of Swiss origin.

Publications

"Ceramics symposium, Crete." *Ceramic Review* 18 (1972): 11.
"35 Years a Potter." *Ceramic Review* 83 (1983): 18–19.

Main Sources

"Workshop by Marianne de Trey." *Ceramic Review* 10 (1971): 4–6.
Barron, Paul. "Marianne de Trey—Porcelain and Stoneware Craftwork." *Ceramic Review* 29 (1974): 18.
Houston, John. "Recent Ceramics by Eric Mellon, Ray Silberman, Marianne de Trey and Mary White." *Crafts* 39 (1979): 52.
Ismay, W. "Marianne de Trey." *Ceramic Review* 12 (1971): 13.
Rogers, Mary. "Marianne de Trey and Colin Kellam." *Ceramic Review* 20 (1973): 16.
Treuherz, Julian. "Four Studio Potters." *Ceramic Review* 25 (1974): 17.

Exhibitions

Watson, Oliver. *British Studio Pottery.* Oxford: Phaidon, 1990.

517   DEBRIL, CLAIRE (1927–)
       French ceramicist.

Main Sources

Deblander, Robert. "Claire Debril: céramiste." *La Revue de la Céramique et du Verre* 34 (May/June 1987): 28–29.
Espagnet, Françoise. "A l'écoute des choses." *La Céramique Moderne* 246 (March 1982): 6.
———. "Claire Debril." *La Revue de la Céramique et du Verre* 19 (November/December 1984): 29–31
———. "Claire Debril." *La Céramique Moderne* 288 (January 1986): 7.
Jaulin, Aline. "Propos d'atelier." *La Céramique Moderne* 303 (May 1987): 6–7.

————. "Paris: Claire Debril." *L'Oeil* 382 (May 1987): 92.

Exhibitions

Collection Fina Gomez: 30 ans de céramique contemporaine. Paris: Musée des Arts Décoratifs, 1991.

518   DECHO, ILSE (1915–1978)
      German designer of glass and ceramics.

Exhibitions

Glaskunst in der DDR. Leipzig: Stadtisches Museum des Kunsthandwerk, 1977.

Mundt, Barbara, Suzanne Netzer, and Innes Hettler. *Interieur + Design in Deutschland, 1945=60.* Berlin: Kunstgewerbemuseum and Dietrich Reimer Verlag, 1994.

519   DECOUX, AGNES (1951–)
      French ceramics designer.

Exhibitions

Brunhammer, Yvonne, and Marie-Laure Perrin. *Céramique française contemporaine: sources et courants.* Paris: Musée des Arts Décoratifs, 1981.

Beeh, Wolfgang, and Carl Benno Heller. *Keramik '88: Ton in Ton.* Darmstadt: Hessiches Landesmuseum, 1988.

520   DEFRAOUI, SILVIA (1935–)
      Swiss designer of ceramics.

Exhibitions

International Ceramics. London: Victoria and Albert Museum, 1972.

521   DEGUTITE, GRAJINA
      Ceramics designer from the former USSR.

Other Sources

Lewenstein, Eileen, and Emmanuel Cooper. *New Ceramics.* London: Studio Vista, 1974.

522   DEL PIERRE, FRANCINE (1913–1968)
      French ceramicist.

Publications

"Le métier et l'art de la céramique. Conférence au Musée Guimet avant la projection de 2 films sur Hamada et Leach, le 25 novembre 1963." *La Céramique Moderne* 51 (June 1964): 8.

"Plaidoyer pour un mot." *La Céramique Moderne* 76 (October 1966): 7, 10.

"L'art et l'artisanat." *La Céramique Moderne* 74 (July/August 1967): 5. Text of an introduction to the catalogue of an exhibition at the Museum of Fine Arts in Caracas.

Main Sources

"Exposition Francine del Pierre au Musée des Beaux-Arts de Caen." *La Céramique Moderne* 187 (November 1986): 3.

Exhibitions

Brunhammer, Yvonne, and Marie-Laure Perrin. *Céramique française contemporaine: sources et courants.* Paris: Musée des Arts Décoratifs, 1981.

Francine del Pierre, Shoji Hamada, Bernard Leach: Keramik. Hamburg: Museum für Kunst und Gewerbe, 1967, 87pp., 46 illus.

Collection Fina Gomez: 30 ans de céramique contemporaine. Paris: Musée des Arts Décoratifs, 1991. Contains a bibliography.

523   DEPLANO, ANNA
    Italian designer of ceramics.

Exhibitions

Bacci, N. *Il Design delle Donne.* Ravenna: Museo dell'Arredo Contemporaneo, 1991.

524   DIONYSE, CARMEN (1921–)
    Belgian ceramicist who produces figurative sculptural work.

Exhibitions

International Ceramics. London: Victoria and Albert Museum, 1972.

Keramik von Carmen Dionyse. Ghent: Museum voor Sierkunst, 1978.

Drei Keramiker aus Belgien: ihr Werk, Ihre Sammlung. Zurich: Kunstgewerbe Museum, 1981, 62pp., illus. Text in German.

Carmen Dionyse. Dusseldorf: Hetjens Museum, 1979.

Carmen Dionyse. Hilversum: Centrun De Vaart, 1979.

Europäische Keramik de Gegenwart: zweiter Internationale Ausstellung in Keramion. Frechen: Museum für zeitgenössische keramische Kunst, 1986.

Other Sources

Lewenstein, Eileen, and Emmanuel Cooper. *New Ceramics.* London: Studio Vista, 1974.

525   DÖRR, ELISABETH (1902–?)
      German designer of ceramics.

Exhibitions

Meister der Deutschen Keramik 1900–1950. Cologne: Kunstgewerbemuseum, 1978.

526   DORAT, MARY
      French designer of ceramics who was president of the Decorative Arts Section at the Salon des Femmes Peintres.

Main Sources

Faré, Michel. *La céramique contemporaine.* Paris: Compagnie des Arts Photoméchaniques, 1954.

527   DRIESCH-FOUCAR, LYDIA (1895–1980)
      German ceramicist who worked at the Bauhaus.

Exhibitions

Weber, Klaus, ed. *Keramik und Bauhaus.* Berlin: Bauhaus-Archiv, 1989.

528   DUCKWORTH, RUTH (1919–)
      German-born ceramicist who worked in England.

Main Sources

Birks, Tony. "Towards Ceramic Sculpture." *Ceramic Review* 29 (1974): 19.
Cooper, Emmanuel. "Ruth Duckworth—a great original." *Ceramic Review* 25 (1974): 4–5.
———. "Ruth Duckworth." *Ceramic Review* 68 (1981): 15–18.
Harrod, Tanya. "Free Spirit." *Crafts* 85 (1987): 32–36.

Exhibitions

International Ceramics. London: Victoria and Albert Museum, 1972.
Beeh, Wolfgang, and Carl Benno Heller. *Keramik '88: Ton in Ton.* Darmstadt: Hessiches Landesmuseum, 1988.
Watson, Oliver. *British Studio Pottery.* Oxford: Phaidon, 1990.

529   DUNN, CONSTANCE E. (née WADE) (c. 1902–?)
      English ceramicist who studied under Dora Billington (q.v.).

Exhibitions

Watson, Oliver. *British Studio Pottery.* Oxford: Phaidon, 1990.

530   DURAY, LILLA (1946–)
Hungarian ceramics designer.

Exhibitions

Varga, Péter. *A VII Országos Kerámia Biennale Pécs* [VII National Ceramics Biennale]. Pécs: Pécsi Galéria, 1982.

531   EBÉZZIYA-SIESBYE, ALEV (1938–)
Turkish-born ceramicist who works in Denmark.

Exhibitions

Europäische Keramik de Gegenwart: zweiter Internationale Ausstellung in Keramion. Frechen: Museum für zeitgenössische keramische Kunst, 1986.

532   EGGER, GABRIELLA (1950–)
Swiss ceramics designer.

Exhibitions

Céramique Suisse '93: 17e Biennale des Céramistes Suisses. Geneva: Musée Adriana, 1993.

533   EISENLOEFFEL, EVA (1917–)
Dutch-born ceramicist who discovered the La Borne groupe of potters in 1965 and has lived in France since 1975.

Exhibitions

Brunhammer, Yvonne, and Marie-Laure Perrin. *Céramique française contemporaine: sources et courants.* Paris: Musée des Arts Décoratifs, 1981.

534   ELENIUS, ELSA (1897–)
Finnish designer of ceramics.

Other Sources

Mäki, Oili. *Taide ja Työ: Finnish Designers of Today.* Helsinki: Werner Söderström Osakeyhtiö, 1954. Gives an outline biography.

535   EPTON, CHARLOTTE (1902–1970)
English ceramicist who worked at the Leach pottery from 1927 to 1930 but ceased to work after her marriage to the artist Edward Bawden in 1932.

Exhibitions

Watson, Oliver. *British Studio Pottery.* Oxford: Phaidon, 1990.

536 ERDÖS, IDA (née MEISINGER) (1897–1985)
German designer of ceramics.

Exhibitions

Meister der Deutschen Keramik 1900–1950. Cologne: Kunstgewerbemuseum, 1978.

Mundt, Barbara, Suzanne Netzer, and Innes Hettler. *Interieur + Design in Deutschland, 1945=60.* Berlin: Kunstgewerbemuseum and Dietrich Reimer Verlag, 1994.

537 EXNER, HILDE (1880–?)
Austrian designer of ceramics.

Other Sources

Pirhofer, G., and A. Gmeiner. *Der Österreichische Werkbund.* Salzburg: Residenz Verlag, 1985.

538 FABRE, CHRISTINE (1951–)
French ceramicist.

Main Sources

C.S. [Colette Save]. "Des pots/objets." *L'Atelier des Métiers d'Art* 87 (April 1984).

S.G. [Sylvie Girard]. "Christine Fabre." *La Revue de la Céramique et du Verre* 6 (September/October 1982): 28.

Deblander, Robert. "Christine Fabre." *La Revue de la Céramique et du Verre* 33 (March/April 1987): 26–27.

Espagnet, Françoise. "Le plaisir de créer." *La Céramique Moderne* 255 (January 1983): 4.

Exhibitions

Collection Fina Gomez: 30 ans de céramique contemporaine. Paris: Musée des Arts Décoratifs, 1991.

539 FAVERGER, PIERETTE (1924–)
Swiss ceramics designer and sculptor.

Exhibitions

15 Schweizer Keramiker: Ausstellung der Nationen. Faenza: Palazzo delle Esposizioni, 1984.

540   FAVRE, ALICE (1932–)
       Swiss ceramics designer.

Exhibitions

Beeh, Wolfgang, and Carl Benno Heller. *Keramik '88: Ton in Ton.*
Darmstadt: Hessiches Landesmuseum, 1988.
Céramique Suisse '93: 17e Biennale des Céramistes Suisses. Geneva: Musée
Adriana, 1993.

541   FEIBLEMAN, DOROTHY (1951–)
       American-born ceramicist who has worked in England since 1973.

Main Sources

"CPA New Members." *Ceramic Review* 35 (1975): 13.
Adamczewski, Fiona. "Ceramics by Dorothy Feibleman." *Crafts* 39 (1979): 49.
Catleugh, John. "Dorothy Feibleman's Agate Porcelain." *Ceramic Review* 68
(1981): 4–6.

Exhibitions

Watson, Oliver. *British Studio Pottery.* Oxford: Phaidon, 1990.

542   FIBICHOV, ZDENA (1933–)
       Czech ceramics designer.

Exhibitions

Beeh, Wolfgang, and Carl Benno Heller. *Keramik '88: Ton in Ton.*
Darmstadt: Hessiches Landesmuseum, 1988.
Klinge, Ekkart. *Tschechesche Keramik.* Dusseldorf: Hetjens-Museum, 1991.
She was one of eight exhibitors.

543   FILLIATREAU, CHRISTINE (1951–)
       French ceramicist.

Exhibitions

Brunhammer, Yvonne, and Marie-Laure Perrin. *Céramique française contemporaine: sources et courants.* Paris: Musée des Arts Décoratifs, 1981.

544   FISCHER-TREYDEN, ELSA (1901–after 1989)
       Russian designer of textiles, ceramics and glass who worked in Germany
       from c. 1925.

See Textiles section.

545   FJELDSAA, KAARE BERVEN (1918–)
      Norwegian sculptor and designer of ceramics.

Other Sources

Opie, Jennifer. *Scandinavia: Ceramics and Glass in the Twentieth Century.* London: Victoria and Albert Museum, 1989.

546   FLECKSTEIN, CATHY (1955–)
      French-born ceramicist who works in Germany.

Exhibitions

Klinge, Ekkart. *Deutsche Keramik Heute.* Dusseldorf: Verlagsanstalt Handwerk, 1984.

Europäische Keramik de Gegenwart:zweiter Internationale Ausstellung in Keramion. Frechen: Museum für zeitgenössische keramische Kunst, 1986.

Beeh, Wolfgang, and Carl Benno Heller. *Keramik '88: Ton in Ton.* Darmstadt: Hessiches Landesmuseum, 1988.

547   FLOCHE, ANN
      Danish ceramicist.

Main Sources

"Two Danish Potters: Inger Rokkjoer and Ann Floche." *Ceramic Review* 139 (1993): 20–21.

548   FOURMANOIR, ANNIE (alt. FOURMANOIR-GORIUS) (1931–)
      French ceramicist.

Publications

Fourmanoir-Gorius, Annie. *Comme l'argile dans la main du potier.* Paris: Dessain et Tolra, n.d. [1979].

Fourmanoir, Annie. "Vive la potérie." *L'Atelier des Métiers d'Art* 43 (November 1979): 14–15.

Main Sources

Brouillard, Florence. "Annie Fourmanoir-Gorius." *La Revue de la Céramique et du Verre* 38 (January/February 1988): 26–29.

R.G. "Les grès et porcelaines d'Annie Fourmanoir-Gorius." *La Céramique Moderne* 277 (January 1985): 6.

Valls, Marie-Françoise. "Annie Fourmanoir: 'On brûle un peu soi-même à chaque cuisson.'" *La Croix,* 19 June 1980. Interview.

Exhibitions

Brunhammer, Yvonne, and Marie-Laure Perrin. *Céramique française contemporaine: sources et courants.* Paris: Musée des Arts Décoratifs, 1981.

Collection Fina Gomez: 30 ans de céramique contemporaine. Paris: Musée des Arts Décoratifs, 1991.

549   FOURNIER, SHEILA (1930–)

English ceramicist who worked with her husband, Robert, to produce tableware and individual pieces. She retired in 1987.

Publications

"Built-in Decoration." *Ceramic Review* 9 (1970): 9.

Main Sources

Dunning, R. "Stoneware and Porcelain by Robert and Sheila Fournier." *Ceramic Review* 32 (1972): 19.

Fieldhouse, Murray. "Robert and Sheila Fournier." *Ceramic Review* 9 (1971): 15.

Thompson, Peter. "Robert and Sheila Fournier." *Crafts* 21 (1976): 48.

Exhibitions

International Ceramics. London: Victoria and Albert Museum, 1972.

Watson, Oliver. *British Studio Pottery.* Oxford: Phaidon, 1990.

Other Sources

Lewenstein, Eileen, and Emmanuel Cooper. *New Ceramics.* London: Studio Vista, 1974.

550   FOX, VALERIE (Alt. BARRY) (1937–)

British ceramicist until the mid-1980s when she became a sculptor.

Publications

Barry, Val. "Porcelain by Lucie Rie, Mary Rogers and Peter Simpson." *Ceramic Review* 20 (1973): 17.

―――. "Tessa Fuchs—Ceramics." *Ceramic Review* 23 (1973): 16.

―――. "'Porcelain': Craftsman Potters' Shop." *Ceramic Review* 22 (1973). Review of exhibition of twenty-six designers, of which four are women.

―――. "'Working with Porcelain' by Alison Sandman." *Ceramic Review* 56 (1979): 21. Book review.

Main Sources

Catleugh, Jon. "Ceramic sculptured forms by Val Barry." Crafts 39 (1979): 52–53.
Cooper, Emmanuel. "The pots of Val Barry." *Ceramic Review* 57 (1979): 28–29.
Orr, J. "CPA new members." *Ceramic Review* 31 (1975): 12.
Sidney, Jonathan. "Val Barry." *Ceramic Review* 13 (1972): 18.

Exhibitions

Feeling through form. London: Barbican Centre, 1986.
Collection Fina Gomez: 30 ans de céramique contemporaine. Paris: Musée des Arts Décoratifs, 1991.

Other Sources

Watson, Oliver. *British Studio Pottery.* Oxford: Phaidon, 1990.

551   FRAGOSO, MARIA LUISA (1907–)
        Portuguese designer of ceramics.

Exhibitions

International Ceramics. London: Victoria and Albert Museum, 1972.

552   FRANCK, FANCE (alt. FRANCE, FRANK) (1931–)
        America ceramicist working in France since 1957. She was inspired by Francine del Pierre (q.v.).

Main Sources

A.G. [Axelle de Gaigneron]. "Fance Franck: céramiste." *Connaissance des Arts,* June 1986, 92–99.

F.C. "Céramiste sur le chemin de Damas." *Connaissance de Paris et de la France* 31 (February 1987): 48–49.

Du Pasquier, Jacqueline. "Die Keramiken Fance Franck." *Keramos* 74 (1976): 49–54.

Save, Colette. "Le secret du rouge chinois." *L'Atelier des Métiers d'Art* 1 (September 1975): 10–13, illus.

Exhibitions

Brunhammer, Yvonne, and Marie-Laure Perrin. *Céramique française contemporaine: sources et courants.* Paris: Musée des Arts Décoratifs, 1981.
Collection Fina Gomez: 30 ans de céramique contemporaine. Paris: Musée des Arts Décoratifs, 1991.

553 FRANCO, DIANA
Italian designer of ceramics.

Exhibitions

Ceramiche del Museo Artistico Industriale di Napoli, 1920–1950. Naples: Museo Artistico Industriale, 1985.

554 FRANKEN, MARIANNA (1928–)
Dutch designer of ceramics.

Exhibitions

Neue Formen der Keramik aus der Niederlanden. Darmstadt: Hessischen Landesmuseum, 1967.
Ceramische Hoogtepunten Nederland Pottenkijker, 1959–1969. Rotterdam: Museum Boymans-van Beuningen, 1969.

555 FRANKLIN, RUTH (1948–)
English ceramicist who turned to painting in the early 1980s.

Main Sources

"CPA New Members." *Ceramic Review* 60 (1979): 36–37.

Exhibitions

Watson, Oliver. *British Studio Pottery.* Oxford: Phaidon, 1990.

556 FRIEDLÄNDER-WILDENHAIN, MARGUERITE (Alt. FRIEDLÄNDER) (1886–1985)
French-born ceramicist who studied at the Bauhaus and worked in Germany before emigrating to America in 1940.

Exhibitions

Meister der Deutschen Keramik 1900–1950. Cologne: Kunstgewerbemuseum, 1978.

Becker, Ingeborg, and Dieter Högermann. *Berliner Porzellan vom Jugenstil zum Funktionalismus, 1899–1939.* Berlin: Bröhan Museum, [1987?].

Oedekoven-Gerischer, Angela, et al., eds. *Frauen im Design: Berufsbilder und Lebenswege seit 1900. Women in Design: Careers and Life Histories since 1900.* Stuttgart: Design Center, 1989.

Weber, Klaus, ed. *Keramik und Bauhaus.* Berlin: Bauhaus-Archiv, 1989.

Mundt, Barbara, Suzanne Netzer, and Innes Hettler. *Interieur + Design in Deutschland, 1945=60.* Berlin: Kunstgewerbemuseum and Dietrich Reimer Verlag, 1994.

Other Sources

Byars, Mel. *The Design Encyclopedia.* London: Lawrence King, 1994.

Weltge, Sigrid Wortmann. *Bauhaus Textiles: Women Artists and the Weaving Workshop.* London: Thames and Hudson, 1993.

557   FRITSCH, ELIZABETH (née HUGHES) (1940–)
Welsh-born ceramicist who is one of the most influential figures to work in England in recent decades.

Publications

"Juggling into jugs." [about Alison Britton q.v.] *Crafts* 40 (1979): 26–31.

"Pots from nowhere." *Crafts* 71 (1984): 20–21.

"Notes on Time in Relation to the Making and Painting of Pots." *Crafts* 97 (1989): 18–19.

Main Sources

Bennet, Ian. "Elizabeth Fritsch." *Crafts* 25 (1977): 45.

Catleugh, John. "Elizabeth Fritsch—Recent Pottery." *Ceramic Review* 30 (1974): 19.

———. "Recents pots by Elizabeth Fritsch." *Ceramic Review* 44 (1977): 7.

Dormer, Peter, and David Cripps. *Elizabeth Fritsch in Studio: A view by Peter Dormer and David Cripps.* London: Bellow, 1985, 96pp., illus. Consists of critical essays on the ideas and influences of Fritsch followed by annotated photographs of her work.

Houston, John. "Traps to fill emptiness." *Crafts* 10 (1974): 13–17.

Inch, Peter. "Pots about Music." *Crafts* 35 (1978): 47.

Russel Taylor, John. "Elizabeth Fritsch—Pots about Music." *Ceramic Review* 58 (1979): 30–34.

Exhibitions

Elizabeth Fritsch: Pots about Music. Leeds Art Galleries, Temple Newsam House, 1978.

Pots from Nowhere. London: Royal College of Art Gallery, 1980.

Bennett, Ian. *British 20th Century Studio Ceramics.* London: Christopher Wood Gallery, 1980.

Houston, John. *The Abstract Vessel. Ceramics in Studio: Forms of Expression and Decoration by Nine Artist Potters.* London: Bellew with the Oriel Gallery and the Welsh Arts Council, 1991.

Fast Forward: New Directions in British Ceramics. London: Institute of Contemporary Art, 1985.

Watson, Oliver. *British Studio Pottery.* Oxford: Phaidon, 1990.

Other Sources

Dormer, Peter. *The New Ceramics: Trends and Traditions.* London: Thames and Hudson, 1986.

558   FRÖSCH, FRANÇOISE (1948–)
        Swiss ceramics designer.

Exhibitions

Beeh, Wolfgang, and Carl Benno Heller. *Keramik '88: Ton in Ton.* Darmstadt: Hessiches Landesmuseum, 1988.

559   FUGINI, LUISA (1954–)
        Swiss ceramics designer.

Exhibitions

Céramique Suisse '93: 17e Biennale des Céramistes Suisses. Geneva: Musée Adriana, 1993.

560   GALLEN, MARIA (1934–)
        Irish designer of ceramics.

Exhibitions

International Ceramics. London: Victoria and Albert Museum, 1972.

561   GALOCSY, EDIT (1928–)
        Hungarian ceramics designer.

Exhibitions

Varga, Péter. *A VII Országos Kerámia Biennale Pécs* [VII National Ceramics Biennale]. Pécs: Pécsi Galéria, 1982.

562   GALTIER-BOISSIRE, MME
        French designer of ceramics.

Exhibitions

Oeuvres des Céramistes Modernes, 1890–1930. Sèvres: Musée Céramique in association with Imprimérie Lapina, Paris, 1931.

563   GARDE, FANNY (1855–1928)
        Danish designer of ceramics.

Exhibitions

Europäischer Keramik des Jugendstils. Art Nouveau Modern Style. Dusseldorf: Hetjens-Museum, 1977. Contains short bibliography.
        Opie, Jennifer. *Scandinavia: Ceramics and Glass in the Twentieth Century.* London: Victoria and Albert Museum, 1989.

564   GASS, MONIKA (1952–)
        German ceramics designer.

Exhibitions

Beeh, Wolfgang, and Carl Benno Heller. *Keramik '88: Ton in Ton.* Darmstadt: Hessiches Landesmuseum, 1988.

565   GAUSH, LIUBOV NIKOLAEVNA (1877–1943)
        Russian designer of ceramics.

Exhibitions

Wardropper, Ian, et al. *News From a Radiant Future: Soviet Porcelain from the Collection of Craig H. and Kay A. Tuber.* Chicago: Art Institute, 1992.

566   GEBHARDT, CHRISTA (1937)
        German ceramicist.

Exhibitions

Klinge, Ekkart. *Deutsche Keramik Heute.* Dusseldorf: Verlagsanstalt Handwerk, 1984.
        Europäische Keramik de Gegenwart: zweiter Internationale Ausstellung in Keramion. Frechen: Museum für zeitgenössische keramische Kunst, 1986.

567   GEBHAUER, GERDA
        Austrian ceramicist working in France since 1979.

Main Sources

Lesein, Nicole. "Des formes elégantes et sobres." *La Céramique Moderne* 300 (February 1987): 4.

Exhibitions

Collection Fina Gomez: 30 ans de céramique contemporaine. Paris: Musée des Arts Décoratifs, 1991.

568 GILBERT, ODILE (1929–)
French designer of ceramics and glass.

Other Sources

Byars, Mel. *The Design Encyclopedia.* London: Lawrence King, 1994.

569 GILES, MAGGI (1938–)
English-born ceramicist who works in the Netherlands.

Exhibitions

Duits, Thimo Te. *Keramiek '90. Moderne Keramiek in Nederland.* The Hague: SDU Uitgevrerij, 1990.

570 GIORIA, FABIENNE (1961–)
Swiss ceramics designer.

Exhibitions

Beeh, Wolfgang, and Carl Benno Heller. *Keramik '88: Ton in Ton.* Darmstadt: Hessiches Landesmuseum, 1988.

571 GIRONS, TERESA (c. 1938–)
Spanish designer of ceramics.

Exhibitions

Soto la magía de Gutenberg: Maria Assumpció Raventós, Teresa Gironès. Barcelona: Museu de Ceramica, 1985, 23pp., illus.

572 GIROUD, NICOLE (1936–)
French ceramicist.

Exhibitions

International Ceramics. London: Victoria and Albert Museum, 1972.
Brunhammer, Yvonne, and Marie-Laure Perrin. *Céramique française contemporaine: sources et courants.* Paris: Musée des Arts Décoratifs, 1981.

573 GLAVE, PATRICIA (1960–)
Swiss ceramics designer.

Exhibitions

Céramique Suisse '93: 17e Biennale des Céramistes Suisses. Geneva: Musée Adriana, 1993.

574 GOLENKINA, ALISSA RUDOLFOVNA (Alt. ALISA) (1884–1970)
Russian designer of ceramics.

Exhibitions

Sovetskii Khoudojestvenyi farfor 1918–1923 [Soviet art porcelain 1918–1923]. Moscow: Museum of Eighteenth Century Ceramics, 1962.

Paris-Moscou 1900–1930. Paris: Centre Nationale d'Art et de Culture Georges Pompidou, 1979.

Wardropper, Ian, et al. *News From a Radiant Future: Soviet Porcelain from the Collection of Craig H. and Kay A. Tuber.* Chicago: Art Institute, 1992.

575 GOMBER, HENRIKE (1955–)
German designer of ceramics.

Exhibitions

Oedekoven-Gerischer, Angela, et al., eds. *Frauen im Design: Berufsbilder und Lebenswege seit 1900* [Women in design: Careers and life histories since 1900]. Stuttgart: Design Center, 1989.

576 GORKA, LIVÍA (1925–)
Hungarian ceramics designer.

Exhibitions

Varga, Péter. *A VII Országos Kerámia Biennale Pécs* [VII National Ceramics Biennale]. Pécs: Pécsi Galéria, 1982.

Other Sources

Pataky-Bretyánsky, Ilona. *Modern Hungarian Ceramics.* Budapest: Corvina, 1961.

577 GRANDPIERRE, JEANNE (1942–)
French ceramicist.

Exhibitions

Brunhammer, Yvonne, and Marie-Laure Perrin. *Céramique française contemporaine: sources et courants.* Paris: Musée des Arts Décoratifs, 1981.

578 GROTE, THOMA GRÄFIN (pseudonym of DORALINE MARIA HELE-
NA GRÄFIN GROTE) (1896–1977)
German ceramicist who worked at the Bauhaus.

Exhibitions

Weber, Klaus, ed. *Keramik und Bauhaus.* Berlin: Bauhaus-Archiv, 1989.

579 GUILLERMAIN, JACQUELINE (1943–)
French ceramicist.

Exhibitions

Brunhammer, Yvonne, and Marie-Laure Perrin. *Céramique française contemporaine: sources et courants.* Paris: Musée des Arts Décoratifs, 1981.

580 GUNN-RUSSEL, LINDA (1953–)
English ceramicist who makes individual pieces using the illusions of
visual perspective.

Exhibitions

Watson, Oliver. *British Studio Pottery.* Oxford: Phaidon, 1990.

581 HAENEN, BABS (1948–)
Dutch ceramicist.

Exhibitions

Beeh, Wolfgang, and Carl Benno Heller. *Keramik '88: Ton in Ton.*
Darmstadt: Hessiches Landesmuseum, 1988.
Gaillard, Karin. *Céramique néerlandaise contemporaine. Contemporary
Dutch Ceramics. Niederlandische Keramik der Gegenwart.* Roanne: Musée Joseph
Dechelette, 1988.

Other Sources

Dormer, Peter. *The New Ceramics: Trends and Traditions.* London: Thames
and Hudson, 1986.

582 HAHN, SUSANNE.
Dutch ceramicist and sculptor.

Exhibitions

Gaillard, Karin. *Céramique néerlandaise contemporaine. Contemporary
Dutch Ceramics. Niederlandische Keramik der Gegenwart.* Roanne: Musée Joseph
Dechelette, 1988.

583   HALLING-KOCH, ANNAGRETE (1947–)
    Danish designer of ceramics and textiles.

Other Sources

Byars, Mel. *The Design Encyclopedia.* London: Lawrence King, 1994.

584   HAMLYN, JANE (1940–)
    English ceramicist who trained as a potter in the 1970s having earlier qualified as a nurse.

Publications

"Paper-resist Decoration." *Ceramic Review* 55 (1979): 8.
Pigott, Gwyn Hannsen, and Jane Hamlyn. "Domestic Pots—Domestic Potters." *Ceramic Review* 92 (1985): 20–21.
"Salt Glaze and Something Else." *Ceramics Monthly,* April 1989, 32–36.

Main Sources

"CPA New Members." *Ceramic Review* 43 (1977): 11.
Cochrane, Rosemary. "For Use and Ornament: Saltglaze Pots by Jane Hamlyn." *Ceramic Review* 139 (1993): 24–25.
Leon, Anne. "Jane Hamlyn at Millfield Pottery." *Ceramic Review* 74 (1982): 4–7.
Miller, Catherine. " New Pottery by Jane Hamlyn, Gary Standige and Jim Malone." *Crafts* 49 (1981): 51–52.
Wren, Rosemary, and Peter Crotty. "Jane Hamlyn: Salt-Glazed Pottery." *Crafts* 20 (1976): 50.

Exhibitions

Shrimpton, Sally. *Jane Hamlyn.* Ceramics Series no. 19. Aberystwyth: Arts Centre, 1987, 4pp., illus.
Watson, Oliver. *British Studio Pottery.* Oxford: Phaidon, 1990.

Other Sources

Dormer, Peter. *The New Ceramics: Trends and Traditions.* London: Thames and Hudson, 1986.

585   HARDING, GILLIAN (1936–)
    English designer of ceramics who worked for Denby.

Exhibitions

Timmers, Margaret. *The Way We Live Now: Designs for Interiors 1950 to the Present Day.* London: Victoria and Albert Museum, 1978.

586   HARKORT, LUISE (née DE LAPORTE)
       German designer of ceramics.

Exhibitions

Meister der Deutschen Keramik 1900–1950. Cologne: Kunstgewerbemuseum, 1978.

587   HATZINICOLI, MARY (1928–)
       Greek designer of ceramics.

Exhibitions

International Ceramics. London: Victoria and Albert Museum, 1972.

588   HEGERMANN-LINDENCRONE, EFFIE (1860–1945)
       Danish designer of ceramics.

Exhibitions

Europäischer Keramik des Jugendstils. Art Nouveau Modern Style. Dusseldorf: Hetjens-Museum, 1977. Contains short bibliography.
       Becker, Ingeborg, and Dieter Högermann. *Berliner Porzellan vom Jugenstil zum Funktionalismus, 1899–1939.* Berlin: Bröhan Museum, [1987?].
       Opie, Jennifer. *Scandinavia: Ceramics and Glass in the Twentieth Century.* London: Victoria and Albert Museum, 1989.

589   HELLUM, CHARLOTTE BLOCK (1911–)
       German-born designer of ceramics and enamels who worked in Norway.

Exhibitions

McFadden, David. *Scandinavian Modern Design, 1880–1980.* New York: Harry Abrams in association with the Cooper-Hewitt Museum, 1982.
       Opie, Jennifer. *Scandinavia: Ceramics and Glass in the Twentieth Century.* London: Victoria and Albert Museum, 1989.

590   HENKELMAN, VILMA.
       Dutch ceramics designer.

Exhibitions

Gaillard, Karin. *Céramique néerlandaise contemporaine. Contemporary Dutch Ceramics. Niederlandische Keramik der Gegenwart.* Roanne: Musée Joseph Dechelette, 1988.

591   HENNIX, MARGARETA (1941–)
       Swedish designer of ceramics, textiles and enamels.

Exhibitions

Opie, Jennifer. *Scandinavia: Ceramics and Glass in the Twentieth Century.* London: Victoria and Albert Museum, 1989.

592 HEYMANN-MARKS, MARGARETE (Alt. GRETE MARKS) (1899/ 1901–?)
German designer of ceramics who worked at the Bauhaus and then in England from 1935.

See under Grete Marks.

593 HILLFON, HERTHA (1921–)
Swedish designer of ceramics who won the Lunning Prize.

Exhibitions

McFadden, David. *Scandinavian Modern Design, 1880–1980.* New York: Harry Abrams and the Cooper-Hewitt Museum, 1982.
The Lunning Prize. Stockholm: Nationalmuseum, 1986.
Opie, Jennifer. *Scandinavia: Ceramics and Glass in the Twentieth Century.* London: Victoria and Albert Museum, 1989.

Other Sources

Byars, Mel. *The Design Encyclopedia.* London: Lawrence King, 1994.
Lewenstein, Eileen, and Emmanuel Cooper. *New Ceramics.* London: Studio Vista, 1974.

594 HLADIHOV, LYDIA
Czech ceramics designer.

Other Sources

Lewenstein, Eileen, and Emmanuel Cooper. *New Ceramics.* London: Studio Vista, 1974.

595 HLAVACOV-CHODEROV, JANA (1925–)
Czech designer of ceramics.

Exhibitions

Art tchèque contemporain: gravure, céramique, verre. Freiburg: Musée d'Art et d'Histoire, 1973.

596 HOCKMAN, MIRJAM
Dutch ceramicist.

Exhibitions

Duits, Thimo Te. *Keramiek '90. Moderne Keramiek in Nederland.* The Hague: SDU Uitgevrerij, 1990.

597   HOLZER-KJELLBERG, ELFRIEDE AMALIE ADOLFINE (1905–)
Austrian-born designer of ceramics who worked in Finland.

Exhibitions

Opie, Jennifer. *Scandinavia: Ceramics and Glass in the Twentieth Century.* London: Victoria and Albert Museum, 1989.

598   HOOFT, MARJA (1946–)
Dutch ceramicist who since the 1980s has worked in partnership with the textile designer Danielle Janssen (q.v.).

Exhibitions

Duits, Thimo Te. *Keramiek '90. Moderne Keramiek in Nederland.* The Hague: SDU Uitgevrerij, 1990.

599   HOPEA-UNTRACHT, SAARA (alt. HOPEA) (1925–1984)
Finnish designer of ceramics, glass, graphics, textiles, furniture, lighting and interiors.

See Glass section.

600   HÖST, MARIANNE (active 1885–1907)
Danish or German designer of ceramic decoration who specialised in flowers and trees.

Exhibitions

Europäischer Keramik des Jugendstils. Art Nouveau Modern Style. Dusseldorf: Hetjens-Museum, 1977. Contains a short bibliography.
Becker, Ingeborg, and Dieter Högermann. *Berliner Porzellan vom Jugenstil zum Funktionalismus, 1899–1939.* Berlin: Bröhan Museum, [1987?].

601   HOY, AGNETE (1914–)
Danish designer of ceramics who lived and worked in England after training in Denmark.

Other Sources

Buckley, Cheryl. *Potters and Paintresses: Women Designers in the Pottery Industry, 1870–1955.* London: Women's Press, 1990.

602   HÖGYE, KATALIN (1952–)
    Hungarian ceramics designer.

Exhibitions

Varga, Péter. *A VII Országos Kerámia Biennale Pécs* [VII National Ceramics Biennale]. Pécs: Pécsi Galéria, 1982.

603   HUGGINS, VERA
    English designer of ceramic decoration.

Other Sources

Buckley, Cheryl. *Potters and Paintresses: Women Designers in the Pottery Industry, 1870–1955.* London: Women's Press, 1990.

604   JACENAITE, GENOVEITE
    Ceramics designer and sculptor from the former USSR.

Other Sources

Lewenstein, Eileen, and Emmanuel Cooper. *New Ceramics.* London: Studio Vista, 1974.

605   JACZ, ZUZANA (1953–)
    Czech-born ceramicist who has lived in France since 1975. She produces small figure sculptures in clay.

Exhibitions

Brunhammer, Yvonne, and Marie-Laure Perrin. *Céramique française contemporaine: sources et courants.* Paris: Musée des Arts Décoratifs, 1981.

606   JANSSEN, DANIELLE (1948–)
    Dutch textile designer who has since the 1980s worked in partnership with the ceramicist Marja Hooft (q.v.).

Exhibitions

Duits, Thimo Te. *Keramiek '90. Moderne Keramiek in Nederland.* The Hague: SDU Uitgevrerij, 1990.

607   JÄDERHOLM-SNELLMAN, GRETA-LISA (1894–1973)
    Finnish designer in glass and ceramics.

Exhibitions

Opie, Jennifer. *Scandinavia: Ceramics and Glass in the Twentieth Century.* London: Victoria and Albert Museum, 1989.

608   JESSER, HILDA (Alt. JESSER-SCHMIDT) (1894–after 1982)
       Austrian designer in many media, including ceramics and glass.

Exhibitions

Kallir, Jane. *Viennese Design and the Wiener Werkstätte.* New York: Braziller in association with the Galérie St. Etienne, 1986.

Leitgeb, Hildegard, Elizabeth Schmuttermeier, and Angela Völker. *Wiener Werkstätte: atelier viennois, 1903–1932.* Brussels: Galérie CGER, 1987.

Hamacher, Bärbel, ed. *Expressive Keramik der Wiener Werkstätte, 1917–1930.* Munich: Bayerische Vereinsbank, 1992. Contains a bibliography.

Other Sources

Arwas, Victor. *Glass: Art Nouveau to Art Déco.* London: Academy Editions, 1977.

Joseph Hoffmann and Wilhelm Wagenfeld: Glaskunst der Moderne. Munich: Klinkhardt and Bierman, 1992.

Neuwirth, Waltraud. *Die Keramik der Wiener Werkstätte.* Vienna: W. Neuwirth, 1981.

Pirhofer, G., and A. Gmeiner. *Der Österreichische Werkbund.* Salzburg: Residenz Verlag, 1985.

Schweiger, W. *Weiner Werkstätte: Kunst und Handwerk, 1903–32.* Vienna: Christian Brandstätter Verlag, 1982.

609   JOHNOV, HELENA (1884–1962)
       Czech ceramics designer.

Other Sources

Byars, Mel. *The Design Encyclopedia.* London: Lawrence King, 1994.

Lewenstein, Eileen, and Emmanuel Cooper. *New Ceramics.* London: Studio Vista, 1974.

Pirhofer, G., and A. Gmeiner. *Der Österreichische Werkbund.* Salzburg: Residenz Verlag, 1985.

Préaud, Tamara. *Ceramics of the Twentieth Century.* Oxford: Phaidon, 1982.

610   JONGMANS, CONNY (1965–)
       Dutch ceramicist.

Exhibitions

Duits, Thimo Te. *Keramiek '90. Moderne Keramiek in Nederland.* The Hague: SDU Uitgevrerij, 1990.

611   JOULIA (Pseudonym of ELISABETH JOULIA) (1925–)
       French ceramicist who works in the group based in La Borne.

Main Sources

"Joulia." *L'Atelier des Métiers d'Art* 3 (November 1975): 4, 24. Interview.

Bertrand, Evariste. "Joulia la grande." *La Céramique Moderne* 228 (May 1980): 9.

Brunhammer, Yvonne. "Joulia." *La Revue de la Céramique et du Verre* (September/October 1986): 34–35.

Canteins, Jean. "Joulia." *La Céramique Moderne* 279 (November 1978): 6.

Gautier Delaye, Pierre. "Le monde de Joulia, potier à La Borne." *La Maison Française* 282 (November 1974): 160–163, mainly illus.

S.G. [Sylvie Girard]. "Rétrospective Joulia 1950–53." *La Revue de la Céramique et du Verre* 14 (January/February 1984): 45. Review of exhibition at the Musée de St. Amand les Eaux.

Save, Colette. "Voyage autour de la terre." *L'Atelier des Métiers d'Art* 24 (December 1977/January 1978): 3–5.

———. "Tendance: sculpture-architecture." *L'Atelier des Métiers d'Art* 27 (April 1978): 14–15.

———. "Joulia comme les tarots." *L'Atelier des Métiers d'Art* 113 (November 1986): 28–31.

Exhibitions

International Ceramics. London: Victoria and Albert Museum, 1972.

Brunhammer, Yvonne, and Marie-Laure Perrin. *Céramique française contemporaine: sources et courants.* Paris: Musée des Arts Décoratifs, 1981.

Collection Fina Gomez: 30 ans de céramique contemporaine. Paris: Musée des Arts Décoratifs, 1991.

612   JUNGE, REGINA (1912–)
      German designer of ceramics.

Exhibitions

International Ceramics. London: Victoria and Albert Museum, 1972.

613   JUNIK, NICOLE
      French ceramicist.

Main Sources

"Simples, lisses et rondes." *La Céramique Moderne* 330 (November 1989): 7.

614   JUURIKAALA, ANJA (1923–)
      Finnish ceramics designer.

Other Sources

Opie, Jennifer. *Scandinavia: Ceramics and Glass in the Twentieth Century.* London: Victoria and Albert Museum, 1989.

615   KADASI, JUDIT (1953–)
      Hungarian ceramics designer.

Exhibitions

Varga, Péter. *A VII Országos Kerámia Biennale Pécs* [VII National Ceramics Biennale]. Pécs: Pécsi Galéria, 1982.

616   KAJANDER, CATHARINA
      Finnish ceramics designer.

Exhibitions

International Ceramics. London: Victoria and Albert Museum, 1972.

Other Sources

Lewenstein, Eileen, and Emmanuel Cooper. *New Ceramics.* London: Studio Vista, 1974.

617   KAMERMANS, KLAARTJE (1954–)
      Dutch ceramicist.

Exhibitions

Duits, Thimo Te. *Keramiek '90. Moderne Keramiek in Nederland.* The Hague: SDU Uitgevrerij, 1990.

618   KANT, GERTRUDE
      German designer of ceramics.

Exhibitions

Becker, Ingeborg, and Dieter Högermann. *Berliner Porzellan vom Jugenstil zum Funktionalismus, 1899–1939.* Berlin: Bröhan Museum, [1987?].

619   KARCZEWSKA, JANINA (1934–)
      Polish designer of ceramics.

Exhibitions

International Ceramics. London: Victoria and Albert Museum, 1972.

620   KEIL, MARIA (Alt. KEIL DO AMARAL) (1914–)
      Portuguese designer of ceramics who specialises in the creation of large murals with tiles.

Exhibitions

Maria Keil: azulejos. Lisbon: Museu Nacional do Azulejo, 1989, 108pp., illus. Contains a useful bibliography.

Waves of Influence: cinco séculos do azulejo português. Staten Island, New York: Snug Harbour Cultural Center, 1995.

621   KEYSER, YVONNE (1956–)
      Dutch ceramicist.

Exhibitions

Duits, Thimo Te. *Keramiek '90. Moderne Keramiek in Nederland.* The Hague: SDU Uitgevrerij, 1990.

622   KING, JESSIE MARION (1875–1949)
      Scottish illustrator, designer of graphics, woven and printed textiles, wallpaper and, from 1914, ceramics and ceramic decoration.

See Volume 2, Graphic Art section.

623   KIPPENBERG, HEIDI (1941–)
      German ceramicist.

Exhibitions

Klinge, Ekkart. *Deutsche Keramik Heute.* Dusseldorf: Verlagsanstalt Handwerk, 1984.

Other Sources

Dormer, Peter. *The New Ceramics: Trends and Traditions.* London: Thames and Hudson, 1986.

624   KISS-ROÓZ, ILONA
      Hungarian designer of ceramics.

Other Sources

Pataky-Brestyánsky, Ilona. *Modern Hungarian Ceramics.* Budapest: Corvina, 1961.

625   KJAERSGAARD, ANNE (1933–1990)
      Danish ceramicist working in France.

Main Sources

Bertrand, Evariste. "'Sois toi-même.'" *La Céramique Moderne* 330 (November 1989): 6.

Exhibitions

Brunhammer, Yvonne, and Marie-Laure Perrin. *Céramique française contemporaine: sources et courants.* Paris: Musée des Arts Décoratifs, 1981.

Collection Fina Gomez: 30 ans de céramique contemporaine. Paris: Musée des Arts Décoratifs, 1991.

626 KJELLBERG, FREIDL (1905–)
Finnish designer of ceramics.

Other Sources

Mäki, Oili. *Taide ja Työ: Finnish Designers of Today.* Helsinki: Werner Söderström Osakeyhtiö, 1954. Gives an outline biography.

627 KLEIN, MAAIKE (1947–)
Dutch ceramicist.

Exhibitions

Duits, Thimo Te. *Keramiek '90. Moderne Keramiek in Nederland.* The Hague: SDU Uitgevrerij, 1990.

628 KLEINVELD, YVONNE (1952–)
Dutch ceramicist.

Other Sources

Dormer, Peter. *The New Ceramics: Trends and Traditions.* London: Thames and Hudson, 1986.

629 No entry 629.

630 KLINGER-RÖMHILD, EVA (1945–)
German ceramics designer.

Exhibitions

Beeh, Wolfgang, and Carl Benno Heller. *Keramik '88: Ton in Ton.* Darmstadt: Hessisches Landesmuseum, 1988.

631 KNAVEN, MARGA (1956–)
Dutch ceramicist.

Exhibitions

Duits, Thimo Te. *Keramiek '90. Moderne Keramiek in Nederland.* The Hague: SDU Uitgevrerij, 1990.

632   KOBYLETSKAYA, ZINAIDA VIKTORIOVNA (1880–1957)
Russian designer of ceramics and botanical illustrator.

Exhibitions

Paris-Moscou, 1900–1939. Paris: Centre Nationale d'Art et de Culture Georges Pompidou, 1979.

Wardropper, Ian, et al. *News from a Radiant Future: Soviet Porcelain from the Collection of Craig H. and Kay A. Tuber.* Chicago: Art Institute, 1992.

Other Sources

Elliott, David, and Valery Dudakov. *100 Years of Russian Art, 1889–1989.* London: Lund Humphries, 1989.

Nikiforova, L. *Russian Porcelain in the Hermitage Collection.* Leningrad: Aurora Art Publishers, 1973.

633   KOCH, GABY (1948–)
German-born ceramicist who trained in London.

Other Sources

Dormer, Peter. *The New Ceramics: Trends and Traditions.* London: Thames and Hudson, 1986.

634   KOCH, LUISE CHARLOTTE (1917–)
German designer who worked in several media, including ceramics and fashion design.

Exhibitions

Mundt, Barbara, Suzanne Netzer, and Innes Hettler. *Interieur + Design in Deutschland, 1945=60.* Berlin: Kunstgewerbemuseum and Dietrich Reimer Verlag, 1994.

635   KOEFOED, INGE-LISA (1939–)
Danish designer of ceramics and graphics.

Other Sources

Opie, Jennifer. *Scandinavia: Ceramics and Glass in the Twentieth Century.* London: Victoria and Albert Museum, 1989.

636   KOLTCHEVA, OLIA
Bulgarain ceramics designer.

Other Sources

Lewenstein, Eileen, and Emmanuel Cooper. *New Ceramics.* London: Studio Vista, 1974.

637   KONZOV, ANTONINA
Bulgarian ceramics designer.

Other Sources

Lewenstein, Eileen, and Emmanuel Cooper. *New Ceramics.* London: Studio Vista, 1974.

638   KOOLBERG, MAIA
Ceramics designer from the former USSR.

Other Sources

Lewenstein, Eileen, and Emmanuel Cooper. *New Ceramics.* London: Studio Vista, 1974.

639   KOPPENHÖFER, RUTH (1922–)
German designer of ceramics.

Exhibitions

International Ceramics. London: Victoria and Albert Museum, 1972.
Klinge, Ekkart. *Deutsche Keramik Heute.* Dusseldorf: Verlagsanstalt Handwerk, 1984.

640   KOPRIVA, ERNA (Alt. ERNESTINE) (1894–1984)
Austrian designer of ceramics who worked in the Wiener Werkstätte.

Exhibitions

Hamacher, Bärbel, ed. *Expressive Keramik der Wiener Werkstätte, 1917–1930.* Munich: Bayerische Vereinsbank, 1992. Contains a bibliography.

Other Sources

Byars, Mel. *The Design Encyclopedia.* London: Lawrence King, 1994.

Neuwirth, Waltraud. *Die Keramik der Wiener Werkstätte.* Vienna: W. Neuwirth, 1981.

Pirhofer, G., and A. Gmeiner. *Der Österreichische Werkbund.* Vienna: 1985.

Schweiger, W. *Weiner Werkstätte: Kunst und Handwerk, 1903–32.* Vienna: Christian Brandstätter Verlag, 1982.

641   KOVCS, MARGIT (1902–)
      Hungarian designer of ceramics, especially sculpture and small figurines.

Main Sources

Pataky-Brestyánsky, Ilona. *Margit Kovács.* Hungarian and English Editions. Budapest: Corvina, 1976, 193pp., illus. Contains critical essays, a catalogue of her work and a bibliography.

————. *Kovács, Margit.* Budapest: Fine Arts Publishing House, 1990, 63pp., illus. Revised translation of the 1974 edition. A small publication which nevertheless contains a thorough account of her life and work; there is also a list of exhibitions and a bibliography.

Other Sources

Pataky-Brestyánsky, Ilona. *Modern Hungarian Ceramics.* Budapest: Corvina, 1961.

642   KRAJTSOVITS, MARGIT (1936–)
      Hungarian ceramics designer.

Exhibitions

Varga, Péter. *A VII Országos Kerámia Biennale Pécs* [VII National Ceramics Biennale]. Pécs: Pécsi Galéria, 1982.

643   KRAJTSOVITS, MARTA (1946–)
      Hungarian ceramics designer.

Exhibitions

Varga, Péter. *A VII Országos Kerámia Biennale Pécs* [VII National Ceramics Biennale]. Pécs: Pécsi Galéria, 1982.

644   KRAMER, BASTIENNE (1961–)
      Dutch ceramicist.

Exhibitions

Duits, Thimo Te. *Keramiek '90. Moderne Keramiek in Nederland.* The Hague: SDU Uitgevrerij, 1990.

645   KRASNIK, ANTOINETTE
Austrian painter and designer of ceramics, glass, silver and jewellery active just after 1900.

Other Sources

Byars, Mel. *The Design Encyclopedia*. London: Lawrence King, 1994.

646   KRAUT, GERTRUD (1883–1980)
German designer of ceramics.

Exhibitions

Oedekoven-Gerischer, Angela, et al., eds. *Frauen im Design: Berufsbilder und Lebenswege seit 1900. Women in Design: Careers and Life Histories since 1900.* Stuttgart: Design Center, 1989.

647   KREBS, NATHALIE (1895–1978)
Danish ceramics designer.

Exhibitions

McFadden, David, ed. *Scandinavian Modern Design, 1880–1980.* New York: Harry Abrams and the Cooper-Hewitt Museum, 1982.
Opie, Jennifer. *Scandinavia: Ceramics and Glass in the Twentieth Century.* London: Victoria and Albert Museum, 1989.

Other Sources

Byars, Mel. *The Design Encyclopedia*. London: Lawrence King, 1994.
Hiort, Esbjørn. *Modern Danish Ceramics*. New York: Museum Books Inc.; London: A. Zwemmer Ltd.; Stuttgart: Verlag Gerd Hatje; Teufen: Arthur Niggli und Willy Verkauf; Copenhagen: Jul Gjellerups Forlag, 1955.
Préaud, Tamara. *Ceramics of the Twentieth Century.* Oxford: Phaidon, 1982.

648   KUCH, ELLY (1927/9–)
German ceramicist.

Exhibitions

Klinge, Ekkart. *Deutsche Keramik Heute.* Dusseldorf: Verlagsanstalt Handwerk, 1984.
Europäische Keramik de Gegenwart:zweiter Internationale Ausstellung in Keramion. Frechen: Frechen, 1986.

Other Sources

Beeh, Wolfgang, and Carl Benno Heller. *Keramik '88: Ton in Ton.* Darmstadt: Hessiches Landesmuseum, 1988.

649   KUCZYNSKA, MARIA TERESA (1948–)
      Polish ceramicist.

Exhibitions

Europäische Keramik de Gegenwart:zweiter Internationale Ausstellung in Keramion. Frechen: Museum für zeitgenössische keramische Kunst, 1986.

650   KUHN, BEATE (1927–)
      German designer of ceramics.

Exhibitions

Ceramics from Germany. London: Primavera Gallery, 1968.
International Ceramics. London: Victoria and Albert Museum, 1972.
Rosenthal: Hundert Jahre Porzellan. Hanover: Kestner-Museum, 1982.
Klinge, Ekkart. *Deutsche Keramik Heute.* Dusseldorf: Verlagsanstalt Handwerk, 1984.
Europäische Keramik de Gegenwart:zweiter Internationale Ausstellung in Keramion. Frechen: Museum für zeitgenössische keramische Kunst, 1986.
Mundt, Barbara, Suzanne Netzer, and Innes Hettler. *Interieur + Design in Deutschland, 1945=60.* Berlin: Kunstgewerbemuseum and Dietrich Reimer Verlag, 1994.

Other Sources

Lewenstein, Eileen, and Emmanuel Cooper. *New Ceramics.* London: Studio Vista, 1974.

651   KUHN, DINA (née BERNHARDINE) (1891–?)
      Austrian designer, especially in ceramics and graphics.

Exhibitions

Hamacher, Bärbel, ed. *Expressive Keramik der Wiener Werkstätte, 1917–1930.* Munich: Bayerische Vereinsbank, 1992. Contains a bibliography.

Other Sources

Neuwirth, Waltraud. *Die Keramik der Wiener Werkstätte.* Vienna: W. Neuwirth, 1981.
Schweiger, W. *Weiner Werkstätte: Kunst und Handwerk, 1903–32.* Vienna: Christian Brandstätter Verlag, 1982.

652   KUN, EVA (1948–)
      Hungarian ceramics designer.

Exhibitions

Varga, Péter. *A VII Országos Kerámia Biennale Pécs* [VII National Ceramics Biennale]. Pécs: Pécsi Galéria, 1982.

653   KÜLZ, WALBURGA (1921–)
        German ceramicist.

Exhibitions

Klinge, Ekkart. *Deutsche Keramik Heute.* Dusseldorf: Verlagsanstalt Handwerk, 1984.

Europäische Keramik de Gegenwart: zweiter Internationale Ausstellung in Keramion. Frechen: Museum für zeitgenössische keramische Kunst, 1986.

654   LALIQUE, SUZANNE (1899–?)
        French designer of textiles, ceramics and painter; daughter of René Lalique.

Exhibitions

Les Années 25. Paris: Musée des Arts Décoratifs, 1966. Includes some of her work which had been shown in the 1925 international exhibition.

Dufresne, Jean-Luc, and Olivier Messac, eds. *Femmes créatrices des années vingt.* Granville: Musée Richard Anacréon, 1988. Wide-ranging catalogue with a short biographical account on each woman included.

655   LANGLEY, SIDDY (1955–)
        English designer of ceramics and glass.

See Glass section.

656   LANGSCH, ELIZABETH (1933–)
        Swiss ceramics designer and sculptor.

Exhibitions

Céramique Suisse '93: 17e Biennale des Céramistes Suisses. Geneva: Musée Adriana, 1993.

15 Schweizer Keramiker: Ausstellung der Nationen. Faenza: Palazzo delle Esposizioni, Faenza, 1984.

657   LARDINOIS, YVETTE (1960–)
        Dutch ceramicist.

Exhibitions

Duits, Thimo Te. *Keramiek '90. Moderne Keramiek in Nederland.* The Hague: SDU Uitgevrerij, 1990.

658   LARPENT-RUFFE, AGATHE (1946–)
      French ceramicist.

Exhibitions

Brunhammer, Yvonne, and Marie-Laure Perrin. *Céramique française contemporaine: sources et courants.* Paris: Musée des Arts Décoratifs, 1981.

659   LARSEN, INGER FOLMER
      Danish ceramics designer.

Other Sources

Hiort, Esbjørn. *Modern Danish Ceramics.* New York: Museum Books Inc.; London: A. Zwemmer Ltd.; Stuttgart: Verlag Gerd Hatje; Teufen: Arthur Niggli und Willy Verkauf; Copenhagen: Jul Gjellerups Forlag, 1955.

660   LAST, MOKI (1955–)
      Dutch ceramicist.

Exhibitions

Duits, Thimo Te. *Keramiek '90. Moderne Keramiek in Nederland.* The Hague: SDU Uitgevrerij, 1990.

661   LE MIGNOT, MARLYSE (1951–)
      Swiss-born ceramicist who works in France.

Exhibitions

Brunhammer, Yvonne, and Marie-Laure Perrin. *Céramique française contemporaine: sources et courants.* Paris: Musée des Arts Décoratifs, 1981.

662   LEACH, JANET (née DARNELL) (1918–1997)
      American-born ceramicist who came to England in 1956 to marry Bernard Leach, after which she worked at St. Ives. In her work she is closer to Hamada than Leach; she was the first Western potter to be trained in the Japanese country potteries.

Publications

"Fifty-One Years of the Leach Pottery." *Ceramic Review* 14 (1972): 4–7.
"Shoji Hamada—a tribute." *Ceramic Review* 50 (1978): 4–5.

"Going to Pot." *Ceramic Review* 71 (1981): 24–25.
"Tribute to Michael Cardew." *Ceramic Review* 81 (1983): 14.
"Pots at the Tate." *Ceramic Review* 92 (1985): 25–26.

Main Sources

"Janet Leach—New Ceramics." *Ceramic Review* 51 (1978): 12.
Birks, Tony. "Janet Leach—Recent Pottery." *Ceramic Review* 32 (1975): 16.
———. "Janet Leach." *Crafts* 63 (1983): 50.
Cooper, Emmanuel. *Janet Leach.* Ceramics Series no. 44. Aberystwyth: Aberystwyth Arts Centre, 1990, 6pp., illus.
Edwards, William. "Recent Ceramics by Janet Leach and ceramics sculpture by David Burnham." *Crafts* 32 (1978): 47.
Ismay, W. "Janet Leach." *Ceramic Review* 17 (1972): 16.
———. "Pottery by Janet Leach." *Crafts* 50 (1981): 51.
Lewenstein, Eileen. "Janet Leach." *Crafts* 15 (1975): 49.
Sidney, Jonathan. "Janet Leach—New Pots." *Ceramic Review* 82 (1983): 30–31.

Exhibitions

Bennett, Ian. *British 20th Century Studio Ceramics.* London: Christopher Wood Gallery, 1980.
Watson, Oliver. *British Studio Pottery.* Oxford: Phaidon, 1990.

Other Sources

Lewenstein, Eileen, and Emmanuel Cooper. *New Ceramics.* London: Studio Vista, 1974.
Rose, Muriel. *Artist Potters in England.* London: Faber and Faber, 1970.
Vincent, Paul, and David Whiting. "Janet Leach: Fired by Her Own Instincts." *The Guardian*, 18 September 1997, 17. Obituary.

663   LEBEDEVA, MARIA VASILIEVNA (1895–1942)
Russian painter, graphic artist and designer of ceramics and decorative arts.

Exhibitions

Paris-Moscou, 1900–1939. Paris: Centre Nationale d'Art et de Culture Georges Pompidou, 1979.

Other Sources

Andreeva, L. *Sovetskii farfor, 1920–1930* [Soviet Porcelain, 1920–1930]. Moscow, 1975.
Byars, Mel. *The Design Encyclopedia.* London: Lawrence King, 1994.
Lobanov-Rostovsky, Nina. *Revolutionary Ceramics.* London: Studio Vista, 1990.

664 LECHNER, SOPHIE (1935–)
 Swiss ceramics designer.

Exhibitions

Céramique Suisse '93: 17e Biennale des Céramistes Suisses. Geneva: Musée Adriana, 1993.

665 LECOEUR, JEANNE
 French designer of ceramics.

Exhibitions

Oeuvres des Céramistes Modernes, 1890–1930. Sèvres: Musée Céramique in association with Imprimérie Lapina, Paris, 1931.

666 LEE, JENNIFER (1956–)
 Scottish ceramicist.

Publications

"Handbuilt Coloured Stoneware." *Ceramic Review* 95 (1985): 6–8.

Exhibitions

Beeh, Wolfgang, and Carl Benno Heller. *Keramik '88: Ton in Ton.* Darmstadt: Hessisches Landesmuseum, 1988.
Watson, Oliver. *British Studio Pottery.* Oxford: Phaidon, 1990.

667 LEIGH, MABEL (1915–1996)
 English designer of ceramics.

Main Sources

Hopwood, Irene, and Gordon. "Mabel Leigh: Fired With Enthusiasm." *The Guardian,* 7 February 1996. Obituary.

668 LEMAÎTRE, MARIE-DOMINIQUE (1951–)
 French ceramicist.

Exhibitions

Brunhammer, Yvonne, and Marie-Laure Perrin. *Céramique française contemporaine: sources et courants.* Paris: Musée des Arts Décoratifs, 1981.

669 LENEVA, ELIZAVETA (1898–)
 Russian designer of ceramics.

Exhibitions

Paris-Moscou, 1900–1939. Paris: Centre Nationale d'Art et de Culture Georges Pompidou, 1979.

Other Sources

Andreeva, L. *Sovetskii farfor, 1920–1930* [Soviet porcelain, 1920–1930]. Moscow, 1975.

670   LEPELTIER, ODETTE (1914–)
      French ceramicist who worked at La Primavera with Guéden (q.v.) in the 1930s. She mainly produced work for interior décor rather than tableware.

Exhibitions

Brunhammer, Yvonne, and Marie-Laure Perrin. *Céramique française contemporaine: sources et courants.* Paris: Musée des Arts Décoratifs, 1981.

Other Sources

Faré, Michel. *La céramique contemporaine.* Paris: Compagnie des Arts Photoméchaniques, 1954.

671   LEPORSKAYA, ANNA ALEXANDROVNA (1900–1982)
      Russian painter, book illustrator and designer of interiors, ceramics and stage designs.

Other Sources

Byars, Mel. *The Design Encyclopedia.* London: Lawrence King, 1994.
Nikiforova, L. *Russian Porcelain in the Hermitage Collection.* Leningrad: Aurora Art Publishers, 1973.

672   LERAT, JACQUELINE (1920–)
      French ceramicist who works jointly with her husband, Jean, in the group of ceramicists at Dieulefit, Savoie.

Main Sources

Deblander, Robert. "Un témoignage exemplaire." *La Céramique Moderne* 246 (March 1982): 10–11.

Exhibitions

International Ceramics. London: Victoria and Albert Museum, 1972.
Brunhammer, Yvonne, and Marie-Laure Perrin. *Céramique française contemporaine: sources et courants.* Paris: Musée des Arts Décoratifs, 1981.

673   LERCH-BRODERSEN, INKE (1946–)
      German ceramics designer.

Exhibitions

Beeh, Wolfgang, and Carl Benno Heller. *Keramik '88: Ton in Ton.*
Darmstadt: Hessiches Landesmuseum, 1988.

674   LEWENSTEIN, EILEEN (1925–)
      English ceramicist and writer. She is co-editor of *Ceramic Review.*

Publications

Lewenstein, Eileen, and Emmanuel Cooper. "Gwyn Hanssen talking."
Ceramic Review 11 (1971): 4–6.
      ———. *New Ceramics.* London: Studio Vista, 1974.
      "Potters Go to China." *Ceramic Review* 54 (1978): 4–10. Describes a CPA
visit to China.
      "International Academy of Ceramics Annual Assembly, Barcelona, October
1979." *Ceramic Review* 61 (1980): 25.
      "Wobage Farm Pottery." *Ceramic Review* 73 (1982): 6–13. Looks at the work
of Michael and Sheila Casson and Andrew McGarva.

Main Sources

"Ceramics by Eileen Lewenstein and Emmanuel Cooper." *Crafts* 7 (1974):
42–43.
      "Eileen Lewenstein and John Ward." *Crafts* 33 (1978): 50.
      Hepburn, Tony. "Eileen Lewenstein." *Ceramic Review* 9 (1971): 15.
      Hyman, Sylvia. "England's Eileen Lewenstein." *Ceramics Monthly,* May
1979, 37–41.
      Pitts, Rosemary. "New Ceramics by Eileen Lewenstein." *Crafts* 44 (1980):
50.

Exhibitions

Watson, Oliver. *British Studio Pottery.* Oxford: Phaidon, 1990.

Other Sources

Lewenstein, Eileen, and Emmanuel Cooper. *New Ceramics.* London: Studio
Vista, 1974.
      Rose, Muriel. *Artist Potters in England.* London: Faber and Faber, 1970.

675   LHOTE, BERNADETTE (c. 1928–)
      French ceramicist.

Exhibitions

Brunhammer, Yvonne, and Marie-Laure Perrin. *Céramique française contemporaine: sources et courants.* Paris: Musée des Arts Décoratifs, 1981.

676   LIKARZ, MARIA (Alt. LIKARZ-STRAUSS) (1893–after 1956)
Austrian designer in many media, including ceramics, glass and graphics.

Exhibitions

Kallir, Jane. *Viennese Design and the Wiener Werkstätte.* New York: Braziller in association with the Galérie St. Etienne, 1986.
Leitgeb, Hildegard, Elizabeth Schmuttermeier, and Angela Völker. *Wiener Werkstätte: atelier viennois, 1903–1932.* Brussels: Galérie CGER, 1987.

Other Sources

Byars, Mel. *The Design Encyclopedia.* London: Lawrence King, 1994.
Fanelli, Giovanni, and Rosalia Fanelli. *Il tessuto art déco e anni trenta: disegno, moda, architettura.* Florence: Cantini, 1986.
Neuwirth, Waltraud. *Die Keramik der Wiener Werkstätte.* Vienna: W. Neuwirth, 1981.
Pirhofer, G., and A. Gmeiner. *Der Österreichische Werkbund.* Salzburg: Residenz Verlag, 1985.
Schweiger, W. *Weiner Werkstätte: Kunst und Handwerk, 1903–32.* Vienna: Christian Brandstätter Verlag, 1982.
Völker, Angela. *Wiener Werkstätte: Wiener Mode und Modefotografie. Die Modeabteilung der Wiener Werkstätte, 1922–1932.* Munich and Paris: Schneider-Henn, 1984.

677   LINCK-DUEPP, MARGRIT (1903–?)
Swiss designer of ceramics.

Exhibitions

International Ceramics. London: Victoria and Albert Museum, 1972.

678   LINDBERG-FREUND, MÄRIT (1934–)
Swedish designer of ceramics.

Exhibitions

International Ceramics. London: Victoria and Albert Museum, 1972.

Other Sources

Lewenstein, Eileen, and Emmanuel Cooper. *New Ceramics.* London: Studio Vista, 1974.

679   LINDH, FRANCESCA (1931–)
      Italian-born ceramicist who has worked in Finland since 1949.

Exhibitions

Keramik i rum. [Ceramics in space]. Copenhagen: Danske Kunstindustri-museum, 1981.
Europäische Keramik de Gegenwart:zweiter Internationale Ausstellung in Keramion. Frechen: Museum für zeitgenössische keramische Kunst, 1986.

680   LINDT, MICHELE (1965–)
      Swiss ceramics designer.

Exhibitions

Céramique Suisse '93: 17e Biennale des Céramistes Suisses. Geneva: Musée Adriana, 1993.

681   LINNEMANN-SCHMIDT, ANNE-LISE
      Danish designer of ceramics.

Other Sources

Hiort, Esbjørn. *Modern Danish Ceramics.* New York: Museum Books Inc.; London: A. Zwemmer Ltd.; Stuttgart: Verlag Gerd Hatje; Teufen: Arthur Niggli und Willy Verkauf; Copenhagen: Jul Gjellerups Forlag, 1955.

682   No entry 682.

683   LIUKKO-SUNDSTRÖM, HELJÄ (1938/9–)
      Finnish designer of ceramics.

Exhibitions

International Ceramics. London: Victoria and Albert Museum, 1972

Other Sources

Opie, Jennifer. *Scandinavia: Ceramics and Glass in the Twentieth Century.* London: Victoria and Albert Museum, 1989.

684   LOFFLER, BARBARA
      German ceramics designer and sculptor.

Other Sources

Lewenstein, Eileen, and Emmanuel Cooper. *New Ceramics.* London: Studio Vista, 1974.

685   LOWNDES, GILLIAN (1930–)
      English ceramicist.

Main Sources

"Gillan Lowndes and Ian Auld." *Crafts* 26 (1977): 49.
Cameron, Elizabeth. "Gillian Lowndes." *Ceramic Review* 83 (1983): 9–11.
Harley, Sue. "Ian Auld and Gillian Lowndes." *Ceramic Review* 44 (1977): 4–6.
Harrod, Tanya. "Transcending Clay." *Crafts* 84 (1987): 16–20.
Suttie, Angus. "The Dangerous Edge of Things." *Crafts* 76 (1982): 49–50.

Exhibitions

Watson, Oliver. *British Studio Pottery.* Oxford: Phaidon, 1990.

686   LUC-LANEL, MARJOLAINE
      French designer of ceramics.

Exhibitions

Oeuvres des Céramistes Modernes, 1890–1930. Sèvres: Musée Céramique in association with Imprimérie Lapina, Paris, 1931.

Other Sources

Kapferer, Simone. "Les artistes céramistes et verriers au Salon des Artistes Décorateurs." *Les Arts du Feu* 2 (June 1938): 62–64.

687   LUNN, DORA (1881–c. 1961)
      English ceramicist.

Publications

Pottery in the Making. A Handbook for Teachers and Individual Workers. Leicester and London: Dryad Press, 1931.
A Potter's Pot-Pourri (Unpublished, Archive, Victoria and Albert Museum, London.)
Life and the Crafts. London, 1947.

Main Sources

Joy, Lilian. "Woman Potter's Work: Miss Dora Lunn's Decorative China." *Yorkshire Post,* 21 July 1922.
McLaren, Graham. "'A Complete Potteress'—the Life and Work of Dora Lunn." *Journal of the Decorative Arts Society 1850 to the Present* 13 (1989): 33–38. Profile of Lunn's work at the Ravenscourt Pottery as an educator.

Exhibitions

Watson, Oliver. *British Studio Pottery.* Oxford: Phaidon, 1990.

Other Sources

Bergesen, Victoria. *Encyclopaedia of British Art Pottery, 1870–1920.* London: Barrie & Jenkins, 1991.

688   MADOLA (Pseudonym of MADOLA ANGELS DOMINGO LAPLANA) (1944–)
        Spanish ceramics designer.

Main Sources

Sanchez-Pacheco, Trinidad. "Deux barcelonaises à Paris." Translated Jacqueline Jacquet. *La Revue de la Céramique et du Verre* 31 (November/ December 1986): 36–37.

Exhibitions

Exposition Barcelone. Barcelona: Museu de Ceramica, 1985.
Collection Fina Gomez: 30 ans de céramique contemporaine. Paris: Musée des Arts Décoratifs, 1991.

689   MADUREIRA, MARIA MANUELA (1931–)
        Portuguese designer of ceramics.

Exhibitions

International Ceramics. London: Victoria and Albert Museum, 1972.

Other Sources

Lewenstein, Eileen, and Emmanuel Cooper. *New Ceramics.* London: Studio Vista, 1974.

690   MAGSON, MAL (née WITHERS) (1950–)
        English ceramicist.

Main Sources

"CPA New Members." *Ceramic Review* 61 (1980): 37.
Ismay, W. "Mal Withers." *Ceramic Review* 27 (1974): 20.

691   MAJOROS, HÉDI (Alt. HEDWIG) (1930–)
        Hungarian ceramics designer.

Exhibitions

Varga, Péter. *A VII Országos Kerámia Biennale Pécs* [VII National Ceramics Biennale]. Pécs: Pécsi Galéria, 1982.

Other Sources

Pataky-Brestyánsky, Ilona. *Modern Hungarian Ceramics.* Budapest: Corvina, 1961.

692   MAKEIG-JONES, DAISY
       English painter and decorator of ceramics.

Main Sources

Des Fontaines, Una. *Wedgwood Fairyland Lustre: The Work of Daisy Makeig-Jones.* New York and London: Born-Hawes and Sotheby Park Bernet, 1975, 298pp., illus. A biographical account with a bibliography.

Exhibitions

Des Fontaines, Una, Lionel Lambourne, and Ann Eatwell. *Miss Jones and her Fairyland: The Work of Daisy Makeig-Jones.* The Weinstein Gift to the Victoria and Albert Museum. London: Victoria and Albert Museum, 1990, 47pp., illus.

Other Sources

Buckley, Cheryl. *Potters and Paintresses: Women Designers in the Pottery Industry, 1870–1955.* London: Women's Press, 1990.

693   MANGEAT-DUC, RENÉE (1947–)
       Swiss ceramics designer.

Exhibitions

Céramique Suisse '93: 17e Biennale des Céramistes Suisses. Geneva: Musée Adriana, 1993.
       15 Schweizer Keramiker: Ausstellung der Nationen. Faenza: Palazzo delle Esposizioni, 1984.
       Beeh, Wolfgang, and Carl Benno Heller. *Keramik '88: Ton in Ton.* Darmstadt: Hessisches Landesmuseum, 1988.

694   MANICUS-HANSEN, THYRA (c. 1870–after 1936)
       Danish designer of ceramics.

Exhibitions

Opie, Jennifer. *Scandinavia: Ceramics and Glass in the Twentieth Century.* London: Victoria and Albert Museum, 1989.

695 MAREGIANO, MONIQUE (1944–)
     French architectural ceramicist.

Exhibitions

Brunhammer, Yvonne, and Marie-Laure Perrin. *Céramique française contemporaine: sources et courants.* Paris: Musée des Arts Décoratifs, 1981.

696 MARKS, GRETE (née MARGARETE; alt. HEYMANN-MARKS) (1901–)
     German-born designer of ceramics who worked in England from 1936.

Exhibitions

Oedekoven-Gerischer, Angela, et al., eds. *Frauen im Design: Berufsbilder und Lebenswege seit 1900. Women in Design: Careers and Life Histories since 1900.* Stuttgart: Design Center, 1989.
Weber, Klaus, ed. *Keramik und Bauhaus.* Berlin: Bauhaus-Archiv, 1989.
Seddon, Jill, and Suzette Worden. *Women Designing: Redefining Design Between the Wars.* Brighton: University of Brighton, 1994.

Other Sources

Buckley, Cheryl. *Potters and Paintresses: Women Designers in the Pottery Industry, 1870–1955.* London: Women's Press, 1990.

697 MARTI-COLL, MAGDA (1946–)
     Spanish designer of ceramics.

Exhibitions

Exposition Barcelone. Barcelona: Museu de Ceramica, 1985.

698 MATEESCU, PATRICIU (1927–)
     Romanian ceramics designer and sculptor.

Exhibitions

International Ceramics. London: Victoria and Albert Museum, 1972.

Other Sources

Lewenstein, Eileen, and Emmanuel Cooper. *New Ceramics.* London: Studio Vista, 1974.

699   McELROY, MARIANNE (1932–)
      Irish designer of ceramics.

Exhibitions

International Ceramics. London: Victoria and Albert Museum, 1972.

700   McNICOLL, CAROL (1943–)
      English ceramicist.

Main Sources

Gough, Piers. "Carol McNicoll Ceramics." *Crafts* 78 (1986): 57.
Harrod, Tanya. "Bridging the divide." *Crafts* 80 (1986): 51.
Street-Porter, Janet. "Tea-time for the Non-Conformist." *Crafts* 47 (1980): 32–35.

Exhibitions

Carol McNicoll Ceramics. London: Crafts Council Gallery, 1985, 32pp., mainly illus. Contains short essays by Oliver Watson and Richard Deacon.
Fast Forward: New Directions in British Ceramics. London: Institute of Contemporary Art, 1985.
Houston, John. *The Abstract Vessel. Ceramics in Studio: Forms of Expression and Decoration by Nine Artist Potters.* London: Bellew with the Oriel Gallery and the Welsh Arts Council, 1991.
Watson, Oliver. *British Studio Pottery.* Oxford: Phaidon, 1990.

Other Sources

Dormer, Peter. *The New Ceramics: Trends and Traditions.* London: Thames and Hudson, 1986.

701   MEEDOM, GUDRUN
      Danish designer of ceramics.

Other Sources

Hiort, Esbjørn. *Modern Danish Ceramics.* New York: Museum Books Inc.; London: A. Zwemmer Ltd.; Stuttgart: Verlag Gerd Hatje; Teufen: Arthur Niggli und Willy Verkauf; Copenhagen: Jul Gjellerups Forlag, 1955.

702   MÉHEUT, MARYVONNE
      French designer of ceramics.

Exhibitions

Oeuvres des Céramistes Modernes, 1890–1930. Sèvres: Musée Céramique in association with Imprimérie Lapina, Paris, 1931.

703   MEHL, ELZBIETA EWA
         Polish ceramics designer and sculptor.

Other Sources

Lewenstein, Eileen, and Emmanuel Cooper. *New Ceramics.* London: Studio Vista, 1974.

704   MEISSNER, YVONNE (1963–)
         Dutch ceramicist.

Exhibitions

Duits, Thimo Te. *Keramiek '90. Moderne Keramiek in Nederland.* The Hague: SDU Uitgevrerij, 1990.

705   MELION, JOTA
         Greek ceramics designer.

Other Sources

Lewenstein, Eileen, and Emmanuel Cooper. *New Ceramics.* London: Studio Vista, 1974.

706   MERCHN, CRISTINA (1926–1987)
         Venezuelan-born ceramicist who has worked in France and Spain since 1958.

Exhibitions

Brunhammer, Yvonne, and Marie-Laure Perrin. *Céramique française contemporaine: sources et courants.* Paris: Musée des Arts Décoratifs, 1981.
Collection Fina Gomez: 30 ans de céramique contemporaine. Paris: Musée des Arts Décoratifs, 1991.

707   METAS, CATHERINE (1957–)
         French ceramicist and sculptor.

Exhibitions

Brunhammer, Yvonne, and Marie-Laure Perrin. *Céramique française contemporaine: sources et courants.* Paris: Musée des Arts Décoratifs, 1981.

708   MEYER, BARBARA (1959–)
         Swiss ceramics designer.

Exhibitions

Céramique Suisse '93: 17e Biennale des Céramistes Suisses. Geneva: Musée Adriana, 1993.

709 MEYER, GRETHE (1918–)
Danish architect and designer of ceramics, glass and furniture.

Exhibitions

McFadden, David, ed. *Scandinavian Modern Design, 1880–1980.* New York: Harry Abrams and the Cooper-Hewitt Museum, 1982.

Hiesinger, Kathryn, and George Marcus III, eds. *Design since 1945.* Philadelphia: Philadelphia Museum of Art, 1983.

Oedekoven-Gerischer, Angela, et al., eds. *Frauen im Design: Berufsbilder und Lebenswege seit 1900. Women in Design: Careers and Life Histories since 1900.* Stuttgart: Design Center, 1989.

Opie, Jennifer. *Scandinavia: Ceramics and Glass in the Twentieth Century.* London: Victoria and Albert Museum, 1989.

Mundt, Barbara, Suzanne Netzer, and Innes Hettler. *Interieur + Design in Deutschland, 1945=60.* Berlin: Kunstgewerbemuseum and Dietrich Reimer Verlag, 1994.

Other Sources

Byars, Mel. *The Design Encyclopedia.* London: Lawrence King, 1994.

Karlsen, Arne. *Møbler tegnet af Børge Mogensen. Furniture designed by Børge Mogensen.* Copenhagen: Danish Architectural Press, 1968, 138pp., illus.

Lassen, Erik. *Dansk Glass 1925–75.* Copenhagen: Busck, 1975.

Naylor, Colin, ed. *Contemporary Designers.* 2nd edition. Chicago and London: St. James Press, 1990. Contains a bibliography.

Opie, Jennifer. *Scandinavia: Ceramics and Glass in the Twentieth Century.* London: Victoria and Albert Museum, 1989.

710 MEYER, JENNY SOFIE (1866–1927)
Danish designer of ceramics.

Exhibitions

Europäischer Keramik des Jugendstils. Art Nouveau Modern Style. Dusseldorf: Hetjens-Museum, 1977. Contains short bibliography.

711 MIROV, DEVANA
Czech ceramics designer.

Other Sources

Lewenstein, Eileen, and Emmanuel Cooper. *New Ceramics.* London: Studio Vista, 1974.

712 MOHR, ANNE-MARIE BACKER
Norwegian ceramics designer.

Other Sources

Lewenstein, Eileen, and Emmanuel Cooper. *New Ceramics*. London: Studio Vista, 1974.

713   MONNIER, RUTH (1948–)
      Swiss ceramics designer who produces both sculpture and reliefs.

Exhibitions

15 Schweizer Keramiker: Ausstellung der Nationen. Faenza: Palazzo delle Esposizioni, 1984.

714   MOREAU-MÉLATON, MME
      French designer of ceramics.

Exhibitions

Oeuvres des Céramistes Modernes, 1890–1930. Sèvres: Musée Céramique in association with Imprimérie Lapina, Paris, 1931.

715   MORGAN, JOYCE
      English ceramicist.

Exhibitions

Watson, Oliver. *British Studio Pottery*. Oxford: Phaidon, 1990.

716   MORTENSEN, INGRID (1941–)
      Norwegian ceramicist.

Other Sources

Dormer, Peter. *The New Ceramics: Trends and Traditions*. London: Thames and Hudson, 1986.

717   MOTTE, VERONIQUE (1944–)
      Belgian-born ceramicist who works in France.

Exhibitions

Brunhammer, Yvonne, and Marie-Laure Perrin. *Céramique française contemporaine: sources et courants*. Paris: Musée des Arts Décoratifs, 1981.

718   MÖCKEL, ELSE (1901–)
      German designer of ceramics.

Exhibitions

Becker, Ingeborg, and Dieter Högermann. *Berliner Porzellan vom Jugenstil zum Funktionalismus, 1899–1939.* Bröhan Museum, Berlin, [1987?].

Mundt, Barbara, Suzanne Netzer, and Innes Hettler. *Interieur + Design in Deutschland, 1945=60.* Berlin: Kunstgewerbemuseum and Dietrich Reimer Verlag, 1994.

719   MÖGELINE, ELSE (Alt. MÖGELIN) (1887–1982)
German painter and designer of textiles and ceramics who worked at the Bauhaus.

See Textiles section.

720   MÖLLER, GRETE (1915–)
Danish designer of ceramics.

Other Sources

Opie, Jennifer. *Scandinavia: Ceramics and Glass in the Twentieth Century.* London: Victoria and Albert Museum, 1989.

721   MUNCH-PETERSEN, URSULA
Danish ceramics designer.

Other Sources

Lewenstein, Eileen, and Emmanuel Cooper. *New Ceramics.* London: Studio Vista, 1974.

722   MUONA, TOINI (1904–)
Finnish designer of ceramics who worked at the Arabia factory.

Other Sources

Mäki, Oili. *Taide ja Työ: Finnish Designers of Today.* Helsinki: Werner Söderström Osakeyhtiö, 1954. Gives an outline biography.

723   MÜHLHAUS, HEIKE (1954–)
German designer of ceramic objects and furniture.

Exhibitions

Oedekoven-Gerischer, Angela, et al., eds. *Frauen im Design: Berufsbilder und Lebenswege seit 1900. Women in Design: Careers and Life Histories since 1900.* Stuttgart: Design Center, 1989.

724   MÜLLER, KAREN (1939–)
      German ceramics designer.

Exhibitions

Beeh, Wolfgang, and Carl Benno Heller. *Keramik '88: Ton in Ton.* Darmstadt: Hessiches Landesmuseum, 1988.

725   MÜLLERTZ, MALENA (1949–)
      Danish designer of ceramics.

Exhibitions

Europäische Keramik de Gegenwart:zweiter Internationale Ausstellung in Keramion. Frechen: Museum für zeitgenössische keramische Kunst, 1986.
Beeh, Wolfgang, and Carl Benno Heller. *Keramik '88: Ton in Ton.* Darmstadt: Hessiches Landesmuseum, 1988.

726   NADLER, SABINE (1946–)
      Swiss ceramics designer.

Exhibitions

15 Schweizer Keramiker: Ausstellung der Nationen. Faenza: Palazzo delle Esposizioni, 1984.
Europäische Keramik de Gegenwart: zweiter Internationale Ausstellung in Keramion. Frechen: Museum für zeitgenössische keramische Kunst, 1986.

727   NANNING, BARBARA (1957–)
      Dutch ceramicist.

Exhibitions

Duits, Thimo Te. *Keramiek '90. Moderne Keramiek in Nederland.* The Hague: SDU Uitgevrerij, 1990.

Other Sources

Dormer, Peter. *The New Ceramics: Trends and Traditions.* London: Thames and Hudson, 1986.

728   NATHANIELSEN, BERTHA (1869–1914)
      Danish designer of ceramics.

Exhibitions

Europäischer Keramik des Jugendstils. Art Nouveau Modern Style. Dusseldorf: Hetjens-Museum, 1977. Contains a short bibliography.

729   NAWOTHNIG, OLGA
German designer of ceramics.

Exhibitions

Mundt, Barbara, Suzanne Netzer, and Innes Hettler. *Interieur + Design in Deutschland, 1945=60.* Berlin: Kunstgewerbemuseum and Dietrich Reimer Verlag, 1994.

730   NEUWALDER, GRETE (Alt. MARGARETE NEUWALDER-BREUER) (1898–after 1939)
Austrian designer of ceramics.

Other Sources

Neuwirth, Waltraud. *Die Keramik der Wiener Werkstätte.* Vienna: W. Neuwirth, 1981.

Schweiger, W. *Weiner Werkstätte: Kunst und Handwerk, 1903–32.* Vienna: Christian Brandstätter Verlag, 1982.

731   NEUWIRTH, ROSA (1883–?)
Austrian designer of ceramics.

Other Sources

Pirhofer, G., and A. Gmeiner. *Der Österreichische Werkbund.* Salzburg: Residenz Verlag, 1985.

732   NISBET, EILEEN (1929–)
English ceramicist and sculptor. Her earlier work consisted of large modelled panels but during the 1980s her work became increasingly sculptural.

Main Sources

Barton, Glenys. "Porcelain and Stoneware by Eileen Nisbet." *Crafts* 27 (1977): 49.

Lane, Peter. "Eileen Nisbet's Porcelain." *Ceramic Review* 61 (1980): 22–24.

Weston, Geoffrey. "Three in Ceramics." *Crafts* 43 (1980): 49.

Exhibitions

International Ceramics. London: Victoria and Albert Museum, 1972.
Watson, Oliver. *British Studio Pottery.* Oxford: Phaidon, 1990.

733   OBERDIECK-DEUTSCHBEIN, EVA (1898–1973)
      German ceramicist who worked at the Bauhuas.

Exhibitions

Weber, Klaus, ed. *Keramik und Bauhaus.* Bauhaus-Archiv, Berlin, 1989.

734   ODERKERK, OLGA (1924–)
      Dutch designer of ceramics.

Exhibitions

Ceramische Hoogtepunten Nederland Pottenkijker, 1959–1969. Rotterdam: Museum Boymans-van Beuningen, 1969.

735   ODUNDO, MAGDALENE (1950–)
      Kenyan-born ceramicist who has worked in England since 1971.

Main Sources

"CPA New Members." *Ceramic Review* 83 (1983): 36.
"Kenyan Heritage." *Crafts* 67 (1984): 24–29.

Exhibitions

New works: Magdalene Odundo. Swansea: Glyn Vivian Art Gallery, 1987, 22pp., illus.
Watson, Oliver. *British Studio Pottery.* Oxford: Phaidon, 1990.
Magdalene Odundo. Hamburg: Museum für Kunst under Gewerbe, 1991, 21pp., illus.
Magdalene Odundo. London: Southern Arts, 1992.
Columbus Drowning. Rochdale: Rochdale Art Gallery, 1992.

736   OESTREICHER, HELLY (1936–)
      Dutch designer of ceramics.

Exhibitions

Neue Formen der Keramik aus der Niederlanden. Darmstadt: Hessischen Landesmuseum, 1967.
Ceramische Hoogtepunten Nederland Pottenkijker, 1959–1969. Rotterdam: Museum Boymans-van Beuningen, 1969.
International Ceramics. London: Victoria and Albert Museum, 1972.

737   ORBN, KATALIN (1950–)
      Hungarian ceramics designer.

Exhibitions

Varga, Péter. *A VII Országos Kerámia Biennale Pécs* [VII National Ceramics Biennale]. Pécs: Pécsi Galéria, 1982.

738   OREHOV, VERONIKA
Ceramics designer from the former USSR.

Other Sources

Lewenstein, Eileen, and Emmanuel Cooper. *New Ceramics*. London: Studio Vista, 1974.

739   OSIPOW, ANNA-MARIA
Finnish ceramics designer and sculptor.

Exhibitions

McFadden, David. *Scandinavian Modern Design, 1880–1980*. New York: Harry Abrams in association with the Cooper-Hewitt Museum, 1982.

Other Sources

Byars, Mel. *The Design Encyclopedia*. London: Lawrence King, 1994.
Lewenstein, Eileen, and Emmanuel Cooper. *New Ceramics*. London: Studio Vista, 1974.

740   OSOL, OLGA (1905–)
Finnish designer of ceramics.

Exhibitions

Opie, Jennifer. *Scandinavia: Ceramics and Glass in the Twentieth Century*. London: Victoria and Albert Museum, 1989.

741   OWEN, ELSPETH (1938–)
English ceramicist who is largely self-taught. She began making pots after taking a history degree at Oxford.

Publications

"A Sense of Balance." *Crafts* 42 (1980): 40–44.
"Rural Rides." *Crafts* 81 (1986).

Main Sources

Fielding, Amanda. "Ceramics by Elspeth Owen." *Crafts* 84 (1987): 51.

Harrod, Tanya. *"Take Utopia to be where you are now": Elspeth Owen.* Ceramic Series no. 30. Aberystwyth: Arts Centre, 1988, 4pp., illus.

Exhibitions

Watson, Oliver. *British Studio Pottery.* Oxford: Phaidon, 1990.

742   PALLEY, CLAUDE.
        French ceramicist who works with Slavik Palley.

Exhibitions

Brunhammer, Yvonne, and Marie-Laure Perrin. *Céramique française contemporaine: sources et courants.* Paris: Musée des Arts Décoratifs, 1981.

743   PANNONHALMI, ZSUZSANNA (1949–)
        Hungarian ceramics designer.

Exhibitions

Varga, Péter. *A VII Országos Kerámia Biennale Pécs* [VII National Ceramics Biennale]. Pécs: Pécsi Galéria, 1982.

744   PAPAGEORGIOU, DINA (1946–)
        Swiss ceramics designer.

Exhibitions

Céramique Suisse '93: 17e Biennale des Céramistes Suisses. Geneva: Musée Adriana, 1993.

745   PASQUIER, NADIA (1940–)
        French ceramicist.

Exhibitions

Brunhammer, Yvonne, and Marie-Laure Perrin. *Céramique française contemporaine: sources et courants.* Paris: Musée des Arts Décoratifs, 1981.

746   PEDERSEN, ANNE LISE BRUUN (1931–)
        Danish designer of ceramics.

Exhibitions

Vaev + Raku. Copenhagen: Dansk Kunstindustrimuseet, 1981.

747   PEDLEY-KEPP, CHRISTINE (1944–)
        English-born ceramicist who has worked in France since 1970.

Exhibitions

Brunhammer, Yvonne, and Marie-Laure Perrin. *Céramique française contemporaine: sources et courants.* Paris: Musée des Arts Décoratifs, 1981.

748   PENICAUD, BRIGITTE (1954–)
      French ceramicist.

Exhibitions

Brunhammer, Yvonne, and Marie-Laure Perrin. *Céramique française contemporaine: sources et courants.* Paris: Musée des Arts Décoratifs, 1981.

749   PERSSON-MELIN, SIGNE (1925–)
      Swedish designer in glass, metal and ceramics who won the Lunning Prize.

Exhibitions

McFadden, David, ed. *Scandinavian Modern Design, 1880–1980.* New York: Harry Abrams and the Cooper-Hewitt Museum, 1982.
The Lunning Prize. Stockholm: Nationalmuseum, 1986.
Opie, Jennifer. *Scandinavia: Ceramics and Glass in the Twentieth Century.* London: Victoria and Albert Museum, 1989.

Other Sources

Beard, Geoffrey. *International Modern Glass.* London: Barrie and Jenkins, 1976.
Byars, Mel. *The Design Encyclopedia.* London: Lawrence King, 1994.
Naylor, Colin, ed. *Contemporary Designers.* 2nd edition. Chicago and London: St. James Press, 1990. Contains a bibliography.

750   PERSSON, INGER (1936–)
      Swedish designer of ceramics.

Exhibitions

International Ceramics. London: Victoria and Albert Museum, 1972.
Opie, Jennifer. *Scandinavia: Ceramics and Glass in the Twentieth Century.* London: Victoria and Albert Museum, 1989.

Other Sources

Lewenstein, Eileen, and Emmanuel Cooper. *New Ceramics.* London: Studio Vista, 1974.

751   PETIT, ISABELLE (1958–)
      French ceramicist who produces elaborate fountains, lamps and wall panels.

Exhibitions

Brunhammer, Yvonne, and Marie-Laure Perrin. *Céramique française contemporaine: sources et courants.* Paris: Musée des Arts Décoratifs, 1981.

752 PETRI-RABEN, TRUDE (1906–1989)
German designer of ceramics.

Exhibitions

Oedekoven-Gerischer, Angela et al., eds. *Frauen im Design: Berufsbilder und Lebenswege seit 1900. Women in Design: Careers and Life Histories since 1900.* Stuttgart: Design Center, 1989.

753 PETROLI GARATI, FRANCA (1935–)
Italian designer of ceramics, lighting, glass and furniture.

Other Sources

Byars, Mel. *The Design Encyclopedia.* London: Lawrence King, 1994.

754 PFEFFER, FRANCESCA (1944–)
Swiss ceramicist.

Exhibitions

Beeh, Wolfgang, and Carl Benno Heller. *Keramik '88: Ton in Ton.* Darmstadt: Hessiches Landesmuseum, 1988.
Céramique Suisse '93: 17e Biennale des Céramistes Suisses. Geneva: Musée Adriana, 1993.

755 PICART, DENISE
French designer of ceramics who also produced sculpture.

Other Sources

Faré, Michel. *La céramique contemporaine.* Paris: Compagnie des Arts Photoméchaniques, 1954.

756 PIERLOT, JEANNE (1917–)
French ceramicist; mother of Nathalie Pierlot (q.v.).

Exhibitions

Brunhammer, Yvonne, and Marie-Laure Perrin. *Céramique française contemporaine: sources et courants.* Paris: Musée des Arts Décoratifs, 1981.

757   PIERLOT, NATHALIE (1951–)
      French ceramicist, daughter of Jeanne Pierlot (q.v.).

Exhibitions

Brunhammer, Yvonne, and Marie-Laure Perrin. *Céramique française contemporaine: sources et courants.* Paris: Musée des Arts Décoratifs, 1981.

758   PINCOMBE, HELEN (1908–)
      English ceramicist who produced both thrown and hand-built pieces.

Publications

"Coiled Pottery." *Athene* 7, nos. 1 & 2 (1955): 23–24.

Main Sources

"Potter's profile." *Potters' Quarterly* 5 (1958): 90–91.

Exhibitions

Thirties: British Art and Design Before the War. London: Hayward Gallery, 1979.
      Bennett, Ian. *British 20th Century Studio Ceramics.* London: Christopher Wood Gallery, 1980.
      Watson, Oliver. *British Studio Pottery.* Oxford: Phaidon, 1990.

Other Sources

Byars, Mel. *The Design Encyclopedia.* London: Lawrence King, 1994.
Rose, Muriel. *Artist Potters in England.* London: Faber and Faber, 1970.

759   PLEYDELL-BOUVERIE, KATHARINE (1895–1985)
      English ceramicist, a pupil of Leach, who specialised in ash-glazed stoneware.

Publications

"Pottery by Graham Newing." *Ceramic Review* 14 (1972): 18.
      "Michael Cardew—a Personal Account." *Ceramic Review* 20 (1973): 4–6.
      "Early days at St. Ives." *Ceramic Review* 50 (1978): 25, 28–29. Describes working with Bernard Leach.
      "Tribute to Michael Cardew." *Ceramic Review* 81 (1983): 13.

Main Sources

"Katharine Pleydell-Bouverie." *Ceramic Review* 66 (1980).

Adamczewski, Fiona. "Katharine Pleydell-Bouverie." *Crafts* 19 (1976): 13–16.

Leach, David. "Katharine Pleydell-Bouverie—Pottery." *Ceramic Review* 28 (1974): 16.

———. "Katharine Pleydell-Bouverie." *Ceramic Review* 92 (1985): 9. Obituary.

Lewenstein, Eileen, and Emmanuel Cooper. "A Visit to Katharine Pleydell-Bouverie." *Ceramic Review* 30 (1974): 4–6.

Exhibitions

Thirties: British Art and Design before the War. London: Hayward Gallery, 1979.

Katharine Pleydell-Bouverie. Bath: Crafts Study Centre, 1980, 26pp., illus.

Bennett, Ian. *British 20th Century Studio Ceramics.* London: Christopher Wood Gallery, 1980.

Hogben, C. *British Art and Design 1900–1960: A Collection in the Making.* London: Victoria and Albert Museum, 1983.

Katharine Pleydell-Bouverie: A Potter's Life, 1895–1985. London: Crafts Council in association with the Crafts Study Centre, Bath, 1986, 80pp., illus. Consists of a series of memoirs of the potter by those who knew her and a chapter by her on vegetable ashes in stoneware glazes. Contains a bibliography.

Watson, Oliver. *British Studio Pottery.* Oxford: Phaidon, 1990.

Other Sources

Byars, Mel. *The Design Encyclopedia.* London: Lawrence King, 1994.

Buckley, Cheryl. *Potters and Paintresses: Women Designers in the Pottery Industry, 1870–1955.* London: Women's Press, 1990.

760   POLISSET, MARTINE (1944–)
     French ceramicist.

Exhibitions

Brunhammer, Yvonne, and Marie-Laure Perrin. *Céramique française contemporaine: sources et courants.* Paris: Musée des Arts Décoratifs, 1981.

761   PONCELET, JACQUELINE (1947–)
     Belgian-born ceramicist who has lived in England since the age of four. She is one of the group of eminent women potters who emerged from the Royal College of Art in the 1970s, along with Fritsch, Briton, McNicoll, Crowley and Barton (qq.v.). Recently her work has become more sculptural.

Main Sources

"Jacqueline Poncelet: New Ceramics." *Ceramic Review* 72 (1981): 22–25.

Adamczewski, Fiona. "Outside Tradition." *Crafts* 2 (1973): 20–23.

Catleugh, John. "Bone China by Jacqueline Poncelet and Glenys Barton." *Ceramic Review* 22 (1973): 15.

Filmer, Paul. "Jacqui Poncelet: New Ceramics." *Crafts* 55 (1982): 50–51.

Margetts, Martina. "Bridging the Divide." *Crafts* 80 (1986): 50–51.

Pitts, Rosemary. "American Graffiti." *Crafts* 50 (1981): 22–25.

Exhibitions

International Ceramics. London: Victoria and Albert Museum, 1972.

Bennett, Ian. *British 20th Century Studio Ceramics.* London: Christopher Wood Gallery, 1980.

Deacon, Richard. *Jacqui Poncelet: New Ceramics.* London: Crafts Council, 1981.

Fast Forward: New Directions in British Ceramics. London: Institute of Contemporary Art, 1985.

Houston, John. *The Abstract Vessel. Ceramics in Studio: Forms of Expression and Decoration by Nine Artist Potters.* London: Bellew with the Oriel Gallery and the Welsh Arts Council, 1991.

Opie, Jennifer. *Scandinavia: Ceramics and Glass in the Twentieth Century.* London: Victoria and Albert Museum, 1989.

Watson, Oliver. *British Studio Pottery.* Oxford: Phaidon, 1990.

Other Sources

Dormer, Peter. *The New Ceramics: Trends and Traditions.* London: Thames and Hudson, 1986.

Lewenstein, Eileen, and Emmanuel Cooper. *New Ceramics.* London: Studio Vista, 1974.

762   PORRET, EVELYNE (1939–)
      French ceramicist working at La Borne.

Exhibitions

Brunhammer, Yvonne, and Marie-Laure Perrin. *Céramique française contemporaine: sources et courants.* Paris: Musée des Arts Décoratifs, 1981.

763   POWELL, LOUISE (Alt. ADA LOUISE) (1882–1956)
      English designer of ceramics who worked for Wedgwood.

Other Sources

Buckley, Cheryl. *Potters and Paintresses: Women Designers in the Pottery Industry, 1870–1955.* London: Women's Press, 1990.

764   No entry 764.

765   PÖSCHL, VERONIKA (1950–)
      Austrian or Dutch ceramicist.

Exhibitions

Europäische Keramik de Gegenwart: zweiter Internationale Ausstellung in Keramion. Frechen: Museum für zeitgenössische keramische Kunst, 1986.
Duits, Thimo Te. *Keramiek '90. Moderne Keramiek in Nederland.* The Hague: SDU Uitgevrerij, 1990.

766   PRESSEL, CLAUDE ALBANA (1934–)
      Swiss designer of ceramics.

Exhibitions

International Ceramics. London: Victoria and Albert Museum, 1972.

767   PROCOPÉ, ULLA (1921–68)
      Finnish designer of ceramics.

Exhibitions

McFadden, David, ed. *Scandinavian Modern Design, 1880–1980.* New York: Harry Abrams and the Cooper-Hewitt Museum, 1982.
Hiesinger, Kathryn, and George Marcus III, eds. *Design since 1945.* Philadelphia: Philadelphia Museum of Art, 1983.
Opie, Jennifer. *Scandinavia: Ceramics and Glass in the Twentieth Century.* London: Victoria and Albert Museum, 1989.

Other Sources

Byars, Mel. *The Design Encyclopedia.* London: Lawrence King, 1994.

768   PRUS, MIRA (1943–)
      German ceramics designer.

Exhibitions

Beeh, Wolfgang, and Carl Benno Heller. *Keramik '88: Ton in Ton.* Darmstadt: Hessisches Landesmuseum, 1988.

769   PURKRABKOV, HANA (1936–)
      Czech ceramics designer and sculptor.

Exhibitions

Beeh, Wolfgang, and Carl Benno Heller. *Keramik '88: Ton in Ton.* Darmstadt: Hessisches Landesmuseum, 1988.

Klinge, Ekkart. *Tschechesche Keramik.* Dusseldorf: Hetjens-Museum, 1991. She was one of eight exhibitors.

770 PUTZ, GABRIELE (1949–)
German ceramicist.

Exhibitions

Klinge, Ekkart. *Deutsche Keramik Heute.* Dusseldorf: Verlagsanstalt Handwerk, 1984.
Europäische Keramik de Gegenwart:zweiter Internationale Ausstellung in Keramion. Frechen: Museum für zeitgenössische keramische Kunst, 1986.

771 QUINEY, FRANÇOISE (1950–)
French ceramicist working at La Borne.

Exhibitions

Brunhammer, Yvonne, and Marie-Laure Perrin. *Céramique française contemporaine: sources et courants.* Paris: Musée des Arts Décoratifs, 1981.

772 RADOV, JINDRISKA (1925–)
Czech ceramics designer.

Exhibitions

International Ceramics. London: Victoria and Albert Museum, 1972

773 RADSTONE, SARA (1955–)
English ceramicist.

Publications

"Builders of Dreams." *Crafts* 84 (1987): 38.

Main Sources

Britton, Alison. "Pots by Sara Radstone." *Crafts* 82 (1986): 54.
Deacon, Richard. "Fragile presences." *Crafts* 62 (1983): 26–29.

Exhibitions

Watson, Oliver. *British Studio Pottery.* Oxford: Phaidon, 1990.

774 RAEBURN, ELIZABETH (1943–)
English ceramicist specialising in hand-built forms which are raku-fired.

Exhibitions

Watson, Oliver. *British Studio Pottery*. Oxford: Phaidon, 1990.

Other Sources

Nine Potters. London: Fischer Fine Art, 1986.

775   RAMAN, INGEGERD (1943–)
       Swedish designer of ceramics and glass.

Exhibitions

Opie, Jennifer. *Scandinavia: Ceramics and Glass in the Twentieth Century*. London: Victoria and Albert Museum, 1989.

776   RAVENTÓS, MARIA ASSUMPCIÓ (c. 1930–)
       Spanish designer of ceramics.

Exhibitions

Soto la magía de Gutenberg: Maria Assumpció Raventós, Teresa Gironès. Barcelona: Museu de Ceramica, 1985, 23pp., illus.

777   RAYMOND, MICHELE
       French ceramics sculptor.

Exhibitions

Brunhammer, Yvonne, and Marie-Laure Perrin. *Céramique française contemporaine: sources et courants*. Paris: Musée des Arts Décoratifs, 1981.

778   REGIUS, LENE (1940–)
       Danish ceramicist.

Other Sources

Dormer, Peter. *The New Ceramics: Trends and Traditions*. London: Thames and Hudson, 1986.

779   REIMERS, LOTTE
       German ceramics designer.

Other Sources

Lewenstein, Eileen, and Emmanuel Cooper. *New Ceramics*. London: Studio Vista, 1974.

780   REISINGER, BARBARA (1955–)
      Austrian ceramicist.

Exhibitions

Europäische Keramik de Gegenwart: zweiter Internationale Ausstellung in Keramion. Frechen: Museum für zeitgenössische keramische Kunst, 1986.

781   REY, MARGARET (1911–)
      Welsh ceramicist, designer, painter and sculptor.

Exhibitions

Watson, Oliver. *British Studio Pottery.* Oxford: Phaidon, 1990.

782   RHEAD, CHARLOTTE (1885–1947)
      English designer of ceramics.

Main Sources

Bumpus, Bernard. "Tube-Line Variations." *The Antique Collector,* December 1985, 59–61.
————. *Charlotte Rhead, Potter and Designer.* London: Kevin Francis Publishing, 1987.

Other Sources

Bergesen, Victoria. *Encyclopaedia of British Art Pottery, 1870–1920.* London: Barrie & Jenkins, 1991.
Buckley, Cheryl. *Potters and Paintresses: Women Designers in the Pottery Industry, 1870–1955.* London: Women's Press, 1990.

783   RICHARDS, CHRISTINE-ANN (1949–)
      English ceramicist working in pure forms and colours and influenced by Chinese ceramics.

Publications

"Colouring Glazes." *Ceramic Review* 54 (1978): 18.
"Travelling in China." *Ceramic Review* 91 (1985): 34–35.

Main Sources

"CPA New Members." *Ceramic Review* 42 (1976): 12.

Exhibitions

Watson, Oliver. *British Studio Pottery.* Oxford: Phaidon, 1990.

784   RICHARDS, FRANCES (c. 1869–1931)
      English ceramicist who was one of the earliest of the studio potters.

Exhibitions

Watson, Oliver. *British Studio Pottery.* Oxford: Phaidon, 1990.

785   RIE, LUCIE (1902–1995)
      Austrian-born ceramicist who worked in England from 1938 when she arrived as a refugee. She is one of the outstanding potters of the century.

Main Sources

"Lucie Rie—New Pots." *Ceramic Review* 50 (1978): 18–19.
      Barry, Val. "Porcelain by Lucie Rie, Mary Rogers and Peter Simpson." *Ceramic Review* 20 (1973): 17.
      Birks, Tony. *Lucie Rie.* Sherborne: Alpha Books, 1987, 224pp., many illus. This contains a useful bibliography.
      Coatts, Margot. *Lucie Rie.* London: Crafts Council, 1992, n.p., illus. Published on the occasion of Rie's 90th birthday. Contains a biographical account and a list of exhibitions.
      Cooper, Emmanuel. "Lucie Rie—Artist Potter." *Ceramic Review* 72 (1981): 4–9.
      ———. "Lucie Rie—Potter." *Ceramic Review* 100 (1986).
      Davenport, Tarby. "Lucie Rie—A Potter of our Time." *Ceramic Review* 27 (1974): 4–5.
      MacCarthy, Fiona. "A Sublime Ceramicist: Lucie Rie." *The Guardian,* 3 April 1995, 2:11. Obituary.
      Reid, Christopher. "Lucie Rie." *Crafts* 53 (1981): 34–39.

Exhibitions

International Ceramics. London: Victoria and Albert Museum, 1972.
      Bennett, Ian. *British 20th Century Studio Ceramics.* London: Christopher Wood Gallery, 1980.
      Houston, John. *Lucie Rie.* London: Crafts Council Gallery, 1981. Contains a full bibliography up to that date.
      Hogben, C. *British Art and Design 1900–1960: A Collection in the Making.* London: Victoria and Albert Museum, 1983.
      Fast Forward: New Directions in British Ceramics. London: Institute of Contemporary Art, 1985.
      Europäische Keramik de Gegenwart: zweiter Internationale Ausstellung in Keramion. Frechen: Museum für zeitgenössische keramische Kunst, 1986.
      Nine Potters. London: Fischer Fine Art, 1986.
      Watson, Oliver. *British Studio Pottery.* Oxford: Phaidon, 1990.
      Collection Fina Gomez: 30 ans de céramique contemporaine. Paris: Musée des Arts Décoratifs, 1991.

Other Sources

Dormer, Peter. *The New Ceramics: Trends and Traditions.* London: Thames and Hudson, 1986.

Lewenstein, Eileen, and Emmanuel Cooper. *New Ceramics.* London: Studio Vista, 1974.

786   RIX, KITTY (Alt. KATHARINA RIX-TICHAK) (1901–)
Austrian designer of ceramics, textiles and fashion; sister of Felice Rix.

Exhibitions

Hamacher, Bärbel, ed. *Expressive Keramik der Wiener Werkstätte, 1917–1930.* Munich: Bayerische Vereinsbank, 1992. Contains a bibliography.

Other Sources

Byars, Mel. *The Design Encyclopedia.* London: Lawrence King, 1994.

Neuwirth, Waltraud. *Die Keramik der Wiener Werkstätte.* Vienna: W. Neuwirth, 1981.

Pirhofer, G., and A. Gmeiner. *Der Österreichische Werkbund.* Vienna, 1985.

Schweiger, W. *Weiner Werkstätte: Kunst und Handwerk, 1903–32.* Vienna: Christian Brandstätter Verlag, 1982.

787   ROGERS, MARY (1929–)
English ceramicist who produces hand-built bowls often derived from forms in nature.

Publications

"Decoration Through Form." *Ceramic Review* 9 (1971): 10–11.

"Marianne de Trey and Colin Kellam." *Ceramic Review* 20 (1973): 16.

"Hand Modelled or Pinched Pottery." *Ceramic Review* 38 (1976): 13.

On Pottery and Porcelain. London: Alphabooks, 1979, 152pp., illus.

Main Sources

"Mary Rogers' 'On Pottery and Porcelain.'" *Ceramic Review* 59 (1979): 30–31. Concerns her book of that title.

Barry, Val. "Porcelain by Lucie Rie, Mary Rogers and Peter Simpson." *Ceramic Review* 20 (1973): 17.

Catleugh, John. "Mary Rogers—English Romantic." *Ceramic Review* 76 (1982): 26–29.

Houghton, Angela. "Spirit of Nature: Mary Rogers and Wendy Ramshaw." *Crafts* 22 (1976): 47.

Ismay, W. "Mary Rogers—ceramics." *Ceramic Review* 23 (1973): 15.

———. "Mary Rogers, Mary Rich and John Malby." *Ceramic Review* 29 (1974): 17.

————. "Ceramics by Mary Rogers." *Crafts* 42 (1980): 49–50.
Margrie, Victor. "Mary Rogers—Porcelain." *Ceramic Review* 36 (1975): 18.

Exhibitions

International Ceramics. London: Victoria and Albert Museum, 1972.
Bennett, Ian. *British 20th Century Studio Ceramics.* London: Christopher Wood Gallery, 1980.
Watson, Oliver. *British Studio Pottery.* Oxford: Phaidon, 1990.

Other Sources

Dormer, Peter. *The New Ceramics: Trends and Traditions.* London: Thames and Hudson, 1986.
Lewenstein, Eileen, and Emmanuel Cooper. *New Ceramics.* London: Studio Vista, 1974.

788 ROKKJOER, INGER (1934–)
     Danish designer of ceramics.

Main Sources

"Two Danish Potters: Inger Rokkjoer and Ann Floche." *Ceramic Review* 139 (1993): 20–21.

Exhibitions

Vaev + Raku. Copenhagen: Dansk Kunstindustrimuseet, 1981.

789 ROLF, JOHNNY
     Dutch ceramics designer.

Other Sources

Lewenstein, Eileen, and Emmanuel Cooper. *New Ceramics.* London: Studio Vista, 1974.

790 RØNNING, GRETE (1937–)
     Norwegian designer of ceramics, glass and textiles.

Exhibitions

Opie, Jennifer. *Scandinavia: Ceramics and Glass in the Twentieth Century.* London: Victoria and Albert Museum, 1989.

791 ROSARIO, LAURA
     Italian designer of ceramics.

Exhibitions

Ceramiche del Museo Artistico Industriale di Napoli, 1920–1950. Naples: Museo Artistico Industriale, 1985.

792   ROSEMEIJER, NICOLA (1955–)
      Dutch ceramicist.

Exhibitions

Duits, Thimo Te. *Keramiek '90. Moderne Keramiek in Nederland.* The Hague: SDU Uitgevrerij, 1990.

793   ROZENDORF, ELIZAVETA BERNGARDOVNA (1898–1984)
      Russian designer of ceramics.

Exhibitions

Wardropper, Ian, et al. *News from a Radiant Future: Soviet Porcelain From the Collection of Craig H. and Kay A. Tuber.* Chicago: Art Institute, 1992.

794   RUEDA, MARISA.
      Argentinian-born ceramic sculptor who works in England.

Main Sources

Shirtliffe, Jean. "Ceramic Sculpture by Marisa Rueda." *Crafts* 49 (1979): 51–52.
Johnson, Pamela. "Subversive Ceramics." *Crafts* Magazine 95 (1988): 34–37.

795   RUELLAND, DANIELLE (c. 1930–)
      French ceramicist.

Exhibitions

Brunhammer, Yvonne, and Marie-Laure Perrin. *Céramique française contemporaine: sources et courants.* Paris: Musée des Arts Décoratifs, 1981.

796   RYCHLIKOV, MARIE
      Czech ceramics designer.

Exhibitions

Art tchèque contemporain: gravure, céramique, verre. Freiburg: Musée d'Art et d'Histoire, 1973.

Other Sources

Lewenstein, Eileen, and Emmanuel Cooper. *New Ceramics*. London: Studio Vista, 1974.

797 SAINT-ANDRE PERRIN, SYLVIE (1945–)
     French ceramicist.

Exhibitions

Brunhammer, Yvonne, and Marie-Laure Perrin. *Céramique française contemporaine: sources et courants*. Paris: Musée des Arts Décoratifs, 1981.

798 SALA, ELISENDA (1950–)
     Spanish ceramicist.

Exhibitions

Europäische Keramik de Gegenwart: zweiter Internationale Ausstellung in Keramion. Frechen: Museum für zeitgenössische keramische Kunst, 1986.

Other Sources

Lewenstein, Eileen, and Emmanuel Cooper. *New Ceramics*. London: Studio Vista, 1974.

799 SALMENHAARA, KYLLIKI (1915–)
     Finnish designer of ceramics and glass.

Other Sources

Mäki, Oili. *Taide ja Työ: Finnish Designers of Today*. Helsinki: Werner Söderström Osakeyhtiö, 1954. Gives an outline biography.

800 SAMMLER, CHRISTA (1932–)
     German designer of ceramics.

Exhibitions

International Ceramics. London: Victoria and Albert Museum, 1972.

801 SAMOHELOV, HELENA (1941–)
     Czech designer of ceramics.

Exhibitions

International Ceramics. London: Victoria and Albert Museum, 1972.
Art tchèque contemporain: gravure, céramique, verre. Freiburg: Musée d'Art et d'Histoire, 1973.

Beeh, Wolfgang, and Carl Benno Heller. *Keramik '88: Ton in Ton.* Darmstadt: Hessisches Landesmuseum, 1988.
Klinge, Ekkart. *Tschechesche Keramik.* Dusseldorf: Hetjens-Museum, 1991. She was one of eight exhibitors.

802 SCAVINI, ELENA
Italian designer of ceramics.

Exhibitions

Mostra della ceramica italiana, 1920–1940. Turin: Palazzo Nervi, 1982.

803 SCHAFFER, ELIZABETH (1935–)
Austrian-born ceramicist who works in Germany.

Exhibitions

Europäische Keramik de Gegenwart: zweiter Internationale Ausstellung in Keramion. Frechen: Museum für zeitgenössische keramische Kunst, 1986.
Beeh, Wolfgang, and Carl Benno Heller. *Keramik '88: Ton in Ton.* Darmstadt: Hessisches Landesmuseum, 1988.

Other Sources

Dormer, Peter. *The New Ceramics: Trends and Traditions.* London: Thames and Hudson, 1986.

804 SCHASCHL, RENI (Alt. IRENE SCHASCHL-SCHUSTER) (1895–1979)
Austrian designer in several media, including ceramics.

Exhibitions

Hamacher, Bärbel, ed. *Expressive Keramik der Wiener Werkstätte, 1917–1930.* Munich: Bayerische Vereinsbank, 1992. Contains a bibliography.

Other Sources

Joseph Hoffmann and Wilhelm Wagenfeld: Glaskunst der Moderne. Munich: Klinkhardt and Bierman, 1992.
Pirhofer, G., and A. Gmeiner. *Der Österreichische Werkbund.* Vienna, 1985.
Neuwirth, Waltraud. *Die Keramik der Wiener Werkstätte.* Vienna: W. Neuwirth, 1981.
Schweiger, W. *Weiner Werkstätte: Kunst und Handwerk, 1903–32.* Vienna: Christian Brandstätter Verlag, 1982.

805 SCHEDLER, MARIET (1935–)
Dutch ceramicist.

Exhibitions

Duits, Thimo Te. *Keramiek '90. Moderne Keramiek in Nederland.* The Hague: SDU Uitgevrerij, 1990.

806   SCHEID, URSULA (1932–)
German ceramics designer.

Exhibitions

International Ceramics. London: Victoria and Albert Museum, 1972.

Klinge, Ekkart. *Deutsche Keramik Heute.* Dusseldorf: Verlagsanstalt Handwerk, 1984.

Europäische Keramik de Gegenwart:zweiter Internationale Ausstellung in Keramion. Frechen: Museum für zeitgenössische keramische Kunst, 1986.

Beeh, Wolfgang, and Carl Benno Heller. *Keramik '88: Ton in Ton.* Darmstadt: Hessisches Landesmuseum, 1988.

Other Sources

Dormer, Peter. *The New Ceramics: Trends and Traditions.* London: Thames and Hudson, 1986.

Lewenstein, Eileen, and Emmanuel Cooper. *New Ceramics.* London: Studio Vista, 1974.

807   SCHETTINI, M. LETIZIA (1961–)
Italian designer of ceramics, textiles and furniture.

Exhibitions

Bacci, N. *Il Design delle Donne.* Ravenna: Museo dell'Arredo Contemporaneo, 1991.

Other Sources

Byars, Mel. *The Design Encyclopedia.* London: Lawrence King, 1994.

Shimuzu, Fumio, and Matteo Thun. *The Descendants of Leonardo da Vinci: The Italian design.* Tokyo: Graphic Publishing, 1987.

808   SCHLEGEL, VALENTINE
French designer of ceramics.

Exhibitions

Paris 1937–Paris 1957. Paris: Centre Nationale d'Art et de Culture Georges Pompidou, 1981.

809   SCHLICHENMAIER, HILDEGUND (1941–)
French ceramicist.

Exhibitions

International Ceramics. London: Victoria and Albert Museum, 1972.
Brunhammer, Yvonne, and Marie-Laure Perrin. *Céramique française contemporaine: sources et courants*. Paris: Musée des Arts Décoratifs, 1981.

810   SCHLOESSINGK, MICKI (Alt. MICKY; née DOHERTY) (1949–)
English ceramicist producing tableware in salt-glazed stoneware.

Main Sources

"CPA New Members." *Ceramic Review* 67 (1981): 35.

Exhibitions

Watson, Oliver. *British Studio Pottery*. Oxford: Phaidon, 1990.
Nuttgens, John. *Micki Schloessingk*. Ceramic Series no. 66. Aberystwyth: Arts Centre, 1994, 6pp., illus.

811   SCHMIDL, HEDWIG (1889–?)
Austrian designer of ceramics.

Exhibitions

Hamacher, Bärbel, ed. *Expressive Keramik der Wiener Werkstätte, 1917–1930*. Munich: Bayerische Vereinsbank, 1992. Contains a bibliography.

Other Sources

Neuwirth, Waltraud. *Die Keramik der Wiener Werkstätte*. Vienna: W. Neuwirth, 1981.
Pirhofer, G., and A. Gmeiner. *Der Österreichische Werkbund*. Vienna: 1985.
Schweiger, W. *Weiner Werkstätte: Kunst und Handwerk, 1903–32*. Vienna: Christian Brandstätter Verlag, 1982.

812   SCHMIDT-REUTHER, GISELA (1915–)
German designer of ceramics.

Exhibitions

International Ceramics. London: Victoria and Albert Museum, 1972.
Klinge, Ekkart. *Deutsche Keramik Heute*. Dusseldorf: Verlagsanstalt Handwerk, 1984.

813   SCHOTT, MARGARETHE (1911–)
German ceramics designer.

Exhibitions

Mundt, Barbara. *Nostalgie warum? Kunsthandwerkliche techniken im Stilwandel vom Historismus zur Moderne.* Berlin: Kunstgewerbemuseum, S.M.P.K., 1982.

Klinge, Ekkart. *Deutsche Keramik Heute.* Dusseldorf: Verlagsanstalt Handwerk, 1984.

Other Sources

Lewenstein, Eileen, and Emmanuel Cooper. *New Ceramics.* London: Studio Vista, 1974.

814   SCHRAMMEL, LILO (1949–)
      Austrian ceramicist.

Other Sources

Dormer, Peter. *The New Ceramics: Trends and Traditions.* London: Thames and Hudson, 1986.

815   SCHULZ-ENDERT, EVA (1912–)
      German designer of ceramics.

Exhibitions

International Ceramics. London: Victoria and Albert Museum, 1972.

816   SCHWETZ-LEHMANN, IDA (Alt. SCHWETZ) (1883–1971)
      Austrian designer in several media but particularly ceramics.

Other Sources

Pirhofer, G., and A. Gmeiner. *Der Österreichische Werkbund.* Vienna, 1985.

Schweiger, W. *Weiner Werkstätte: Kunst und Handwerk, 1903–32.* Vienna: Christian Brandstätter Verlag, 1982.

817   SCHWICHTENBERG, MARTEL (1896–1945)
      German designer of graphics and ceramics.

Exhibitions

Oedekoven-Gerischer, Angela, et al., eds. *Frauen im Design: Berufsbilder und Lebenswege seit 1900. Women in Design: Careers and Life Histories since 1900.* Stuttgart: Design Center, 1989.

818   SEREGÉLY, MART (1935)
      Hungarian ceramics designer.

Exhibitions

Varga, Péter. *A VII Országos Kerámia Biennale Pécs* [VII National Ceramics Biennale]. Pécs: Pécsi Galéria, 1982.

819 SHCHEKOTIKHINA-POTOTSKAIA, ALEXANDRA VASILIEVNA (1892–1967)
Russian designer of ceramics, book illustration and theatre costumes.

Exhibitions

Paris-Moscou, 1900–1939. Paris: Centre Nationale d'Art et de Culture Georges Pompidou, 1979.
Wardropper, Ian, et al. *News from a Radiant Future: Soviet Porcelain from the Collection of Craig H. and Kay A. Tuber.* Chicago: Art Institute, 1992.

Other Sources

Byars, Mel. *The Design Encyclopedia.* London: Lawrence King, 1994.
Elliott, David, and Valery Dudakov. *100 Years of Russian Art, 1889–1989.* London: Lund Humphries, 1989.
Lobanov-Rostovsky, Nina. *Revolutionary Ceramics.* London: Studio Vista, 1990.
Nikiforova, L. *Russian Porcelain in the Hermitage Collection.* Leningrad: Aurora Art Publishers, 1973.

820 SIELCKEN, HARRIET (1929–)
Dutch designer of ceramics.

Exhibitions

Neue Formen der Keramik aus der Niederlanden. Darmstadt: Hessischen Landesmuseum, 1967.
Ceramische Hoogtepunten Nederland Pottenkijker, 1959–1969. Rotterdam: Museum Boymans-van Beuningen, 1969.

821 SIIMES, AUNE (1909–)
Finnish designer of ceramics.

Other Sources

Mäki, Oili. *Taide ja Työ: Finnish Designers of Today.* Helsinki: Werner Söderström Osakeyhtiö, 1954. Gives an outline biography.

822 SIKA, JUTTA (1877–1964)
Austrian designer in several media, including ceramics, glass and textiles.

Exhibitions

Europäischer Keramik des Jugendstils. Art Nouveau Modern Style. Dusseldorf: Hetjens-Museum, 1977. Contains short bibliography.

Kallir, Jane. *Viennese Design and the Wiener Werkstätte.* New York: Braziller in association with the Galérie St. Etienne, 1986.

Oedekoven-Gerischer, Angela, et al., eds. *Frauen im Design: Berufsbilder und Lebenswege seit 1900. Women in Design: Careers and Life Histories since 1900.* Stuttgart: Design Center, 1989.

Other Sources

Byars, Mel. *The Design Encyclopedia.* London: Lawrence King, 1994.

Joseph Hoffmann and Wilhelm Wagenfeld: Glaskunst der Moderne. Munich: Klinkhardt and Bierman, 1992.

Pirhofer, G., and A. Gmeiner. *Der Österreichische Werkbund.* Vienna: 1985.

Schweiger, W. *Weiner Werkstätte: Kunst und Handwerk, 1903–32.* Vienna: Christian Brandstätter Verlag, 1982.

823 SILVERFANT, SUSANNE (1961–)
     Dutch ceramicist.

Exhibitions

Duits, Thimo Te. *Keramiek '90. Moderne Keramiek in Nederland.* The Hague: SDU Uitgevrerij, 1990.

824 SIMMANCE, ELIZA C. (c. 1851–after 1928)
     English decorator of ceramics who worked for Doulton.

Other Sources

Bergesen, Victoria. *Encyclopaedia of British Art Pottery, 1870–1920.* London: Barrie & Jenkins, 1991.

825 SIMMULSON, MARI (1911–)
     Estonian-born designer of ceramics who worked in Sweden.

Other Sources

Opie, Jennifer. *Scandinavia: Ceramics and Glass in the Twentieth Century.* London: Victoria and Albert Museum, 1989.

826 SIMON, ARLETTE (1950–)
     French ceramics designer.

Exhibitions

Beeh, Wolfgang, and Carl Benno Heller. *Keramik '88: Ton in Ton.* Darmstadt: Hessisches Landesmuseum, 1988.

827 SINGER, SUSI (1891–1965)
Austrian designer of ceramics who worked for the Wiener Werkstätte and emigrated to America in 1937.

Exhibitions

Kallir, Jane. *Viennese Design and the Wiener Werkstätte.* New York: Braziller in association with the Galérie St. Etienne, 1986.
Hamacher, Bärbel, ed. *Expressive Keramik der Wiener Werkstätte, 1917–1930.* Munich: Bayerische Vereinsbank, 1992. Contains a bibliography.

Other Sources

Neuwirth, Waltraud. *Die Keramik der Wiener Werkstätte.* Vienna: W. Neuwirth, 1981.
Pirhofer, G., and A. Gmeiner. *Der Österreichische Werkbund.* Salzburg: Residenz Verlag, 1985.
Schweiger, W. *Weiner Werkstätte: Kunst und Handwerk, 1903–32.* Vienna: Christian Brandstätter Verlag, 1982.

828 SKÅLTEIT, GRO (1942–)
Danish ceramics designer.

Exhibitions

Beeh, Wolfgang, and Carl Benno Heller. *Keramik '88: Ton in Ton.* Darmstadt: Hessisches Landesmuseum, 1988.

829 SMEUNINX, LOTTE (1964–)
Belgian designer of furniture, ceramics and glass.

See Interior Design section.

830 SMITH, GILLIAN (1960–)
British-born ceramicist working in the Netherlands.

Exhibitions

Duits, Thimo Te. *Keramiek '90. Moderne Keramiek in Nederland.* The Hague: SDU Uitgevrerij, 1990.

831   SORMA, AGNES (1865–1925)
      German designer of ceramics.

Exhibitions

Becker, Ingeborg, and Dieter Högermann. *Berliner Porzellan vom Jugenstil zum Funktionalismus, 1899–1939*. Berlin: Bröhan Museum, [1987?].

832   SPANNRING, LOUISE (1894–)
      Austrian sculptor and designer of ceramics.

Other Sources

Pirhofer, G., and A. Gmeiner. *Der Österreichische Werkbund*. Salzburg: Residenz Verlag, 1985.
Schweiger, W. *Weiner Werkstätte: Kunst und Handwerk, 1903–32*. Vienna: Christian Brandstätter Verlag, 1982.

833   SPARKES, CATHERINE ADELAIDE (née EDWARDS) (1842–1891)
      English painter of genre, illustrator and designer of ceramic decoration for Lambeth Doulton. A large tile painting by her was exhibited at the 1876 Philadelphia Centennial Exposition.

Main Sources

Clayton, Ellen. *English Female Artists*. Vol. 2. London: Tinsley, 1876

Other Sources

Bergesen, Victoria. *Encyclopaedia of British Art Pottery, 1870–1920*. London: Barrie & Jenkins, 1991.
Callen, Anthea. *Angel in the Studio*. London: Architectural Press, 1979.
Dunford, Penny. *Biographical Dictionary of Women Artists in Europe and America since 1850*. Hemel Hempstead: Harvester Wheatsheaf, 1990. Contains a bibliography.
Mallalieu, Hugh. *Dictionary of British Watercolour Artists*. Woodbridge: Antique Collectors Club, 1976.
Wood, Christopher. *The Dictionary of Victorian Painters*. Woodbridge: Antique Collectors Club, 1978.

834   SPIERS, CHARLOTTE.
      English painter of ceramics who worked for Mintons and, after it closed, continued freelance with Ellen Welby; she also exhibited as a painter in all the main London venues.

Other Sources

Bergesen, Victoria. *Encyclopaedia of British Art Pottery, 1870–1920*. London: Barrie & Jenkins, 1991.

835 SPUREY, GERDA
   Austrian ceramics designer.

Exhibitions

International Ceramics. London: Victoria and Albert Museum, 1972.

Other Sources

Lewenstein, Eileen, and Emmanuel Cooper. *New Ceramics.* London: Studio Vista, 1974.

836 STABLER, PHOEBE
   English designer of ceramics and jewellery.

Exhibitions

Hogben, C. *British Art and Design 1900–1960: A Collection in the Making.* London: Victoria and Albert Museum, 1983.

Other Sources

Buckley, Cheryl. *Potters and Paintresses: Women Designers in the Pottery Industry, 1870–1955.* London: Women's Press, 1990.

837 STAINDL, KATALIN
   Hungarian designer of ceramics.

Other Sources

Pataky-Brestyánsky, Ilona. *Modern Hungarian Ceramics.* Budapest: Corvina, 1961.

838 STEHR, BARBARA (1936–)
   German ceramicist.

Exhibitions

Klinge, Ekkart. *Deutsche Keramik Heute.* Dusseldorf: Verlagsanstalt Handwerk, 1984.
   Europäische Keramik de Gegenwart:zweiter Internationale Ausstellung in Keramion. Frechen: Museum für zeitgenössische keramische Kunst, 1986.

839 STEINEMANN-REIS, BRIGITTE (1948–)
   Swiss ceramics designer.

Exhibitions

Céramique Suisse '93: 17e Biennale des Céramistes Suisses. Geneva: Musée Adriana, 1993.

840   STEPANOV, IOANA
        Romanian ceramics designer and sculptor.

Other Sources

Lewenstein, Eileen, and Emmanuel Cooper. *New Ceramics.* London: Studio Vista, 1974.

841   STORR-BRITZ, HILDEGARD
        German designer of ceramics.

Publications

International Keramik der Gegenwart. Cologne: DuMont, 1980.

Exhibitions

International Ceramics. London: Victoria and Albert Museum, 1972.

Mundt, Barbara. *Nostalgie warum? Kunsthandwerkliche techniken im Stilwandel vom Historismus zur Moderne.* Berlin: Kunstgewerbemuseum, S.M.P.K., 1982.

Mundt, Barbara, Suzanne Netzer, and Innes Hettler. *Interieur + Design in Deutschland, 1945=60.* Berlin: Kunstgewerbemuseum and Dietrich Reimer Verlag, 1994.

842   STÖCKER, ANNETTE (1962–)
        Swiss ceramics designer.

Exhibitions

Céramique Suisse '93: 17e Biennale des Céramistes Suisses. Geneva: Musée Adriana, 1993.

843   STURM, ORSOLYA (1947–)
        Hungarian ceramics designer.

Exhibitions

Varga, Péter. *A VII Országos Kerámia Biennale Pécs* [VII National Ceramics Biennale]. Pécs: Pécsi Galéria, 1982.

844   SVENSSON, INEX GUDRUN LINNEA (1932–)
        Swedish designer of textiles and ceramics.

Exhibitions

McFadden, David. *Scandinavian Modern Design, 1880–1980.* New York: Harry Abrams in association with the Cooper-Hewitt Museum, 1982.

Other Sources

Martin, Edna, and Beata Sydhoff. *Svensk textilkonst. Swedish Textile Art.* Stockholm: Liber Forlag, 1980.

Naylor, Colin, ed. *Contemporary Designers.* 2nd edition. Chicago and London: St. James Press, 1990. Contains a bibliography.

845   SZAB, ANTNIA SZ (1938–)
        Hungarian designer of ceramics.

Exhibitions

Varga, Péter. *A VII Országos Kerámia Biennale Pécs* [VII National Ceramics Biennale]. Pécs: Pécsi Galéria, 1982.

846   SZAVOSZT, KATALIN (1941–)
        Hungarian ceramics designer.

Exhibitions

Varga, Péter. *A VII Országos Kerámia Biennale Pécs* [VII National Ceramics Biennale]. Pécs: Pécsi Galéria, 1982.

847   TABÉRYOV, MARTA (1930–)
        Czech designer of ceramics.

Exhibitions

International Ceramics. London: Victoria and Albert Museum, 1972
Art tchèque contemporain: gravure, céramique, verre. Freiburg: Musée d'Art et d'Histoire, 1973.

848   TAIT, JESSIE (1928–)
        English designer of ceramic decoration.

Other Sources

Buckley, Cheryl. *Potters and Paintresses: Women Designers in the Pottery Industry, 1870–1955.* London: Women's Press, 1990.

849   TAPLIN, MILLIE (née MILLICENT JANE TAPLIN) (1902–1980)
        English designer and painter of ceramics at Wedgwood.

Other Sources

Buckley, Cheryl. *Potters and Paintresses: Women Designers in the Pottery Industry, 1870–1955.* London: Women's Press, 1990.

850   TAUB, SUZANNE (1937–)
        Dutch designer of ceramics.

Exhibitions

Neue Formen der Keramik aus der Niederlanden. Darmstadt: Hessischen Landesmuseum, 1967.

Ceramische Hoogtepunten Nederland Pottenkijker, 1959–1969. Rotterdam: Museum Boymans-van Beuningen, 1969.

851   TCHALENKO, JANICE (1942–)
English ceramicist who produces brightly coloured tableware that takes on increasingly sculptural forms.

Main Sources

"CPA New Members." *Ceramic Review* 30 (1974): 12.

"7 Deadly Sins: Janice Tchalenko and Spitting Image Workshop." *Ceramic Review* 143 (1993): 32–33.

Cooper, Emmanuel. "Janice Tchalenko." *Ceramic Review* 80 (1983): 21–25.

———. *Janice Tchalenko: A Potter who Decorates.* Ceramics Series no. 2. Aberystwyth: Arts Centre, n.d. The text is a revised version of Cooper's 1983 article.

Dormer, Peter. "Tchalenko, Eclectic." *Crafts* 72 (1985): 16–23, 59.

Sherratt, Rachel. "Dart/Tchalenko: Designer Workshop." *Crafts* 87 (1987): 51–52.

Exhibitions

Fast Forward: New Directions in British Ceramics. London: Institute of Contemporary Art, 1985.

Watson, Oliver. *British Studio Pottery.* Oxford: Phaidon, 1990.

Other Sources

Dormer, Peter. *The New Ceramics: Trends and Traditions.* London: Thames and Hudson, 1986.

852   TER KUILE, LILY (1926–)
Dutch designer of ceramics.

Exhibitions

Ceramische Hoogtepunten Nederland Pottenkijker, 1959–1969. Rotterdam: Museum Boymans-van Beuningen, 1969.

853   TERNES, RITA (1955–)
German ceramicist.

Exhibitions

Europäische Keramik de Gegenwart:zweiter Internationale Ausstellung in Keramion. Frechen: Museum für zeitgenössische keramische Kunst, 1986.

854   TEUTEBERG, SABINA
   Swiss-born ceramicist who trained in ceramics and has worked in England since the late 1970s. Originally trained as a fine artist, her main output is tableware.

Main Sources

"CPA New Members." *Ceramic Review* 85 (1984): 29.
Briers, David. *Sabina Teuteberg.* Ceramic Series no. 26. Aberystwyth: Arts Centre, n.d., 4pp., illus.

855   THIENOT, MARCELLE (?–1946)
   French designer of ceramics.

Other Sources

Faré, Michel. *La céramique contemporaine.* Paris: Compagnie des Arts Photoméchaniques, 1953.

856   TOVOLLGYI, KATALIN (1948–)
   Hungarian ceramics designer.

Exhibitions

Varga, Péter. *A VII Országos Kerámia Biennale Pécs* [VII National Ceramics Biennale]. Pécs: Pécsi Galéria, 1982.

857   TRETHAN, THERESE (1879–?)
   Austrian designer of ceramics.

Exhibitions

Oedekoven-Gerischer, Angela, et al., eds. *Frauen im Design: Berufsbilder und Lebenswege seit 1900. Women in Design: Careers and Life Histories since 1900.* Stuttgart: Design Center, 1989.

858   TRILLER, INGRID (née ABENIUS) (1905–1980)
   German ceramicist who worked at the Bauhaus.

Exhibitions

Weber, Klaus, ed. *Keramik und Bauhaus.* Berlin: Bauhaus-Archiv, 1989.

859   TRITSCHLER, HELGA (1941–)
   German ceramicist.

Other Sources

Dormer, Peter. *The New Ceramics: Trends and Traditions.* London: Thames and Hudson, 1986.

860   TULLIO, ANITA (1935–)
      French ceramicist.

Exhibitions

Brunhammer, Yvonne, and Marie-Laure Perrin. *Céramique française contemporaine: sources et courants.* Paris: Musée des Arts Décoratifs, 1981.

861   TURGEL, MARGUERITE
      French designer of ceramics.

Other Sources

Faré, Michel. *La céramique contemporaine.* Paris: Compagnie des Arts Photoméchaniques, 1953.

862   TURNER, ANNE (1958–)
      English ceramicist.

Other Sources

Dormer, Peter. *The New Ceramics: Trends and Traditions.* London: Thames and Hudson, 1986.

863   ULLMANN, SILVIA (1947–)
      German ceramics designer.

Exhibitions

Klinge, Ekkart. *Deutsche Keramik Heute.* Dusseldorf: Verlagsanstalt Handwerk, 1984.
Beeh, Wolfgang, and Carl Benno Heller. *Keramik '88: Ton in Ton.* Darmstadt: Hessisches Landesmuseum, 1988.

864   URBN, TERÉZ (1936–)
      Hungarian ceramics designer.

Exhibitions

Varga, Péter. *A VII Országos Kerámia Biennale Pécs* [VII National Ceramics Biennale]. Pécs: Pécsi Galéria, 1982.

865   VALLIEN, ULRICA (Alt. HYDMAN-VALLIEN) (1938–)
      Swedish designer of glass and ceramics.

See Glass section.

866   VAN AGTHOVEN, DOROTHY (1950–)
      Dutch ceramicist.

Exhibitions

Duits, Thimo Te. *Keramiek '90. Moderne Keramiek in Nederland.* The Hague: SDU Uitgevrerij, 1990.

867   VAN BAARDA, EVELYN (1953–)
      Dutch ceramicist.

Exhibitions

Duits, Thimo Te. *Keramiek '90. Moderne Keramiek in Nederland.* The Hague: SDU Uitgevrerij, 1990.
      Gaillard, Karin. *Céramique néerlandaise contemporaine. Contemporary Dutch Ceramics. Niederlandische Keramik der Gegenwart.* Roanne: Musée Joseph Dechelette, 1988.

868   VAN DEN HEUVEL, NETTY
      Dutch ceramicist.

Exhibitions

Gaillard, Karin. *Céramique néerlandaise contemporaine. Contemporary Dutch Ceramics. Niederlandische Keramik der Gegenwart.* Roanne: Musée Joseph Dechelette, 1988.

869   VAN LANGEN, BETTIE (1941–)
      Dutch designer of ceramics.

Exhibitions

Neue Formen der Keramik aus der Niederlanden. Darmstadt: Hessischen Landesmuseum, 1967.
      Ceramische Hoogtepunten Nederland Pottenkijker, 1959–1969. Rotterdam: Museum Boymans-van Beuningen, 1969.

870   VAN OS, MARIJKE (1950–)
      Dutch ceramicist.

Exhibitions

Duits, Thimo Te. *Keramiek '90. Moderne Keramiek in Nederland.* The Hague: SDU Uitgevrerij, 1990.

871   VAN REES, ETIE (née EELCOLINE VAN REES) (1890–?)
      Indonesian-born designer of ceramics who works in the Netherlands.

Exhibitions

Neue Formen der Keramik aus der Niederlanden. Darmstadt: Hessischen Landesmuseum, 1967.

Ceramische Hoogtepunten Nederland Pottenkijker, 1959–1969. Rotterdam: Museum Boymans-van Beuningen, 1969.

872   VAN VLAARDINGEN, MARIJKE (1942–)
      Dutch designer of ceramics.

Exhibitions

Neue Formen der Keramik aus der Niederlanden. Darmstadt: Hessischen Landesmuseum, 1967.

Ceramische Hoogtepunten Nederland Pottenkijker, 1959–1969. Rotterdam: Museum Boymans-van Beuningen, 1969.

873   VANIER, CATHERINE (1943–)
      French ceramicist.

Exhibitions

Brunhammer, Yvonne, and Marie-Laure Perrin. *Céramique française contemporaine: sources et courants.* Paris: Musée des Arts Décoratifs, 1981.

874   VASEGAARD, GERTRUD (1913–)
      Danish ceramics designer.

Exhibitions

McFadden, David, ed. *Scandinavian Modern Design, 1880–1980.* New York: Harry Abrams and the Cooper-Hewitt Museum, 1982.

Hiesinger, Kathryn, and George Marcus III, eds. *Design since 1945.* Philadelphia: Philadelphia Museum of Art, 1983.

Opie, Jennifer. *Scandinavia: Ceramics and Glass in the Twentieth Century.* London: Victoria and Albert Museum, 1989.

Eidelberg, Martin, ed. *Design 1935–1965: What Modern Was.* New York: Abrams in association with the Musée des Arts Décoratifs, Montreal, 1991.

Other Sources

Byars, Mel. *The Design Encyclopedia.* London: Lawrence King, 1994.

Hiort, Esbjørn. *Modern Danish Ceramics.* New York: Museum Books Inc.; London: A. Zwemmer Ltd.; Stuttgart: Verlag Gerd Hatje; Teufen: Arthur Niggli und Willy Verkauf; Copenhagen: Jul Gjellerups Forlag, 1955.

875   VASEGAARD, MYRE (1936–)
      Danish ceramics designer.

Exhibitions

International Ceramics. London: Victoria and Albert Museum, 1972.
McFadden, David, ed. *Scandinavian Modern Design, 1880–1980.* New York:
Harry Abrams and the Cooper-Hewitt Museum, 1982.

876   VEHRING, VERA (1944–)
      German ceramicist.

Exhibitions

Klinge, Ekkart. *Deutsche Keramik Heute.* Dusseldorf: Verlagsanstalt
Handwerk, 1984.
*Europäische Keramik de Gegenwart:zweiter Internationale Ausstellung in
Keramion.* Frechen: Museum für zeitgenössische keramische Kunst, 1986.

877   VERNADAKI
      Greek ceramics designer.

Other Sources

Lewenstein, Eileen, and Emmanuel Cooper. *New Ceramics.* London: Studio
Vista, 1974.

878   VÉN, EDIT (1937–)
      Hungarian ceramics designer.

Exhibitions

Varga, Péter. *A VII Országos Kerámia Biennale Pécs* [VII National Ceramics
Biennale]. Pécs: Pécsi Galéria, 1982.

879   VIALLET, CHRISTINE (Alt. VIALLET-KUHN) (1942–)
      French ceramicist.

Main Sources

Espagnet, Françoise. "Une oeuvre à sa mesure." *La Céramique moderne* 262
(September 1983): 9. Exhibition review.

Exhibitions

Brunhammer, Yvonne, and Marie-Laure Perrin. *Céramique française contemporaine: sources et courants.* Paris: Musée des Arts Décoratifs, 1981.

880   VIKOV, JINDRA (1946–)
      Czech ceramics designer.

Exhibitions

Europäische Keramik de Gegenwart: zweiter Internationale Ausstellung in Keramion. Frechen: Museum für zeitgenössische keramische Kunst, 1986.

Beeh, Wolfgang, and Carl Benno Heller. *Keramik '88: Ton in Ton.* Darmstadt: Hessisches Landesmuseum, 1988.

Klinge, Ekkart. *Tschechesche Keramik.* Dusseldorf: Hetjens-Museum, 1991. She was one of eight exhibitors.

881 VIOTTI, ULLA
       Swedish ceramicist.

Main Sources

"Ulla Viotti's ceramic landscape." *Ceramic Review* 82 (1983): 4–5.

Exhibitions

Keramik i rum [Ceramics in space]. Copenhagen: Danske Kunstindustri-museum, 1981.

Europäische Keramik de Gegenwart:zweiter Internationale Ausstellung in Keramion. Frechen: Museum für zeitgenössische keramische Kunst, 1986.

882 VOET, PETRI (1943–)
       Dutch ceramicist.

Exhibitions

Duits, Thimo Te. *Keramiek '90. Moderne Keramiek in Nederland.* The Hague: SDU Uitgevrerij, 1990.

883 VON BOCH, HELEN (1938–)
       German designer of ceramics; member of the Boch family of designers of ceramics and glass.

Exhibitions

Hiesinger, Kathryn, and George Marcus III, eds. *Design since 1945.* Philadelphia: Philadelphia Museum of Art, 1983.

Other Sources

Byars, Mel. *The Design Encyclopedia.* London: Lawrence King, 1994.

884 VON BREVERN, RENATE (1942–)
       German designer of ceramic objects and furniture.

Exhibitions

Oedekoven-Gerischer, Angela, et al., eds. *Frauen im Design: Berufsbilder und Lebenswege seit 1900. Women in Design: Careers and Life Histories since 1900.* Stuttgart: Design Center, 1989.

885   VON ROTZ-KAMMER, MAJA (1924–)
       Swiss ceramics designer.

Exhibitions

Céramique Suisse '93: 17e Biennale des Céramistes Suisses. Geneva: Musée Adriana, 1993.

886   VON RUCKTESCHELL-TRÜB, CLARA (1882–?)
       German designer of ceramics.

Exhibitions

Meister der Deutschen Keramik 1900–1950. Cologne: Kunstgewerbe-museum, 1978.

887   VON STARK, ADELE (1859–1923)
       Austrian designer of ceramics, ceramic decoration and furniture who became a professor at the Vienna School of Arts and Crafts in 1914.

Exhibitions

Oedekoven-Gerischer, Angela, et al., eds. *Frauen im Design: Berufsbilder und Lebenswege seit 1900. Women in Design: Careers and Life Histories since 1900.* Stuttgart: Design Center, 1989.

888   VONCK, IRENE (1950–)
       Irish-born ceramicist who trained in England and then lived in the Netherlands.

Exhibitions

Duits, Thimo Te. *Keramiek '90. Moderne Keramiek in Nederland.* The Hague: SDU Uitgevrerij, 1990.

Gaillard, Karin. *Céramique néerlandaise contemporaine. Contemporary Dutch Ceramics. Niederlandische Keramik der Gegenwart.* Roanne: Musée Joseph Dechelette, 1988.

Other Sources

Dormer, Peter. *The New Ceramics: Trends and Traditions.* London: Thames and Hudson, 1986.

889   VOYATZGLOU, MARIA (1930–)
      Greek ceramics designer.

Exhibitions

Europäische Keramik de Gegenwart: zweiter Internationale Ausstellung in Keramion. Frechen: Museum für zeitgenössische keramische Kunst, 1986.

Other Sources

Lewenstein, Eileen, and Emmanuel Cooper. *New Ceramics.* London: Studio Vista, 1974.

890   WALKER, CASSANDIA ANNIE
      English decorator of ceramics who was one of the Della Robbia Pottery's most prolific designers and decorators.

Other Sources

Bergesen, Victoria. *Encyclopaedia of British Art Pottery, 1870–1920.* London: Barrie & Jenkins, 1991.

891   WALTON, HANNAH MOORE (1863–1940)
      Scottish miniature painter and designer who painted on glass and ceramics; sister of Helen (q.v.) and Constance.

Exhibitions

Burkhauser, Jude, ed. *'Glasgow Girls': Women in Art and Design, 1880–1920.* Edinburgh: Canongate, 1990.
      Cumming, Elizabeth. *Glasgow 1900: Art and Design.* Zwolle: Waanders Publishers in association with the Van Gogh Museum, Amsterdam, 1992.

892   WALTON, HELEN (1850–1921)
      Scottish designer who painted glass and ceramics. She set up a studio with her sisters Hannah (q.v.) and Constance.

See Hannah Walton.

893   WALTON, SARAH (1945–)
      English ceramicist.

Publications

"Salt-glaze." *Crafts* 23 (1976): 12–13.
"Nursing the kiln." *Crafts* 36 (1979): 28–31.
"Salt and form." *Ceramics Monthly,* November 1983, 55–59.

Sarah Walton: Salt-Glaze Potter. Ceramic Series no. 14. Aberystwyth: Arts Centre, n.d.

Exhibitions

Watson, Oliver. *British Studio Pottery.* Oxford: Phaidon, 1990.

894 WÄRFF, ANN (1937–)
 German-born glass and ceramics designer who works in Sweden.

See Glass section.

895 WEDGWOOD, STAR (née CECILY STELLA WEDGWOOD) (1903–?)
 English designer and painter of ceramics at Wedgwood.

Other Sources

Buckley, Cheryl. *Potters and Paintresses: Women Designers in the Pottery Industry, 1870–1955.* London: Women's Press, 1990.

896 WEIGEL, GOTLIND (1932–)
 German ceramicist.

Exhibitions

Klinge, Ekkart. *Deutsche Keramik Heute.* Dusseldorf: Verlagsanstalt Handwerk, 1984.
 Europäische Keramik de Gegenwart:zweiter Internationale Ausstellung in Keramion. Frechen: Museum für zeitgenössische keramische Kunst, 1986.

Other Sources

Lewenstein, Eileen, and Emmanuel Cooper. *New Ceramics.* London: Studio Vista, 1974.

897 WEINBERGER, TRUDE (née GERTRUDE) (1897–1945)
 Austrian designer in ceramics and other media.

Exhibitions

Leitgeb, Hildegard, Elizabeth Schmuttermeier, and Angela Völker. *Wiener Werkstätte: atelier viennois, 1903–1932.* Brussels: Galérie CGER, 1987.

Other Sources

Joseph Hoffmann and Wilhelm Wagenfeld: Glaskunst der Moderne. Munich: Klinkhardt and Bierman, 1992.

898   WEISS, PETRA (1947–)
      Swiss ceramics designer.

Exhibitions

15 Schweizer Keramiker: Ausstellung der Nationen. Faenza: Palazzo delle
Esposizioni, 1984.
*Europäische Keramik de Gegenwart: zweiter Internationale Ausstellung in
Keramion.* Frechen: Museum für zeitgenössische keramische Kunst, 1986.

899   WHITTALL, ELEANOR (1900–?)
      English ceramicist.

Exhibitions

Watson, Oliver. *British Studio Pottery.* Oxford: Phaidon, 1990.

900   WIERTZ, PAULINE
      Dutch ceramics designer.

Exhibitions

Gaillard, Karin. *Céramique néerlandaise contemporaine. Contemporary
Dutch Ceramics. Niederlandische Keramik der Gegenwart.* Roanne: Musée Joseph
Dechelette, 1988.

901   WIESELTHIER, VALLY (Alt. VALERIE) (1895–1945)
      Austrian designer in several media, particularly ceramics and glass; she
      moved to America in 1929.

See Glass section.

902   WISSE, CHRISTIAN (1956–)
      Dutch ceramicist.

Exhibitions

Duits, Thimo Te. *Keramiek '90. Moderne Keramiek in Nederland.* The
Hague: SDU Uitgevrerij, 1990.
Gaillard, Karin. *Céramique néerlandaise contemporaine. Contemporary
Dutch Ceramics. Niederlandische Keramik der Gegenwart.* Roanne: Musée Joseph
Dechelette, 1988.

903   WOLFF, ANN (née ANNELIESE SCHAEFER) (1937–)
      German-born designer of glass and ceramics who worked in Sweden
      from 1960.

Exhibitions

Oedekoven-Gerischer, Angela, et al., eds. *Frauen im Design: Berufsbilder und Lebenswege seit 1900. Women in Design: Careers and Life Histories since 1900.* Stuttgart: Design Center, 1989.

Other Sources

Naylor, Colin, ed. *Contemporary Designers.* 2nd edition. Chicago and London: St. James Press, 1990. Contains a bibliography.

904   WOOD, HELEN MUIR (1864–1930)
   Scottish designer of metalwork, stained glass and decorated ceramics.

Exhibitions

Burkhauser, Jude, ed. *'Glasgow Girls': Women in Art and Design, 1880–1920.* Edinburgh: Canongate, 1990.

905   WREN, DENISE (née TUCKFIELD) (1891–1979)
   English ceramicist who founded the Oxshott Pottery. Her daughter Rosemary (q.v.) was also a potter.

Publications

Wren, Denise, and Henry. *Oxshott Handmade Pottery.* London: Central Hall, Westminster, 1924. Exhibition catalogue.
   Handcraft Pottery for Workshop and School. London, 1928.
   Pottery, the Finger-Built Methods. London, 1932.
   Wren, Denise, and Rosemary. *Pottery Making.* London, 1952.

Main Sources

Coatts, Margot. "Denise and Henry Wren—Pioneer Potters." *Ceramic Review* 87 (1984): 22–24.
   Fournier, Robert. "Handbuilt ceramics: Denise and Rosemary Wren, Terry and Beverley Bell-Hughes." *Ceramic Review* 10 (1971).
   Lewenstein, Eileen. "Denise Wren, 1891–1979." *Ceramic Review* 59 (1979): 38. Obituary.
   Wren, Rosemary. "Denise K. Wren: Sixty-one Years a potter." *Ceramic Review* 15 (1972): 12–13.

Exhibitions

Coatts, Margot. *The Oxshott Pottery.* Bath: Bath Craft Study Centre, 1984, 60pp., illus. Contains a chronological study of the Wrens and the context of the pottery, a personal account by their daughter, Rosemary Wren (q.v.), a list of exhibitions and a bibliography.
   Watson, Oliver. *British Studio Pottery.* Oxford: Phaidon, 1990.

Other Sources

Lewenstein, Eileen, and Emmanuel Cooper. *New Ceramics*. London: Studio Vista, 1974.

Rose, Muriel. *Artist Potters in England*. London: Faber & Faber, 1970.

906   WREN, ROSEMARY D. (1922–)

English ceramicist and writer who, as the daughter of Denise Wren (q.v.), took over the family pottery at Oxshott in 1947 before setting up independently close by in 1950.

Publications

Wren, Denise, and Rosemary. *Pottery Making*. London, 1952.

"Why Raku?" *Ceramic Review* 1 (1970).

"CPA New Members." *Ceramic Review* 7 (1971): 12–13.

Wren, Rosemary, and Peter Crotty. "New Members." *Ceramic Review* 8 (1971): 8–9; 9 (1971): 14; 11 (1971): 12; 12 (1971): 8.

———. "Potters: Survey of some recently elected members of the Craftsman Potters Association." *Ceramic Review* 10 (1971): 12–13.

———. "CPA New Members." *Ceramic Review* 13 (1972): 12–13; 14 (1972): 12.

"Denice K. Wren: Sixty-one Years a Potter." *Ceramic Review* 15 (1972): 12–13.

"The Secret Life of Ian Godfrey." *Ceramic Review* 16 (1972): 12–13.

"Walter Keeler." *Ceramic Review* 18 (1972): 4–6.

"Potters' Aches and Pains." *Ceramic Review* 93 (1985): 27–28.

Main Sources

"Rosemary Wren—animals and birds." *Ceramic Review* 67 (1981): 9.

Colavecchia, Lyn. "Rosemary D. Wren and Peter Crotty." *Ceramic Review* 16 (1972): 18.

Fournier, Robert. "Handbuilt ceramics: Denise and Rosemary Wren, Terry and Beverley Bell-Hughes." *Ceramic Review* 10 (1971).

Ismay, W. "Rosemary D. Wren—Ceramics." *Ceramic Review* 22 (1973): 17.

Exhibitions

Rosemary D. Wren: Ceramics. London: Commonwealth Art Gallery, Commonwealth Institute, 1973.

Watson, Oliver. *British Studio Pottery*. Oxford: Phaidon, 1990.

907   WYNE REEVES, ANN (1929–)

English ceramicist and designer of tilework.

Exhibitions

Watson, Oliver. *British Studio Pottery.* Oxford: Phaidon, 1990.

908   WYNN, PATRICIA (1914–)
      Irish designer of ceramics.

Exhibitions

International Ceramics. London: Victoria and Albert Museum, 1972.

909   YOUNG, JOANNA (1950–)
      English ceramicist who works with Andrew Young to produce tableware
      that is both refined and practical.

Main Sources

"CPA New Members." *Ceramic Review* 51 (1978): 13.

Exhibitions

Joanna Young. Ceramic Series no. 24. Aberystwyth: Arts Centre, n.d.
Watson, Oliver. *British Studio Pottery.* Oxford: Phaidon, 1990.

910   ZALUDOV, NATASHA DRAHOMIRA (1936–)
      Czech-born designer of ceramics who works in the Netherlands.

Exhibitions

Neue Formen der Keramik aus der Niederlanden. Darmstadt: Hessischen
Landesmuseum, 1967.
Ceramische Hoogtepunten Nederland Pottenkijker, 1959–1969. Rotterdam:
Museum Boymans-van Beuningen, 1969.

911   ZAVADSKY, ÉVA (1953–)
      Hungarian ceramics designer.

Exhibitions

Varga, Péter. *A VII Országos Kerámia Biennale Pécs* [VII National Ceramics
Biennale]. Pécs: Pécsi Galéria, 1982.

912   ZEISEL, EVA (née POLANYI STRICKER) (1906–)
      Hungarian designer of ceramics and, later, furniture. She was deported
      and went to America in 1938.

Publications

See Naylor below.

Exhibitions

Hiesinger, Kathryn, and George Marcus III, eds. *Design since 1945.* Philadelphia: Philadelphia Museum of Art, 1983.

Oedekoven-Gerischer, Angela, et al., eds. *Frauen im Design: Berufsbilder und Lebenswege seit 1900. Women in Design: Careers and Life Histories since 1900.* Stuttgart: Design Center, 1989.

Mundt, Barbara, Suzanne Netzer, and Innes Hettler. *Interieur + Design in Deutschland, 1945=60.* Berlin: Kunstgewerbemuseum and Dietrich Reimer Verlag, 1994.

Other Sources

Byars, Mel. *The Design Encyclopedia.* London: Lawrence King, 1994.

Naylor, Colin, ed. *Contemporary Designers.* 2nd edition. Chicago and London: St. James Press, 1990. Contains a bibliography.

Fashion

REFERENCE

913 ADRIAENSSEN, AGNES. *Encyclopédie de la mode: De grote Mode-Encyclopedie.* Paris: Nathan, and Tielt, Editions Lannoo, 1989, 240pp., illus.
Dictionary of international fashion designers, fashion photographers and writers about fashion. A very useful source for women.

914 McDOWELL, COLIN. *McDowell's Dictionary of Twentieth Century Fashion.* London: Frederick Muller, 1984, 320pp., illus.
After an introductory overview to the topic, the alphabetical entries are primarily for individuals who may be fashion designers, fabric designers, fashion illustrators or photographers. At the end are lists of autobiographies for designers, of fashion awards, fashion educational institutions and relevant organisations. The entries give a useful summary of the career and character-istics of individuals.

915 MARTIN, RICHARD (ED.). *Contemporary Fashion. Contemporary Arts Series.* New York and London: St. James Press, 1995, illus.
Like the other books in this series, each individual is given an outline biography, a few paragraphs describing their style, characteristics and career, a list of exhibitions and a select bibliography.

916 O'HARA, GEORGINA. *The Encyclopedia of Fashion from 1840 to the 1980s.* London: Thames and Hudson, 1986, 272pp., illus.
Comprehensive alphabetical listing of many aspects of the fashion indus-try: fabrics, couture houses, styles, periodicals, garments, photographers and designers. Includes many women fashion designers. Contains a bibliography.

917 REMAURY, BRUNO (ED.). *Dictionnaire de la Mode au XXe siecle.* Paris: Editions du Regard, 1994, 592pp., illus.

The entries cover not only designers, amongst which many women are included, but also styles, accessories, fashion photographers, periodicals, journalists and other aspects of the fashion world. The countries on which the text concentrates are Europe, the United States and Japan. The biographical accounts vary in length and can be quite detailed and useful.

OTHER PUBLICATIONS

918   ARAGNO, BONIZZA GIORDANI (ED.). *Creativity and Technology in the Italian Fashion System. Creatività, impresa e tecnologia nel sistema italiano della moda.* Milan: Editoriale Domus, 1988, 198pp., illus.

Text in Italian and English. After four essays on the Italian fashion industry, there are shorter essays on eight designers, of whom three are women: Krizia, Biagiotti and Missoni.

919   BERTIN, CELIA. *Paris à la mode: A Voyage of Discovery.* London: Gollancz Ltd., 1956, 254pp., illus.

Consists of anecdotal reminiscences of aspects of the fashion industry in the early 1950s. Included in the chapter on the major couturiers of the time are several women: Vionnet, Chanel, Schaparelli, Grès and Lanvin, about each of whom there is a short biographical account and any personal reminiscences from the author.

920   BOWMAN, SARA. *A Fashion for Extravagance: Art Déco Fabrics and Fashions.* London: Bell and Hyman, 1985, 125pp., illus.

This provides a survey of the fashions which used luxurious and embroidered fabrics in Paris in the 1920s and 1930s. There are chapters on Poiret, the Atelier Martine, la Maison Lallement, Fortúny, Sonia Delaunay, Erté, Raymond Duncan, Ugo lo Monaco, and fashion accessories. Apart from Delaunay there is information on Alice Rutter, a designer at Martine, Suzanne Lallement, who took over the craft embroidery workshop started by her father, which produced embroidered fabrics for couturiers, Margarette Callot, a painter and designer for Lallement, and fabric designer Mme Claussen Smith.

921   DE PETRI, STEPHAN, and MELISSA LEVENTON. *New Look to Now: French haute couture, 1947–1987.* San Francisco: Fine Arts Museum and New York: Rizzoli, 1987, illus.

Consists of several essays which address the problem of costume in museums in addition to the fashion history of the forty years covered by the book. As an American publication it also looks at the influence of French haute couture in the U.S. In the biographies of designers whose work is included in the museum, several women are included: Chanel, Mme Grès, Jeanne Lanvin and Maggy Rouff.

922 DESLANDRES, YVONNE, and FLORENCE MÜLLER. *Histoire de la mode au XXe siècle.* Paris: Editions Somogy, 1986, 404pp., illus.

A chronological account of twentieth-century fashion is followed by an alphabetical list of the principal designers, each with an informative biography. A considerable number of women are included.

923 DORNER, JANE. *Fashion in the Forties and Fifties.* London: Ian Allan Ltd., 1975, 160pp., illus.

A chronological survey of changes in fashion over the two decades done mainly through extended captions to illustrations. Chanel, Grès and Quant all mentioned (qq.v.).

924 KENNETT, FRANCES. *Collector's Book of Twentieth Century Fashion.* London: Granada, 1983.

An introductory text which reviews each decade of fashion in turn from the point of view of collectors of fashion items. There are a number of women designers mentioned but the information is not detailed. Of particular interest are those from the turn of the century: Mme Paquin, Caillot Soeurs, Mme Cheruit, and Lucile Lady Duff Gordon. From the 1920s and 1930s are Vionnet, Chanel, Sonia Delaunay, Schaparelli, Maria Monaci Gallenga, Mme Babani and Angèle Delanghe. From more recent decades are Mary Quant, Barbara Hulanicki (Biba), Jean Muir, Zandra Rhodes, Sonia Rykiel and Mariuccia Mandelli (Krizia) (qq.v.).

925 LEY, SUSAN. *Fashion for Everyone: The Story of Ready-to-Wear 1870s–1970s.* New York: Charles Scribner's Sons, 153pp., illus.

After an introduction to pre-1870s dress designers, which includes Rose Berlin, the official dressmaker to Marie-Antionette, as well as Palmyre, Victorine and Vignon, the book is divided into decades. The short text contentrates on styles more than designers but seven women are mentioned in the early-twentieth-century chapters.

926 MULASSANO, ADRIANA. *The Who's Who of Italian Fashion.* Florence: Edizioni G. Spinelli & C., 1979, 363pp., illus.

The early chapters are devoted to aspects of the history of Italian fashion and textiles, principally after 1950. The largest part of the book consists of chapters on forty individual designers written in an anecdotal rather than analytical style. The photographs by Alfa Castaldi reinforce this with their snapshot appearance. The women included are Laura Biagiotti, Roberta da Camerino [Giuliana], the Fendi family (Adele, Paola, Anna, Carla), Wanda, Fiamma and Giovanna Ferragamo, Marina Ferrari, Grazia Gherardini, Mariuccia Mandelli (Krizia), Enrica Massi, Rosita Missoni, Paola Sanlorenzo, Mila Schön.

927 ROBINSON, JULIAN. *Fashion in the '30s.* London: Oresko, 1978, 104pp., mainly illus.

A chronological account of the revivial of feminine fashions in the 1930s, including Lanvin, Chanel, Schiaparelli, Vionnet and Callot Soeurs (qq.v.).

928 STEELE, VALERIE. *Paris Fashion: A Cultural Context.* New York and Oxford: Oxford University Press, 1988, 317pp., illus.

Examines critically the significance and symbolism of fashion in French society from the eighteenth century. In the discussion many women designers are mentioned and Steele draws attention to the lack of research on their activities.

929 STEELE, VALERIE. *Women of Fashion.* New York: Rizzoli International, 1991, 224pp., illus.

The most comprehensive publication to date which examines the role of women fashion designers and related professions. Scholarly , with extensive footnotes and bibliography, it analyses the sociohistorical context which allowed women to emerge as designers.

930 STRIJÉNOVA, TATIANA. *La mode en Union Soviétique, 1917–45.* Paris: Flammarion, 1991, 225pp., illus.

A chronological account from c. 1900, but particularly from the Revolution, of a surprisingly rich subject. Using paintings, graphics and photographs as evidence, the author traces the history of Soviet fashion. The main figure to emerge is that of the designer Nadejda Lamanova (1861–1941), who successfully made the transition from supplying the Tzars' court to that of the State Department of Crafts. A number of her female followers are also examined: Mukhina, Exter, Pribylaskaya as well as Lamanova's niece, Nadejda Makarova. The contructivist clothing designs of Popova, Stepanova and Oudaltsova are included, together with other lesser known figures of the 1920s.

931 VAUDOYER, MARY. *Le livre de la haute couture.* Paris: V et O Editions, 1990, 300pp., illus.

Text in English and French. Covering the period from 1865 to 1990, the book is divided into sections according to the type of garment, for example, daywear, garden party clothes, informal dinner and cocktail gowns. Within each section there are examples by different fashion houses. The last 100 pages consist of a biographical dictionary of the principal designers and fashion houses in which many women are included.

932 VÖLKER, ANGELA. *Wiener Werkstätte: Wiener Mode und Modefotografie. Die Modeabteilung der Wiener Werkstätte, 1922–1932.* Munich and Paris: Schneider-Henn, 1984, 283pp., mainly illus.

Text in German. The two introductory essays which precede the plates make mention of eight women involved in either fashion design and its photography: Marianne Zels, Maria Likarz, Gertrude Brandt, Erna Putz, Gabriele Lagus Möschl, Fritzi Löw, Mela Kohler and Heddi Hirsch-Landesmann.

Further women are listed as present in the Wiener Werkstätte archive but no information is given about them. There are no biographies but a list of the exhibitions in which fashion featured.

933   ZALETOVA, LIDIJA, and FABIO CIOFI. *L'Abito della rivoluzione: tessuti, abiti, costumi nell'Unione Sovietica degli anni 20.* Venice: Cataloghi Marsilio, 1987, 193pp., illus.

Text in Italian. Examines textile design and fashion in the years immediately following the Revolution, a field in which women were active.

INDIVIDUALS

934   AGNS B. (née TROUBLE; alt. AGNES CLARET DE FLEURIEU) (1941–) French fashion designer.

Main Sources

See Naylor below.

Other Sources

Naylor, Colin, ed. *Contemporary Designers.* 2nd edition. Chicago and London: St. James Press, 1990.
Steele, Valerie. *Women of Fashion.* New York: Rizzoli International, 1991.

935   ASHLEY, LAURA (née MOUNTNEY) (1926–88) English fabric and fashion designer.

Main Sources

Gandee, Charles. "Nick Ashley: Life after Laura." *House and Garden,* April 1991, 212.

Other Sources

Byars, Mel. *The Design Encyclopedia.* London: Lawrence King, 1994.
Naylor, Colin, ed. *Contemporary Designers.* 2nd edition. Chicago and London: St. James Press, 1990.
Steele, Valerie. *Women of Fashion.* New York: Rizzoli International, 1991.

936   BEDIN, MARTINE (1957–) French designer of lighting, furniture, interiors and fashion accessories.

See Interior Design section.

937   BERETTA, ANNE-MARIE (1935–)
      French fashion designer.

Exhibitions

Correspondence vêtement revêtement. Paris: Union des Arts Décoratifs and Musée des Arts de la Mode, 1986, 72pp., illus.

Other Sources

Naylor, Colin, ed. *Contemporary Designers.* 2nd edition. Chicago and London: St. James Press, 1990.
Steele, Valerie. *Women of Fashion.* New York: Rizzoli International, 1991.

938   BIAGIOTTI, LAURA (1943–)
      Italian fashion designer.

Main Sources

Aragno, Bonizza Gordani, ed. *Creativity and Technology in the Italian Fashion System. Creatività, impresa e technologia nel sistema italiano di moda.* Milan: Editoriale Domus, 1988.
Mulassano, Adriana. *The Who's Who of Italian Fashion.* Florence: Edizioni G. Spinelli & C., 1979.

Other Sources

Naylor, Colin, ed. *Contemporary Designers.* 2nd edition. Chicago and London: St. James Press, 1990. Contains bibliography.
Steele, Valerie. *Women of Fashion.* New York: Rizzoli International, 1991.

939   BIBA (Pseudonym of BARBARA HULANICKI) (1938–)
      Polish-born designer of fashion and accessories who worked in London during the 1960s and later moved to America.

Publications

A to Biba. London: Hutchinson, 1983. Autobiography.

Other Sources

Steele, Valerie. *Women of Fashion.* New York: Rizzoli International, 1991.

940   BOULANGER, LOUISE
      French fashion designer who trained with Cheruit (q.v.) and opened her own fashion house in 1923.

Exhibitions

Dufresne, Jean-Luc, and Olivier Messac, eds. *Femmes créatrices des années vingt.* Granville: Musée Richard Anacréon, 1988. Wide-ranging catalogue with a short biographical account on each woman included.

941 CALLOT SOEURS (MARIE, MARTHE, RÉGINA and JOSÉPHINE) (Flourished 1895–c.1950)
French fashion designers known especially for their use of lace and braiding.

Exhibitions

Dufresne, Jean-Luc, and Olivier Messac, eds. *Femmes créatrices des années vingt.* Granville: Musée Richard Anacréon, 1988. Wide-ranging catalogue with biographical outlines on each woman included.

Other Sources

Steele, Valerie. *Paris Fashion: A Cultural History.* New York and Oxford: Oxford University Press, 1988.
———. *Women of Fashion.* New York: Rizzoli International, 1991.

942 CHANEL, COCO (née GABRIELLE CHANEL) (1883–1971)
French fashion designer who opened her first salon in 1908.

Main Sources

Baillen, Claude. *Chanel Solitaire.* Paris: N.R.F., 1971, 216pp., illus.
Charles-Roux, Edmonde. *L'irrégulière.* Paris: Editions Grasset, 1974.
Charles-Roux, Edmonde. *Le Temps Chanel.* Paris: Chêne-Grasset, 1979, 382pp., illus. Looks at the era in which Chanel worked.
Galante, Pierre. *Les années Chanel.* Paris: Mercure de France, 1972, 341pp., illus. A biographical and anecdotal account.
Haedrich, Marcel. *Coco Chanel secrète.* Series Vécu. Paris: Laffont, 1971, 327pp., illus.
———. *Coco Chanel.* Paris: P. Belfond, 1987, 234pp., illus. Biographical account including transcripts of conversations which the author held with Chanel during the period 1959–71.
Kent, Malhia. *La Pharaonne.* Paris: Editions Acropole, 1980, 218pp., illus.
Leymarie, Jean, and Catherine Huebschmann. *Chanel.* Geneva: Skira, 1987, 225pp., illus. Combines a biographical account with a wider consideration of fashion.
Marquand, Lilou. *Chanel m'a dit.* Paris: J.C. Lattès, 1990, 163pp., illus.
Mauries, Patrick. *Jewellery by Chanel.* London: Thames and Hudson, 1993, 143pp., 136 illus. Discusses the influences of Iribe and Cocteau, her imagery and the makers of her designs. Contains a bibliography.
Morand, Paul. *L'allure de Chanel.* Paris: Editions Hermann, 1976, 166pp., illus.

Exhibitions

Dufresne, Jean-Luc, and Olivier Messac, eds. *Femmes créatrices des années vingt.* Granville: Musée Richard Anacréon, 1988. Wide-ranging catalogue with biographical outlines on each woman included.

Aveline, M. *Chanel: ouverture pour la mode à Marseille.* Musées de Marseille, 1989, 111pp., illus.

Other Sources

Bertin, Celia. *Paris à la Mode: A Voyage of Discovery.* London: Gollancz Ltd., 1956.

Kennett, Frances. *Collector's Book of Twentieth Century Fashion.* London: Granada, 1983.

Naylor, Colin, ed. *Contemporary Designers.* 2nd edition. Chicago and London: St. James Press, 1990. Contains a bibliography.

Petri, Stephan de, and Melissa Leventon. *New Look to Now: French Haute Couture, 1947–1987.* San Francisco: Fine Arts Museum and New York: Rizzoli, 1987.

Robinson, Julian. *Fashion in the '30s.* London: Oresko, 1978.

Steele, Valerie. *Paris Fashion: A Cultural History.* New York and Oxford: Oxford University Press, 1988.

———. *Women of Fashion.* New York: Rizzoli International, 1991.

943   CHERUIT, MME (Active 1880s–1923)
French fashion designer who founded her own *maison de couture* in 1905 and worked there until her retirement in 1923.

Exhibitions

Dufresne, Jean-Luc, and Olivier Messac, eds. *Femmes créatrices des années vingt.* Granville: Musée Richard Anacréon, 1988. Wide-ranging catalogue with biographical outlines on each woman included.

Other Sources

Steele, Valerie. *Women of Fashion.* New York: Rizzoli International, 1991.

944   CYBER (Pseudonym of LUCY TOBOUL)
French fashion designer who, with her husband, Robert, established the fashion house Cyber in 1920.

Exhibitions

Dufresne, Jean-Luc, and Olivier Messac, eds. *Femmes créatrices des années vingt.* Granville: Musée Richard Anacréon, 1988. Wide-ranging catalogue with biographical outlines on each woman included.

945   DA CAMERINO, ROBERTA
      Italian fashion designer.

Main Sources

Mulassano, Adriana. *The Who's Who of Italian Fashion.* Florence: Edizioni G. Spinelli & C., 1979.

946   DE RAUCH, MADELEINE
      French fashion designer who specialised in sportswear.

Exhibitions

Dufresne, Jean-Luc, and Olivier Messac, eds. *Femmes créatrices des années vingt.* Granville: Musée Richard Anacréon, 1988. Wide-ranging catalogue with a short biographical account on each woman included.

947   DELAUNAY, SONIA (1885–1979) (née SOFIA ILINITCHNA STERN TERK from 1890; alt. DELAUNAY-TERK)
      Russian-born abstract painter and designer of textiles, fashion, stage designs and costumes who worked in France.

See Textiles section.

948   DUFF-GORDON, LUCILLE (LADY)
      English fashion designer who worked in London and France.

Publications

Discretions and Indiscretions. London: Jarrolds, 1932.

Other Sources

Kennett, Frances. *Collector's Book of 20th Century Fashion.* London: Granada, 1983.

Steele, Valerie. *Paris Fashion: A Cultural History.* New York and Oxford: Oxford University Press, 1988.

———. *Women of Fashion.* New York: Rizzoli International, 1991. Contains a bibliography.

949   FENDI SISTERS (ADELE, PAOLA, ANNA, CARLA)
      Italian fashion designers.

Other Sources

Mulassano, Adriano. *The Who's Who of Italian Fashion.* Florence: Edizioni G. Spinelli & C., 1979.

Steele, Valerie. *Women of Fashion.* New York: Rizzoli International, 1991. Contains a bibliography.

950   FRATINI, GINA (née GEORGIA CAROLINE BUTLER) (1931–)
       English fashion designer.

Other Sources

Naylor, Colin, ed. *Contemporary Designers.* 2nd edition. Chicago and London: St. James Press, 1990. Contains a bibliography.

951   GHERARDINI, GRAZIA
       Italian fashion designer.

Main Sources

Mulassano, Adriana. *The Who's Who of Italian Fashion.* Florence: Edizioni G. Spinelli & C., 1979.

952   GRS, MADAME ALIX (pseudonym of ALICE BARTON)
       French fashion designer.

Main Sources

Sciaky, Françoise. "Lovely Grès." *American Fabrics and Fashions* 128 (1983): 6–9.
Villiers Le Moy, Pascale. "The Timeless Fashions of Madame Grès." *Connoisseur* 211, no. 846 (August 1982): 94–99.

Other Sources

Dorner, Jane. *Fashion in the Forties and Fifties.* London: Ian Allan Ltd., 1975.
Petri, Stephan de, and Melissa Leventon. *New Look to Now: French Haute Couture, 1947–1987.* San Francisco: Fine Arts Museum and New York: Rizzoli, 1987.
Steele, Valerie. *Paris Fashion: A Cultural History.* New York and Oxford: Oxford University Press, 1988.
———. *Women of Fashion.* New York: Rizzoli International, 1991. Contains a bibliography.

953   GROULT, NICOLE (flourished 1910–1936)
       French fashion designer, sister of Paul Poiret, who opened her own *maison de couture* in 1910.

Exhibitions

Garnier, Guillaume, et al. *Paule Poiret and Nicole Groult: maîtres de la mode Art Déco.* Paris: Musée de la Mode, 1986.

Dufresne, Jean-Luc, and Olivier Messac, eds. *Femmes créatrices des années vingt.* Granville: Musée Richard Anacréon, 1988. Wide-ranging catalogue with a short biographical account on each woman included.

Other Sources

Steele, Valerie. *Women of Fashion.* New York: Rizzoli International, 1991. Contains a bibliography.

954   HAMNETT, KATHERINE
      English fashion designer.

Other Sources

Buckley, Richard. "Katherine the Great: Miss Hamnett Talks." *DNR: The Magazine,* February 1985, 41–42.
      Etherington Smith, Meredith. "New Guard, Old Guard: Fashion Designers Katherine Hamnett and Jean Muir." *Ultra,* December 1984.
      Mower, Sarah. "Katherine Hamnett." *Vogue,* February 1987, 131–134.
      Steele, Valerie. *Women of Fashion.* New York: Rizzoli International, 1991. Contains a bibliography.

955   HIRSCH, HEDDI (née LEOPOLDINE; alt. HIRSCH-LANDESMANN)
      (1895–1947)
      Austrian designer, especially of textiles, fashion and graphics.

Exhibitions

Kallir, Jane. *Viennese Design and the Wiener Werkstätte.* New York: Braziller in association with the Galérie St. Etienne, 1986.
      Leitgeb, Hildegard, Elizabeth Schmuttermeier, and Angela Völker. *Wiener Werkstätte: atelier viennois, 1903–1932.* Brussels: Galérie CGER, 1987.

Other Sources

Schweiger, W. *Weiner Werkstätte: Kunst und Handwerk, 1903–32.* Vienna: Christian Brandstätter Verlag, 1982.
      Völker, Angela. *Wiener Werkstätte: Wiener Mode und Modefotografie. Die Modeabteilung der Wiener Werkstätte, 1922–1932.* Munich and Paris: Schneider-Henn, 1984.

956   IRFÉ (Couture house founded by PRINCESS YPOUSSOUPOV) (1924–)
      Russian fashion designer who lived in France.

Exhibitions

Dufresne, Jean-Luc, and Olivier Messac, eds. *Femmes créatrices des années vingt.* Granville: Musée Richard Anacréon, 1988. Wide-ranging catalogue with a short biographical account on each woman included.

957   JACKSON, BETTY (1949–)
      English fashion designer.

Main Sources

Frankel, Susannah. "The Comfort Zone." *The Guardian Weekend,* 12 October 1996, 42–44.

958   JENNY
      French fashion designer who opened her own *maison de couture* in 1908 and in 1933 worked in partnership with Lucille Paray.

Exhibitions

Dufresne, Jean-Luc, and Olivier Messac, eds. *Femmes créatrices des années vingt.* Granville: Musée Richard Anacréon, 1988. Wide-ranging catalogue with a short biographical account on each woman included.

Other Sources

Steele, Valerie. *Paris Fashion: A Cultural History.* New York and Oxford: Oxford University Press, 1988.
————. *Women of Fashion.* New York: Rizzoli International, 1991. Contains a bibliography.

959   KHANH, EMMANUELLE (née RENÉE MEZIRE) (1937–)
      French fashion designer.

Exhibitions

Correspondence vêtement revêtement. Paris: Union des Arts Décoratifs and Musée des Arts de la Mode, 1986, 72pp., illus.

Other Sources

Naylor, Colin, ed. *Contemporary Designers.* 2nd edition. Chicago and London: St. James Press, 1990. Contains a bibliography.
Steele, Valerie. *Women of Fashion.* New York: Rizzoli International, 1991. Contains a bibliography.

960   KOCH, LUISE CHARLOTTE (1917–)
      German designer who worked in several media including ceramics and fashion design.

Exhibitions

Mundt, Barbara, Suzanne Netzer, and Innes Hettler. *Interieur + Design in Deutschland, 1945=60.* Berlin: Kunstgewerbemuseum and Dietrich Reimer Verlag, 1994.

961   KRIZIA
         See MARIUCCIA MANDELLI below.

962   LAMANOVA, NADEJDA (1861–1941)
         Russian/Soviet fashion designer.

Publications

"Rousskaïa moda." *Krasnaia Niva* [Red Field] 30 (1923).
"O sovremennom kostioume." [Contemporary dress] *Krasnaia Niva* 27 (1924).

Main Sources

Strijenova, Tatiana. *La Mode en Union Soviétique, 1917–45.* Paris:
Flammarion, 1991.

Exhibitions

Paris-Moscou, 1900–1939. Paris: Centre Nationale d'Art et de Culture
Georges Pompidou, 1979.

963   LANVIN, JEANNE (1867–1946)
         French fashion designer who founded her own fashion house about 1890.

Main Sources

Schlumberger, E. "Au 16 rue Barbet de Jouy avec Jeanne Lanvin."
Connaissance des Arts, August 1963.

Exhibitions

Mathey, François. *Les années 25: Art Déco, Bauhaus, De Stijl. Esprit
Nouveau.* Paris: Musée des Arts Décoratifs, 1966.
      Cinquantenaire de l'Exposition de 1925. Paris: Musée des Arts Décoratifs,
1976.
      Paris-Moscou, 1900–1939. Paris: Centre Nationale d'Art et de Culture
Georges Pompidou, 1979.
      Dufresne, Jean-Luc, and Olivier Messac, eds. *Femmes créatrices des années
vingt.* Granville: Musée Richard Anacréon, 1988. Wide-ranging catalogue with a
short biographical account on each woman included.

Other Sources

Bertin, Celia. *Paris à la Mode: A Voyage of Discovery.* London: Gollancz
Ltd., 1956.
      Brunhammer, Yvonne. *1925.* Paris: Les Presses de la Connaissance, 1976.
      Byars, Mel. *The Design Encyclopedia.* London: Lawrence King, 1994.
      Petri, Stephan de, and Melissa Leventon. *New Look to Now: French Haute
Couture, 1947–1987.* San Francisco: Fine Arts Museum and New York: Rizzoli, 1987.
      Robinson, Julian. *Fashion in the '30s.* London: Oresko, 1978.

Steele, Valerie. *Paris Fashion: A Cultural History*. New York and Oxford: Oxford University Press, 1988.

————. *Women of Fashion*. New York: Rizzoli International, 1991. Contains a bibliography.

964 MAKAROVA, NADEJDA (1898–1966)
Soviet fashion designer.

Main Sources

Strijenova, Tatiana. *La Mode en Union Soviétique, 1917–45*. Paris: Flammarion, 1991.

965 MANDELLI, MARIUCCIA (1933–)
Italian fashion designer and cofounder of the Krizia company.

Main Sources

Aragno, Bonizza Gordani, ed. *Creativity and Technology in the Italian Fashion System. Creatività, impresa e tecnologia nel sistema italiano di moda*. Milan: Editoriale Domus, 1988.

Mulassano, Adriana. *The Who's Who of Italian Fashion*. Florence: Edizioni G. Spinelli & C., 1979.

Other Sources

Naylor, Colin, ed. *Contemporary Designers*. 2nd edition. Chicago and London: St. James Press, 1990. Contains a bibliography.

Steele, Valerie. *Women of Fashion*. New York: Rizzoli International, 1991. Under both Mandelli and Krizia. Contains a bibliography.

966 MARCE, ROSER
Spanish fashion designer.

Other Sources

Dent-Coad, Emma. *Spanish Design and Architecture*. London: Studio Vista, 1990.

967 MENNI, ROSA GIOLLI
Italian designer of fashion and furnishing textiles.

Other Sources

Fanelli, Giovanni, and Rosalia Fanelli. *Il tessuto art déco e anni trenta: disegno, moda, architettura*. Florence: Cantini, 1986.

968 MISSONI, ROSITA (née JELMINI) (1931–)
Italian fashion designer.

Main Sources

Aragno, Bonizza Gordani, ed. *Creativity and Technology in the Italian Fashion System. Creatività, impresa e tecnologia nel sistema italiano di moda.* Milan: Editoriale Domus, 1988.

Mulassano, Adriana. *The Who's Who of Italian Fashion.* Florence: Edizioni G. Spinelli & C., 1979.

Other Sources

Naylor, Colin, ed. *Contemporary Designers.* 2nd edition. Chicago and London: St. James Press, 1990. Contains a bibliography.

Steele, Valerie. *Women of Fashion.* New York: Rizzoli International, 1991. Contains a bibliography.

969   MÖSCHL, GABI (Alt. GABRIELE MARIA MÖSCHL-LAGUS) (1887– after 1939)

Austrian designer, especially of textiles and fashion.

Other Sources

Schweiger, Werner. *Weiner Werkstätte: Kunst und Handwerk, 1903–32.* Vienna: Christian Brandstätter Verlag, 1982.

970   MUIR, JEAN ELIZABETH (1933–1995)

English fashion designer.

Publications

Jean Muir. London, 1981.

Main Sources

Etherington Smith, Meredith. "New Guard, Old Guard: Fashion Designers Katherine Hamnett and Jean Muir." *Ultra,* December 1984.

Gilroy, Griselda. "Jean Muir." *Crafts* 46 (1980): 56.

Hill, Rosemary. "Outlook." *Crafts* 80 (1986): 49. Conversation with Muir.

Webb, Iain. "Secure with Miss Muir." *Harper and Queen,* March 1991, 166–170.

Exhibitions

Jean Muir. Leeds: City Art Gallery, 1980.

Other Sources

Naylor, Colin, ed. *Contemporary Designers.* 2nd edition. Chicago and London: St. James Press, 1990. Contains a bibliography.

Steele, Valerie. *Women of Fashion.* New York: Rizzoli International, 1991. Contains a bibliography.

971   NAVARRO, SARA (1957–)
Spanish fashion designer specialising in shoe design.

Other Sources

Dent-Coad, Emma. *Spanish Design and Architecture.* London: Studio Vista, 1990.
Martin, Richard, ed. *Contemporary Fashion.* Contemporary Arts Series. New York and London: St. James Press, 1995.

972   NEWBERY, JESSIE (née ROWAT) (1864–1948)
Scottish designer of textiles, especially embroidery, and fashion who taught at the Glasgow School of Art; she also designed metalwork.

See Textiles section.

973   ÖSTREICHER, LISBETH (Alt. BIRMAN) (1902–1989)
German designer of textiles and fashion who worked in the Netherlands from 1930.

Other Sources

Gunta Stölzl: Weberei am Bauhaus und aus eigener Werkstatt. Berlin: Bauhaus Archiv in association with Kupfergraben Verlag, 1987. Contains individual bibliographies.
Weltge, Sigrid Wortmann. *Bauhaus Textiles: Women Artists and the Weaving Workshop.* London: Thames and Hudson, 1993.

974   PANIZON, MADELEINE
French fashion designer who specialised in hats and collaborated with Poiret from 1920–1928.

Exhibitions

Dufresne, Jean-Luc, and Olivier Messac, eds. *Femmes créatrices des années vingt.* Granville: Musée Richard Anacréon, 1988. Wide-ranging catalogue with a short biographical account on each woman included.

975   PAQUIN, JEANNE (Pseudonym of JEANNE MARIE CHARLOTTE BECKER)
French fashion designer who opened her own fashion house in 1891 in Paris and who later worked in England, Argentina and Spain.

Exhibitions

Dufresne, Jean-Luc, and Olivier Messac, eds. *Femmes créatrices des années vingt.* Granville: Musée Richard Anacréon, 1988. Wide-ranging catalogue with a short biographical account on each woman included.

Biro, Adam. *Paquin: une Rétrospective de 60 ans de Haute Couture.* Lyon: Musée Historique des Tissus de Lyon, 1989.

Other Sources

Steele, Valerie. *Paris Fashion: A Cultural History.* New York and Oxford: Oxford University Press, 1988.

————. *Women of Fashion.* New York: Rizzoli International, 1991. Contains a bibliography.

976   PRIBYLSKAYA, EVGENIA (1878–1949)
Soviet fashion designer.

Publications

Pribylskaya, Evgenia. "La broderie dans la production actuelle." *Atelier* 1 (1923): 7.

Main Sources

Strijenova, Tatiana. *La Mode en Union Soviétique, 1917–45.* Paris: Flammarion, 1991.

977   PUPPA, DANIELA (1947–)
Italian designer of furniture, textiles and fashion accessories.

See Interior Design section.

978   QUANT, MARY (1934–)
English fashion designer who opened her first shop in the King's Road, Chelsea, in 1955 and became prominent in the 1960s.

Publications

Quant by Quant. London: Cassell, 1965. Autobiography.

Exhibitions

Mary Quant's London. London: The London Museum, 1973.

Other Sources

Dorner, Jane. *Fashion in the Forties and Fifties.* London: Ian Allan Ltd., 1975.

Kennett, Frances. *Collector's Book of Twentieth Century Fashion*. London: Granada, 1983.

Steele, Valerie. *Women of Fashion*. New York: Rizzoli International, 1991. Contains a bibliography.

979   REBOUX, CAROLINE (flourished from 1860)
French fashion designer who designed robes for the empress in the 1870s and founded her own *maison de couture*.

Exhibitions

Dufresne, Jean-Luc, and Olivier Messac, eds. *Femmes créatrices des années vingt*. Granville: Musée Richard Anacréon, 1988. Wide-ranging catalogue with biographical outlines on each woman included.

980   REICH, LILLY (1885–1947)
German designer of interiors, furniture, textiles and fashion.

See Interior Design section.

981   RÉGNY, JANE
French fashion designer whose *maison de couture* specialised in sportswear.

Exhibitions

Dufresne, Jean-Luc, and Olivier Messac, eds. *Femmes créatrices des années vingt*. Granville: Musée Richard Anacréon, 1988. Wide-ranging catalogue with a short biographical account on each woman included.

Other Sources

Steele, Valerie. *Women of Fashion*. New York: Rizzoli International, 1991. Contains a bibliography.

982   RHODES, ZANDRA LINDSEY (1940–)
English fashion and textile designer.

Publications

Rhodes, Zandra, and Anne Knight. *The Art of Zandra Rhodes*. Boston: Houghton Mifflin Co., 1984. Autobiography.

Main Sources

Coleman, Marigold. "Zandra Rhodes." *Crafts* 13 (1975): 17–21.

Other Sources

Naylor, Colin, ed. *Contemporary Designers.* 2nd edition. Chicago and London: St. James Press, 1990. Contains a bibliography.

Steele, Valerie. *Women of Fashion.* New York: Rizzoli International, 1991. Contains a bibliography.

983   RIX, FELICE (1893–1967)
Austrian designer of textiles and fashion who worked in Japan from 1935; sister of Kitty Rix (q.v.).

Other Sources

Byars, Mel. *The Design Encyclopedia.* London: Lawrence King, 1994.

984   RIX, KITTY (Alt. KATHARINA RIX-TICHAK) (1901–)
Austrian designer of ceramics, textiles and fashion; sister of Felice Rix.

See Ceramics section.

985   RUGGIERI, CINZIA (1945–)
Italian fashion and industrial designer.

Other Sources

Naylor, Colin, ed. *Contemporary Designers.* 2nd edition. Chicago and London: St. James Press, 1990. Contains a bibliography.

Steele, Valerie. *Women of Fashion.* New York: Rizzoli International, 1991. Contains a bibliography.

986   RYKIEL, SONIA (née FLIS) (1930–)
French fashion designer.

Publications

'*Et je la voudrai nue.*' Paris: Bernard Grasset, 1979. Autobiography.

Main Sources

Chapsall, Madeleine, Helene Cixious, and Sonia Rykiel. *Rykiel.* Paris: Editions Herscher, 1985, 215pp., illus. Text in French. Each of the authors contributes one chapter. Rykiel's own contribution is an autobiographical account.

Exhibitions

Correspondence vêtement revêtement. Paris: Union des Arts Décoratifs and Musée des Arts de la Mode, 1986, 72pp., illus.

Other Sources

Naylor, Colin, ed. *Contemporary Designers.* 2nd edition. Chicago and London: St. James Press, 1990. Contains a bibliography.

Steele, Valerie. *Women of Fashion.* New York: Rizzoli International, 1991. Contains a bibliography.

987 SCHIAPARELLI, ELSA LUISA MARIA (1890–1973)
 Italian-born fashion designer who lived in France from 1913.

Publications

Shocking Life. New York: Dutton, 1954. Autobiography.

Berard, Christian. *Shocking: Souvenirs d'Elsa Schiaparelli avec 7 dessins de Christian Berard.* Paris: Denöel, 1954, 253pp., illus. French edition of her autobiography.

Main Sources

White, Palmer. *Elsa Schiaparelli: Empress of Paris Fashion.* New York: Rizzoli, 1986, 224pp., illus.

Exhibitions

Hommage à Elsa Schiaparelli. Musée de la Mode et du Costume, Paris, 1984, 159pp., illus. Contains one essay in French and another in English by different authors. There are also interviews with those who knew Schiaparelli.

Dufresne, Jean-Luc, and Olivier Messac, eds. *Femmes créatrices des années vingt.* Granville: Musée Richard Anacréon, 1988. Wide-ranging catalogue with a short biographical account on each woman included.

Other Sources

Bertin, Celia. *Paris à la Mode: A Voyage of Discovery.* London: Gollancz Ltd., 1956.

Kennett, Frances. *Collector's Book of Twentieth Century Fashion.* London: Granada, 1983.

Robinson, Julian. *Fashion in the '30s.* London: Oresko, 1978.

Steele, Valerie. *Paris Fashion: A Cultural History.* New York and Oxford: Oxford University Press, 1988.

———. *Women of Fashion.* New York: Rizzoli International, 1991. Contains a bibliography.

988 SCHÖN, MILA
 Italian fashion designer.

Main Sources

Mulassano, Adriana. *The Who's Who of Italian Fashion*. Florence: Edizioni G. Spinelli & C., 1979.

Other Sources

Steele, Valerie. *Women of Fashion*. New York: Rizzoli International, 1991. Contains a bibliography.

989 STÜBCHEN-KIRCHNER, ELSE.
Austrian designer of textiles and fashion.

Other Sources

Fanelli, Giovanni, and Rosalia Fanelli. *Il tessuto art déco e anni trenta: disegno, moda, architettura*. Florence: Cantini, 1986.

990 SYBILLA (née SYBILLA SORONDO) (1963–)
Born in America to Argentinian-Polish parents, she is a fashion designer who works in Spain.

Other Sources

Dent-Coad, Emma. *Spanish Design and Architecture*. London: Studio Vista, 1990.
Steele, Valerie. *Women of Fashion*. New York: Rizzoli International, 1991. Contains a bibliography.

991 THOMASS, CHANTAL (1947–)
French fashion designer.

Other Sources

Naylor, Colin, ed. *Contemporary Designers*. 2nd edition. Chicago and London: St. James Press, 1990. Contains a bibliography.
Steele, Valerie. *Women of Fashion*. New York: Rizzoli International, 1991. Contains a bibliography.

992 VIONNET, MADELEINE (1876–1975)
French fashion designer who opened her first fashion house in 1912–14 and then again from 1919.

Main Sources

Chapsall, Madeleine. *La Chair et la robe*. Paris: Fayard, 1989, 377pp., illus. Text in French.
Demornex, Jacqueline. *Madeleine Vionnet (1876–1975)*. Paris: Editions du Regard, 1990, 305pp., mainly illus. English edition, London: Thames and Hudson,

1991. A relatively small amount of text but drawn from primary sources. Contains many photographs of Vionnet and her collections.

Frechet, Andre. "Une grande maison de couture moderne." *Mobilier et Décoration* 5 (1923): 3–11. Describes the work of Georges de Feure in the interior design of Vionnet's *maison de couture*, of which there are several photographs.

Exhibitions

Cinquantenaire de l'Exposition de 1925. Paris: Musée des Arts Décoratifs, 1976.

Dufresne, Jean-Luc, and Olivier Messac, eds. *Femmes créatrices des années vingt.* Granville: Musée Richard Anacréon, 1988. Wide-ranging catalogue with a short biographical account on each woman included.

Madeleine Vionnet: l'art de la couture, 1876–1975. Centre de la Vieille Charité, Marseille, 1991, 75pp., illus. Text in French. Consists of nineteen short essays by different authors on aspects of Vionnet's work.

Other Sources

Bertin, Celia. *Paris à la Mode: A Voyage of Discovery.* London: Gollancz Ltd., 1956.

Kennett, Frances. *Collector's Book of Twentieth Century Fashion.* London: Granada, 1983.

Naylor, Colin, ed. *Contemporary Designers.* 2nd edition. Chicago and London: St. James Press, 1990. Contains a bibliography.

Robinson, Julian. *Fashion in the '30s.* London: Oresko, 1978.

Steele, Valerie. *Paris Fashion: A Cultural History.* New York and Oxford: Oxford University Press, 1988.

———. *Women of Fashion.* New York: Rizzoli International, 1991. Contains a bibliography.

993   WESTWOOD, VIVIENNE
   English fashion designer who works in London and Paris known for her controversial designs.

Other Sources

Steele, Valerie. *Women of Fashion.* New York: Rizzoli International, 1991. Contains a bibliography.

994   WILLE, FIA (1868–1920)
   German of interiors and fashion.

Exhibitions

Oedekoven-Gerischer, Angela, et al., eds. *Frauen im Design: Berufsbilder und Lebenswege seit 1900. Women in Design: Careers and Life Histories since 1900.* Stuttgart: Design Center, 1989.

Garden Design

995 DESMOND, RAY. *Dictionary of British and Irish Botanists and Horticulturalists including Plant Collectors, Flower Painters and Garden Designers.* 2nd rev. ed. London: Taylor and Francis with the Natural History Museum, 1994, 825pp., illus.

This very comprehensive reference work is enhanced by indices by profession of the categories mentioned in the title. These indices are in turn organised into chronological order. The majority of people included are British but those born abroad who worked in Britain or Ireland are also included. Most women occur in the category of flower painting but are also represented under garden designers.

996 HADFIELD, MILES, ROBERT HARLING, and LEONIE HIGHTON. *British Gardeners: A Biographical Dictionary.* London: Zwemmer in association with Condé Nast Publications Ltd., 1980, 320pp., illus.

The key figures are all included in this text, in which the entries vary in length. In addition there are also some lesser known women garden designers, including a number from the nineteenth century.

997 JELLICOE, GEOFFREY, and SUSAN. *Oxford Companion to Gardens.* Oxford & New York: Oxford University Press, 1986, 635pp., illus.

Consists of alphabetically arranged entries on gardens, styles, landscape architects, writers on gardens and designers. Because of the international range of the book, only the better known women landscape architects (e.g., Sylvia Crowe, Brenda Colvin) and designers are included although an interesting entry on Maria Shephard Parpagliolo is given.

OTHER PUBLICATIONS

998   BROWN, JANE. *The English Garden in our Time from Gertrude Jekyll to Geoffrey Jellicoe.* Woodbridge: Antique Collectors' Club, 1986, 272pp., illus.

     In addition to Gertrude Jekyll, Vita Sackville-West, Frances Wolseley, Norah Lindsay and Marjorie Fish (qq.v.) are discussed.

999   BROWN, JANE. *Eminent Gardeners: Some People of Influence and Their Gardens, 1880–1980.* London: Viking, 1990, 183pp., illus.

     Consists of seven chapters about individuals, families or small groups who contributed to garden design and history in Britain from 1880. The women included are Frances Wolseley (q.v.), Norah Lindsay (q.v.), Gertrude Cleveland Waterbury, Vita Sackville-West (q.v.), Anne Jemima Clough (q.v.), Blanche Clough, Nora Sidgwick and Gertrude Jekyll (q.v.).

1000 CRITCHLEY, LAURIE (ED.). *A Glimpse of Green: Women Writing on Gardens.* London: Women's Press, 1996, 144pp.

     An anthology of women writing on various aspects of gardens. Some of them are writers who are keen amateur gardeners or who happen to have written about a garden while others, a minority, are garden designers who also write. Short biographies of the contributors are included.

1001 ELLIOTT, BRENT. *Victorian Gardens.* 2nd ed. London: Batsford, 1990, 285pp., illus.

     A thorough examination of the development of British gardens in the nineteenth century. A number of women garden designers and writers are included, such as Jane Loudon, Gertrude Jekyll, Ellen Willmott (qq.v.) and Eleanour Rohde.

1002 KELLAWAY, DEBORAH (ED.). *The Virago Book of Women Gardeners.* London: Virago, 1995, 274pp., illus.

     An anthology from the writings of women gardeners, garden designers, garden writers, horticulturalists, poets and authors. They are mainly concerned with British gardens and gardening in the nineteenth and twentieth centuries.

1003 MASSINGHAM, BETTY. "Three famous women gardeners." *Country Life* 15 (September 1960): 540–42.

     Discusses the work of Gertrude Jekyll, Maria Thérèse Earle and Ellen Willmott (qq.v.).

1004 PENN, HELEN. *An Englishwoman's Garden.* London: BBC Books, 1993, 224pp., illus.

     A historical survey of the activities of women gardeners, garden designers and some flower painters from the eighteenth century but with the emphasis on the period from 1850.

INDIVIDUALS

1005 CLOUGH, ANNE JEMIMA (1820–1892)
English philanthopist who was the first Principal of Newnham College, Cambridge, and designer of its gardens.

Other Sources

Brown, Jane. *Eminent Gardeners. Some People of Influence and Their Gardens, 1880–1980.* London: Viking, 1990.

1006 COLVIN, BRENDA (1897–1981)
English garden designer.

Main Sources

Jellicoe, Geoffrey, and Susan. *Oxford Companion to Gardens.* Oxford and New York: Oxford University Press, 1986.

1007 CONNOLLY, SYBIL
Irish designer of textiles and interiors.

Publications

Connolly, Sybil, and Helen Dillon, eds. *In an Irish Garden,* London: Weidenfeld and Nicolson, 1986, 160pp., illus. A series of short chapters by the creator-owners of gardens in Ireland, two of which are the editors.

1008 EARLE, THERESA (née MARIA THERESA VILLIERS) (1836–1925)
English gardener, designer and writer.

Publications

Pot-Pourri from a Surrey Garden. London: Smith, Elder & Co., 1897, 381pp., illus.
More Pot-Pourri. London: Smith, Elder & Co., 1899, 453pp., illus.
Memoirs and Memories. London: Smith, Elder & Co., 1911, 388pp., illus.
A Third Pot-Pourri. London: Smith, Elder & Co., 1903, 440pp., illus.
Pot-Pourri Mixed by Two. London, 1914.

Main Sources

Massingham, Betty. "Three Famous Women Gardeners." *Country Life* 15 (September 1960): 540–542.

Other Sources

Brown, Jane. *Eminent Gardeners. Some People of Influence and Their Gardens, 1880–1980.* London: Viking, 1990.

Elliott, Brent. *Victorian Gardens.* London: Batsford, 1990.

Kellaway, Deborah. *The Virago Book of Women Gardeners.* London: Virago, 1995.

MacLeod, Dawn. *Down-to-Earth Women: Those Who Care for the Soil.* Edinburgh: William Blackwood, 1982.

Penn, Helen. *An Englishwoman's Garden.* London: BBC Books, 1993.

1009 FISH, MARGERY (1892–1969)
English garden designer and plantswoman.

Publications

We Made a Garden. London: Collingridge, 1956, 120pp., illus. 2nd ed. London: Faber & Faber, 1984.

An All the Year Garden. London: Collingridge and Florida: Transatlantic Arts, 1958, 144pp., illus.

Cottage Garden Flowers. London: Collingridge, 1961, 127pp., illus.

Ground Cover Plants. London: Collingridge, 1963, 144pp., illus.

Gardening in the Shade. London: Collingridge, 1964, 160pp., illus.

A Flower for Every Day. London: Studio Vista, 1965, 208pp., illus.

Carefree Gardening. London: Collingridge, 1966, 160pp., illus.

Other Sources

Kellaway, Deborah. *The Virago Book of Women Gardeners.* London: Virago, 1995.

MacLeod, Dawn. *Down-to-Earth Women: Those Who Care for the Soil.* Edinburgh: William Blackwood, 1982.

Penn, Helen. *An Englishwoman's Garden.* London: BBC Books, 1993.

1010 HAMILTON, CAROLINE (1780–?)
Irish garden designer and writer.

Publications

Hamilton, Caroline. *Garden Notebook.* Unpublished MS., National Library of Ireland.

Other Sources

Bell, Eva Mary. *The Hamwood Papers of the Ladies of Llangollen and Caroline Hamilton.* London: Macmillan, 1930, 417pp.

MacLeod, Dawn. *Down-to-Earth Women: Those Who Care for the Soil.* Edinburgh: William Blackwood, 1982.

1011 HOBHOUSE, PENELOPE
English garden designer.

Publications

Gertrude Jekyll on gardening. London: Collins and the National Trust, 1983.
Colour in your garden. London: Collins, 1985, 240pp., illus.
Private gardens of England. London: Weidenfeld and Nicolson, 1986, 223pp., illus.
Hobhouse Penelope, and Christopher Wood. *Painted Gardens: English Watercolours 1850–1914.* New York, Atheneum, 1988, illus.
Plants in Garden History. London: Pavilion, 1992, 336pp., illus.

Other Sources

Kellaway, Deborah. *The Virago Book of Women Gardeners.* London: Virago, 1995.
Penn, Helen. *An Englishwoman's Garden.* London: BBC Books, 1993.

1012 JEKYLL, GERTRUDE (1843–1932)
English garden designer.

Publications

Wood and garden: Notes and thoughts, practical and critical, of a working amateur. London: Longmans, Green and Co., 1899, 286pp., illus.
Home and Garden: Notes and thoughts, practical and critical, by a worker in both. London: Longmans, Green and Co., 1900, 301pp., 53 illus.
Lilies for English Gardens: A guide for amateurs. Compiled from information published lately in 'The Garden,' with the addition of some original chapters. London: The Country Life Library, 1901, 72pp.
Wall and water gardens. London: The Country Life Library, 1901, 177pp., illus.
Jekyll, Gertrude, and Edward Mawley. *Roses for English gardens.* London: The Country Life Library, 1902, 166pp., illus.
Old West Surrey: Some notes and memories. London: Longmans, Green and Co., 1904, 320pp., 330 illus.
Some English gardens. After drawings by George Elgood. Notes by G. Jekyll. London: Longmans, Green and Co., 1904, 131pp., illus.
Colour in the flower garden. London: The Country Life Library, 1908, 148pp., illus. Subsequent editions entitled *Colour schemes for the flower garden.*
Children and gardens. London: The Country Life Library, 1908, 110pp., 106 illus.
Jekyll, Gertrude, and Lawrence Weaver. *Gardens for small country houses.* London: Country Life, 1912, 260pp.
Annuals and biennials: The best annual and biennial plants and their uses in the garden, with cultural notes by E.H. Jenkins. London: Country Life, 1916, xiv + 174pp.
Garden ornament. London: Country Life, 1918, xii + 460 pp.
Old English household life: Some accounts of cottage objects and country folk. (Revised and rewritten from *Old West Surrey*.) London: Batsford Ltd., 1925, xix + 222pp.

Main Sources

"A famous Surrey garden: Miss Jekyll at home." *The Surrey Times,* Summer number, 1899.

"Munstead House and its mistress." *Country Life,* Christmas number, 1900.

Barron, Leonard. "The passing of Gertrude Jekyll." *American Rose Annual,* 1933.

Brown, Jane. *Miss Gertrude Jekyll, 1843–1932, Gardener.* London: Architectural Association, 1981.

———. *Gardens of a golden afternoon. The story of a partnership: Edwin Lutyens and Gertrude Jekyll.* London: Viking, 1992.

Cowley, Herbert. "Gertrude Jekyll V.M.H." *Gardening Illustrated* (17 December 1932).

Cran, Marion. *I know a garden.* London: Jenkins, 1933,

Hutchinson, Martha B. "An appreciation of Miss Jekyll." *Bulletin of the Garden Club of America* (March 1933).

Jekyll, Francis. *Gertrude Jekyll: A Memoir.* London: Jonathan Cape, 1934, 248pp., illus. Foreword by Sir Edwin Lutyens and introduction by Agnes Jekyll [sister-in-law]. Francis Jekyll was her nephew. Contains a list of her publications.

King, Frances. "Gertrude Jekyll." *National Horticultural Magazine* [Baltimore, Md.] (April 1933).

Massingham, Betty. "Three Famous Women Gardeners." *Country Life* 15 (September 1960): 540–42.

Massingham, Betty. *Miss Jekyll: Portrait of a Great Gardener.* London: Country Life, 1966.

———. *Gertrude Jekyll. An illustrated life of Gertrude Jekyll. 1843–1932.* Lifelines no. 37. Aylesbury: Shire Publications, 1975, 48pp., illus. A short biographical account written in an accessible style.

Smith, Logan Pearsall. "Gertrude Jekyll." *Life and Letters,* June 1933.

Tooley, Michael, ed. *Gertrude Jekyll: Artist, gardener, craftswoman.* Witton-le Wear: Michaelmas Books, 1984. Contains a bibliography compiled by the editor and Margaret Hastings of all Jekyll's published works.

Tankard, Judith, and Van Valkenberg, Michael. *A vision of garden and wood.* London: John Murray and New York: Sagapress, 1989. Contains some photographs from Jekyll's collection with commentary and essays.

Tipping, H. Avray. "English gardens: Munstead Wood." *Country Life,* 1925.

1013 LINDSAY, NORAH (1876–1948)
    English garden designer.

Main Sources

Jellicoe, Geoffrey, and Susan. *Oxford Companion to Gardens.* Oxford and New York: Oxford University Press, 1986.

Other Sources

Brown, Jane. *Eminent Gardeners. Some People of Influence and Their Gardens, 1880–1980*. London: Viking, 1990.

Kellaway, Deborah. *The Virago Book of Women Gardeners*. London: Virago, 1995.

MacLeod, Dawn. *Down-to-Earth Women: Those Who Care for the Soil*. Edinburgh: William Blackwood, 1982.

Penn, Helen. *An Englishwoman's Garden*. London: BBC Books, 1993.

1014 LOUDON, JANE (née WEBB) (1807–1858)
English writer and garden designer.

Publications

Practical Instructions in Gardening for Ladies. London: John Murray, 1840, 343pp., illus.

Ladies' Companion to the Flower Garden. London: W. Smith, 1841, 316pp., illus.

Botany for Ladies. London, 1842.

The Ladies' Flower Garden of Ornamental Perennials. London: W. Smith, 1843.

The Lady's Country Companion. London, 1845.

British Wild Flowers. London, 1846

The Amateur Gardener's Calendar. London: 1846

Most of these and her other books went through several editions. She also edited for republication many books by her husband, John Claudius Loudon, including:

Loudon, John. *An Encyclopedia of Gardening. Improved by Mrs Loudon*. London: Longman, Brown, Green and Longmans, 1850.

————. *An Encyclopedia of Plants. Edited by Mrs Loudon*. London: Longman, Brown, Green and Longmans, 1855, 1574pp.

Main Sources

Howe, Bea. *Lady With Green Fingers. The Life of Jane Loudon*. London: Country Life, 1961, 184pp. A biographical account which provides the main source for Loudon.

Other Sources

Elliott, Brent. *Victorian Gardens*. London: Batsford, 1990.

Kellaway, Deborah. *The Virago Book of Women Gardeners*. London: Virago, 1995.

MacLeod, Dawn. *Down-to-Earth Women: Those Who Care for the Soil*. Edinburgh: William Blackwood, 1982.

1015 MARKIEWICZ, MAEVE DE
Irish garden designer.

Other Sources

Haverty, A. *Constance Markiewicz.* London: Pandora Press, 1988. Like all the books in this section this is primarily about her mother, a political activist, with Maeve being mentioned as a child and young woman.

Marecco, A. *The Rebel Countess.* London: Weidenfeld and Nicolson, 1967.

Norman, D. *Terrible Beauty.* London: Poolbeg Press, 1988.

1016 PARPAGLIOLO, MARIA SHEPHARD (?–1974)
English garden designer.

Main Sources

Jellicoe, Geoffrey, and Susan. *Oxford Companion to Gardens.* Oxford and New York: Oxford University Press, 1986.

1017 RUYS, MIEN (1905–)
Dutch garden designer.

Main Sources

Pearson, Dan. "Dutch Treat." *Style,* 5 March 1995, 34. A conversation with the 90-year-old designer.

1018 SACKVILLE-WEST, VITA
English writer and garden designer.

Publications

Only those relevant to garden design have been included.

Country Notes. 2nd ed. London: Michael Joseph, 1940, 219pp., illus.

English Country Houses. Britain in Pictures. London: Collins, 1944, 46pp., illus.

The Garden. London: Michael Joseph, 1946, 135pp.

In Your Garden. London: Michael Joseph, 1951, 231pp., illus. Reprint of articles for *The Observer.*

In Your Garden Again. London: Michael Joseph, 195, 178pp., illus.

Even More for your Garden. London: Michael Joseph, 19, 199pp., 7 illus. Collection of articles written for *The Observer.*

A Joy of Gardening. New York: Dolphin, 1958, 199pp. A selection for Americans by Hermine [*sic*] Popper.

'The Land' and 'The Garden.' New edition. London: Webb & Bower, Michael Joseph, 1989, 190pp., illus. New illustrated edition of her two poems which were first published in 1927 and 1946 respectively.

Main Sources

Brown, Jane. *Vita's Other World.* London: Viking, 1985.
―――. *Sissinghurst: Portrait of a Garden.* London: Weidenfeld & Nicolson, in association with The National Trust, 1990, 136pp., illus.
Scott-James, Anne. *Sissinghurst: The Making of a Garden.* London: Michael Joseph, 1975, 160pp., illus.

Other Sources

Kellaway, Deborah. *The Virago Book of Women Gardeners.* London: Virago, 1995.
MacLeod, Dawn. *Down-to-Earth Women: Those Who Care for the Soil.* Edinburgh: William Blackwood, 1982.
Penn, Helen. *An Englishwoman's Garden.* London: BBC Books, 1993.

1019 SAWYER, MAIRI (née MacKENZIE; alt. HANBURY) (c. 1875–1953)
    Scottish gardener and designer of Inverewe Gardens.

Other Sources

MacLeod, Dawn. *Down-to-Earth Women: Those Who Care for the Soil.* Edinburgh: William Blackwood, 1982.

1020 VEREY, ROSEMARY
    English garden designer.

Publications

The Herb Growing Book. London: 1980, 41pp., illus.
Verey, Rosemary, and Alvide Lees-Milne, eds. *The Englishwoman's Garden.* London: Chatto & Windus, 1980, 156pp., illus.
The Scented Garden. London: Joseph, 1981, 168pp., illus.
The Englishman's Garden. London: Allen Lane, 1982.
Classic Garden Design: How to Adapt and Recreate Garden Features of the Past. Harmondsworth: Viking Press, 1984, 160pp., illus.
Verey, Rosemary, and Ellen Samuels. *The American Woman's Garden.* Boston: Little, Brown & Co., 1984, 191pp., illus.
Verey, Rosemary, and Alvide Lees-Milne. *The New Englishwoman's Garden.* London: Chatto & Windus, 1987, 151pp., illus.
The Garden in Winter. London: Frances Lincoln, 1988, 168pp., illus.
The Flower Arranger's Garden. London: Conran Octopus, 1989.
Verey, Rosemary, and Katherine Lambert. *The American Man's Garden.* Boston: Little, Brown & Co., Bullfinch Press, 1990, 166pp., illus.
Good Planting. London: Frances Lincoln, 1990, 168pp., illus.
A Countrywoman's Notes. Revised ed. London: Frances Lincoln, 1991. Articles reprinted from *Country Life* between 1979 and 1987, selected and edited by Eileen Stamers-Smith.

The Garden Gate. The Library of Garden Detail. London: Pavilion Books., 1991, 64pp., illus.

A Gardener's Book of Days. London: Frances Lincoln, 1992, 110pp., illus.

Rosemary Verey's Garden Plants. London: Frances Lincoln, 1993, 144pp., illus. Describes the plants she has used to create a variety of commissioned gardens.

Rosemary Verey's Garden Plans. Special photography by Andrew Lawson, watercolours by Jean Sturgis. London: Frances Lincoln, 1993, 144pp., illus.

Secret Gardens Revealed by their Owners. London: Ebury Press, 1994, 207pp., illus.

Main Sources

Berridge, Vanessa. "A Countrywoman's View." *The Lady,* 24–30 May 1994, 32–33.

Other Sources

Kellaway, Deborah. *The Virago Book of Women Gardeners.* London: Virago, 1995.

Penn, Helen. *An Englishwoman's Garden.* London: BBC Books, 1993.

1021 WILLMOTT, ELLEN ANN (1858–1934)
       English garden designer and plantswoman.

Publications

Warley Garden in Spring and Summer. London: Bernard Quaritch, 1909.
The Genus Rosa. 2 vols. London: John Murray, 1910, 551 pp., illus.

Main Sources

Jellicoe, Geoffrey, and Susan. *Oxford Companion to Gardens.* Oxford and New York: Oxford University Press, 1986.

Massingham, Betty. "Three Famous Women Gardeners." *Country Life* 15 (September 1960): 540–542.

Other Sources

Brown, Jane. *Eminent Gardeners. Some People of Influence and Their Gardens, 1880–1980.* London: Viking, 1990.

Elliott, Brent. *Victorian Gardens.* London: Batsford, 1990.

Kellaway, Deborah. *The Virago Book of Women Gardeners.* London: Virago, 1995.

MacLeod, Dawn. *Down-to-Earth Women: Those Who Care for the Soil.* Edinburgh: William Blackwood, 1982.

Penn, Helen. *An Englishwoman's Garden.* London: BBC Books, 1993.

1022 WOLSELEY, FRANCES GARNETT (VISCOUNTESS) (1872–1936)
English garden designer.

Publications

Gardening for women. London: Cassell, 1908, 289pp., illus.

Women and the land. London: Chatto and Windus, 1916, 222pp., illus.

In a College garden. London: John Murray, 1916, 255pp., illus. An account of the making of Glynde College for Lady Gardeners which she founded to teach women horticulture.

Gardens: Their form and design. London: Edward Arnold, 1919, 284pp., illus.

The Countryman's Log Book. London: Warner and Jonathan Cape, 1921, 325pp., illus.

Some of the smaller manor houses of Sussex. London: Medici Society, 1925.

Main Sources

Tipping, H. Avray. "King Edward VII Sanitorium." *Country Life* 26 (20 November 1909): 701. Describes the garden created by Wolseley's pupils at Glynde College in 1906–1907.

Other Sources

Brown, Jane. *Eminent Gardeners. Some People of Influence and Their Gardens, 1880–1980.* London: Viking, 1990.

Kellaway, Deborah. *The Virago Book of Women Gardeners.* London: Virago, 1995.

MacLeod, Dawn. *Down-to-Earth Women: Those Who Care for the Soil.* Edinburgh: William Blackwood, 1982.

Penn, Helen. *An Englishwoman's Garden.* London: BBC Books, 1993.

Glass

1023 BLOCH-DERMANT, JANINE. *Le verre en France: les années 80*. Paris: Les Editions des Amateurs, n.d. [c. 1990], 158pp., illus.

Text in French. Alphabetical survey of seventy-four active glass artists, of whom eleven are women: Hélène Chantemerle, Elizabeth Cibot, Nicole Cipres, Jutta Cuny, Minica Damian-Eyrignoux, Ingrid Maillot, Isabelle and Véronique Monod, Josette Rispal, Claire de Rougemeont, Catherine Zoritchak. The length of the entries varies but all contain informative biographical material together with details of the work of each artist.

1024 GROVER, LEE, and RAY. *Contemporary Art Glass*. New York: Crown Publishers, 1975, 208pp., many illus.

A reference book that organises individuals and manufacturers into an alphabetical sequence within countries. For each individual designer a brief biographical outline is given, together with an description of the type of work and an illustration. Thirteen European women are included: for the Czech Republic and Slovakia, Jaroslava Brychtová-Lipenska, Miluse Kytková-Roubicková; for Britain, Dillon Clarke and Pauline Solven; for Finland, Nanny Still and Helen Tynell; the Norwegians Gro Sommerfelt, Benny Motzfeldt and the Swedes Monica Backstrom, Mona Morales-Schildt, Ann Warff, Ingeborg Lundin and Eva Englund.

1025 *Who's Who in Contemporary Glass Art: A Comprehensive World Guide to Glass Artists—Craftsmen—Designers*. Munich: Waldrich Verlag, 1993, 650pp.

An alphabetical sequence in which each person is given a biographical outline, information on their working arrangements (e.g., own workshop, for manufacturer), list of collections where their work is found, exhibitions, symposia to which they have contributed and a bibliography. The entries vary in length. An invaluable source for information on women.

233

OTHER SOURCES

1026 *II Rocník trienále rezaného skla [Second glass triennial]*. Brno: Moravská
Galerie, 1968, 14pp. plus 71pp. illus.

Text in Czech with summary in English. Contemporary glass exhibited
by twenty-two artists. Six of these are women: Jitka Forejtová-Pelikánová,
Marie Glückhaufová, Erika Hellerová, Antonie Jankovcová-Skoková, Jirina
Pastrnková and Ludvika Smrčková.

1027 *3 trienále rezaneho skla [3rd triennial of cut glass]*. Brno: Moravská
Galerie, 1971, 40pp., illus.

Text in Czech with a summary in English. The introduction is followed
by the list of exhibits, which includes very brief outline biographies of the
exhibitors. Ten women designers are included, the oldest born in 1903 and
the youngest in 1947.

1028 *150 Years of Danish Glass: Kastrup and Holmegaard Glassworks*.
Copenhagen: Kunstindustrimuseet, 1981, n.p., mainly illus.

Survey of glass production at the two glassworks from the 1830s. The
first designers were used in the early twentieth century, but women are not
mentioned until the 1970s, when Christel Holmgren was employed and a
number of freelance designers, three of whom were women, were involved.
There is no specific information about individuals.

1029 ADLEROVÁ, ALENA. "Les artistes tchécoslovaques au Deuxième Prix de
Coburg." *Revue de Verre* 41, no. 1 (1986): 18–23.

Text in French. An account of the organisation of this prestigious competition for contemporary studio glass where, in 1985, a considerable number
of prizewinners were from Czechoslovakia, of whom several were women.

1030 ADLEROVÁ, ALENA. "Le verre moderne." *Revue du verre* 36, no. 9
(1981): 7–11.

Text in French. Review of the exhibition in Paris of Czech Glass between
1350 and 1980, in which the modern works are discussed in particular detail.

1031 ADLEROVÁ, ALENA. *Böhmisches Glas der Gegenwart*. Hamburg:
Museum für Kunst und Gewerbe, 1973, 143pp., illus.

Text in German. An introductory essay on contemporary Bohemian glass
is followed by an alphabetical listing of fifty artists from the former
Czechoslovakia, of whom ten are women: Kapka Tousková, Antonie
Jankovcová, Jirina Jechcová, Jaroslava Brychtová, Vera Lišková, Miluse
Roubicková, Eliska Rozatová, Ludvika Smrčková, Dana Vachtová and Jirina
Zertová. For each there is a photograph of the artist and at least one photo-
graph of their work, an outline biography and a few lines about the charac-
teristics of their glass production.

1032 ARWAS, VICTOR. *Glass: Art Nouveau to Art Déco*. London: Academy Editions, 1977, 256pp., illus.

An introduction to the subject, including technical developments, is followed by chapters on the principal designers and producers. Women feature as associates to the masters but overall a useful number are identified.

1033 BALDOUY-MATERNATI, DANIELLE. *La verrerie européene des années 50*. Marseille: Musées de Marseille, in association with Michel Aveline, 1988, 159pp., illus.

Text in French. After an introductory essay there are sections on the work of individuals and factories from each of nine European countries. In all, six women working in Europe feature among the fifty-five designers: Saraa Hopea-Untracht, Gunnel Nyman and Nanny Still from Finland, Irene Stephens from Britain, the Italian Serena del Maschio and Ingeborg Lundin from Sweden.

1034 BEARD, GEOFFREY. *International Modern Glass*. London: Barrie and Jenkins, 1976, 264pp., many illus.

Begins with a brief authoritative review of modern glass from 1870 to 1974. This is followed by a select list of manufacturers, including the names of their chief designers, and bibliographical references. The final section is a list of approximately three hundred designers, among whom are thirty-nine women, each with a biographical outline and a minority with details of exhibitions and bibliography.

1035 BETTAGNO, ALESSANDRO (ED.). *Gli artisti di Veneni: per una storia del vetro d'arte veneziano*. Cataloghi di Mostre 31. Milan: Electa and Fondazione Giorgio Cini, Venice, 1996, 234pp., illus.

Text in Italian. Four essays on the development of glass design in Venice precede the catalogue. Gae Aulenti and Tyra Lundgren are included.

1036 BLOCH-DERMANT, JANINE. *Le Verre en France d'Emile Gallé à nos jours*. Paris: Editions de l'Amateur, 1983, 312pp., illus.

While the principal figures, particularly in the earlier years discussed, are men, a number of women are included. Marie-Claude Lalique is the only woman featured in the chapter on *les verreries artistiques;* Yvonne Brunet (jewellery), Marcelle Wahl, a doctor who decorated and enamelled blue and grey vases, and Colette Guedin, who was head of the Primavera workshop, are included among the glassmakers and decorators. In the section on contemporary glass artists, Isabelle and Veronique Monod, Catherine Zoritchak and Jutta Cuny are discussed (qq.v.).

1037 *British Studio Glass*. Sunderland: Sunderland Arts Centre, 1983, 74pp., illus.

Short introductory essays deal with developments in British studio glass, the problems of setting up as an independent glass artist (by Alison Kinnaird) and the setting up of courses in studio glass. Of the twenty-five exhibitors, twelve are women.

1038 BROOS, KEES. *Beelden in Glas; Glass Sculpture.* Utrecht: Stichting Glas, 1986, 120pp., illus.

Text in Dutch and English. Essays on the history of glass-making at Leerdam and the use of glass in modern art precede biographical outlines of the twenty artists in the exhibition. Only two are women: Marijke de Goey and Mieke Groot.

1039 BÜCHNER, THOMAS, and WILLIAM WARMUS. *Czechoslovakian diary: 1980. 23 Glassmakers.* Corning, New York: Corning Museum of Glass, 1980, 16pp., illus.

After a short introduction there are a few paragraphs on each of the glass-makers. There are several husband and wife partnerships included, and over-all there are seven women.

1040 CARTERON, PHILIPPE (ED.). *Ceci n'est plus du verre.* Paris: Editions vers les Arts, 1994, 270pp., mainly illus.

Text in French with an English summary. A series of critical essays on a number of glass designers whose work is judged to be on the boundaries of previous creations in the medium. Three women are included: Liane Allibert, Marisa Begou and Isabelle Monod.

1041 CHAVANCE, RENE. *La céramique et la verrerie. L'art français depuis vingt ans.* Paris: Les Editions Rieder, 1928, 127pp., illus.

Text in French. Divided into two sections, each deals in turn with devel-opments from c. 1900 to 1925 in ceramics and glass. More women are men-tioned in the former section, particularly in connection with the production at Sèvres. Little information about individuals is given.

1042 *Contemporary British Glass.* London: Crafts Council, 1993, 103pp., illus.

Consists of a short history of glass in Britain and an outline of the growth in glass courses in British higher education. There are also interviews with five glassmakers, three of whom are women, and a review of the state of British glass in the 1990s. In the catalogue section itself, biographical out-lines are provided and the exhibitors include a majority of women.

1043 *Contemporary Crystal and Glass Sculptures from the Countries of the European Community.* Brussels, 293pp., illus.

Organised by country, the number of exhibitors in each varies from one to eighteen. Several women are included.

1044 COOK, JOHN. "Czech Glass." *Crafts* 8 (1974): 28–29.

An account of visits to the studios of several glass designers.

1045 *Czechoslovakian Glass, 1350–1980*. Corning, New York, and Museum of Decorative Arts, Prague: Corning Museum of Glass, 1981, 176pp., 144 illus.

A historical survey of the subject is followed by a catalogue of the items exhibited and brief biographies of the artists, eleven of whom are women.

1046 *Dansk Glas '94*. Ebeltoft: Glasmuseum, 1994, 97pp., illus.

Text in Danish and English. After a short introduction, there is one page devoted to each exhibitor. This includes a biographical outline. More than half the exhibitors are women, many of them young. Photographs but no dates of birth are given.

1047 DAWSON, JACK. *Finnish Post-War Glass (1945–1996)*. Sunderland: Reg Vardy Gallery at the University of Sunderland, 1996, 118pp., illus.

Analyses the development of Finnish glass in its political and socio-economic context from the eighteenth century, but with particular emphasis on the last hundred years. Some ten women designers are included.

1048 DODSWORTH, ROGER (ED.). *British glass between the wars*. Kingswinford: Broadfield House Glass Museum, 1987, 115pp., illus.

The essays and the catalogue entries are organised around the chief figures of the period. Only one of these is a woman: Elizabeth Graydon Stannus, an Irish antique dealer who set up the Gray-Stan glassmaking studio in Battersea, London. There are references to other women, both as glass designer/makers—Anna Fogelberg and Moira Forsyth—and as artists who designed for glassware, including Dod Procter and Laura Knight.

1049 DORMER, PETER. "Review of 'British Artists in Glass,' 'German Glass Today' and 'Glass of '83.'" *Crafts* 66 (1984): 49–50.

The author points out the lack of ideas present in glassworks in comparison with a sculpture exhibition showing concurrently at the Hayward Gallery, London.

1050 *Glass 1959: A special exhibition of international contemporary glass*. Corning, New York: Corning Museum of Glass, 1959, 329pp., 292 illus.

Organised in alphabetical order of country, the choice of work was made by selection committee. Each object is illustrated and details of the manufacturer, designer and relevant literature are given. Twenty-four women are included, the largest numbers being from Czechoslovakia (nine) and Sweden (five).

1051 *Glaskunst in der DDR*. Leipzig: Städtisches Museum des Kunsthandwerks, 1977, n.p., 44 illus.

Text in German. A short essay is followed by information about the exhibitors. They are presented in alphabetical order, with an outline biography and a paragraph on their work. Four of the sixteen participants are women: Ilse Decho, Irmgard Kotte-Weidaner, Ulrike Oelzner and Ilse Scharge-Nebel.

1052 *Joseph Hoffmann and William Wagenfeld: Glaskunst der Moderne.* Munich: Klinkhardt & Bierman, 1992, 477pp., many illus.

Text in German. A thorough survey of German glass produced by the studios and pupils of Hoffmann and Wagenfeld in the early decades of the twentieth century. The main essay is followed by illustrations and biographies of the designers, of whom thirteen are women.

1053 HETTJEŠ, KAREL. *Glass in Czechoslovakia.* Translated by Georgina A. Evans. Prague: SNTL, 1958, 65pp., 88 illus.

A historical survey of Czech glass from its earliest times, but with almost half the text devoted to the twentieth century. Some women designers are included: Zdenka Braunerová, Marie Stabilková, M. Veliöková, Vera Lišková, Ludvika Smrčková, Jirina Zertová, Miluse Roubícková are all briefly mentioned. The emphasis is on the organisation and technical developments of the glass industry. Zdenka Braunerová is also active in painting and typesetting.

1054 KILPATRICK, PATRICIA. "The Guild of Glass Engravers' Jubilee Exhibition." *Crafts* 28 (1977): 48.

Review of this exhibition, which includes several women.

1055 KLEIN, DAN. *Glass: A Contemporary Art.* London: Collins, 1989, 224pp., illus.

An international survey of glass that is organised by geographical area. Chapters 3 to 5 cover Europe, and women are well represented throughout.

1056 LANGHAMER, ANTONIN. "Le verre Tchécoslovaque." *Revue du Verre* 30, no. 9 (1985): 3–45.

Text in French. Historical account of the development of glass in Czechoslovakia since 1945 that mentions the main women designers. There are many illustrations.

1057 LASSEN, ERIK. *Dansk Glas 1925–75.* Copenhagen: Busck, 1975, 64pp., illus.

Text in Danish. A survey of the principal glass factories in Denmark and their designers over fifty years. Extensive treatment is given to those included, but the total number is small. Four women feature: Orla Juul Nielsen, who designed for Holmegaard in the 1920s, Grethe Meyer, who worked for Kastrup, and Nanna Ditzel and Charlotte Rude, who worked for Odense.

1058 LAYTON, P. "Studio Glass." *Crafts* 7 (1974).

Exhibition review.

1059 LINDKVIST, LENNART (ED.). *Design in Sweden.* Stockholm: Swedish Institute, 1972, 144pp., illus.

After an overview of the situation for design in Sweden between 1917 and 1970, there are chapters on glass, ceramics, silver, textiles, furniture, industrial design, the design schools and the employment situation for designers. In most, the work of the principal designers is described, and many of these are women.

1060 LOTZ, FRANÇOIS. *Femmes peintres sous verre.* Pfaffenhoffen: Musée de l'Imagérie Peinte et Populaire Alsacienne, 1984, 16pp., illus.

Text in French. Painting under glass is a regionally important artistic practice in Alsace that involves considerable numbers of women. Some of these are well known as painters on other surfaces.

1061 LUTTEMAN, HELENA DAHLBACK (ED.). *Svenskt glas 1915–60.* Stockholm: National Museum, 1987, 75pp., illus.

Text in Swedish. After the introduction, the catalogue is organised around a number of manufacturers. Increasingly, designers were employed by them during the period, but by 1960 the number of women was still small. Those included here are Gerda Stromberg, Gunnar Nyland, Margaretha Schlyter-Stiernstedt and Greta Runeborg-Tell.

1062 *Metamorfózy skla [New tendencies in glass sculpture].* Brno: Moravská Galerie, 1973, n.p.

Text in Czech with summaries in German, English and Russian. A short essay precedes a list of exhibits, but a significant number of the exhibitors are women: Jitka Forejtová, Jaroslava Brychtová, Vera Lišková, Miluse Roubícková, Eliška Rozatová, Kapka Toušková, Dana Vachtová and Jirina Zertová.

1063 *Moderne Hollandsk Tekstilkunst og Glas.* Copenhagen: Kunstindustrimuseet, 1979.

Text in Danish, Dutch and English. Introductory essays for each of the sections on glass and textiles precede information on the individual exhibitors. Of the seven textile designers, six are women, while six of the fourteen glass designers are women.

1064 *Modernes Glas aus Amerika, Europa und Japan.* Frankfurt-am-Main: Museum fur Kunsthandwerk, 1976, 191pp., illus.

Text in German. Of the two sections to the catalogue, each organised by country and then by individual, the second has information about the designers. Women are not particularly well represented, with two for Germany, five for Britain, one for Norway and two each from Czechoslovakia and Sweden. None of the other sections on European countries include women.

1065 MZYKOVÁ, MARIE. "Les activités créatrices des jeunes verriers." *Revue du Verre* 40, no. 7 (1985): 22–24, illus.

Text in French. Discusses the work of three pupils of Stanislav Libensky in Prague, of whom one, Tatána Vojteková, is a woman.

1066 NEUWIRTH, WALTRAUD. *Bimini: Wiener Glaskunst des Art Deco.* Walter Neuwirth: Vienna, 1992, 470pp., illus.

Text in German with English summary. An extremely thorough treatment of this area of glass history consisting of small blown-glass decorative objects, some of which were vases and perfume bottles but most of which were figures, flowers, animals and birds. Neuwirth has located over six hundred pieces, of which some of the designers and makers were women. Biographical details of all the participants were obscure, and he notes the need for a monograph on the main woman designer, Marianne von Allesch. Other women designers were Suzanne Fontan and Dina Kuhn.

1067 *New Glass: A Worldwide Survey.* Corning, New York: Corning Museum of Glass, 1979, 288pp., illus.

Statements by members of the jury and an overview of developments in glass since the last similar exhibition at Corning in 1959 are followed by the catalogue. This consists of photographs of the works with captions. At the end of this section there are brief biographies of the designers. Twenty-six women are included.

1068 NILLONEN, KIRTTU. *Finnish Glass.* Helsinki: Tammi, 1966, 112pp., mainly illus.

After a brief history of glass in Finland, it describes the role of the designers in the three largest glassworks of the time. The works of designers are then illustrated. Included are Gunnel Nyman, Nanny Still and Helena Tynell (qq.v.).

1069 *Nordisk glass '88.* Trondheim with Nordisk Kulturformidling: Nordenfjeldske Kunstindustriemuseum, 1988, 19pp., illus.

An exhibition of seventeen glass artists from Scandinavia, of whom ten are women: Åsa Brandt, Ulla Forsell, Ulrica Vallien, Karen Klim and Kari Ullberg, all from Sweden, Pia Sverresdottir and Sigrum Olöf Einarsdottir from Iceland, Ulla-Mari Brantenberg from Norway, and Anja Kjoer and Tchai Munch of Denmark. The oldest of these was born in 1938, the youngest in 1956.

1070 OPIE, JENNIFER. *Scandinavia: Ceramics and Glass in the Twentieth Century.* London: Victoria and Albert Museum, 1989, 183pp., illus.

Based on the collection in the Victoria and Albert Museum, London, the book provides an analysis of the ceramics and glass produced in each of the four Scandinavian countries. For each country there is also a list of key exhibitions. Following this are biographies of the artists and designers whose work features in the collection, among whom are many women.

1071 PETROVÁ, SILVA. "Une exposition d'oeuvres contemporaines de verre tchèque en Finlande." *Revue du Verre* 44, no. 1 (1989): 11–13, illus.

Text in French. Revue of exhibition that included works by Stanislava Grebecniková, Ivana Houserová, Gizela Saboková, Ivana Solková and Dana Zanecniková.

1072 PETROVÁ, SYLVA. "Le verre et la céramique contemporains des collections du Musée des Arts décoratifs de Prague." *Revue du Verre* 42, no. 7 (1987): 14–19, mainly illus.

Text in French. A short account of the formation of the contemporary collection is followed by some illustrations of individual works. Women whose works are illustrated are Edita Devinská, Dagmar Hendrychová, Grethe Meyer (Denmark), Marta Taberyová, Dana Zanecniková and Jirina Zertová.

1073 PETROVÁ, SYLVIA, and OLIVIE, JEAN-LUC. *Verres de Bohème 1400–1989: chef d'oeuvres des musées de Tchécoslovaquie.* Paris: Musée des Arts Décoratifs; Flammarion, 1989; 239pp., illus.

Seven short essays provide a chronological introduction to the collection of glass in the Museum of Decorative Arts in Prague. Details follow of the items featured in the exhibition. Where these have been produced by an individual rather than a factory, there are biographical details. Sixteen women are included, the oldest, Marie Kirschner, born in 1852, and the youngest, Ivana Mašitová, born in 1961.

1074 PHILIPPE, JOSEPHE. *Sculpture contemporaine en cristal et en verre des pays de la Communauté Européenne.* Liege: Générale de Banque, 1992, 322pp., illus.

Text in French and English. Catalogue of an exhibition held on the formation of the single European market. After a history of exhibitions of glass that had a specifically European character, the catalogue is organised by country and then by individual. Each is given a biographical paragraph together with a succinct account of the development and characteristics of their work and illustrations of the works in the current exhibition.

1075 POLAK, ADA. *Modern glass.* Faber monographs on glass. London: Faber and Faber, 1962, 94pp., 96 illus.

Twenty-three women from nine countries are included in this short survey of studio and industrial glass in Europe from the turn of the century to the date of publication. For the majority there is a clear indication of their contribution to the field and illustrations of their work.

1076 PROCTOR, STEPHEN. "Masters of Czech Glass, New Czech Glass and Czechoslovakian Crafts." *Crafts Magazine* 66 (1984): 50.

Review of three exhibitions in which the work of several women is included. Specifically mentioned are Vera Lišková, Stanislava Grebeničková, Vladimira Klumparová and Blanka Adensamová.

1077 RABAN, JOSEF. *Le verre moderne de Bohème.* Prague: Artia Praga, 1963, 191pp., illus.

Text in French. An account of the development of modern Czech glass done in collaboration with the designer Smrčkovà. This is followed by biographies of the designers and details of 315 works. Fifteen women are included.

1078 RICKE, HELMUT. *Neues Glas in Europa: 50 Künstler—50 Konzepte; New Glass in Europe: 50 Artists—50 Concepts.* Dusseldorf: Kunstmuseum, 1990, 352pp., illus.

Text in German and English. Following introductory essays are two alphabetical sequences for the designers, one with a statement about their work and several colour illustrations and the second with biographical and detailed bibliographical lists. Of the fifty-one exhibitors, fourteen are European women. There is also a full bibliography of glass exhibitions.

1079 RICKE, HELMUT. *Neues Glas in Deutschland: New Glass in Germany.* Dusseldorf: Verlagsanstalt Handwerk and the Kunstmuseum, 1983, 311pp., illus.

Parallel text in German and English. After chapters on new glass in German, contemporary glass painting, the glass panel and glass art there are catalogue entries on fifty-nine artists, of whom thirteen are women. Each artist has a brief biographical outline. Included are: Birgit Becker, Ingrid Conrad-Lindig, Sigrid Glöggler, Tina Grunert-Bott, Ursula Huth, Ada Isensee, Rosemarie Lierke, Uta Majmuder, Isgarol Moje-Wohlgemuth, Angelika Müller, Freia Schulze, Eva Sperner and Karin Stöckle-Krumbein, all of whom were born between 1935 and 1955.

1080 RICKE, HELMUT, and GRONERT ULRICH. *Glass in Sweden, 1915–60.* Munich: Prestel in association with the Kunstmuseum, Dusseldorf, 1987, 309pp., illus.

Text in German. The organisation of this historical survey is based around the firms involved in glass production, but of the twenty-five designers listed at the end, only six are women: Monica Bratt, Eva Janke-Bjørk, Tyra Lundgren, Ingeborg Lundin, Mona Morales-Schmidt and Gerda Stromberg.

1081 *Ryté sklo: pruní prehlidka soudobé tvorby.* Brno: Moravská Galerie, 1965, n.p., illus.

Text in Czech. A short introductory essay is followed by a list of the exhibits of work in glass with minimal biographical information on the designers, among whom are six women: Jitka Forejtová-Pelikanová, Eliška Havlová, Erika Hellerová, Jaromira Lipská-Straková, Jirina Patrnková and Ludvika Smrčková.

1082 SCHOU-CHRISTENSEN, JORGEN. "Hot Glass Now." *Crafts* 22 (1976): 21–28.
Report on a conference held at the Royal College of Art, London, and an exhibition of German glass.

1083 SCHROEDER, CHRISTINA. "Metaphors in Glass: die Rolle des Glases in der Zeitgenössichen Kunst. The Role of Glass in Contemporary Art." *Neues Glas* 96, no. 2.
The second of two articles under this title, it contains references to four women: Barbara Holub, Christiane Möbus, Gloria Friedman and Maria Roosen.

1084 STEENBERG, ELISA. *Modern Swedish Glass.* Stockholm: Lindqvists, 1949, n.p., illus.
An early appreciation of the seminal role of Swedish glass. The introductory essay examines the developments from 1917, with particular emphasis on the firms of Orrefors and Kosta. Women designers appear in the later years; Ingeborg Lundin, Gerda Strømberg, Greta Runeborg-Tell, Monica Bratt and Inga Hallenborg-Nordstrøm are mentioned.

1085 *Suomen Lasi—Finnish Glass.* Sunderland: Sunderland Arts Centre, 1979, n.p., illus.
A short contextual essay precedes an alphabetical catalogue of the fifteen designers, of whom five are women: Kaija Aarikka, Saara Hopea, Kerttu Nurminen, Inkeri Toikka and Helena Tynell. Under each there is a biographical outline, a list of selected exhibitions, awards, and collections in which their work may be found. There is also a statement by the designer.

1086 *Svenskt Glas '83: Prisbelont design.* Stockholm: National Museum, 1984, n.p., illus.
Text in Swedish. Survey of designs for glass produced in Swedish factories in 1983. Women designers include Monica Backstrøm, Ulrica Hydman-Vallien, Anna Ehrner, Ingegerd Räman, Anne Nilsson, Lisa Bauer and Eva Englund.

1087 *Vetri Murano Oggi.* Milan: Electa, 1981, 154pp., illus.
Text in Italian with an English summary. Consists of essays on the history of glass-making in Murano, including technological developments. Included are Federica Marangoni and Bertha Sarasin.

1088 *World Glass Now.* Hokkaido: Museum of Modern Art, 1982, 273pp., mainly illus.

Text in Japanese and English. Begins with five personal views on contemporary glass. This is followed by a list of the prizewinning works from the competition section, together with biographies of the designers. In addition there is a section for invited designers. Several women are included, among them Mieke Groot, Benny Motzfeldt, Jaroslava Brychtová and Ann Wärff.

INDIVIDUALS

1089 AARIKKA, KAIJA (1929–)
Finnish glass designer.

Exhibitions

Suomen Lasi—Finnish Glass. Sunderland Arts Centre, Sunderland, 1979.

1090 ADENSAMOVÁ, BLANKA (1948–)
Czech glass designer.

Exhibitions

Büchner, Thomas, and William Warmus. *Czechoslovakian Diary: 1980. 23 Glassmakers.* Corning, New York: Corning Museum of Glass, 1980, 16 pp., illus.
New Glass: A Worldwide Survey. Corning Museum of Glass, Corning, New York, 1979

1091 AHO, KAARINA (1925–)
Finnish glass designer.

Exhibitions

Opie, Jennifer. *Scandinavia: Ceramics and Glass in the Twentieth Century.* London: Victoria and Albert Museum, 1989.

1092 ALADIN, TAMARA (1932–)
Finnish glass and ceramics designer.

Other Sources

Beard, Geoffrey. *International Modern Glass.* London: Barrie and Jenkins, 1976.

1093 ASELIUS-LIDBECK, CATHERINA (1941–)
Swedish designer in glass and ceramics.

Other Sources

Beard, Geoffrey. *International Modern Glass.* London: Barrie and Jenkins, 1976.

1094 ATTERBERG, INGRID (1920–)
   Swedish designer of glass, ceramics and textiles.

Exhibitions

Opie, Jennifer. *Scandinavia: Ceramics and Glass in the Twentieth Century.* *London:* Victoria and Albert Museum, 1989.

1095 BACKSTRÖM, MONICA (1939–)
   Swedish glass designer.

Main Sources

Form, no. 9 (1965): 608–609.

Exhibitions

Hiesinger, Kathryn, and George Marcus III, eds. *Design since 1945.* Philadelphia: Philadelphia Museum of Art, 1983.
   New Glass: A Worldwide Survey. Corning, New York: Corning Museum of Glass, 1979.
   Opie, Jennifer. *Scandinavia: Ceramics and Glass in the Twentieth Century.* London: Victoria and Albert Museum, 1989.

Other Sources

Beard, Geoffrey. *International Modern Glass.* London: Barrie and Jenkins, 1976.
   Byars, Mel. *The Design Encyclopedia.* London: Lawrence King, 1994.
   Grover, Ray, and Lee Grover. *Contemporary Art Glass.* New York: Crown Publishers Inc., 1975.

1096 BALSAMO-STELLA, ANNA
   Swedish engraver of glass who worked in Italy with her husband, the glass designer Guido Balsamo-Stella, and introduced him to key Swedish designers.

Other Sources

Arwas, Victor. *Glass: Art Nouveau to Art Deco.* London: Academy Editions, 1977.

1097 BARTOVÁ, MILENA (Alt. BARTOVÁ-KOROUSOVÁ) (1921/1924–)
   Czech designer of glass.

Exhibitions

Glass 1959: A Special Exhibition of International Contemporary Glass. Corning, New York: Corning Museum of Glass, 1959.

Other Sources

Raban, Josef. *Le Verre Moderne de Bohème.* Prague: Artia Praga, 1963.

1098 BATHORY, JULIA (1909–)
      Hungarian glass designer.

Other Sources

Beard, Geoffrey. *International Modern Glass.* London: Barrie and Jenkins, 1976.

1099 BAUER, LISA (1920–)
      Swedish glass designer.

Exhibitions

McFadden, David. *Scandinavian Modern Design, 1880–1980.* New York: Harry Abrams and the Cooper-Hewitt Museum, 1982.

Other Sources

Byars, Mel. *The Design Encyclopedia.* London: Lawrence King, 1994.

1100 BECKERT, MAREY (née SCHIDER) (1883–1975)
      German painter and glass designer.

Other Sources

Joseph Hoffmann and Wilhelm Wagenfeld: Glaskunst der Moderne. Munich: Klinkhardt and Bierman, 1992.

1101 BEGOU, MARISA (1948–)
      Italian-born glass designer who has worked in France with her husband
      since 1981.

Exhibitions

Ricke, Helmut. *Neues Glas in Europa: 50 Künstler—50 Konzepte.* Dusseldorf: Kunstmuseum, 1990. Contains bibliography.

Other Sources

Carteron, Philippe, ed. *Ceci n'est plus du verre.* Paris: Editions vers les Arts, 1994.

1102 BELZ-SCHLIERER, HEIDI-ASTRID.
German glass designer.

Exhibitions

New Glass: A Worldwide Survey. Corning Museum of Glass, Corning, New York, 1979

1103 BLOCH, LUCIENNE (1905–)
Dutch glass designer and sculptor.

Exhibitions

Duits, Thimo Te. *Geperst Glas uit Leerdam.* Leerdam: Glasmuseum, 1991. 152pp., illus. Bloch is the only woman included in this exhibition.

1104 BOHNERT, GERTRUDE (fl. 1945–60)
Swiss glass engraver.

Main Sources

Heddle, G.M. *A manual on etching and engraving glass.* London: Tiranti, 1961.

Other Sources

Beard, Geoffrey. *International Modern Glass.* London: Barrie and Jenkins, 1976.

1105 BOHN, IRMGARD (Alt. HILKER-BOHN) (1907–)
German designer and engraver of glass.

Other Sources

Joseph Hoffmann and Wilhelm Wagenfeld: Glaskunst der Moderne. Munich: Klinkhardt and Bierman, 1992.

1106 BOISSIER, PHYLLIS (fl. 1946–70)
English glass engraver.

Main Sources

"Artist with a Diamond." *Pottery and Glass,* November 1957, 347.
Pottery Gazette, September 1958, 1124.

Exhibitions

Glass 1959: A Special Exhibition of International Contemporary Glass. Corning, New York: Corning Museum of Glass, 1959.

Other Sources

Beard, Geoffrey. *International Modern Glass.* London: Barrie and Jenkins, 1976.

1107 BÖGEL, ULRIKE (1954–)
German designer of glass, metalwork and other items.

Exhibitions

Oedekoven-Gerischer, Angela, et al., eds. *Frauen im Design: Berufsbilder und Lebenswege seit 1900. Women in Design: Careers and Life Histories since 1900.* Stuttgart: Design Center, 1989.

1108 BRANDT, ÅSA (1940–)
Swedish glass designer.

Main Sources

Dansk Brugkunst 41, no. 3 (1969): 73–75.

Exhibitions

McFadden, David, ed. *Scandinavian Modern Design, 1880–1980.* New York: Harry Abrams and the Cooper-Hewitt Museum, 1982.

Nordisk Glass '88. Trondheim: Nordernfjeldske Kunstindustriemuseum, 1988. 17 designers featured in the exhibition.

Ricke, Helmut. *Neues Glas in Europa: 50 Künstler—50 Konzepte.* Dusseldorf: Kunstmuseum, 1990. Contains a bibliography.

Other Sources

Beard, Geoffrey. *International Modern Glass.* London: Barrie and Jenkins, 1976.

Byars, Mel. *The Design Encyclopedia.* London: Lawrence King, 1994.

1109 BRANTENBERG, ULLA-MARI (1947–)
Norwegian glass designer.

Exhibitions

Nordisk Glass '88. Trondheim: Nordernfjeldske Kunstindustriemuseum, 1988. She was one of seventeen designers featured in the exhibition.

Opie, Jennifer. *Scandinavia: Ceramics and Glass in the Twentieth Century,* London: Victoria and Albert Museum, 1989.

1110 BRATT, MONICA (alt. BRATT-WIJKANDER) (1913–1958/61)
Swedish glass designer and painter.

Main Sources

Å. H. "Monica Bratt: Glaskonstnär." *Form* 47, no. 2 (1951): 40–41.

Glas av Monica Bratt. Formgivare vid Rejmyre Glasbruk under Üren 1937–1958. Stockholm: Bellmansmiljö, 1981, 100pp., mostly illus. Text in Swedish.

Exhibitions

Glass 1959: A Special Exhibition of International Contemporary Glass. Corning, New York: Corning Museum of Glass, 1959.

Opie, Jennifer. *Scandinavia: Ceramics and Glass in the Twentieth Century.* London: Victoria and Albert Museum, 1989.

Other Sources

Polak, Ada. *Modern Glass.* London: Faber and Faber, 1962.

Ricke, Helmut, and Ulrich Gronert, eds. *Glas in Schweden 1915–60.* Munich: Prestel, 1987.

Steenberg, Elisa. *Modern Swedish Glass.* Stockholm: Lindqvists, 1949.

1111 BRUNNER, MARIA VERA (Alt. FRIEDBERGER) (1895–1965)
German painter and glass designer.

Other Sources

Joseph Hoffmann and Wilhelm Wagenfeld: Glaskunst der Moderne. Munich: Klinkhardt and Bierman, 1992.

1112 BRYCHTOVÁ (Alt. BRYCHTOVÁ-ZAHRADNIKOVÁ), JAROSLAVA (1924–)
Czech glass designer.

Main Sources

"Derrière le rideau de verre: Libenský/Brychtová." *L'Atelier* 1 (1989): 35–40, illus. Interview with the designers.

Drdácká, Pavla. "The Sculptures of Jaroslava Brychtová and Stanislav Libenský in the U.S.A." *Glass Review* 36, no. 1 (1981): 10–13, illus.

Langhamer, Antonin. "Une haute appréciation des artistes verriers tchécoslovaques." *Revue du Verre* 40, no. 4 (1985): 27–28.

Libenský, Stanislav. "The 20th Century Revival of Glassmaking in Czechoslovakia." *Glass Art Society Journal* (1981): 33–35, illus. Gives an account of the activities of himself and Jaroslava Brychtová in this revival. Describes their careers from the immediate postwar period.

Libenský, Stanislav. "Stanislav Libenský and Jaroslava Brychtová: A 40 Year Retrospective. Czechoslovakian Glass Art." *Neues Glas* (1982): 2–10, illus. Text in German and English. Largely biographical account from 1945.

Raban, Josef. *Modern Bohemian Glass,* Prague: Artia, 1963.
Czechoslovakia Glass Review, no. 4 (1966): 125.
Czechoslovakia Glass Review, no. 24 (1969).

Exhibitions

Glass 1959: A Special Exhibition of International Contemporary Glass.
Corning, New York: Corning Museum of Glass, 1959.
Adlerová, Alena. *Böhmisches Glas der Gegenwart.* Hamburg: Museum für
Kunst und Gewerbe, 1973.
Metamorfózy skla [New tendencies in glass sculpture]. Brno: Moravská
Gallery, 1973.
New Glass: A Worldwide Survey. Corning, New York: Corning Museum of
Glass, 1979.
Büchner, Thomas, and William Warmus. *Czechoslovakian Diary: 1980. 23
Glassmakers.* Corning, New York: Corning Museum of Glass, 1980, illus.
World Glass Now '82. Hokkaido: Museum of Modern Art, 1982. The work
of prizewinners and their biographies are included.
Petrová, Sylvia, and Jean-Luc Olivie. *Verres de Bohème 1400–1989: Chef
d'oeuvres des Musées de Tchécoslovaquie.* Paris: Musée des Arts Décoratifs in
association with Flammarion, 1989.
Ricke, Helmut. *Neues Glas in Europa: 50 Künstler—50 Konzepte.*
Kunstmuseum, Dusseldorf, 1990. Contains bibliography.

Other Sources

Beard, Geoffrey. *International Modern Glass.* London: Barrie and Jenkins,
1976.
Grover, Ray, and Lee Grover. *Contemporary Art Glass.* New York: Crown
Publishers, 1975.

1113 BÜLOW-HÜBE, TORUN VIVIANNA (1927–)
Swedish designer of metalwork, ceramics, glass and jewellery.

Exhibitions

McFadden, David. *Scandinavian Modern Design, 1880–1980.* New York:
Harry Abrams in association with the Cooper-Hewitt Museum, 1982.

Other Sources

Naylor, Colin, ed. *Contemporary Designers.* 2nd edition. Chicago and
London: St. James Press, 1990. Contains a bibliography.

1114 CHANTEMERLE, HÉLNE
French designer of glass.

Other Sources

Bloch-Dermant, Janine. *Le verre en France: les années 80.* Paris: les Editions des Amateurs, n.d. [c. 1990]. Informative biographical entry.

1115 CIBOT, ELIZABETH
French designer of glass.

Other Sources

Bloch-Dermant, Janine. *Le verre en France: les années 80.* Paris: les Editions des Amateurs, n.d. [c. 1990]. Informative biographical entry.

1116 CLARKE, DILLON (1946–)
English glass designer.

Publications

"Sam Herman/Peter Layton/Glasshouse." *Crafts* 23 (1976): 45. Mentions Annette Meech.
"Pauline Solven." *Crafts* 29 (1977): 49.

Main Sources

Brown, Michael. "Seven Studio Glass Blowers." *Crafts* 32 (1978): 45–46.

Exhibitions

New Glass: A Worldwide Survey. Corning, New York: Corning Museum of Glass, 1979.
Dillon Clarke, Neue Glas. Hamburg: Galerie L, 1982.
British Studio Glass. Sunderland: Sunderland Arts Centre, 1983.

Other Sources

Grover, Ray, and Lee Grover. *Contemporary Art Glass.* New York: Crown Publishers, 1975.

1117 COSTA, DONATELLA
Italian designer of furnishings, including glass.

Exhibitions

Bacci, N. *Il Design delle Donne.* Ravenna: Museo dell'Arredo Contemporaneo, 1991.

1118 COTTER, MAUD
Irish glass designer.

Main Sources

Pyle, Hilary. "Cork Glass Now: A Review of the Work of James Scanlon and Maud Cotter." *Irish Arts Review Yearbook 1990–1,* 1991, 45–52.

1119 CUNY, JUTTA (1944–)
German-born glass artist who has worked in France since 1966.

Publications

"Au sujet de mes scultures de verre." *La Revue de la Céramique et du Verre,* April/May 1982, 30–31.

Main Sources

"Art et moiroiterie: la fontaine de Jutta Cuny." *Verre Actualité* 56 (March 1984): 22–26, illus. Account of commission carried out for offices of Saint-Gobain Vitrage at La Défense, Paris.

Exhibitions

Jutta Cuny: sculptures, verre, bronze. Paris: Galéries Gérard Laubie et Associés, 1982.
Verriers français contemporains: Art et industrie. Paris: Musée des Arts Décoratifs, 1982.

Other Sources

Bloch-Dermant, Janine. *Le verre en France d'Emile Gallé à nos jours.* Paris: Editions de l'Amateur, 1983.
———. *Le verre en France: les années 80.* Paris: les Editions des Amateurs, n.d. [c. 1990]. Informative biographical entry.

1120 DAMIAN-EYRIGNOUX, MONICA
French designer of glass.

Exhibitions

Verriers français contemporains: Art et industrie. Paris: Musée des Arts Décoratifs. 1982.

Other Sources

Bloch-Dermant, Janine. *Le verre en France: les années 80.* Paris: les Editions des Amateurs, n.d. [c. 1990]. Informative biographical entry.

1121 DE BRAUN, FELICIA FUSTE
Spanish designer of glass who worked in France.

Exhibitions

Glass 1959: A Special Exhibition of International Contemporary Glass. Corning, New York: Corning Museum of Glass, 1959.

1122 DE GOEY, MARIJKE (1947–)
      Dutch textile and glass designer.

See Textiles section.

1123 DE SANTILLANA, LAURA
      Italian glass designer.

Exhibitions

New Glass: A Worldwide Survey. Corning, New York: Corning Museum of Glass, 1979.

1124 DECHO, ILSE (1915–1978)
      German designer of glass and ceramics.

Exhibitions

Glaskunst in der DDR. Leipzig: Stadtisches Museum des Kunsthandwerk, 1977.
      Mundt, Barbara, Suzanne Netzer, and Innes Hettler. *Interieur + Design in Deutschland, 1945=60.* Berlin: Kunstgewerbemuseum and Dietrich Reimer Verlag, 1994.

1125 DEL MASCHIO, SERENA
      Italian glass designer.

Other Sources

Polak, Ada. *Modern Glass.* London: Faber and Faber, 1962.

1126 DOLEJSLOVÁ, EVA (1947–)
      Czech designer of glass.

Exhibitions

3 Trienále řezaneho skla [3rd triennial of cut glass]. Brno: Moravská Gallery, 1971. Contains a biographical outline.

1127 DRIOUT, LISE (c. 1923–)
      French designer of glass.

Exhibitions

Glass 1959: A Special Exhibition of International Contemporary Glass. Corning, New York: Corning Museum of Glass, 1959.

Other Sources

Karlikow, A. "Gemmaux: Paintings in Glass." *Craft Horizons* 17 (November–December 1957): 20–23.

1128 EISCH, MARGARETE
    German glass designer.

Exhibitions

New Glass: A Worldwide Survey. Corning, New York: Corning Museum of Glass, 1979.

1129 ELMHIRST, SHIELA (1920–)
    English glass engraver.

Publications

"The Aesthetic and Practical Applications of Diamond-Point Glass Engraving." Paper read at the Eighth International Congress on Glass, Brussels, June 1965.

Exhibitions

Glass 1959: A Special Exhibition of International Contemporary Glass. Corning, New York: Corning Museum of Glass, 1959.

Other Sources

Beard, Geoffrey. *International Modern Glass.* London: Barrie and Jenkins, 1976.
    Polak, Ada. *Modern Glass.* London: Faber and Faber, 1962.

1130 ENGELS-NEUHOLD, FELICITAS (c. 1938–)
    Austrian-born glass designer who works in the Netherlands.

Exhibitions

Moderne Hollandsk Tekstilkunst og Glas. Copenhagen: Dansk Kunstindustrimuseum, 1979.

1131 ENGLUND, EVA (1937–)
Swedish sculptor and designer of ceramics and glass.

Exhibitions

McFadden, David, ed. *Scandinavian Modern Design, 1880–1980*. New York: Harry Abrams and the Cooper-Hewitt Museum, 1982.
Opie, Jennifer. *Scandinavia: Ceramics and Glass in the Twentieth Century*. London: Victoria and Albert Museum, 1989.

Other Sources

Byars, Mel. *The Design Encyclopedia*. London: Lawrence King, 1994.
Grover, Ray, and Lee Grover. *Contemporary Art Glass*. New York: Crown Publishers, 1975.

1132 EYRIGNOUX, MONICA DAMIAN (1936–)
French designer in glass and metal; also a sculptor.

See Monica Damian-Eyrignoux.

1133 FAHLSTRÖM, ELSA (1930–)
Swedish designer of glass.

Exhibitions

Glass 1959: A Special Exhibition of International Contemporary Glass. Corning, New York: Corning Museum of Glass, 1959.

1134 FLADGATE, DEBORAH (1957–)
English glass designer.

Exhibitions

British Studio Glass. Sunderland: Sunderland Arts Centre, 1983.

1135 FLANDER, BRITA (1957–)
Finnish designer of glass.

Exhibitions

Dawson, Jack. *Finnish Post-War Glass (1945–1996)*. Sunderland: Reg Vardy Gallery at the University of Sunderland, 1996.

1136 FOREJTOVÁ, JITKA (Alt. FOREJTOVÁ-PELIKANOVÁ) (1923–)
Czech designer of glass.

Exhibitions

Ryté sklo: pruní prehlídka soudobé tvorby. Brno: Moravská Gallery, 1965. Very brief biographical outline given.

3 Trienále řezaneho skla [3rd triennial of cut glass]. Brno: Moravská Gallery, 1971. Contains a biographical outline.

Metamorfózy skla [New tendencies in glass sculpture]. Brno: Moravská Gallery, 1973.

1137 FORSELL, ULLA (1944–)
Swedish glass designer.

Exhibitions

New Glass: A Worldwide Survey. Corning, New York: Corning Museum of Glass, 1979.

McFadden, David, ed. *Scandinavian Modern Design, 1880–1980.* New York: Harry Abrams and the Cooper-Hewitt Museum, 1982.

Nordisk Glass '88. Trondheim: Nordernfjeldske Kunstindustriemuseum, 1988. She was one of seventeen designers featured in the exhibition.

Opie, Jennifer. *Scandinavia: Ceramics and Glass in the Twentieth Century.* London: Victoria and Albert Museum, 1989.

Other Sources

Byars, Mel. *The Design Encyclopedia.* London: Lawrence King, 1994.

1138 GILLE, MARIANNE
Swedish glass designer.

Exhibitions

New Glass: A Worldwide Survey. Corning, New York: Corning Museum of Glass, 1979.

1139 GRAYDON STANNUS, ELIZABETH (Alt. BILLINGHURST)
Irish designer of glass who established the Gray-Stan Glass Studio in London.

Exhibitions

Thirties: British Art and Design before the War. London: Arts Council of Great Britain at the Hayward Gallery, 1979.

Dodsworth, Roger, ed. *British Glass Between the Wars.* Kingswinford: Broadfield Glass Museum, 1987.

1140 GROOT, MIEKE (DE) (1949–)
Dutch ceramicist and glass designer.

Exhibitions

Moderne Hollandsk Tekstilkunst og Glas. Copenhagen: Dansk Kunstindustrimuseum, 1979.

World Glass Now '82. Hokkaido: Museum of Modern Art, 1982. The work of prizewinners and their biographies are included.

Broos, Kees. *Beelden in Glass: Glass Sculpture.* Copenhagen: Stichting Glas, 1986.

Duits, Thimo Te. *Keramiek '90. Moderne Keramiek in Nederland.* The Hague: SDU Uitgevrerij, 1990.

Ricke, Helmut. *Neues Glas in Europa: 50 Künstler—50 Konzepte.* Dusseldorf: Kunstmuseum, 1990. Contains a bibliography.

1141 GULBRANDSEN, NORA (1894–1978)
Norwegian designer of ceramics, glass, metal and graphics.

Exhibitions

McFadden, David. *Scandinavian Modern Design, 1880–1980.* New York: Harry Abrams and the Cooper-Hewitt Museum, 1982.

Opie, Jennifer. *Scandinavia: Ceramics and Glass in the Twentieth Century.* London: Victoria and Albert Museum, 1989.

Wichstrøm, Anne. *Rooms with a View: Women's Art in Norway, 1880–1990.* Oslo: Royal Ministry of Foreign Affairs, 1989.

Other Sources

Byars, Mel. *The Design Encyclopedia.* London: Lawrence King, 1994.

1142 HAKATIE, ANNALEENA (1965–)
Finnish designer of glass.

Exhibitions

Dawson, Jack. *Finnish Post-War Glass (1945–1996).* Sunderland: Reg Vardy Gallery at the University of Sunderland, 1996.

1143 HAVLOVÁ, ELIŠKA (1937–)
Czech designer of glass.

Exhibitions

Ryté sklo: pruní prehlídka soudobé tvorby. Brno: Moravská Gallery, 1965. Very brief biographical outline given.

1144 HELLEROVÁ, ERIKA (1924–)
Czech designer of glass.

Exhibitions

Ryté sklo: pruní prehlídka soudobé tvorby. Brno: Moravská Gallery, 1965. Very brief biographical outline given.

3 Trienále řezaneho skla [3rd triennial of cut glass]. Brno: Moravská Gallery, 1971. Contains a biographical outline.

Other Sources

Raban, Josef. *Le Verre Moderne de Bohème.* Prague: Artia Praga, 1963.

1145 HOBSON, DIANA (1943–)
English glass designer.

Exhibitions

British Studio Glass. Sunderland: Sunderland Arts Centre, 1983.

1146 HOUSEROVÁ, IVANA (1957–)
Czech glass designer.

Exhibitions

Büchner, Thomas, and William Warmus. *Czechoslovakian Diary: 1980. 23 Glassmakers.* Corning, New York: Corning Museum of Glass, 1980, p. 15, illus.

Petrová, Sylvia, and Jean-Luc Olivie. *Verres de Bohème 1400–1989: chef d'oeuvres des Musées de Tchécoslovaquie.* Paris: Musée des Arts Décoratifs in association with Flammarion, 1989.

1147 HUBERT, KARIN (until 1986 KARIN STÖCKLE-KRUMBEIN) (1939–)
German glass designer.

Exhibitions

Ricke, Helmut. *Neues Glas in Europa: 50 Künstler—50 Konzepte.* Dusseldorf: Kunstmuseum, 1990. Contains a bibliography.

1148 ISENSEE, ADA
German glass designer.

Exhibitions

New Glass: A Worldwide Survey. Corning, New York: Corning Museum of Glass, 1979.

1149 JÄDERHOLM-SNELLMAN, GRETA-LISA (1894–1973)
Finnish designer in glass and ceramics.

Exhibitions

Opie, Jennifer. *Scandinavia: Ceramics and Glass in the Twentieth Century.* London: Victoria and Albert Museum, 1989.

1150 KATON, ERZSEBET
   Hungarian glass designer.

Exhibitions

New Glass: A Worldwide Survey. Corning, New York: Corning Museum of Glass, 1979

1151 KERHARTOVÁ-PEŘINOVÁ, MARTA (Alt. KERHASRTOVÁ) (1921/35–)
   Czech glass designer.

Exhibitions

Glass 1959: A Special Exhibition of International Contemporary Glass. Corning, New York: Corning Museum of Glass, 1959.
   Petrová, Sylvia, and Jean-Luc Olivie. *Verres de Bohème 1400–1989: chef d'oeuvres des Musées de Tchécoslovaquie.* Paris: Musée des Arts Décoratifs in association with Flammarion, 1989.

1152 KINNAIRD, ALISON (1949–)
   Scottish glass designer and engraver.

Exhibitions

British Studio Glass. Sunderland: Sunderland Arts Centre, 1983.

1153 KIRSCHNER, MARIE LOUISA (Alt. KIRSCHNEROVÁ) (1852–1931)
   Czech designer of glass and interiors.

Exhibitions

České secese umení 1900 [Art Nouveau in Bohemia]. Brno: Moravská Gallery, 1966. She is one of the few women included.
   Oedekoven-Gerischer, Angela, et al., eds. *Frauen im Design: Berufsbilder und Lebenswege seit 1900. Women in Design: Careers and Life Histories since 1900.* Stuttgart: Design Center, 1989.
   Petrová, Sylvia, and Jean-Luc Olivie. *Verres de Bohème 1400–1989: chef d'oeuvres des Musées de Tchécoslovaquie.* Paris: Musée des Arts Décoratifs in association with Flammarion, 1989.

Other Sources

Raban, J. *Modern Bohemian Glass.* Prague: Artia, 1963.
   Arwas, Victor. *Glass: Art Nouveau to Art Deco.* London: Academy Editions, 1977.

Joseph Hoffmann and Wilhelm Wagenfeld: Glaskunst der Moderne. Munich: Klinkhardt and Bierman, 1992.

1154 KJOER, ANJA (1956–)
Danish designer of glass.

Exhibitions

Nordisk Glass '88. Trondheim: Nordernfjeldske Kunstindustriemuseum, 1988. She was one of seventeen designers featured in the exhibition.

1155 KLEYN-ALTENBURGER, BRIGITTE (Alt. ALTEN BURGER; KLEIN-ALTENBURGER) (1942–)
Austrian-born glass designer who works in the Netherlands.

Exhibitions

Ricke, Helmut, ed. *Leerdam Unica: 50 Jahre modernes niederländisches Glas. 50 jaar modern nederlands glas.* Dusseldorf: Kunstmuseum, 1977, 148pp., illus. Text in German and Dutch. Altenburger is the only woman included.
Moderne Hollandsk Tekstilkunst og Glas. Copenhagen: Dansk Kunstindustrimuseum, 1979.

1156 KLIM, KAREN (1951–)
Norwegian glass designer.

Exhibitions

Nordisk Glass '88. Trondheim: Nordernfjeldske Kunstindustriemuseum, 1988. She was one of seventeen designers featured in the exhibition.
Opie, Jennifer. *Scandinavia: Ceramics and Glass in the Twentieth Century.* London: Victoria and Albert Museum, 1989.

1157 KOTTE-WEIDAUER, IRMGARD (1907–)
German designer of glass.

Exhibitions

Glaskunst in der DDR. Leipzig: Stadtisches Museum des Kunsthandwerk, 1977.

1158 KUDROVÁ, DAGMAR (1934–)
Czech designer of glass.

Other Sources

Raban, Josef. *Le Verre Moderne de Bohème.* Prague: Artia Praga, 1963.

1159 KUPETZ, SIGRID (1926–)
      German designer of glass.

Exhibitions

Glass 1959: A Special Exhibition of International Contemporary Glass. Corning, New York: Corning Museum of Glass, 1959.

1160 LALIQUE, MARIE-CLAUDE
      French designer of glass; since 1977 chair of and designer for the Lalique firm.

Publications

Lalique, Marc, and Marie-Claude. *Lalique par Lalique.* Lausanne: Edipop, 1977.

Other Sources

Byars, Mel. *The Design Encyclopedia.* London: Lawrence King, 1994.

1161 LANGLEY, SIDDY (1955–)
      English designer of ceramics and glass.

Exhibitions

British Studio Glass. Sunderland: Sunderland Arts Centre, 1983.

1162 LATVA-SOMPPI, RIKKA (1969–)
      Finnish designer of glass.

Exhibitions

Dawson, Jack. *Finnish Post-War Glass (1945–1996).* Sunderland: Reg Vardy Gallery at the University of Sunderland, 1996.

1163 LECJAKS, MARIA (1943–)
      Hungarian glass designer.

Other Sources

Beard, Geoffrey. *International Modern Glass.* London: Barrie and Jenkins, 1976.

1164 LIŠKOVÁ, VERA (1924–1985)
      Czech glass designer.

Main Sources

Marsiková, Jaromira. "Une exposition de verre de Vera Lišková." *Revue du Verre* 37, no. 9 (1972): 270–274, illus.

Rehl, René. "Une idée originale de l'artiste Vera Lišková." *Revue du Verre* 23, no. 2 (1968): 47–49, illus.

Stehlík, Frantisek. "Le monde imaginaire de Vera Lišková." *Revue du Verre* 29, no. 7 (1974): 23–25, illus.

Exhibitions

Glass 1959: A Special Exhibition of International Contemporary Glass. Corning, New York: Corning Museum of Glass, 1959.

Adlerová, Alena. Böhmisches Glas der Gegenwart. Hamburg: Museum für Kunst und Gewerbe, 1973.

Metamorfózy skla [New tendencies in glass sculpture]. Brno: Moravská Gallery, 1973.

New Glass: A Worldwide Survey. Corning, New York: Corning Museum of Glass, 1979.

Büchner, Thomas, and William Warmus. *Czechoslovakian Diary: 1980. 23 Glassmakers.* Corning, New York: Corning Museum of Glass, 1980, p. 8, illus.

Petrová, Sylvia, and Jean-Luc Olivie. *Verres de Bohème 1400–1989: chef d'oeuvres des Musées de Tchécoslovaquie.* Paris: Musée des Arts Décoratifs in association with Flammarion, 1989.

Other Sources

Beard, Geoffrey. *International Modern Glass.* London: Barrie and Jenkins, 1976.

Polak, Ada. *Modern Glass.* London: Faber and Faber, 1962.

Raban, Josef. *Le Verre Moderne de Bohème.* Prague: Artia Praga, 1963.

1165 LOWE, LIZ (1956–)
English glass designer.

Exhibitions

British Studio Glass. Sunderland: Sunderland Arts Centre, 1983.

1166 LUGOSSY, MARIA (1950–)
Hungarian glass designer.

Main Sources

Halasi, Rita. "Under the Spell of Glass." *Neues Glas* (1996): 28–33.

Exhibitions

Ricke, Helmut. *Neues Glas in Europa: 50 Künstler—50 Konzepte.* Kunstmuseum, Dusseldorf, 1990. Contains a bibliography.

1167 LUNDGREN, TYRA (1897–1979)
Swedish designer in glass and ceramics, painter and sculptor.

Main Sources

Stw, Å. "Tyra Lundgren och Paolo Venini." *Form* 36, no. 2 (1940): 32–33.
Widman, Dag. "Tyra Lundgren och europé." *Form* 76, no. 1 (1980): 34–35.

Exhibitions

Tyra Lundgren: A Life in Art. Stockholm: Swedish Academy of Fine Arts, 1978. A retrospective which featured a group of fifteen previously unexhibited self-portraits.

Bettagno, Alessandro, ed. *Gli artisti de Veneni: per una storia del vetro d'arte veneziano.* Milan: Electa in association with the Fondazione Cini, Venice, 1996.

Other Sources

Beard, Geoffrey. *International Modern Glass.* London: Barrie and Jenkins, 1976.

Dunford, Penny. *A Biographical Dictionary of Women Artists in Europe and America since 1850.* Hemel Hempstead: Harvester Wheatsheaf and Philadelphia: University of Pennsylvania Press, 1990. Contains a bibliography.

Grover, Ray, and Lee Grover. *Contemporary Art Glass.* New York: Crown Publishers, 1975.

Ingelman, Ingrid. "Women Artists in Sweden." *Woman's Art Journal* 5, no. 1 (spring–summer 1984): 1–7.

Kapferer, Simone. "Les artistes céramistes et verriers au Salon des Artistes Décorateurs." *Les Arts du Feu* 2 (June 1938): 62–64.

Kim, Jacques. "Les arts du feu au Salon des Artistes Décorateurs." *Les Arts du Feu* 11 (May 1939): 147–151.

Ricke, Helmut, and Ulrich Gronert, eds. *Glas in Schweden 1915–60.* Munich: Prestel, 1987.

Wollin, Nils. *Swedish Textiles 1943–1950.* Leigh-on-Sea: Frank Lewis, 1952.

1168 LUNDIN, INGEBORG (1921–)
Swedish glass designer and winner of the Lunning Prize.

Main Sources

S.F. "Graverad kristallpremiär." *Form* 59, no.8 (1963): 525–526.
Penfield, Louis. "Ingeborg Lundin of Orrefors." *American-Scandinavian Review* 57 (1969): 44–49.

Exhibitions

Glass 1959: A Special Exhibition of International Contemporary Glass. Corning, New York: Corning Museum of Glass, 1959.

McFadden, David, ed. *Scandinavian Modern Design, 1880–1980.* New York: Harry Abrams and the Cooper-Hewitt Museum, 1982.

The Lunning Prize. Stockholm: Nationalmuseum, 1986.

Baldouy-Maternati, Danielle. *La verrerie européene des années 50.* Marseille: Musées de Marseille, 1988.

Mundt, Barbara, Suzanne Netzer, and Innes Hettler. *Interieur + Design in Deutschland, 1945=60.* Berlin: Kunstgewerbemuseum and Dietrich Reimer Verlag, 1994.

Other Sources

Beard, Geoffrey. *International Modern Glass.* London: Barrie and Jenkins, 1976.

Byars, Mel. *The Design Encyclopedia.* London: Lawrence King, 1994.

Grover, Ray, and Lee Grover. *Contemporary Art Glass.* New York: Crown Publishers., 1975.

Polak, Ada. *Modern Glass.* London: Faber and Faber, 1962.

Ricke, Helmut, and Ulrich Gronert, eds. *Glas in Schweden 1915–60.* Munich: Prestel, 1987.

Steenberg, Elisa. *Modern Swedish Glass.* Stockholm: Lindqvists, 1949.

1169 MADERNA, MARIANNE
Austrian glass designer.

Exhibitions

New Glass: A Worldwide Survey. Corning, New York: Corning Museum of Glass, 1979.

1170 MARANGONI, FEDERICA (1940–)
Italian glass designer.

Exhibitions

New Glass: A Worldwide Survey. Corning, New York: Corning Museum of Glass, 1979.

Ricke, Helmut. *Neues Glas in Europa: 50 Künstler—50 Konzepte.* Dusseldorf: Kunstmuseum, 1990. Contains a bibliography.

Bacci, N. *Il Design delle Donne.* Ravenna: Museo dell'Arredo Contemporaneo, 1991.

Other Sources

Vetri Murano Oggi. Milan: Electa, 1981.

1171 MARSH, HONORIA DIANA (1923–)
English glass engraver.

Other Sources

Beard, Geoffrey. *International Modern Glass*. London: Barrie and Jenkins, 1976.

1172 MASITOVÁ, IVANA (1961–)
    Czech glass designer.

Exhibitions

Petrová, Sylvia, and Jean-Luc Olivie. *Verres de Bohème 1400–1989: chef d'oeuvres des Musées de Tchécoslovaquie*. Paris: Musée des Arts Décoratifs in association with Flammarion, 1989.

1173 MASKE, CATHERINE (1966–)
    Finnish designer of glass.

Exhibitions

Dawson, Jack. *Finnish Post-War Glass (1945–1996)*. Sunderland: Reg Vardy Gallery at the University of Sunderland, 1996.

1174 McCONACHIE, ALISON (1953–)
    Scottish glass designer.

Exhibitions

British Studio Glass. Sunderland: Sunderland Arts Centre, 1983.

1175 McKINNEY, NANNY STILL (Alt. STILL) (1926–)
    Finnish designer of glass, ceramics, metals, wood and graphics.

Exhibitions

Hiesinger, Kathryn, and George Marcus III, eds. *Design since 1945*. Philadelphia: Philadelphia Museum of Art, 1983.

Baldouy-Maternati, Danielle. *La verrerie européene des années 50*. Marseille: Musées de Marseille, 1988.

Opie, Jennifer. *Scandinavia: Ceramics and Glass in the Twentieth Century*. London: Victoria and Albert Museum, 1989.

Dawson, Jack. *Finnish Post-War Glass (1945–1996)*. Sunderland: Reg Vardy Gallery at the University of Sunderland, 1996.

Other Sources

Beard, Geoffrey. *International Modern Glass*. London: Barrie and Jenkins, 1976.

Byars, Mel. *The Design Encyclopedia*. London: Lawrence King, 1994.

Grover, Ray, and Lee Grover. *Contemporary Art Glass.* New York: Crown Publishers, 1975.

Mäki, Oili. *Taide ja Työ: Finnish Designers of Today.* Helsinki: Werner Söderström Osakeyhtiö, 1954. Includes an outline biography.

Nillonen, Kerttu. *Finnish Glass.* Helsinki: Tammi, 1966.

1176 MEECH, ANNETTE (1948–)

German-born glass designer who works in England.

Exhibitions

British Studio Glass. Sunderland: Sunderland Arts Centre, 1983.

Other Sources

Clark, Dillon. "Sam Herman/Peter Layton/Glasshouse." *Crafts* 23 (1976): 45. Mentions Annette Meech.

1177 MESZAROS, MARIA

Hungarian glass designer.

Exhibitions

New Glass: A Worldwide Survey. Corning, New York: Corning Museum of Glass, 1979.

1178 MOJE-WOLGEMUTH, ISGARD (1941–)

German glass designer.

Exhibitions

Ricke, Helmut. *Neues Glas in Europa: 50 Künstler—50 Konzepte.* Dusseldorf: Kunstmuseum, 1990. Contains a bibliography.

1179 MONCRIEFF, MARIANNE ISOBEL (1874–1961)

Scottish glass designer.

Exhibitions

Seddon Jill, and Suzette Worden, eds. *Women Designing: Redefining Design in Britain between the Wars.* Brighton: University of Brighton, 1994.

Other Sources

1180 MONOD, ISABELLE (née FERRIRE) (1945–)

French glass designer, sister-in-law of Véronique Monod (q.v.).

Exhibitions

Verriers français contemporains: Art et industrie. Paris: Musée des Arts Décoratifs. 1982.

Other Sources

Bloch-Dermant, Janine. *Le verre en France d'Emile Gallé à nos jours.* Paris: Editions de l'Amateur, 1983.

————. *Le verre en France: les années 80.* Paris: les Editions des Amateurs, n.d. [c.1990]. Informative biographical entry.

Carteron, Philippe, ed. *Ceci n'est plus du verre.* Paris: Editions vers les Arts, 1994.

1181 MONOD, VERONIQUE (1954–)
French glass designer, sister-in-law of Isabelle Monod (q.v.).

Main Sources

Houssard, Françoise. "Véronique Monod: verreries soufflées au couleur du temps." *Revue des Industries d'Art* 178 (March 1982): 154–157.

Labbe, Robert. "Véronique Monod." *Revue de la Céramique du Verre* 9 (March–April 1983): 20–21, illus.

Exhibitions

Verriers français contemporains: art et industrie. Paris: Musée des Arts Décoratifs, 1982.

Other Sources

Bloch-Dermant, Janine. *Le verre en France d'Emile Gallé à nos jours.* Paris: Editions de l'Amateur, 1983.

————. *Le verre en France: les années 80.* Paris: les Editions des Amateurs, n.d. [c.1990]. Informative biographical entry.

1182 MONRO, HELEN (Alt. TURNER or MONRO-TURNER).
Scottish glass designer and engraver who founded the Juniper Workshop with Val Rossi (q.v.).

Publications

"The Training of Students as Glass Artists." *Atti del III Congresso Internazionale del Vetro, Venezia,* 650—653. Rome 1954.

"Glass engraving." *The Studio,* October 1960.

Exhibitions

Glass 1959: A Special Exhibition of International Contemporary Glass. Corning, New York: Corning Museum of Glass, 1959.

Other Sources

Arwas, Victor. *Glass: Art Nouveau to Art Deco.* London: Academy Editions, 1977.

Beard, Geoffrey. *International Modern Glass.* London: Barrie and Jenkins, 1976.

Polak, Ada. *Modern Glass.* London: Faber and Faber, 1962.

1183 MORALES-SCHILDT, MONA (1908–)
Swedish glass designer.

Main Sources

Björkman, Gunvor. "Juveler i glas." *Form* 60, no. 1 (1964): 34–37.

Other Sources

Beard, Geoffrey. *International Modern Glass.* London: Barrie and Jenkins, 1976.

Grover, Ray, and Lee Grover. *Contemporary Art Glass.* New York: Crown Publishers, 1975.

Polak, Ada. *Modern Glass.* London: Faber and Faber, 1962.

Ricke, Helmut, and Ulrich Gronert, eds. *Glas in Schweden 1915–60.* Munich: Prestel, 1987.

1184 MORCH, IBI (Alt. ELIZABETH TRIER) (1910–1980)
Danish architect and designer of glass.

Exhibitions

Mundt, Barbara, Suzanne Netzer, and Innes Hettler. *Interieur + Design in Deutschland, 1945=60.* Berlin: Kunstgewerbemuseum and Dietrich Reimer Verlag, 1994.

1185 MOTZFELDT, BENNY (1909–)
Norwegian designer of glass.

Exhibitions

Mundt, Barbara. *Nostalgie warum? Kunsthandwerkliche techniken im Stilwandel vom Historismus zur Moderne.* Berlin: Kunstgewerbemuseum, S.M.P.K., 1982.

World Glass Now '82. Hokkaido: Museum of Modern Art, 1982. The work of prizewinners and their biographies are included.

Wichstrøm, Anne. *Rooms with a View: Women's Art in Norway, 1880–1990.* Oslo: Royal Ministry of Foreign Affairs, 1989.

Other Sources

Grover, Ray, and Lee Grover. *Contemporary Art Glass.* New York: Crown Publishers, 1975.

1186 MURRAY, SUE
Scottish glass designer.

Exhibitions

New Glass: A Worldwide Survey. Corning, New York: Corning Museum of Glass, 1979.

1187 NÉMETH, MAGDA VADESZI (1941–)
Hungarian glass designer.

Other Sources

Beard, Geoffrey. *International Modern Glass.* London: Barrie and Jenkins, 1976.

1188 NORDSTRÖM, TIINA (1957–)
Finnish glass designer.

Exhibitions

Dawson, Jack. *Finnish Post-War Glass (1945–1996).* Sunderland: Reg Vardy Gallery at the University of Sunderland, 1996.

1189 NURMINEN, KERTTU (1943–)
Finnish designer of glass.

Exhibitions

Dawson, Jack. *Finnish Post-War Glass (1945–1996).* Sunderland: Reg Vardy Gallery at the University of Sunderland, 1996.

1190 NYMAN, GUNNEL GUSTAFSSON (1909–1948)
Finnish designer of glass, textiles, metal and furniture who was one of the early practitioners of modern glass design.

Exhibitions

McFadden, David. *Scandinavian Modern Design, 1880–1980.* New York: Harry Abrams in association with the Cooper-Hewitt Museum, 1982.

Baldouy-Maternati, Danielle. *La verrerie européene des années 50.* Marseille: Musées de Marseille, 1988.

Opie, Jennifer. *Scandinavia: Ceramics and Glass in the Twentieth Century.* London: Victoria and Albert Museum, 1989.

Eidelberg, Martin, ed. *Design 1935–1965: What Modern Was.* New York: Abrams in association with the Musée des Arts Décoratifs, Montreal, 1991.

Mundt, Barbara, Suzanne Netzer, and Innes Hettler. *Interieur + Design in Deutschland, 1945–1960.* Berlin: Kunstgewerbemuseum and Dietrich Reimer Verlag, 1994.

Dawson, Jack. *Finnish Post-War Glass (1945–1996).* Sunderland: Reg Vardy Gallery, University of Sunderland, 1996

Other Sources

Beard, Geoffrey. *International Modern Glass.* London: Barrie and Jenkins, 1976.

Byars, Mel. *The Design Encyclopedia.* London: Lawrence King, 1994.

Grover, Ray, and Lee Grover. *Contemporary Art Glass.* New York: Crown Publishers, 1975.

Mäki, Oili. *Taide ja Työ: Finnish Designers of Today.* Helsinki: Werner Söderström Osakeyhtiö, 1954. Includes an outline biography.

Nillonen, Kerttu. *Finnish Glass.* Helsinki: Tammi, 1966.

1191 ÖLZNER, ULRIKE (1939–)

German designer of glass who worked with Thomas Ölzner.

Exhibitions

Glaskunst in der DDR. Leipzig: Stadtisches Museum des Kunsthandwerk, 1977.

1192 ORTLIEB, NORA (1904–)

German glass designer and engraver.

Publications

Wilhelm von Eiff. Bamburg, 1950.

Exhibitions

Glass 1959: A Special Exhibition of International Contemporary Glass. Corning, New York: Corning Museum of Glass, 1959.

Norah Ortlieb: Glaskunst. Freiburg im Breisgau: Augustinermuseum, 1985, 33pp., illus. Contains a biographical essay, a bibliography and a catalogue of 100 works with prices.

Other Sources

Beard, Geoffrey. *International Modern Glass.* London: Barrie and Jenkins, 1976.

Joseph Hoffmann and Wilhelm Wagenfeld: Glaskunst der Moderne. Munich: Klinkhardt and Bierman, 1992.

Polak, Ada. *Modern Glass.* London: Faber and Faber, 1962.

1193 PASTRNKOVÁ, JIRINA (1908–)
Czech designer of glass.

Exhibitions

Ryté sklo: pruní prehlídka soudobé tvorby. Brno: Moravská Gallery, 1965. Very brief biographical outline given.

3 Trienále řezaneho skla [3rd triennial of cut glass]. Brno: Moravská Gallery, 1971. Contains a biographical outline.

Other Sources

Raban, Josef. *Le Verre Moderne de Bohème.* Prague: Artia Praga, 1963.

1194 PAULIN, IDA (1890–1955)
German painter, designer of graphics and in glass.

Other Sources

Joseph Hoffmann and Wilhelm Wagenfeld: Glaskunst der Moderne. Munich: Klinkhardt and Bierman, 1992.

1195 PERSSON-MELIN, SIGNE (1925–)
Swedish designer in glass, metal and ceramics who won the Lunning Prize.

Exhibitions

McFadden, David, ed. *Scandinavian Modern Design, 1880–1980.* New York: Harry Abrams and the Cooper-Hewitt Museum, 1982.

The Lunning Prize. Stockholm: Nationalmuseum, 1986.

Opie, Jennifer. *Scandinavia: Ceramics and Glass in the Twentieth Century.* London: Victoria and Albert Museum, 1989.

Other Sources

Beard, Geoffrey. *International Modern Glass.* London: Barrie and Jenkins, 1976.

Byars, Mel. *The Design Encyclopedia.* London: Lawrence King, 1994.

Naylor, Colin, ed. *Contemporary Designers.* 2nd edition. Chicago and London: St. James Press, 1990. Contains a bibliography.

1196 POPESCU, ADRIANA (1954–)
Romanian glass designer.

Exhibitions

Ricke, Helmut. *Neues Glas in Europa: 50 Künstler—50 Konzepte.* Dusseldorf: Kunstmuseum, 1990. Contains a bibliography.

1197 RØNNING, GRETE (1937–)
Norwegian designer of ceramics, glass and textiles.

See Ceramics section.

1198 RATH, MARIANNE (1904–)
Austrian designer of glass.

Other Sources

Polak, Ada. *Modern Glass.* London: Faber and Faber, 1962.

1199 ROTTENBERG, ENA (née EMMA HELENA) (1893–1950)
Hungarian-born designer of glass who trained and worked in Austria.

Other Sources

Joseph Hoffmann and Wilhelm Wagenfeld: Glaskunst der Moderne. Munich: Klinkhardt and Bierman, 1992.
Polak, Ada. *Modern Glass.* London: Faber and Faber, 1962.

1200 ROUBÍČKOVÁ, MILUŠE (Alt. KYTKOVÁ-ROUBÍČKOVÁ) (1922–)
Czech glass designer.

Main Sources

Henteš, Karel. "Miluše Roubíčková und ihr Glas." *Für Sie aus der Tschechoslowakei,* no. 3 (1975): 38–40.

Exhibitions

Adlerová, Alena. *Böhmisches Glas der Gegenwart.* Hamburg: Museum für Kunst und Gewerbe, 1973.
Metamorfózy skla [New tendencies in glass sculpture]. Brno: Moravská Gallery, 1973.
Büchner, Thomas, and William Warmus. *Czechoslovakian Diary: 1980. 23 Glassmakers.* Corning, New York: Corning Museum of Glass, 1980, p. 5, illus.
Petrová, Sylvia, and Jean-Luc Olivie. *Verres de Bohème 1400–1989: chef d'oeuvres des Musées de Tchécoslovaquie.* Paris: Musée des Arts Décoratifs in association with Flammarion, 1989.

New Glass: A Worldwide Survey. Corning, New York: Corning Museum of Glass, 1979.

Other Sources

Grover, Ray, and Lee Grover. *Contemporary Art Glass.* New York: Crown Publishers, 1975.

Hetteš, Karel. *Glass in Czechoslovakia.* Prague: S.N.T.L., 1958.

Raban, Josef. *Le Verre Moderne de Bohème.* Prague: Artia Praga, 1963.

1201 ROZÁTOVÁ, ELIŠKA (1940–)
    Czech glass designer.

Exhibitions

Adlerová, Alena. *Böhmisches Glas der Gegenwart.* Hamburg: Museum für Kunst und Gewerbe, 1973.

Metamorfózy skla [New tendencies in glass sculpture]. Brno: Moravská Gallery, 1973.

Petrová, Sylvia, and Jean-Luc Olivie. *Verres de Bohème 1400–1989: chef d'oeuvres des Musées de Tchécoslovaquie.* Paris: Musée des Arts Décoratifs in association with Flammarion, 1989.

1202 SABOKOVÁ, GIZELA (1952–)
    Czech glass designer.

Exhibitions

Petrová, Sylvia, and Jean-Luc Olivie. *Verres de Bohème 1400–1989: chef d'oeuvres des Musées de Tchécoslovaquie.* Paris: Musée des Arts Décoratifs in association with Flammarion, 1989.

1203 SASS, ELIZABETH
    Danish designer of glass.

Other Sources

Polak, Ada. *Modern Glass.* London: Faber and Faber, 1962.

1204 SCHARGE-NEBEL, ILSE (1904–)
    German designer of glass.

Exhibitions

Glaskunst in der DDR. Leipzig: Stadtisches Museum des Kunsthandwerk, 1977.

1205 SCHLYTER-STIERNSTEDT, MARGARETHA (BARONESS) (1927–)
Swedish designer of glass.

Exhibitions

Glass 1959: A Special Exhibition of International Contemporary Glass.
Corning, New York: Corning Museum of Glass, 1959.

1206 SCHODER, MARIANNE (1903–1987)
German glass designer and engraver.

Exhibitions

Glass 1959: A Special Exhibition of International Contemporary Glass.
Corning, New York: Corning Museum of Glass, 1959.

Other Sources

Beard, Geoffrey. *International Modern Glass.* London: Barrie and Jenkins,
1976.
Joseph Hoffmann and Wilhelm Wagenfeld: Glaskunst der Moderne. Munich:
Klinkhardt and Bierman, 1992.
Polak, Ada. *Modern Glass.* London: Faber and Faber, 1962.

1207 SCHRADER, ÅSE VOSS
Danish designer of glass.

Other Sources

Polak, Ada. *Modern Glass.* London: Faber and Faber, 1962.

1208 SIIKAMMÄKI, RAIJA (1964–)
Finnish designer of glass.

Exhibitions

Dawson, Jack. *Finnish Post-War Glass (1945–1996).* Sunderland: Reg Vardy
Gallery at the University of Sunderland, 1996.

1209 SIPOS, JUDIT KEKESI (1937–)
Hungarian glass designer.

Other Sources

Beard, Geoffrey. *International Modern Glass.* London: Barrie and Jenkins,
1976.

1210 SLANG, GERD BOESEN (1925–)
Norwegian glass designer.

Other Sources

Beard, Geoffrey. *International Modern Glass*. London: Barrie and Jenkins, 1976.

1211 SMRČKOVÁ, LUDVIKA (1903–1991)
Czech glass designer.

Publications

"Nové hutní sklo." *Ceskovlovensky Sklar* 1 (1951): 19.
"Nové tvary užitkového skla." *Ceskovlovensky Sklar* 1 (1951): 67.
"Novinky ve foukačském skle." *Ceskovlovensky Sklar* 1 (1951): 117.
"Ruzné druhy váz." *Ceskovlovensky Sklar* 1 (1951): 117.
"Upominkové a darkovésklo." *Ceskovlovensky Sklar* 1 (1951): 170.
"Hutní sklo ze závadu Chřibská." *Ceskovlovensky Sklar* 1 (1951): 280.
"Technicko-výtvarné středisko Borské sklo." *Ceskovlovensky Sklar* 1 (1951): 313

Raban, Josef, with Smrčková. *Le Verre Moderne de Bohème*. Prague: Artia Praga, 1963.

Main Sources

Adlerová, Alena. "Le double jubilé de Ludvika Smrčkov." *Revue du Verre* 28, no. 2 (1973): 3–7, illus.

Hofmeisterová, Jana. "Le soixantième anniversaire de Mme Ludvika Smrčková." *Revue du Verre* 18, no. 2 (1963): 33–38.

———. "Les nouvelles oeuvres de verre de Ludvika Smrčková." *Revue du Verre* 25, no. 7 (1970): 197–202, illus.

Holubová, Miloslava. *Ludvika Smrčková*. Prague: Nakladatelství Ceskoslovenských Výtvarných Umelcú, 1961, 74pp., illus. Monograph in Czech with summaries in English, French, Russian and German.

Langhamer, A. "L'oeuvre de Ludvika Smrčková." *Revue du Verre* 43, no. 2 (1988): 22–27, illus. Written on the occasion of her eighty-fifth birthday.

Exhibitions

Glass 1959: A Special Exhibition of International Contemporary Glass. Corning, New York: Corning Museum of Glass, 1959.

Ryté sklo: pruní prehlídka soudobé tvorby. Brno: Moravská Gallery, 1965. Very brief biographical outline given.

3 Trienále řezaneho skla [3rd triennial of cut glass]. Brno: Moravská Gallery, 1971. Contains a biographical outline.

Adlerová, Alena. *Böhmisches Glas der Gegenwart*. Hamburg: Museum für Kunst und Gewerbe, 1973.

Petrová, Sylvia, and Jean-Luc Olivie. *Verres de Bohème 1400–1989: chef d'oeuvres des Musées de Tchécoslovaquie*. Paris: Musée des Arts Décoratifs in association with Flammarion, 1989.

Other Sources

Beard, Geoffrey. *International Modern Glass*. London: Barrie and Jenkins, 1976.

Byars, Mel. *The Design Encyclopedia*. London: Lawrence King, 1994 (under both LUDVIKA and SMRČKOVÁ).

1212 SOLCOVÁ, IVANA (1960–)
    Czech glass designer.

Exhibitions

Petrová, Sylvia, and Jean-Luc Olivie. *Verres de Bohème 1400–1989: chef d'oeuvres des Musées de Tchécoslovaquie*. Paris: Musée des Arts Décoratifs in association with Flammarion, 1989.

1213 SOLVEN, PAULINE (1943–)
    English glass designer.

Main Sources

"Artists in Glass." *Crafts* 35 (1978).
Clarke, Dillon. "Pauline Solven." *Crafts* 29 (1977): 49.

Exhibitions

British Studio Glass. Sunderland: Sunderland Arts Centre, 1983.

Other Sources

Beard, Geoffrey. *International Modern Glass*. London: Barrie and Jenkins, 1976.

Grover, Ray, and Lee Grover. *Contemporary Art Glass*. New York: Crown Publishers, 1975.

1214 STENGER, NICOLE (1947–)
    French designer of glass.

Exhibitions

Verriers français contemporains: art et industrie. Paris: Musée des Arts Décoratifs, 1982.

1215 STEVENS, IRENE M.
    English designer of glass.

Exhibitions

Baldouy-Maternati, Danielle. *La verrerie européene des années 50*. Marseille: Musées de Marseille, 1988.

Other Sources

Polak, Ada. *Modern Glass*. London: Faber and Faber, 1962.

1216 STILL, NANNY
Finnish designer of glass, ceramics, metal, wood and graphics.

See Nanny McKinney Still above.

1217 STROBACHOVÁ, ZDENA (1932–)
Czech designer of glass.

Other Sources

Raban, Josef. *Le Verre Moderne de Bohème*. Prague: Artia Praga, 1963.

1218 STRÖMBERG, ASTA
Swedish designer of glass.

Exhibitions

Mundt, Barbara, Suzanne Netzer, and Innes Hettler. *Interieur + Design in Deutschland, 1945=60*. Berlin: Kunstgewerbemuseum and Dietrich Reimer Verlag, 1994.

Other Sources

Polak, Ada. *Modern Glass*. London: Faber and Faber, 1962.

1219 STRÖMBERG, GERDA
Swedish glass designer.

Exhibitions

Glass 1959: A Special Exhibition of International Contemporary Glass. Corning, New York: Corning Museum of Glass, 1959.
Lutteman, Helena Dahlback, ed. *Svenskt Glass 1915–1960*. Stockholm: National Museum, 1987.

Other Sources

Polak, Ada. *Modern Glass*. London: Faber and Faber, 1962.
Ricke, Helmut, and Ulrich Gronert, eds. *Glas in Schweden 1915–60*. Munich: Prestel, 1987.
Steenberg, Elisa. *Modern Swedish Glass*. Stockholm: Lindqvists, 1949.

1220 SVESTKOVÁ, EVA (1945–)
Czech designer of glass.

Exhibitions

3 Trienále řezaneho skla [3rd triennial of cut glass]. Brno: Moravská Gallery, 1971. Contains a biographical outline.

1221 TAR, SUZANNA (1953–)

Romanian-born designer of glass who works in France.

Exhibitions

Verriers français contemporains: art et industrie. Paris: Musée des Arts Décoratifs, 1982.

1222 TEUNISSEN VAN MANEN, CARINA (1950–)

Dutch glass designer.

Exhibitions

Moderne Hollandsk Tekstilkunst og Glas. Copenhagen: Dansk Kunstindustrimuseum, 1979.

1223 TEUNISSEN VAN MANEN, CORINA (1950–)

Dutch designer of glass who carries out diamond-point engraving.

Exhibitions

Moderne hollandsk tekstilkunst og glass. Copenhagen: Dansk Kunstindustriemuseum, 1979.

1224 TOIKKA, INKERI (1931–)

Finnish glass designer.

Exhibitions

Suomen Lasi—Finnish Glass. Sunderland: Sunderland Arts Centre, 1979.
New Glass: A Worldwide Survey. Corning, New York: Corning Museum of Glass, 1979.
Dawson, Jack. *Finnish Post-War Glass (1945–1996).* Sunderland: Reg Vardy Gallery at the University of Sunderland, 1996.

1225 TOUSKOVÁ, KAPKA

Bulgarian glass designer working in the Czech Republic.

Exhibitions

Metamorfózy skla [New tendencies in glass sculpture]. Brno: Moravská Gallery, 1973.
New Glass: A Worldwide Survey. Corning, New York: Corning Museum of Glass, 1979.

1226 TUOMINEN, KATI (Alt. TUOMINEN-NIITYLÄ) (1947–)
     Finnish designer of glass.

Exhibitions

Dawson, Jack. *Finnish Post-War Glass (1945–1996)*. Sunderland: Reg Vardy Gallery at the University of Sunderland, 1996.

1227 TYNELL, HELENA (1918–)
     Finnish glass designer.

Main Sources

"Möbel." *Interior Design* 12 (1967): 82–83

Exhibitions

Suomen Lasi—Finnish Glass. Sunderland: Sunderland Arts Centre, 1979.
McFadden, David, ed. *Scandinavian Modern Design, 1880–1980*. New York: Harry Abrams and the Cooper-Hewitt Museum, 1982.
Dawson, Jack. *Finnish Post-War Glass (1945–1996)*. Sunderland: Reg Vardy Gallery at the University of Sunderland, 1996.

Other Sources

Beard, Geoffrey. *International Modern Glass*. London: Barrie and Jenkins, 1976.
Byars, Mel. *The Design Encyclopedia*. London: Lawrence King, 1994.
Grover, Ray, and Lee Grover. *Contemporary Art Glass*. New York: Crown Publishers, 1975.
Mäki, Oili. *Taide ja Työ: Finnish Designers of Today*. Helsinki: Werner Söderström Osakeyhtiö, 1954. Contains an outline biography.
Nillonen, Kerttu. *Finnish Glass*. Helsinki: Tammi, 1967, pp. 89–97.

1228 ULLBERG, KARI (1954–)
     Norwegian designer of glass.

Exhibitions

Nordisk Glass '88. Trondheim: Nordernfjeldske Kunstindustriemuseum, 1988. She was one of seventeen designers featured in the exhibition.

1229 VACHTOVÁ, DANA (1937–)
     Czech glass designer.

Main Sources

Marsiková, J. "Socharka skla" [A woman sculptor in glass]. *Domov* 5 (1977): 28–31, illus.

Exhibitions

Art tchèque contemporain: gravure, céramique, verre. Freiburg: Musée d'Art et d'Histoire, 1973.

Adlerová, Alena. *Böhmisches Glas der Gegenwart.* Hamburg: Museum für Kunst und Gewerbe, 1973.

Metamorfózy skla [New tendencies in glass sculpture]. Brno: Moravská Gallery, 1973.

Büchner, Thomas, and William Warmus. *Czechoslovakian Diary: 1980. 23 Glassmakers.* Corning, New York: Corning Museum of Glass, 1980, p. 15, illus.

Petrová, Sylvia, and Jean-Luc Olivie. *Verres de Bohème 1400–1989: chef d'oeuvres des Musées de Tchécoslováquie.* Paris: Musée des Arts Décoratifs in association with Flammarion, 1989.

1230 VALLIEN, ULRICA (Alt. HYDMAN-VALLIEN) (1938–)
Swedish designer of glass and ceramics.

Exhibitions

New Glass: A Worldwide Survey. Corning, New York: Corning Museum of Glass, 1979.

McFadden, David, ed. *Scandinavian Modern Design, 1880–1980.* New York: Harry Abrams and the Cooper-Hewitt Museum, 1982.

Nordisk Glass '88. Trondheim:Nordernfjeldske Kunstindustriemuseum, 1988. She was one of seventeen designers featured in the exhibition.

Opie, Jennifer. *Scandinavia: Ceramics and Glass in the Twentieth Century.* London: Victoria and Albert Museum, 1989.

Ricke, Helmut. *Neues Glas in Europa: 50 Künstler—50 Konzepte.* Dusseldorf: Kunstmuseum, 1990. Contains a bibliography.

Um seculo de Artes do Fogo (1890–1990):coleccao Padua Ramos; un siècle d'Arts du Feu (1890–1990): collection Padua Ramos. Lisbon: Musseu Nacional do Azulejo, 1994. The only woman included in this exhibition.

Other Sources

Byars, Mel. *The Design Encyclopedia.* London: Lawrence King, 1994.

Beard, Geoffrey. *International Modern Glass.* London: Barrie and Jenkins, 1976.

Lewenstein, Eileen, and Emmanuel Cooper. *New Ceramics.* London: Studio Vista, 1974.

Naylor, Colin, ed. *Contemporary Designers.* 2nd edition. Chicago and London: St. James Press, 1990. Contains a bibliography.

1231 VAN MEURS, SIEN (1953–)
Dutch glass designer.

Exhibitions

Moderne Hollandsk Tekstilkunst og Glas. Copenhagen: Dansk Kunstindustrimuseum, 1979.

Ricke, Helmut. *Neues Glas in Europa: 50 Künstler—50 Konzepte.* Dusseldorf: Kunstmuseum, 1990. Contains a bibliography.

Other Sources

1232 VELIŠKOVÁ, MILENA (1917–)
Czech glass designer.

Exhibitions

Glass 1959: A Special Exhibition of International Contemporary Glass. Corning, New York: Corning Museum of Glass, 1959.
Petrová, Sylvia, and Jean-Luc Olivie. *Verres de Bohème 1400–1989: chef d'oeuvres des Musées de Tchécoslovaquie.* Paris: Musée des Arts Décoratifs in association with Flammarion, 1989.

Other Sources

Raban, Josef. *Le Verre Moderne de Bohème.* Prague: Artia Praga, 1963.

1233 VERVEY, KEA (1945–)
Dutch glass designer.

Exhibitions

Moderne Hollandsk Tekstilkunst og Glas. Copenhagen: Dansk Kunstindustrimuseum, 1979.

1234 VIDA, ZSUSZSA
Hungarian glass designer.

Exhibitions

New Glass: A Worldwide Survey. Corning, New York: Corning Museum of Glass, 1979.

1235 VON BOCH, HELEN (1938–)
German designer of ceramics; member of the Boch family of designers of ceramics and glass.

Exhibitions

Hiesinger, Kathryn, and George Marcus III, eds. *Design since 1945.* Philadelphia: Philadelphia Museum of Art, 1983.

Other Sources

Byars, Mel. *The Design Encyclopedia.* London: Lawrence King, 1994.

1236 WAHL, MARCELLE
>   French designer of glass and enameller who originally trained as a doctor.

Other Sources

Bloch-Dermant, J. *Le verre en France d'Emile Gallé à nos jours.* Paris: Editions de l'Amateur, 1983.

1237 WALTON, HANNAH MOORE (1863–1940)
>   Scottish miniature painter and designer who painted on glass and ceramics; sister of Helen (q.v.).

See Ceramics section.

1238 WALTON, HELEN (1850–1921)
>   Scottish designer who painted glass and ceramics. She set up a studio with her sisters Hannah (q.v.) and Constance.

See Ceramics section.

1239 WÄRFF, ANNE (née WOLFF) (1937–)
>   German glass designer who works in Sweden; a winner of the Lunning Prize with Goran Wärff.

Exhibitions

New Glass: A Worldwide Survey. Corning, New York: Corning Museum of Glass, 1979.

McFadden, David, ed. *Scandinavian Modern Design, 1880–1980.* New York: Harry Abrams and the Cooper-Hewitt Museum, 1982.

World Glass Now '82. Hokkaido: Museum of Modern Art, 1982. The work of prizewinners and their biographies are included.

The Lunning Prize. Stockholm: Nationalmuseum, 1986.

Opie, Jennifer. *Scandinavia: Ceramics and Glass in the Twentieth Century.* London: Victoria and Albert Museum, 1989.

Other Sources

Beard, Geoffrey. *International Modern Glass.* London: Barrie and Jenkins, 1976.

Byars, Mel. *The Design Encyclopedia.* London: Lawrence King, 1994.

Grover, Ray, and Lee Grover. *Contemporary Art Glass.* New York: Crown Publishers, 1975.

1240 WEBSTER, JANE (c. 1935–)
>   English-based glass designer.

Main Sources

Heddle, G. M. *A manual of etching and engraving glass.* London: Tiranti, 1961.

Other Sources

Beard, Geoffrey. *International Modern Glass.* London: Barrie and Jenkins, 1976.

1241 WIESELTHIER, VALLY (née VALERIE) (1895–1945)
Austrian designer in several media, particularly ceramics and glass; she moved to America in 1929.

Exhibitions

Kallir, Jane. *Viennese Design and the Wiener Werkstätte.* New York: Braziller in association with the Galérie St. Etienne, 1986.
Leitgeb, Hildegard, Elizabeth Schmuttermeier, and Angela Völker. *Wiener Werkstätte: Atelier viennois, 1903–1932.* Brussels: Galérie CGER, 1987.
Hamacher, Bärbel, ed. *Expressive Keramik der Wiener Werkstätte, 1917–1930.* Munich: Bayerische Vereinsbank, 1992. Contains a bibliography.

Other Sources

Arwas, Victor. *Glass: Art Nouveau to Art Deco.* London: Academy Editions, 1977.
Byars, Mel. *The Design Encyclopedia.* London: Lawrence King, 1994. *Joseph Hoffmann and Wilhelm Wagenfeld: Glaskunst der Moderne.* Munich: Klinkhardt and Bierman, 1992.
Neuwirth, Waltraud. *Die Keramik der Wiener Werkstätte.* Vienna: W. Neuwirth, 1981.
Schweiger, W. *Weiner Werkstätte: Kunst und Handwerk, 1903–32.* Vienna: Christian Brandstätter Verlag, 1982.

1242 WLODARCZYK-PUCHALA, REGINA
Polish glass designer.

Exhibitions

New Glass: A Worldwide Survey. Corning, New York: Corning Museum of Glass, 1979.

1243 WOLFF, ANN (née ANNELIESE SCHAEFER) (1937–)
German-born designer of glass and ceramics who worked in Sweden from 1960.

Exhibitions

Oedekoven-Gerischer, Angela, et al., eds. *Frauen im Design: Berufsbilder und Lebenswege seit 1900. Women in Design: Careers and Life Histories since 1900.* Stuttgart: Design Center, 1989.

Other Sources

Naylor, Colin, ed. *Contemporary Designers.* 2nd edition. Chicago and London: St. James Press, 1990. Contains a bibliography.

1244 WOLOWSKA, ALINA
Polish glass designer.

Exhibitions

New Glass: A Worldwide Survey. Corning Museum of Glass, Corning, New York, 1979.

1245 ZÁMEČNIKOVÁ, DANA
Czech glass designer and sculptor.

Main Sources

Chambers, Karen. "Dana Zámečníková: Artist and Magician." *Craft International* 1985 (January–March): 20–21, illus.

Suda, Kristian. "Spiel im Raum-Raum im Spiel. Play of space-space of play." *Neues Glas* 4 (1984): 187–191, illus. Article in German and English.

Vondra, Viktor. "Exposition aux Etats-Unis." *Revue du Verre,* vol. 42, part 12 (1987): 23–25, illus. Interview with the designer and her husband who shared an exhibition.

Exhibitions

Büchner, Thomas, and William Warmus. *Czechoslovakian Diary: 1980. 23 Glassmakers.* Corning, New York: Corning Museum of Glass, 1980, p. 11, illus.

Petrová, Sylvia, and Jean-Luc Olivie. *Verres de Bohème 1400–1989: chef d'oeuvres des Musées de Tchécoslovaquie.* Paris: Musée des Arts Décoratifs in association with Flammarion, 1989.

Ricke, Helmut. *Neues Glas in Europa: 50 Künstler—50 Konzepte.* Dusseldorf: Kunstmuseum, 1990. Contains a bibliography.

1246 ZERTOVÁ, JIRINA (1932–)
Czech glass designer.

Exhibitions

3 Trienále řezaneho skla [3rd triennial of cut glass]. Brno: Moravská Gallery, 1971. Contains a biographical outline.

Art tchèque contemporain: gravure, céramique, verre. Freiburg: Musée d'Art et d'Histoire, 1973.

Adlerová, Alena. *Böhmisches Glas der Gegenwart.* Hamburg: Museum für Kunst und Gewerbe, 1973.

Metamorfózy skla [New tendencies in glass sculpture]. Brno: Moravská Gallery, 1973.

New Glass: A Worldwide Survey. Corning, New York: Corning Museum of Glass, 1979.

Petrová, Sylvia, and Jean-Luc Olivie. *Verres de Bohème 1400–1989: chef d'oeuvres des Musées de Tchécoslovaquie.* Paris: Musée des Arts Décoratifs in association with Flammarion, 1989.

Ricke, Helmut. *Neues Glas in Europa: 50 Künstler—50 Konzepte.* Dusseldorf: Kunstmuseum, 1990. Contains a bibliography.

Other Sources

Raban, Josef. *Le Verre Moderne de Bohème.* Prague: Artia Praga, 1963.

1247 ZORITCHAK, CATHERINE (1947–)
       French glass designer.

Exhibitions

Verriers français contemporains: art et industrie. Paris: Musée des Arts Décoratifs, 1982.

Other Sources

Bloch-Dermant, Janine. *La verre en France d'Emile Gallé à nos jours.* Paris: Editions de l'Amateur, 1983.

————. *Le verre en France: les années 80.* Paris: les Editions des Amateurs, n.d. [c. 1990]. Informative biographical entry.

Stained Glass

REFERENCE

1248 ANON. *Directory of Stained Glass Windows Executed within the Past Twenty Years.* London: British Society of Master Glass-Painters, 1955, 109pp.

Arranged as a gazetteer, it provides a geographical listing by county under an alphabetical sequence of designers. Eight women are included: Trena Cox, Clare Dawson, Mrs. R. M. de Montmorency, Marion Grant, Edith Norris, Margaret Thompson, Nora Yoxall and Elsie Whitford (q.v.). These last two worked together.

OTHER PUBLICATIONS

1249 FAUX, MONIQUE. *Le vitrail et les peintres a Reims 1957–59.* Reims: Maison de la Culture, 1969, 80pp., illus.

Text in French. An introductory essay on the value and quality of stained glass in general is followed by an introduction to the exhibition in which each work originated from the Atelier Simon at Rheims. These works are the result of twelve years of cooperation between artists and glass makers. The Atelier is run by Brigitte Simon and Charles Marq, who took the initiative to write to artists to invite their collaboration in the production of stained glass. An alphabetical catalogue follows with a biographical introduction to each artist together with details of the windows installed. Three women featured: Geneviève Asse (q.v., vol. 2), Brigitte Simon (q.v.) and Maria Helena Vieira da Silva (q.v.).

1250 GORDON BOWE, NICOLA. "Women stained glass artists." *Irish Arts Review* 4, no. 3 (1986): 66–67, illus.

Review of an exhibition *of Women Stained Glass Artists of the Arts and Crafts Movement* (q.v.) at the William Morris Gallery, Walthamstow.

1251 MILLER, FRED. "Women Workers in the Art Crafts." *Art Journal* (1896): 116–118.

Description of work executed by six women in the Arts and Crafts style, with the greatest detail being given about the stained glass designer Mary Lowndes (q.v.), whom the author visited. The others are Mary Nevill, Esther Moore, Miss Birkenruth, M. Reeks and M. Hussey, the last three being bookbinders.

1252 MOORE, ANDREW. *Contemporary Stained Glass: A Guide to the Potential of Modern Stained Glass in Architecture.* London: Mitchell Beazley, 1989, 143pp., illus.

Written primarily from the technical point of view, the book includes the work of designers mainly to illustrate a historical survey of postwar stained glass in the United States, Britain, France and Germany and to provide exemplars of different types of work. There are two German women included: Maria Katzgrau and Margarete Keith; and eight British women designers.

1253 MORRIS, ELIZABETH. *Stained and Decorative Glass.* London: Quintet Publishing Ltd., 1988, 128pp., illus.

An historical account of glass in the nineteenth and twentieth centuries, mainly in Britain but with references to mainland Europe and the United States. Women of the Arts and Crafts movement in Britain and Eire are mentioned, and a few contemporary women are also included.

1254 PERROT, FRANÇOISE, and JACQUES BONY. *Le vitrail français contemporain.* L'Oeil et la Main. Lyon: La Manufacture, 1984, 169pp., illus.

Text in French. The focus of the book is on the collaboration of artists and glass artists in stained glass in France. Brief introductory essays on the topic are followed by information on sixty individuals working collaboratively in this field, of whom nine are women: Genevieve Asse and Maria Elena Vieira da Silva (qq.v. vol. 2), who are artists providing designs for glass, and Sylvie Gaudin, Marie-Jo Guevel, Mireille Juteau, Anne Le Chevallier, Brigitte Simon (q.v.), Marie-Cécile Tellier and Jeannette Weiss, who all work in glass.

1255 *Verriers français contemporains: art et industrie.* Paris: Musée des Arts Décoratifs, 1982, 136pp., illus.

A traveling exhibition with introductory texts on contemporary stained glass, the qualities of glass and links between art and industry. Seven women featured in the contemporary section: Jutta Cuny, Monica Damian Eyrignoux, Isabelle and Véronique Monod, Nicole Stenger, Suzanna Tar and Catherine Zoritchak (qq.v.). All are French or based in France.

1256 *Women Stained Glass Artists of the Arts and Crafts Movement.* Waltham Forest: William Morris Gallery, 1985, 25pp., illus.

Examines women who produced stained glass between 1880 and 1950. Detailed information and references are given for the eleven women included as well as notes on the exhibits.

INDIVIDUALS

1257 CAMM, FLORENCE (1874–1960)
English designer of metalwork and stained glass.

Exhibitions

Crawford, Alan. *By Hammer and Hand: The Arts and Crafts Movement in Birmingham.* Birmingham: City Museum and Art Gallery, 1984.
Women Stained Glass Artists of the Arts and Crafts Movement. Waltham Forest: William Morris Gallery, 1985.

1258 CHILTON, MARGARET (1875–c. 1962)
English designer of stained glass who worked with Marjorie Kemp (q.v.).

Exhibitions

Women Stained Glass Artists of the Arts and Crafts Movement. Waltham Forest: William Morris Gallery, 1985.

1259 COX, TRENA
English designer of stained glass.

Other Sources

Day, Michael. *Modern Art in Church: A Gazetteer.* London, 1982.
Directory of Stained Glass Windows Executed within the Past Twenty Years. London: British Society of Master Glass-Painters, 1955.

1260 DAWSON, CLARE
English designer of stained glass.

Other Sources

Directory of Stained Glass Windows Executed within the Past Twenty Years. London: British Society of Master Glass-Painters, 1955.

1261 ELVERY, BEATRICE (Alt. LADY GLENAVY) (1883–1968)
Irish stained glass designer and, later, painter.

Publications

Beatrice, Lady Glenavy. *Today we will only gossip.* London, 1964.

Other Sources

Gordon Bowe, Nicola, David Caron, and Michael Wynne. *Gazetteer of Irish Stained Glass. The Works of Harry Clarke and the Artists of An Tur Gloine, 1903–63.* Dublin: Irish Academic Press, 1988, 112pp., illus. Lists the stained glass executed by these artists by geographical location.

1262 ESPLIN, MABEL (1874–1921)
    English designer of stained glass.

Exhibitions

Women Stained Glass Artists of the Arts and Crafts Movement. Waltham
Forest: William Morris Gallery, 1985.

1263 FORSYTH, MOIRA (1905–)
    English designer of ceramics and stained glass.

Exhibitions

Thirties: British Art and Design Before the War. London: Arts Council of
Great Britain at the Hayward Gallery, 1979.
    Dodsworth, Roger. *British Glass Between the Wars.* Kingswinford:
Broadfield House Glass Museum, 1987.

Other Sources

Buckley, Cheryl. *Potters and Paintresses: Women Designers in the Pottery
Industry, 1870–1955.* London: Women's Press, 1990.
    Byars, Mel. *The Design Encyclopedia.* London: Lawrence King, 1994.
    Day, Michael. *Modern Art in Church: A Gazetteer.* London, 1982

1264 FULLEYLOVE, JOAN (1886–1947)
    English designer of stained glass.

Exhibitions

Women Stained Glass Artists of the Arts and Crafts Movement. Waltham
Forest: William Morris Gallery, 1985.

1265 GEDDES, WILHELMINA (1887–1955)
    Irish stained glass designer.

Main Sources

Gordon Bowe, Nicola. "Wilhelmina Geddes: Ireland's Extraordinary Artist."
Journal of the Stained Glass Association of America 76, no. 1 (spring 1981): 41–43,
illus.
    ———. "Wilhelmina Geddes." *Irish Arts Review,* part 3 (1987): 53–59, illus.
Defends Geddes against unfavourable comparisons with her pupil Evie Hone.
    ———. "Wilhelmina Geddes (1887–1955)," in *New Perspectives in Art
History, Essays in Honour of Anne Crookshank,* 207–218. Dublin: Irish Academic
Press, 1987.
    ———. "Wilhelmina Geddes (1887–1955): Her Life and Work: A

Reappraisal." *Journal of Stained Glass,* vol. 18, part 3 (1988): 275–301, 11 illus. Biographical account.

————. "Wilhelmina Geddes, Harry Clarke and Their Part in the Arts and Crafts Movement in Ireland." *Journal of the Decorative and Propaganda Arts, 1875–1945* (spring 1988): 58–69.

Exhibitions

Women Stained Glass Artists of the Arts and Crafts Movement. Waltham Forest: William Morris Gallery, 1985.

Seddon Jill, and Suzette Worden, eds. *Women Designing: Redefining Design in Britain between the Wars.* Brighton: University of Brighton, 1994.

Other Sources

Day, Michael. *Modern Art in Church: A Gazetteer.* London, 1982.

Gordon Bowe, Nicola, David Caron, and Michael Wynne. *Gazetteer of Irish Stained Glass. The Works of Harry Clarke and the Artists of An Tur Gloine, 1903–63.* Dublin: Irish Academic Press, 1988, 112pp., illus. Lists the stained glass executed by these artists by geographical location.

1266 GRANT, MARION
  English designer of stained glass.

Other Sources

Directory of Stained Glass Windows Executed within the Past Twenty Years. London: British Society of Master Glass-Painters, 1955.

1267 HONE, EVIE (1894–1955)
  Irish painter and designer of stained glass.

Main Sources

Gordon Bowe, Nicola. "Wilhelmina Geddes." *Irish Arts Review,* vol. 4, part 3 (1987): 53–59, illus. Defends Geddes against unfavourable comparisons with her pupil Evie Hone.

Other Sources

Day, Michael. *Modern Art in Church: A Gazetteer.* London: 1982.

Dunford, Penny. *A Biographical Dictionary of Women Artists in Europe and America since 1850.* Hemel Hempstead: Harvester Wheatsheaf and Philadelphia: University of Pennsylvania Press, 1990. Contains a bibliography.

Gordon Bowe, Nicola, David Caron, and Michael Wynne. *Gazetteer of Irish Stained Glass. The Works of Harry Clarke and the Artists of An Tur Gloine, 1903–63.* Dublin: Irish Academic Press, 1988, 112pp., illus. Lists the stained glass executed by these artists by geographical location.

1268 KATZGRAU, MARIA
German designer of stained glass.

Other Sources

Moore, Andrew. *Contemporary Stained Glass: A Guide to the Potential of Modern Stained Glass in Architecture*. London: Mitchell Beazley, 1989.

1269 KEITH, MARGARETE
German designer of stained glass.

Other Sources

Moore, Andrew. *Contemporary Stained Glass: A Guide to the Potential of Modern Stained Glass in Architecture*. London: Mitchell Beazley, 1989.

1270 KEMP, MARJORIE (1886–1975)
English designer of stained glass.

Exhibitions

Women Stained Glass Artists of the Arts and Crafts Movement. Waltham Forest: William Morris Gallery, 1985.

1271 LOWNDES, MARY (1857–1929)
English designer of stained glass.

Main Sources

Miller, Fred. "Women Workers in the Art Crafts." *Art Journal* (1896): 116–118.

Exhibitions

Women Stained Glass Artists of the Arts and Crafts Movement. Waltham Forest: William Morris Gallery, 1985.

1272 McDONALD, JANE
English stained glass designer.

Main Sources

Darley, Gillian. "Hong Kong Jazz." *Crafts* 79 (1986): 42.

1273 NEWILL, MARY J. (1860–1947)
English painter, book illustrator, designer of stained glass and textiles, embroiderer.

Exhibitions

Crawford, Alan. *By Hammer and Hand: The Arts and Crafts Movement in Birmingham.* Birmingham: City Museum and Art Gallery, 1984. Information on her in the sections on different media.

Other Sources

Marsh, Jan, and Pamela Gerrish Nunn. *Women Artists and the Pre-Raphaelite Movement.* London: Virago, 1989.

Miller, Fred. "Women Workers in the Art Crafts." *Art Journal* (1896): 116–118.

Parry, Linda. *Textiles of the Arts and Crafts Movement.* London: Thames and Hudson, 1988.

Vallance, Aymer. "British Decorative Art in 1899 and the Arts and Crafts Exhibition." *Studio* 18 (1900): 179–194, 247–272.

1274 O'BRIEN, KITTY (née CATHERINE O'BRIEN) (1881–1963)
Irish stained glass designer.

Other Sources

Gordon Bowe, Nicola, David Caron, and Michael Wynne. *Gazetteer of Irish Stained Glass. The Works of Harry Clarke and the Artists of An Tur Gloine, 1903–63.* Dublin: Irish Academic Press, 1988, 112pp., illus. Lists the stained glass executed by these artists by geographical location.

1275 POCOCK, LILIAN (1883–1974)
English designer of stained glass, graphic artist and painter.

Exhibitions

Women Stained Glass Artists of the Arts and Crafts Movement. Waltham Forest: William Morris Gallery, 1985.

1276 RHIND, ETHEL (c.1879–1952)
Irish stained glass designer.

Other Sources

Gordon Bowe, Nicola, David Caron, and Michael Wynne. *Gazetteer of Irish Stained Glass. The Works of Harry Clarke and the Artists of An Tur Gloine, 1903–63.* Dublin: Irish Academic Press, 1988, 112pp., illus. Lists the stained glass executed by these artists by geographical location.

1277 ROPE, MARGARET ALDRICH (1891–)
English designer of stained glass, niece of the sculptor Mary Ellen Rope (q.v. vol. 2).

Exhibitions

Women Stained Glass Artists of the Arts and Crafts Movement. Waltham Forest: William Morris Gallery, 1985.

1278 ROPE, MARGARET (1882–1953)
      English designer of stained glass.

Exhibitions

Crawford, Alan. *By Hammer and Hand: The Arts and Crafts Movement in Birmingham.* Birmingham: City Museum and Art Gallery, 1984.
Women Stained Glass Artists of the Arts and Crafts Movement. Waltham Forest: William Morris Gallery, 1985.

1279 RUTHERFORD, ROSEMARY E. (active 1951–66)
      English designer of stained glass.

Other Sources

Day, Michael. *Modern Art in Church: A Gazetteer.* London, 1982.

1280 SIMON, BRIGITTE (1926–)
      French stained glass designer.

Exhibitions

Faux, Monique. *Le vitrail et les peintres à Reims,* 1957–9. Maison de la Culture, Reims, 1969.

Other Sources

Perrot, Françoise, and Jacques Bony. *Le vitrail français contemporain.* Lyon: La Manufacture, 1984.

1281 TANCOCK, RACHEL (Alt. LADY DE MONTMORENCY) (1891–1961)
      English designer of stained glass.

Exhibitions

Women Stained Glass Artists of the Arts and Crafts Movement. Waltham Forest: William Morris Gallery, 1985.

Other Sources

Directory of Stained Glass Windows Executed within the Past Twenty Years. London: British Society of Master Glass-Painters, 1955.

1282 TOWNSHEND, CAROLINE (1878–1944)
English designer of stained glass who worked with Joan Howson from 1920.

Exhibitions

Women Stained Glass Artists of the Arts and Crafts Movement. Waltham Forest: William Morris Gallery, 1985.

1283 TRAHERNE, MARGARET
English designer of stained glass.

Other Sources

Day, Michael. *Modern Art in Church: A Gazetteer.* London: 1982.

1284 WHALL, VERONICA (1887–1967)
English designer of stained glass who trained with her father Christopher and, after his death in 1924, took over his studio and workshop.

Exhibitions

Women Stained Glass Artists of the Arts and Crafts Movement. Waltham Forest: William Morris Gallery, 1985.

1285 WHITFORD, ELSIE
English designer of stained glass who worked with Norah Yoxall (q.v.).

Other Sources

Directory of Stained Glass Windows Executed within the Past Twenty Years. London: British Society of Master Glass-Painters, 1955.

1286 WOOD, HELEN MUIR (1864–1930)
Scottish designer of metalwork, stained glass and decorated ceramics.

Exhibitions

Burkhauser, Jude, ed. *'Glasgow Girls': Women in Art and Design, 1880–1920.* Edinburgh: Canongate, 1990.

1287 YOXALL, NORAH
English designer of stained glass and painter who worked with Elsie Whitford (q.v.).

Exhibitions

Crawford, Alan. *By Hammer and Hand: The Arts and Crafts Movement in Birmingham.* Birmingham: City Museum and Art Gallery, 1984.

Other Sources

Directory of Stained Glass Windows Executed within the Past Twenty Years. London: British Society of Master Glass-Painters, 1955.

Interior Design, Furniture, Lighting and Metalwork

PUBLICATIONS

1288 ANARGYROS, SOPHIE. *Le style des années 80: architecture, décorations, design.* Rivages—styles. Paris: Rivages, 1986, 111pp., illus.

Text in French. After an introductory essay, the three chapters examine the architecture, interior design and furniture of the 1980s. There are references back to Eileen Gray (q.v.) in the second chapter, while several women designers feature in the final one: Elyzabeth Garouste, Mattia Bonetti and Martine Bedin (q.v.).

1289 BACCI, NICOLETTA, ANNA LUPPI, and MILLY MAZZEI. *Il design delle donne.* Milan: Arnaldo Mondadori, 1991, mainly illus.

Text in Italian. Five chapters deal with the work of fifty-nine women designers. The first chapter looks at the redesigning of everyday utensils and objects in order to make them more practical. The emphasis is on furniture, product and interior design.

1290 BANGERT, ALBRECHT, and KARL ARMER. *Design: les années 80.* Paris: Editions du Chêne, 1990, 240pp., many illus.

Text in French. Surveys products of the 1980s in chapters on furniture, lighting, table arts, textiles and industrial design. Biographies of the designers, who are mainly European, are also given. There are sixteen European women included.

1291 BIRJUKOVA, N. J., and V. A. SUSLOV. *Prikladnoe iskusstvo konca XIX—nacala XX veka katalog vystavki* [The decorative arts in the late 19th and early 20th centuries]. Leningrad [St. Petersburg]: Hermitage Museum, 1974.

Text in Russian. An introductory essay describes the decorative arts in Russia up to the nineteenth century, bringing in references to developments in other countries, such as William Morris and Jugendstil. The largest part of the book is a catalogue with the names of artists given in Russian and transcriptions provided for those who are not Russian. Outline biographies are included. Areas covered include ceramics, fabric design, furniture, glass and fashion. Some women are included.

1292 CRAWFORD, ALAN (ED.). *By Hammer and Hand: The Arts and Crafts Movement in Birmingham.* Birmingham: City Museum and Art Gallery, 1984, 169pp., illus.

After an introduction to the Arts and Crafts in Birmingham, there are sections on activities in the different media, including wall-painting, ceramics, metalwork, stained glass, book illustration and binding. There is also a gazetteer. Apart from the better-known figures, such as Kate and Myra Bunce, about thirty other women are mentioned.

1293 DUNCAN, ALASTAIR. *Art Deco Furniture.* London: Thames and Hudson, 1984, 187pp., illus.

The main part of the text consists of alphabetical entries giving a biographical account of the mainly French designers. Each entry is quite detailed but varies according to the information available. Included are Charlotte Alix, Eileen Gray, Charlotte Chauchet-Guilleré, Suzanne Guiguichon, Renée Kinsbourg, Blanche-J. [*sic*] Klotz, Charlotte Perriand and Lucie Renaudot (qq.v.).

1294 GARNIER, PHILIPPE. *The contemporary decorative arts from 1940 to the present day.* Oxford: Phaidon, 1980, 224pp., illus.

Separate chapters are devoted to furniture, metalwork, ceramics, jewellery, glass, textiles, fashion, industrial design, graphic design, film and photography in Europe and the United States. Provides an overview to the subject, in which quite a number of women designers are included.

1295 *Images of Finnish design, 1960–1990. Published on the occasion of the 80th anniversary of the Finnish Association of Designers (Ornamo).* Espoo: Kustannusosakeyhtiö Tietopuu, 1991, 276pp., illus.

This catalogue is organised by decade. Within each, details are given of individuals active at that time together with an illustration of their work. Media covered include glass, ceramics, industrial design, fashion, jewellery, furniture and interior design. The length of each entry varies. Overall, an excellent source for women.

1296 LINDKVIST, LENNART (ED.). *Design in Sweden.* Stockholm: Swedish Institute, 1972, 144pp., illus.

After an overview of the situation for design in Sweden between 1917 and 1970, there are chapters on glass, ceramics, silver, textiles, furniture, industrial design, the Design Schools and the employment situation for designers. In most, the work of the principal designers is described and many of these are women.

1297 McNEIL, PETER. "Designing Women: Gender, Sexuality and the Interior Decorator, c. 1890–1940." *Art History* 17, no. 4 (1994): 631–657.

Discusses the debates around the social status of women interior decorators and whether such activity could be regarded as real progress for women's employment or whether it merely continued women's association with the home. Many women active in Britain and France are mentioned.

1298 McQUISTON, LIZ. *Women in Design: A Contemporary View.* London: Trefoil Publications, 1988, 144pp., many illus.

Profiles forty-three women, mainly from Europe and the United States, who are engaged in various kinds of design. Maintains that women involved in craft and decorative art activities have received more attention than those in design areas more closely related to industry and production. The emphasis here is on women involved in fields such as furniture design, product design, architecture, animation, television and computer graphics, graphic design, advertising and textile design.

1299 MUNDT, BARBARA, SUSANNE NETZER and INES HETTLER. *Interieur + Design in Deutschland, 1945–1960.* Berlin: Kunstgewerbemuseum in association with Dietrich Reimer Verlag, 1994, 254pp., illus.

Text in German. Essays on interior design in Germany since 1945 and on the development of certain media, including glass, ceramics and furniture, precede the catalogue itself. The work of twenty-eight women is included.

1300 PEACOCK, NETTA. "The new movement in Russian decorative art." *Studio* (1901): 268–276.

Helen Polenoff (d. 1899) was the first to revive the decorative arts in Russia through the use of folk art. In Moscow there arose a group of artists who turned to decorative art indigenous to Russia for their designs for furniture, embroidery and carved wooden objects. Among them were Marie Jacounchikoff and Nathalie Davidoff. Princess Ternichev also followed these ideas.

1301 SCHOESER, MARY. *Fabrics and wallpapers.* Twentieth century design. London: Belland Hyman, 1986, 112pp., illus.

A chronological survey with particular emphasis on the period from the late nineteenth century to 1964. A considerable number of women are included in the account, the majority from Britain.

1302 SEDDON, JILL, and SUZETTE WORDEN (EDS.). *Women Designing. Redefining Design in Britain between the Wars.* Brighton: University of Brighton, 1994, 140pp., illus.

A collection of essays on women designers active in the 1920s and 1930s. The essays are in three main sections: Women and art and design education, Women, industry and institutions, while the last, Women designing, is devoted to studies of individuals. They worked in many different media, including textile design, graphics and interiors.

1303 "Studio Talk." *Studio* 21 (1901): 265–268.

Discusses the success of Mount Street School in Liverpool in the recent National Competition and at the Paris International Exposition of 1900. The article also reviews an exhibition of student work from this school then open in Liverpool. More than fifteen women are mentioned, with metalwork being a particularly strong field.

1304 VALLANCE, AYMER. "British Decorative Art in 1899 and the Arts and Crafts Exhibition." *Studio* 18 (1900): 179–194, 247–272.

Reviews the state of the decorative arts at the end of the nineteenth century and an Arts and Crafts exhibition. Mary Newill (stained glass), Mrs. Gaskin (metalwork), Adele Hay (metalwork), Nelia Casella (metalwork and enamelling) and Ellen M. Rope (plaster reliefs) are among the women mentioned.

1305 VERONESI, GIULIA. *Into the Twenties: Style and Design 1909–1929.* Florence: Valecchi Editore, 1966. Translation: London: Thames and Hudson, 1968, 371pp., 10 pl., 246 illus.

Seeks to map the history of design in Europe from Art Nouveau to 1930 as two principal strands: continuity from earlier traditions and revolt from those traditions. Chapters are devoted to Germany, Paris and Italy before World War I, design during the war, the postwar period in Paris, Germany, England, the United States and Italy, the International Exhibition of the Decorative Arts in 1925 and its aftermath. A glossary and brief biographies of the main participants ends the book. A small number of women are included.

1306 WOOD, ESTHER. "The National Competition at South Kensington, 1899." *Studio* 17 (1899): 250–266.

This review mentions the work of at least ten women designers in stained glass, metalwork and tapestry.

1307 WOOD, ESTHER. "The National Competition, 1901." *Studio* 23 (1901): 257–268.

Almost twenty women designers are included in this review. The work ranges from a plaster relief panel to wallpaper design, embroidered screens, bookbinding and designs for furniture and stained glass.

INDIVIDUALS

1308 ALIX, CHARLOTTE (1897–)

French designer of interiors and furniture.

Other Sources

Barre-Despond, Arlette. *U.A.M.* Paris: Editions du Regard, 1986.
Byars, Mel. *The Design Encyclopedia.* London: Lawrence King, 1994.

1309 ANDERSEN, RIGMOR (1903–after 1989)
Danish designer of furniture who collaborated with Annelise Bjørner (q.v.) from 1962 to 1982.

Exhibitions

Oedekoven-Gerischer, Angela, et al., eds. *Frauen im Design: Berufsbilder und Lebenswege seit 1900. Women in Design: Careers and Life Histories since 1900.* Stuttgart: Design Center, 1989.

1310 ASTORI, ANTONIA (1940–)
Italian furniture designer.

Other Sources

Byars, Mel. *The Design Encyclopedia.* London: Lawrence King, 1994.

1311 AULENTI, GAE (Alt. GAETANO AULENTI) (1927–)
Italian designer of furniture and lamps; also an architect who was part of the team redesigning the Musée d'Orsay in Paris.

Publications

See Naylor below.

Main Sources

See Naylor below.

Exhibitions

Hiesinger, Kathryn, and George Marcus III, eds. *Design since 1945.* Philadelphia: Philadelphia Museum of Art, 1983.
Bacci, N. *Il Design delle Donne.* Ravenna: Museo dell'Arredo Contemporaneo, 1991.
Bettagno, Alessandro, ed. *Gli artisti di Veneni: per una storia del vetro d'arte veneziano.* Milan: Electa in association with the Fondazione Cini, Venice, 1996.

Other Sources

Byars, Mel. *The Design Encyclopedia.* London: Lawrence King, 1994.
Grassi, Alfonso, and Anty Pansera. *Atalante del design italiano, 1940–1980.* Milan: Fabbri, 1980.

Naylor, Colin, ed. *Contemporary Designers*. 2nd edition. Chicago and London: St. James Press, 1990.

1312 BANDIERA CERANTOLA, MARISA (1924–)
Italian designer of furniture and textiles.

Other Sources

Byars, Mel. *The Design Encyclopedia*. London: Lawrence King, 1994.

1313 BECKER, MARTINA (1959–)
German designer of furniture, lighting, ceramics and metalwork.

Exhibitions

Oedekoven-Gerischer, Angela, et al., eds. *Frauen im Design: Berufsbilder und Lebenswege seit 1900. Women in Design: Careers and Life Histories since 1900*. Stuttgart: Design Center, 1989.

1314 BEDIN, MARTINE (1957–)
French designer of lighting, interiors and furniture.

Exhibitions

Oedekoven-Gerischer, Angela, et al., eds. *Frauen im Design: Berufsbilder und Lebenswege seit 1900. Women in Design: Careers and Life Histories since 1900*. Stuttgart: Design Center, 1989.

Other Sources

Anargyros, Sophie. *Le style des années 80: Architecture, décorations, design.* Paris: Rivages, 1986.
Byars, Mel. *The Design Encyclopedia*. London: Lawrence King, 1994.

1315 BERNALL ROSELL, GEMMA (1949–)
Spanish designer of furniture, metalwork and interiors.

Exhibitions

Oedekoven-Gerischer, Angela, et al., eds. *Frauen im Design: Berufsbilder und Lebenswege seit 1900. Women in Design: Careers and Life Histories since 1900*. Stuttgart: Design Center, 1989.

1316 BJØRNER, ANNELISE (1932–)
Danish designer of furniture and metalwork who collaborated from 1962 to 1982 with Rigmor Andersen (q.v.).

Exhibitions

Oedekoven-Gerischer, Angela, et al., eds. *Frauen im Design: Berufsbilder und Lebenswege seit 1900. Women in Design: Careers and Life Histories since 1900.* Stuttgart: Design Center, 1989.

1317 BLOCK-HELLUM, CHARLOTTE (1911–)

German designer of ceramics, metalwork and in enamel who also worked in Oslo.

Exhibitions

McFadden, David. *Scandinavian Modern Design, 1880–1980.* New York: Harry Abrams and the Cooper-Hewitt Museum, 1982.

Other Sources

Byars, Mel. *The Design Encyclopedia.* London: Lawrence King, 1994.

1318 BOERI, CINI (1924–)

Italian designer of objects, interiors and architecture.

Publications

See Naylor below.

Exhibitions

Oedekoven-Gerischer, Angela, et al., eds. *Frauen im Design: Berufsbilder und Lebenswege seit 1900. Women in Design: Careers and Life Histories since 1900.* Stuttgart: Design Center, 1989.

Bacci, N. *Il Design delle Donne.* Ravenna: Museo dell'Arredo Contemporaneo, 1991.

Other Sources

Grassi, Alfonso, and Anty Pansera. *Atalante del design italiano, 1940–1980.* Milan: Fabbri, 1980.

McQuiston, Liz. *Women in Design: A Contemporary View.* London: Trefoil Publications, 1988.

Naylor, Colin, ed. *Contemporary Designers.* 2nd edition. Chicago and London: St. James Press, 1990. Contains a bibliography.

Shimuzu, Fumio, and Matteo Thun. *The Descendants of Leonardo da Vinci: The Italian Design.* Tokyo: Graphic Publishing, 1987.

1319 BOLZ, ANNE (1958–)

German designer of furniture.

Exhibitions

Oedekoven-Gerischer, Angela, et al., eds. *Frauen im Design: Berufsbilder und Lebenswege seit 1900. Women in Design: Careers and Life Histories since 1900.* Stuttgart: Design Center, 1989.

1320 BÖGEL, ULRIKE (1954–)
    German designer of glass, metalwork and other items.

Exhibitions

Oedekoven-Gerischer, Angela, et al., eds. *Frauen im Design: Berufsbilder und Lebenswege seit 1900. Women in Design: Careers and Life Histories since 1900.* Stuttgart: Design Center, 1989.

1321 BONAZZI, EMMA (née TIGIÙ) (1881–1959)
    Italian designer in many media, including metalwork, glass and graphics.

Other Sources

Bossaglia, Rossana. *Il 'Déco' italiana: fisionomia dello stile 1925 in Italia.* Milan: Rizzoli, 1975.

1322 BÜLOW-HÜBE, TORUN VIVIANNA (1927–)
    Swedish designer of metalwork, ceramics, glass and jewellery.

See Glass section.

1323 CAMPI, ISABEL (1951–)
    Spanish designer of furniture, lighting and interiors.

Exhibitions

Oedekoven-Gerischer, Angela, et al., eds. *Frauen im Design: Berufsbilder und Lebenswege seit 1900. Women in Design: Careers and Life Histories since 1900.* Stuttgart: Design Center, 1989.

1324 CASTELLI FERRIERI, ANNA (1920–)
    Italian designer of furniture and interiors; also an architect.

Publications

See Naylor below.

Exhibitions

Oedekoven-Gerischer, Angela, et al., eds. *Frauen im Design: Berufsbilder und Lebenswege seit 1900. Women in Design: Careers and Life Histories since 1900.* Stuttgart: Design Center, 1989.

Bacci, N. *Il Design delle Donne.* Ravenna: Museo dell'Arredo Contemporaneo, 1991.

Other Sources

Byars, Mel. *The Design Encyclopedia.* London: Lawrence King, 1994.

Grassi, Alfonso, and Anty Pansera. *Atalante del design italiano 1940–1980.* Milan: Fabbri Editori, 1980.

Naylor, Colin, ed. *Contemporary Designers.* 2nd edition. Chicago and London: St. James Press, 1990. Contains a bibliography.

Shimuzu, Fumio, and Matteo Thun. *The Descendants of Leonardo da Vinci: The Italian Design.* Tokyo: Graphic Publishing, 1987.

1325 CHARALAMBIDES-DIVANIS, SONIA (1948–)
Greek furniture designer.

Exhibitions

Oedekoven-Gerischer, Angela, et al., eds. *Frauen im Design: Berufsbilder und Lebenswege seit 1900. Women in Design: Careers and Life Histories since 1900.* Stuttgart: Design Center, 1989.

Other Sources

Byars, Mel. *The Design Encyclopedia.* London: Lawrence King, 1994.

1326 CHAUCHET-GUILLRE, CHARLOTTE (née CHAUCHET) (1878–1964)
French designer of interiors and administrator of the Primavera Atelier in Paris; also a painter.

Other Sources

Brunhammer, Yvonne, and Suzanne Tise. *Les artistes décorateurs, 1900–42.* Paris: Flammarion, 1990.

Byars, Mel. *The Design Encyclopedia.* London: Lawrence King, 1994.

Duncan, Alastair. *Art Deco Furniture: the French Designers.* London: Thames and Hudson, 1984.

1327 CONNOLLY, SYBIL
Irish designer of textiles and interiors.

Publications

Connolly, Sybil, and Helen Dillon, eds. *In an Irish Garden.* London: Weidenfeld and Nicolson, 1986, 160pp., illus. A series of short chapters by the creator-owners of gardens in Ireland, two of which are the editors.

1328 CRIPPA, FLORA (1954–)
Italian designer of ceramics and interiors who collaborates with Giulio Manzoni.

Other Sources

Shimuzu, Fumio, and Matteo Thun. *The Descendants of Leonardo da Vinci: The Italian Design.* Tokyo: Graphic Publishing, 1987.

1329 DAWSON, EDITH (née ROBINSON) (c. 1870–after 1914)
English designer of metalwork, enamels and a painter.

Main Sources:

Strange, E.F. "A Chat With Mr and Mrs Nelson Dawson on Enamelling." *Architectural Review* 1 (1897): 174–178.
————. "Some Recent Work by Nelson and Edith Dawson." *Studio* 22 (1901): 169–174.

Other Sources

Callen, Anthea. *Angel in the Studio: Women in the Arts and Crafts Movement 1870–1914,* London: Architectural Press, 1979.

1330 DILLON, JANE (1943–)
English designer of furniture.

Other Sources

Byars, Mel. *The Design Encyclopedia.* London: Lawrence King, 1994.
McQuiston, Liz. *Women in Design: A Contemporary View.* London: Trefoil Publications, 1988.

1331 DITZEL, NANNA (1923–)
Danish designer of furniture, textiles and glass who worked in London from 1968; winner of the Lunning Prize.

Main Sources

J.W. "Nanna Ditzel: An Exhibition." *Interiors* 123 (December 1963): 102–103.

Exhibitions

Timmers, Margaret. *The Way We Live Now: Designs for Interiors 1950 to the Present Day.* London: Victoria and Albert Museum, 1978.
McFadden, David, ed. *Scandinavian Modern Design, 1880–1980.* New York: Harry Abrams and the Cooper-Hewitt Museum, 1982.
The Lunning Prize. Stockholm: Nationalmuseum, 1986.

Oedekoven-Gerischer, Angela, et al., eds. *Frauen im Design: Berufsbilder und Lebenswege seit 1900. Women in Design: Careers and Life Histories since 1900.* Stuttgart: Design Center, 1989.

Other Sources

Byars, Mel. *The Design Encyclopedia.* London: Lawrence King, 1994.
Hiesinger, Kathryn, and George Marcus III, eds. *Design since 1945.* Philadelphia: Philadelphia Museum of Art, 1983.
Lassen, Erik. *Dansk Glas 1925–75.* Copenhagen: Busck, 1975.
Salicath, Bent, and Arne Karlsen, eds. *Modern Danish Textiles.* Copenhagen: Danish Society of Arts and Crafts and Industrial Design, 1959.

1332 DORNER, MARIE CHRISTINE (1960–)
French designer of ceramics, glass, lighting, furniture and graphics.

Exhibitions

Oedekoven-Gerischer, Angela, et al., eds. *Frauen im Design: Berufsbilder und Lebenswege seit 1900. Women in Design: Careers and Life Histories since 1900.* Stuttgart: Design Center, 1989.

1333 DU PASQUIER, NATHALIE (1957–)
French designer of furniture and textiles who works in Italy.

Main Sources

Radice, Barbara. "Mosaici Morbidi." *Modo* 54 (November 1982): 68–69.

Exhibitions

Hiesinger, Kathryn, and George Marcus III, eds. *Design since 1945.* Philadelphia: Philadelphia Museum of Art, 1983.

Other Sources

Byars, Mel. *The Design Encyclopedia.* London: Lawrence King, 1994.
McQuiston, Liz. *Women in Design: A Contemporary View.* London: Trefoil Publications, 1988.
Shimuzu, Fumio, and Matteo Thun. *The Descendants of Leonardo da Vinci: The Italian Design.* Tokyo: Graphic Publishing, 1987.

1334 DUMAS, RENA (1937–)
Greek designer of interiors and furniture.

Other Sources

Byars, Mel. *The Design Encyclopedia.* London: Lawrence King, 1994.

1335 FAULKNER, KATE (?–1898)
English designer of Arts and Crafts embroidered textiles, wallpaper and china painting; founder member of Morris, Marshall, Faulkner and Co.; sister of Lucy Faulkner (q.v.).

Main Sources

Callen, Anthea. *Angel in the Studio: Women in the Arts and Crafts Movement 1870–1914.* London: Architectural Press, 1979.

1336 FAULKNER, LUCY (Alt. ORRINSMITH) (c. 1840–?)
English designer of Arts and Crafts embroidered textiles, china painting and wood engraving; sister of Kate Faulkner (q.v.).

Publications

Orrinsmith, Lucy. *The Drawing Room: Is Decoration and Furniture.* London: Macmillan, 1878.

Other Sources

Callen, Anthea. *Angel in the Studio: Women in the Arts and Crafts Movement 1870–1914.* London: Architectural Press, 1979.

1337 GAROUSTE, ELIZABETH (Alt. BONETTI) (1949–)
French furniture designer.

Other Sources

Byars, Mel. *The Design Encyclopedia.* London: Lawrence King, 1994.

1338 GEYER-RAACK, RUTH HILDEGARD (1894–1975)
German designer of interiors, textiles and wallpaper.

Exhibitions

Oedekoven-Gerischer, Angela, et al., eds. *Frauen im Design: Berufsbilder und Lebenswege seit 1900. Women in Design: Careers and Life Histories since 1900.* Stuttgart: Design Center, 1989.

1339 GILI, ANNA (1960–)
Italian designer of ceramics, lighting, textiles, furniture and jewellery.

Exhibitions

Bacci, N. *Il Design delle Donne.* Ravenna: Museo dell'Arredo Contemporaneo, 1991.

Other Sources

Byars, Mel. *The Design Encyclopedia*. London: Lawrence King, 1994.

1340 GILMOUR, MARGARET (1860–1942)
Scottish designer of metalwork, textiles especially embroidery, and other objects who studied at the Glasgow School of Art and set up a studio with her sister Mary Ann (q.v.).

Exhibitions

Burkhauser, Jude, ed. *'Glasgow Girls': Women in Art and Design, 1880–1920*. Edinburgh: Canongate, 1990.
Cumming, Elizabeth. *Glasgow 1900: Art and Design*. Zwolle: Waanders Publishers in association with the Van Gogh Museum, Amsterdam, 1992.

1341 GILMOUR, MARY ANN BELL (1872–1938)
Scottish designer of metalwork, ceramic decoration, textiles especially embroidery, and other objects who trained at the Glasgow School of Art and set up a studio with her sister Margaret (q.v.).

Exhibitions

Burkhauser, Jude, ed. *'Glasgow Girls': Women in Art and Design, 1880–1920*. Edinburgh: Canongate, 1990.

1342 GRAY, EILEEN (1878–1976)
Irish designer of interiors and furniture who worked mainly in France.

Main Sources

Adam, Peter. *Eileen Gray: Architect/Designer: A Biography*. London: Thames and Hudson, 1987, 400pp., illus. A thorough biographical account. Contains the most extensive bibliography to this date which includes both general books which mention Gray and reviews from the United States and Europe.
Berman, Avis. "Eileen Gray: In the Vanguard of Twentieth Century Design." *Architectural Digest* 44 (1987): 62–70.
Doumato, Lamia. *Eileen Gray, 1879–1976. Vance Bibiographies in Architecture no. 412*. 1981, 5pp. This bibliography is divided in sections according to the type of publication.
Garner, Philippe. *Eileen Gray: Design and Architecture, 1878–1976*, Cologne: Benedikt Taschen, 1993, 160pp., many illus. Text in German, English and French.
Loye, Brigitte. *Eileen Gray, 1879–1976: Architecture, Design*. Paris: Analeph/J.P.Viguier, 1983, 159pp., illus. Text in French. Contains a bibliography.
Rayon, J.-P. "Eileen Gray: un manifeste 1926–29." *Architecture, mouvement, Continuité* 37 (November 1975).
Stewart Johnson, J. "E.G. at Richmond." *Arts in Virginia* 27 (1987): 34–43,

illus. A discussion of the five examples of her work at the Virginia Museum of Fine Arts.

Exhibitions

Cinquantenaire de l'Exposition de 1925. Paris: Musée des Arts Décoratifs, 1976. Contains a brief biography.

Paris-Moscou 1900–1939. Paris: Centre Nationale d'Art et de Culture Georges Pompidou, 1979.

Stewart-Johnson, J. *Eileen Gray: Designer.* New York: Debrett's Peerage for the Museum of Modern Art and the Victoria and Albert Museum, London, 1979, 67pp., illus. Contains a biographical account which uses primary material from interviews and documents.

Dufresne, Jean-Luc, and Olivier Messac, eds. *Femmes créatrices des années vingt.* Granville: Musée Richard Anacréon, 1988. Wide-ranging catalogue with a short biographical account on each woman included.

Les années UAM, 1929–1958. Paris: Musée des Arts Décoratifs, 1988.

Oedekoven-Gerischer, Angela, et al., eds. *Frauen im Design: Berufsbilder und Lebenswege seit 1900. Women in Design: Careers and Life Histories since 1900.* Stuttgart: Design Center, 1989.

Other Sources

Byars, Mel. *The Design Encyclopedia.* London: Lawrence King, 1994.

Duncan, Alastair. *Art Deco Furniture: The French Designers.* London: Thames and Hudson, 1984.

Naylor, Colin, ed. *Contemporary Designers.* 2nd edition. Chicago and London: St. James Press, 1990. Contains a bibliography.

1343 GREAVES-LORD, SALLY (1957–)
English designer of textiles for furniture and interiors.

See Textiles section.

1344 GUEDEN, COLETTE
French designer of ceramics, metalwork and furnishings.

Main Sources

"L'Atelier Primavera—deuxième petite foire des Arts Décoratifs." *Céramique et Verrerie* 786 (December 1927): 1207.

Varenne, Gaston. "Colette Gueden ou l'aimable fantaisie." *Art et Décoration* (January 1933): 21–30.

Exhibitions

Paris-Paris 1937–1957. Paris: Centre Nationale d'Art et de Culture Georges Pompidou, 1981.

Other Sources

Bloch-Demant, Janine. *Le Verre en France d'Emil Gallé à nos jours.* Paris: Editions de l'Amateur, 1983.

Brunhammer, Yvonne, and Suzanne Tise. *Les artistes décorateurs, 1900–42.* Paris: Flammarion, 1990.

Byars, Mel. *The Design Encyclopedia.* London: Lawrence King, 1994.

Chavance, René. *La céramique et la verrerie.* Paris: Rieder, 1928.

Kim, Jacques. "Les Art du Feu au Salon des Artistes Décorateurs." *Les Arts du Feu* 11 (May 1939): 147–151.

Rogalier, J. "La participation de la France à la Triennale à Milan." *L'Art Ménager,* September 1936, 512–3.

1345 GUIGUICHON, SUZANNE (1900–?)
French designer.

Other Sources

Brunhammer, Yvonne, and Suzanne Tise. *Les artistes décorateurs, 1900–42.* Paris: Flammarion, 1990.

Byars, Mel. *The Design Encyclopedia.* London: Lawrence King, 1994.

Duncan, Alastair. *Art Deco Furniture: The French Designers.* London: Thames and Hudson, 1984.

1346 HARVEY, AGNES BANKIER (1874–1947)
Scottish designer of metalwork and enamels who taught at the Glasgow School of Art.

Exhibitions

Burkhauser, Jude, ed. *'Glasgow Girls': Women in Art and Design, 1880–1920.* Edinburgh: Canongate, 1990.

1347 HIESTAND, URSULA (1936–)
Swiss designer of graphics and interiors who works with her husband, Ernst.

Other Sources

Naylor, Colin, ed. *Contemporary Designers.* 2nd edition. Chicago and London: St. James Press, 1990. Contains a bibliography.

1348 JALK, GRETE (1920–)
Danish designer of textiles, wallpapers, furniture and metalwork.

Exhibitions

Oedekoven-Gerischer, Angela, et al., eds. *Frauen im Design: Berufsbilder und Lebenswege seit 1900. Women in Design: Careers and Life Histories since 1900.* Stuttgart: Design Center, 1989.

Eidelberg, Martin, ed. *Design 1935–1965: What Modern Was.* New York: Abrams in association with the Musée des Arts Décoratifs, Montreal, 1991.

1349 JOEL, BETTY (1896–)
English designer of furniture and interiors.

Exhibitions

Thirties: British Art and Design before the War. London: Arts Council of Great Britain at the Hayward Gallery, 1979.

Other Sources

Anscombe, Isabelle. *A Woman's Touch: Women in Design from 1860 to the Present Day.* London: Virago, 1984.

1350 JOHANSSON-PAPE, LISA (c. 1906–)
Finnish designer of interiors.

Main Sources

Kaipainen, Marja. "Generations in Design." *Form Function Finland* 3 (1982): 6–11. Interview.

Exhibitions

McFadden, David, ed. *Scandinavian Modern Design, 1880–1980.* New York: Harry Abrams and the Cooper-Hewitt Museum, 1982.

1351 JUNGE, MARGARETE (1874–1966)
German designer of furniture.

Exhibitions

Oedekoven-Gerischer, Angela, et al., eds. *Frauen im Design: Berufsbilder und Lebenswege seit 1900. Women in Design: Careers and Life Histories since 1900.* Stuttgart: Design Center, 1989.

1352 KARRA, ALEXANDRA (1962–)
Greek designer of furniture and lighting.

Exhibitions

Oedekoven-Gerischer, Angela et al., eds. *Frauen im Design: Berufsbilder und Lebenswege seit 1900. Women in Design: Careers and Life Histories since 1900.* Stuttgart: Design Center, 1989.

1353 KINSBOURG, RENÉ (c. 1985–?)
French designer of furniture and interiors.

Other Sources

Duncan, Alastair. *Art Deco Furniture: The French Designers.* London: Thames and Hudson, 1984.

1354 KLEINHEMPEL, GERTRUD (1875–1948)
German designer of furniture, metalwork, glass and ceramic decoration.

Exhibitions

Oedekoven-Gerischer, Angela, et al., eds. *Frauen im Design: Berufsbilder und Lebenswege seit 1900. Women in Design: Careers and Life Histories since 1900.* Stuttgart: Design Center, 1989.

Other Sources

1355 KLOTZ, BLANCHE-J. (c. 1900–?)
French designer of furniture and interiors.

Exhibitions

Les Années 25. Paris: Musée des Arts Décoratifs, 1966. Includes some of her furniture designs shown in the 1925 International Exposition.

Other Sources

Byars, Mel. *The Design Encyclopedia.* London: Lawrence King, 1994.
Duncan, Alastair. *Art Deco Furniture: The French Designers.* London: Thames and Hudson, 1984.

1356 KNIPS, SONJA (née Baroness POTIER DES ECHELLES) (c. 1900–?)
Austrian designer of furniture and furnishings.

Other Sources

Pirhofer, G., and A. Gmeiner. *Der Österreichische Werkbund.* Salzburg: Residenz Verlag, 1985.

1357 KURRER, ANGELA (1945–)
German designer of furniture, lighting and home accessories.

Exhibitions

Oedekoven-Gerischer, Angela, et al., eds. *Frauen im Design: Berufsbilder und Lebenswege seit 1900. Women in Design: Careers and Life Histories since 1900.* Stuttgart: Design Center, 1989.

1358 LEVEY, AUDREY
English designer whose wallpaper won design awards.

Exhibitions

Hogben, C. *A Collection in the Making: British Art & Design, 1900–1860.* London: Victoria and Albert Museum, 1983.

1359 LEWTHWAITE DEWAR, MARGARET DE COURCY (1878–1959)
Scottish designer of metalwork and enamel who trained at the Glasgow School of Art.

Exhibitions

A Centenary Exhibition to Celebrate the Founding of the Glasgow Society of Lady Artists in 1882. Glasgow: Collins Gallery, 1882.

Burkhauser, Jude, ed. *'Glasgow Girls': Women in Art and Design, 1880–1920.* Edinburgh: Canongate, 1990.

Cumming, Elizabeth. *Glasgow 1900: Art and Design.* Zwolle: Waanders Publishers in association with the Van Gogh Museum, Amsterdam, 1992.

1360 LITTLE, MARY (1958–)
Irish designer of furniture who works in Italy.

Other Sources

McQuiston, Liz. *Women in Design: A Contemporary View.* London: Trefoil Publications, 1988.

1361 LOVARINI, LUISA.
Italian designer of furniture.

Other Sources

Bossaglia, Rossana. *Il 'Déco' italiana: fisionomia dello stile 1925 in Italia.* Milan: Rizzoli, 1975.

1362 MACDONALD, FRANCES (Alt. MACNAIR) (1974–1921)
English designer of graphics, interiors, metalwork and painter who worked mainly in Scotland; sister of Margaret (q.v.).

Main Sources

Gear, J. "Trapped Women: Two Artist Designers: Margaret and Frances Macdonald." *Heresies* 1 (winter 1978): 48–51.

Helland, Janice. *The Studios of Frances and Margaret Macdonald.* Manchester: Manchester University Press, 1996.

Exhibitions

Women's Art Show, 1550–1970. Nottingham, Castle Museum, 1982. Contains a brief biography.

Hogben, C. *British Art and Design 1900–1960: A Collection in the Making.* Victoria and Albert Museum, London, 1983.

Sellars, Jane. *Women's Works.* Liverpool: Walker Art Gallery, 1988.

The Last Romantics: The Romantic Tradition in British Art. Burne-Jones to Stanley Spencer. London: Barbican Gallery, 1989.

Oedekoven-Gerischer, Angela, et al., eds. *Frauen im Design: Berufsbilder und Lebenswege seit 1900. Women in Design: Careers and Life Histories since 1900.* Stuttgart: Design Center, 1989.

Burkhauser, Jude, ed. *'Glasgow Girls': Women in Art and Design, 1880–1920.* Edinburgh: Canongate, 1990.

Cumming, Elizabeth. *Glasgow 1900: Art and Design.* Zwolle: Waanders Publishers in association with the Van Gogh Museum, Amsterdam, 1992.

Other Sources

Modern Bookbindings and their Designers. London: The Studio, Winter 1899–1900. Contains little on individual designers.

Callen, Anthea. *The Angel in the Studio.* London: Architectural Press, 1979.

Dunford, Penny. *A Biographical Dictionary of Women Artists in Europe and America since 1850.* Hemel Hempstead: Harvester Wheatsheaf and Philadelphia: University of Pennsylvania Press, 1990. Contains a bibliography.

Gleeson-White, J. "Some Glasgow Designers and their Work." *Studio* 11 (1897): 86–100.

Marsh, Jan, and Pamela Gerrish Nunn. *Women Artists and the Pre-Raphaelite Movement.* London: Virago, 1989.

Parry, Linda. *Textiles of the Arts and Crafts Movement.* London: Thames and Hudson, 1988.

1363 MACDONALD, MARGARET (Alt. MACKINTOSH) (1865–1933)

English designer of interiors, textiles, metalwork, graphics and painter who worked mainly in Scotland; sister of Frances (q.v.).

Main Sources

Helland, Janice. "The Critics and the Arts and Crafts: the Instance of Margaret Macdonald and Charles Rennie Mackintosh." *Art History* 17, no. 2 (June 1994): 209–227.

See under Frances Macdonald.

1364 MARTIN, SADIE (née SPEIGHT) (1906–1992)
English designer of interiors and furniture; also an architect.

Publications

Martin, J. L., and S. Speight. *The Flat Book.* London: Heinemann, 1939.

Main Sources

Parkin, Michael. "Sadie Martin." *The Independent,* 28 October 1992. Obituary.

Exhibitions

Seddon, Jill, and Suzette Worden. *Women Designing: Redefining Design Between the Wars.* Brighton: University of Brighton, 1994.

1365 MAUGHAM, SYRIE (née BARNARDO; alt. WELLCOME) (1879–1955)
English designer of interiors.

Exhibitions

Thirties: British Art and Design before the War. London: Hayward Gallery, 1979.

Other Sources

Anscombe, Isabelle. *A Woman's Touch: Women in Design from 1860 to the Present Day.* London: Virago, 1984.

1366 MILLS, ERNESTINE EVANS (née BELL) (1871–1959)
English designer of metalwork and enamelling.

Other Sources

Callen, Anthea. *Angel in the Studio: Women in the Arts and Crafts Movement 1870–1914.* London: Architectural Press, 1979.

1367 MILNER, ALISON (1958–)
English designer of furniture and sculptor.

Other Sources

McQuiston, Liz. *Women in Design: A Contemporary View.* London: Trefoil Publications, 1988.

1368 MÜHLHAUS, HEIKE (1954–)
German designer of ceramic objects and furniture.

Exhibitions

Oedekoven-Gerischer, Angela, et al., eds. *Frauen im Design: Berufsbilder und Lebenswege seit 1900. Women in Design: Careers and Life Histories since 1900.* Stuttgart: Design Center, 1989.

1369 PERRIAND, CHARLOTTE
French designer of interiors and furniture.

Publications

"Pour un intérieur moderne." *France-Outremer* 248 (May 1950): 159–160.
"L'art d'habiter." *Techniques et Architecture* 9–10 (1950): 33.
"Une tradition vivante." *Architecture d'Aujourd'hui* 65 (May 1956): 14–19, mainly illus. Reflections upon Japan.

Main Sources

"Charlotte Perriand." *Architecture d'Aujourd'hui* 113–114 (April–May 1964): 60–61, illus. Brief chronology of her activities up to this date.
"Charlotte Perriand est de retour." *Le Décor d'Aujourd'hui* 37 (1948): 59.
H.R. "Monologue in a London flat" *The Architect and Building News,* October 1930, 467. Fictional version of conversation with Perriand as she supervised erection of a stand at Olympia.
J.V. "Le siège—l'expérience japonaise de Charlotte Perriand." *Art Présent* 3 (1947): 53–56, illus. In French with short summary in English. Concerns the effects of her visit to Japan in 1940–1941 on her designs for chairs.
A.F. "Le Chalet de Charlotte Perrian [*sic*] en Savoie." *Plaisir de France* 327 (January 1966): 54–57.
M.A.F. "L'équipement de l'habitat étudié au Japon avec des modèles de série et des procédés traditionnels par Charlotte Perriand." *Architecture d'Aujourd'hui* 10 (1947): 104–109, many illus. Reviews designs for chairs brought back by Perriand from her cooperation with Japanese producers.
Clerc, Christine. "Un architecture de l'anti-nostalgie." *Elle* 1677 (27 February 1978): 16–24, mainly illus.
Ellis, Charlotte, and Norman Meade. "Charlotte Perriand looks back (and forward)." *Architectural Review* 176 (November 1984): 64–69, illus. Interview with Perriand.
Filion, Odile. "Portrait de Charlotte Perriand." *Architecture Intérieure* 203 (January–February 1985): 70–79, illus. Interview with Perriand and review of solo exhibition at Musée des Arts Décoratifs, Paris.
Lacroix, Boris. "Mobiliers et ensembles de vacances: Charlotte Perriand décorateur." *Art et Décoration,* 2e Trimestre 9 (1948): xxé12–x.
MacCarthy, Fiona. "A long view of Modernism." *The Guardian,* 19 October

1996, 60–62. Discusses Perriand, whom MacCarthy interviewed for the article, in the context of an exhibition at the Design Museum in London (for which there was no catalogue) opening in October 1996.

Milleret, Marie Edith. "Paris: Charlotte Perriand." *Beaux-Arts* Magazine 21 (February 1985): 90–91, illus. Review of solo exhibition at Musée des Arts Décoratifs, Paris.

Renous, Pascal. "Une intervue par Charlotte Periand." *Revue de l'Ameublement* 6 (June 1963): 25–31.

Sert, Jose Luis. "Charlotte Perriand." *Aujourd'hui* 7 (1956): 58.

Tougard, Daniel. "Perriand c'est fou." *Architectes-Architecture* 156 (April 1985): 28–29.

Exhibitions

Di Fagiolo, Maurizio, and Maria Luisa Madonna. *Le Corbusier, Charlotte Perriand, Pierre Jeanneret: la machine à s'asseoir.* Palazzo dei Convegni, Rome, 1976, 143pp., illus.

Un art de vivre. Paris: Flammarion for the Musée des Arts Décoratifs, 1985, 78pp., illus. Consists of a biographical outline with a commentary by Perriand.

Dufresne, Jean-Luc, and Olivier Messac, eds. *Femmes créatrices des années vingt. Granville: Musée Richard Anacréon,* 1988. Wide-ranging catalogue with a short biographical account on each woman included.

Les années UAM, 1929–1958. Paris: Musée des Arts Décoratifs, 1988.

Oedekoven-Gerischer, Angela, et al., eds. *Frauen im Design: Berufsbilder und Lebenswege seit 1900. Women in Design: Careers and Life Histories since 1900.* Stuttgart: Design Center, 1989.

Other Sources

Byars, Mel. *The Design Encyclopedia.* London: Lawrence King, 1994.

Duncan, Alastair. *Art Deco Furniture: The French Designers.* London: Thames and Hudson, 1984.

1370 PETROLI GARATI, FRANCA (1935–)
Italian designer of ceramics, lighting, glass and furniture.

Other Sources

Byars, Mel. *The Design Encyclopedia.* London: Lawrence King, 1994.

1371 PFAEHLER, JOSEPHINE (née STOLL) (1926–)
German designer of furniture.

Exhibitions

Oedekoven-Gerischer, Angela, et al., eds. *Frauen im Design: Berufsbilder und Lebenswege seit 1900. Women in Design: Careers and Life Histories since 1900.* Stuttgart: Design Center, 1989.

1372 PUPPA, DANIELA (1947–)
Italian designer of furniture, textiles and fashion accessories.

Exhibitions

Bacci, N. *Il Design delle Donne.* Ravenna: Museo dell'Arredo Contemporaneo, 1991.

Other Sources

McQuiston, Liz. *Women in Design: A Contemporary View.* London: Trefoil Publications, 1988.

Shimuzu, Fumio, and Matteo Thun. *The Descendants of Leonardo da Vinci: The Italian Design.* Tokyo: Graphic Publishing, 1987.

1373 RANZO, PATRIZIA (1953–)
Italian designer of furniture.

Other Sources

McQuiston, Liz. *Women in Design: A Contemporary View.* London: Trefoil Publications, 1988.

1374 REICH, LILLY (1885–1947)
German designer of interiors, furniture, textiles and fashion.

Exhibitions

La Tessitura del Bauhaus, 1919–33 nelle collezioni della Repubblica Democratica Tedesca. Venice: Palazzo Ducale and Cataloghi Marsilio, 1985.

Oedekoven-Gerischer, Angela, et al., eds. *Frauen im Design: Berufsbilder und Lebenswege seit 1900. Women in Design: Careers and Life Histories since 1900.* Stuttgart: Design Center, 1989.

Other Sources

Byars, Mel. *The Design Encyclopedia.* London: Lawrence King, 1994.

Droste, Magdalena. *Bauhaus: 1919–1933.* Berlin: Bauhaus Archiv Museum and Benedict Taschen Verlag GmbH & Co KG, 1990.

Gunta Stölzl: Weberei am Bauhaus und aus eigener Werkstatt. Berlin: Bauhaus Archiv in association with Kupfergraben Verlag, 1987. Contains individual bibliographies.

Sparke, Penny. *An Introduction to Design and Culture in the Twentieth Century.* London: Hyman and Unwin, 1986.

Weltge, Sigrid Wortmann. *Bauhaus Textiles: Women Artists and the Weaving Workshop.* London: Thames and Hudson, 1993.

1375 RENAUDET, LUCIE (Alt. RENAUDOT) (c.1895–1939)
French designer of furniture and interiors.

Other Sources

Brunhammer, Yvonne, and Suzanne Tise. *Les artistes décorateurs, 1900–42.* Paris: Flammarion, 1990.

Byars, Mel. *The Design Encyclopedia.* London: Lawrence King, 1994.

Duncan, Alastair. *Art Deco Furniture: The French Designers.* London: Thames and Hudson, 1984.

1376 SARASIN, BETHA (1930–)
Swiss designer of glass and furniture.

Other Sources

Beard, Geoffrey. *International Modern Glass.* London: Barrie and Jenkins, 1976.

1377 SCHETTINI, M. LETIZIA (1961–)
Italian designer of ceramics, textiles and furniture.

See Ceramics section.

1378 SCHMIDT, ANITA (1934–)
German designer of furniture and furnishing textiles.

Exhibitions

Oedekoven-Gerischer, Angela, et al., eds. *Frauen im Design: Berufsbilder und Lebenswege seit 1900. Women in Design: Careers and Life Histories since 1900.* Stuttgart: Design Center, 1989.

1379 SMEUNINX, LOTTE (1964–)
Belgian designer of furniture, ceramics and glass.

Exhibitions

Oedekoven-Gerischer, Angela, et al., eds. *Frauen im Design: Berufsbilder und Lebenswege seit 1900. Women in Design: Careers and Life Histories since 1900.* Stuttgart: Design Center, 1989.

1380 SPEIGHT, SADIE (1906–1992)
Â Â Â Â Â Â English designer of interiors and furniture; also an architect.

See Martin, Sadie above.

1381 TAUSSIG, MELANIE (Alt. STEINITZ) (1881–?)
Â Â Â Â Â Â Austrian designer of furniture, textiles and wallpaper.

Other Sources

Pirhofer, G., and A. Gmeiner. *Der Österreichische Werkbund.* Salzburg: Residenz Verlag, 1985.

1382 THEW, MARY (1876–1953)
Â Â Â Â Â Â Scottish designer of metalwork, especially jewellery.

Exhibitions

A Centenary Exhibition to Celebrate the Founding of the Glasgow Society of Lady Artists in 1882. Glasgow: Collins Gallery, 1982.
Â Â Â Â Burkhauser, Jude, ed. *'Glasgow Girls': Women in Art and Design, 1880–1920.* Edinburgh: Canongate, 1990.

1383 TRAQUAIR, PHOEBE ANNA (née MOSS) (1852–1936)
Â Â Â Â Â Â Irish-born painter and designer in the Arts and Crafts movement who worked in Scotland; she produced metalwork, decorated furniture, jewellery, bookbindings and enamels.

Main Sources

Marsh, Jan, and Pamela Gerrish Nunn. *Women Artists and the Pre-Raphaelite Movement.* London: Virago, 1989.
Â Â Â Â Morris, A.F. "A Versatile Art Worker: Mrs Traquair." *Studio* 34 (1905): 339–43.

Exhibitions

Cumming, Elizabeth. *Phoebe Anna Traquair 1852–1936.* Edinburgh: National Galleries of Scotland, 1993, 96pp., illus. The most thorough source on Traquair. Contains an extensive catalogue and a bibliography.

Other Sources

Modern Bookbindings and their Designers. The Studio, Winter no. 1899–1900.
Â Â Â Â Parry, Linda. *Textiles of the Arts and Crafts Movement.* London: Thames and Hudson, 1988.

1384 UNGER, ELSE (Alt. HOLZINGER) (1873–c. 1930)
Austrian designer of furniture, metalwork, textiles, bookbindings and other decorative items.

Exhibitions

Gronwoldt, Ruth, and Sabine Hesse. *Art Nouveau: Textil: Dekor um 1900.* Stuttgart: Wurtimburgisches Landesmuseum, 1980.
Oedekoven-Gerischer, Angela, et al., eds. *Frauen im Design: Berufsbilder und Lebenswege seit 1900. Women in Design: Careers and Life Histories since 1900.* Stuttgart: Design Center, 1989.

Other Sources

Pirhofer, G., and A. Gmeiner. *Der Österreichische Werkbund.* Salzburg: Residenz Verlag, 1985.

1385 VENOSTA, CARLA
Italian designer of glass, ceramics, lighting, furniture and interiors.

Exhibitions

Oedekoven-Gerischer, Angela, et al., eds. *Frauen im Design: Berufsbilder und Lebenswege seit 1900. Women in Design: Careers and Life Histories since 1900.* Stuttgart: Design Center, 1989.

1386 VERSCHUUREN, NEL (1943–)
Dutch designer of furniture and interiors.

Exhibitions

Oedekoven-Gerischer, Angela, et al., eds. *Frauen im Design: Berufsbilder und Lebenswege seit 1900. Women in Design: Careers and Life Histories since 1900.* Stuttgart: Design Center, 1989.

1387 VIGO, NANDA
Italian designer of furniture and interiors.

Exhibitions

Bacci, N. *Il Design delle Donne.* Ravenna: Museo dell'Arredo Contemporaneo, 1991.

Other Sources

Byars, Mel. *The Design Encyclopedia.* London: Lawrence King, 1994.
McQuiston, Liz. *Women in Design: A Contemporary View.* London: Trefoil Publications, 1988.

Shimuzu, Fumio, and Matteo Thun. *The Descendants of Leonardo da Vinci: The Italian Design.* Tokyo: Graphic Publishing, 1987.

1388 VON BREVERN, RENATE (1942–)
    German designer of ceramic objects and furniture.

Exhibitions

Oedekoven-Gerischer, Angela, et al., eds. *Frauen im Design: Berufsbilder und Lebenswege seit 1900. Women in Design: Careers and Life Histories since 1900.* Stuttgart: Design Center, 1989.

1389 VON STARK, ADELE (1859–1923)
    Austrian designer of ceramics, ceramic decoration and furniture who became a Professor at the Vienna School of Arts and Crafts in 1914.

Exhibitions

Oedekoven-Gerischer, Angela, et al., eds. *Frauen im Design: Berufsbilder und Lebenswege seit 1900. Women in Design: Careers and Life Histories since 1900.* Stuttgart: Design Center, 1989.

1390 VRETZAKI, HELEN (1960–)
    Greek designer of furniture, interiors and graphics.

Exhibitions

Oedekoven-Gerischer, Angela, et al., eds. *Frauen im Design: Berufsbilder und Lebenswege seit 1900. Women in Design: Careers and Life Histories since 1900.* Stuttgart: Design Center, 1989.

Other Sources

1391 WAGER, RHODA (c.1875–1953)
    English designer of metalwork who trained at the Glasgow School of Art.

Exhibitions

Burkhauser, Jude, ed. *'Glasgow Girls': Women in Art and Design, 1880–1920.* Edinburgh: Canongate, 1990.

1392 WILLE, FIA (1868–1920)
    German designer of interiors and fashion.

Exhibitions

Oedekoven-Gerischer, Angela, et al., eds. *Frauen im Design: Berufsbilder und Lebenswege seit 1900. Women in Design: Careers and Life Histories since 1900.* Stuttgart: Design Center, 1989.

1393 WILSON, LYNNE (1952–)
English designer of furniture and printed textiles who works in Italy.

Other Sources

McQuiston, Liz. *Women in Design: A Contemporary View*. London: Trefoil Publications, 1988.

1394 WILSON, MARION HENDERSON (1869–1956)
Scottish designer of metalwork who trained at the Glasgow School of Art.

Exhibitions

Burkhauser, Jude, ed. *'Glasgow Girls': Women in Art and Design, 1880–1920*. Edinburgh: Canongate, 1990.

1395 WOOD, HELEN MUIR (1864–1930)
Scottish designer of metalwork, stained glass and decorated ceramics.

Exhibitions

Burkhauser, Jude, ed. *'Glasgow Girls': Women in Art and Design, 1880–1920*. Edinburgh: Canongate, 1990.

Textiles

OTHER SOURCES

1396 *9. Fal-Es Tertextyil Biennale. 9th Textile Biennale.* Szombathely: Savaria Muzeum, 1986, n.p., illus.

Text in Hungarian and English. One of a series of exhibitions of contemporary textiles in which almost all the participants are women. For each, a list of solo and group exhibitions, the date of birth and the institution where s/he trained is given.

1397 *20th Century Craftsmanship.* Bath: Holburne of Menstrie Museum, 1972, 63pp., illus.

An exhibition of work from the Crafts Study Centre Trust in Bath. The catalogue is little more than a list of exhibits. Women are well represented in textiles, by four out of twelve ceramicists and in small numbers elsewhere.

1398 *Actuelle keramiek en textielkunst uit antwerpen.* Het Sterckshof: Provinciaal Museum voor Kunstambrachten, 1974, n.p., illus.

Text in Flemish. After short introductory essays there is only very brief information on the artists and the exhibits. Several women are included in both sections although the proportion is greater in that on textiles.

1399 BARBER, BARRY. "Tapestry Traditions." *Crafts Magazine* 74 (1985): 48.

Review of the exhibition *Textiles from Poland* from the collection of the Central Museum, Łodz.

1400 BARNETT, PENINA. *The Subversive Stitch: Embroidery and Women's Lives, 1300–1900.* Manchester: Whitworth Art Gallery and *Women and Textiles Today*, Manchester: Cornerhouse, 1988, 64pp., illus.

Catalogue of two exhibitions on the ambiguous relationship of women to needlework, one on historical aspects and the other on contemporary artists dealing with this theme.

1401 BOURQUIN-WALFARD, C., DISCH-BRACK, M-L., and FROSSARD, C. *Tapisséries suisses: artistes d'aujourd'hui. Schweizerische Tapisserien: Künstler von heute.* Lausanne: Genoud, 1977, 73pp., illus.

Text in French, English and German. This is the catalogue of a travelling exhibition for which the artists were chosen by a national contest organised by the Groupe de Cartonniers-lissiers romands. The exhibition included thirty-four works by twenty-eight artists, of whom all but two are women.

1402 BOWMAN, SARA. *A Fashion for Extravagance: Art Déco Fabrics and Fashions.* London: Bell and Hyman, 1985, 125pp., illus.

This provides a survey of the fashions which used luxurious and embroidered fabrics in Paris in the 1920s and 1930s. There are chapters on Poiret, the atelier Martine, la Maison Lallement, Fortúny, Sonia Delaunay, Erté, Raymond Duncan, Ugo lo Monaco, and fashion accessories. Apart from Delaunay there is information on Alice Rutter, a designer at Martine, Suzanne Lallement, who took over the craft embroidery workshop started by her father, which produced embroidered fabrics for couturiers, Margarette Callot, a painter and designer for Lallement, and fabric designer Mme Claussen Smith.

1403 BURY, HESTER. *A Choice of Design, 1850–1980: Fabrics by Warner and Sons Ltd.* Colchester: The Minories, 1981, 113pp., illus.

Contains an extended essay on the history of silk weaving and fabric design by this firm who produced fabrics for royal wedding and coronation robes as well as furnishings for Windsor Castle. After the catalogue of 313 items there is an index of designers included with short biographical outline. Twenty women are included.

1404 *Céramique et Tapissérie contemporains en Belgique.* Brussels. Published Ghent: Snoek-Ducaju & Zoon: Musées Royaux d'Art et d'Histoire, 1978, n.p., illus.

Text in French and Flemish. The exhibition catalogue is organised into sections on sculptural ceramics, everyday and decorative ceramics and tapestry. After several short introductory essays there is very brief information about the designers and the exhibits. Women are well represented.

1405 COATTS, MARGOT. *Colour with Cloth.* London: Crafts Council, 1994, 56pp., illus.

Catalogue of an exhibition of British printed, painted and dyed craft textiles of the twentieth century. The exhibitors are almost exclusively women and biographies are provided. There are interviews with Susan Bosence, Sally Greaves-Lord, Georgina von Etzdorf and Sharon Ting.

1406 COHEN, FRANÇOISE. *La matière pensée: art textile: Michèle Morreau, Martine Salzmann, Jocelyne Toupet-Poutier, Fiep Zwann.* Le Havre: Musée des Beaux-Arts, 1986.

The introductory essay to this catalogue discusses the fibre art tradition and these artists produce sculptural work in fabric. There are biographical outlines and a statement by each artist, three of whom are French and one, Dutch.

1407 COLCHESTER, CHLOE. *The New Textiles: Trends and Traditions.* London: Thames and Hudson, 1991, 191pp., illus.

Discusses contemporary textiles in Europe and America under three headings: design (fashion and furnishing fabrics), craft textiles and textile art. There are biographies of the eighty artists/designers included, of which sixty-three are women and thirty-seven are women from Europe. Lists museums and galleries with collections of contemporary textiles and important exhibitions.

1408 CONSTANTINE, MILDRED, and JACK LENOR LARSEN. *The Art Fabric: Mainstream.* New York: Van Nostrand Reinhold, 1981, 272pp., illus.

The authors argue for the acceptance of textiles within the Fine Art establishment, pointing out the range of work, similarity of concerns and aesthetics between the two fields. In the course of the argument many designers from America and Europe are included. A useful biographical section gives details of their training, exhibitions and awards. Nearly thirty European women are included.

1409 *Contemporary Polish Weavers.* Edinburgh: Weavers' Workshop Gallery, 1972, 19pp., illus.

Of the eighteen designers exhibited, one is a man. A brief biographical outline and a list of exhibitions in given for each person together.

1410 *Correspondence vêtement revêtement.* Paris: Union des Arts Décoratifs and Musée des Arts de la Mode, 1986, 72pp., illus.

Text in French. Examines the links and exchanges between furnishing and fashion fabrics in the work of contemporary fabric designers, of which seven are women: Anne Marie Beretta, Françoise Chassin, Emmanuelle Khanh, Maryll Lanvin, Popy Moreni, Sonia Rykiel and Elizabeth de Senneville.

1411 DORMER, PETER, TANYA HARROD, ROSEMARY HILL, and BARLEY ROSCOE. *Arts and Crafts to Avant-Garde. Essays on the Crafts from 1880 to the Present.* London: South Bank Centre, 1992, 34pp., illus.

Consists of four critical essays on aspects of the crafts in Britain over the past century. The essays eschew the survey approach in favour of the analytical. Several women are mentioned, particularly in the essay on textiles.

1412 FANELLI, GIOVANNI, and ROSALIA FANELLI. *Il tessuto art deco e anni trenta: disegno, moda, architettura.* Florence: Cantini, 1986, 310pp., illus.

Text in Italian. Divided into two periods—Art Nouveau to Art Deco and the thirties—the book provides detailed information subdivided by country. It covers textile design for clothes and interiors, fashion, small scale production and designs for industrial production. There are many women included.

1413 FANELLI, GIOVANNI, and ROSALIA FANELLI. *Il tessuto Art Nouveau: disegno, moda, architettura.* Florence: Cantini, 1986, 318pp., illus.

Text in Italian. After a consideration of the beginnings of modern design, here placed c. 1850, notably in Britain with the ideas of Ruskin and the designs of William Morris, there is a survey of the contribution to Art Nouveau textiles made by individual European countries. A small number of women are included.

1414 FANELLI, GIOVANNI, and ROSALIA FANELLI. *Il tessuto moderno: disegno, moda, architettura 1890–1940.* Florence: Vallecchi, 1976, 256pp., 740 illus., 147 pl.

Text in Italian. A chronological survey of the development of textile design and fashion during the period from Art Nouveau to Art Deco. A considerable number of women are included in the later periods.

1415 *Fibres art 85.* Paris: Musée des Arts Décoratifs in conjunction with the association Textil/art/langage, 1985, 157pp., illus.

Text in French and English. The introduction focuses on the art/craft debate in relation to textiles. The catalogue which follows is divided into three sections: a portfolio of images; articles addressing basic themes in fibre art and, third, a list of artists by country. The countries with the strongest representation are France, Hungary and the Netherlands. The majority of artists included are women.

1416 GANE, LUCINDA. "Patchwork: The Quilters' Guild Exhibition." *Crafts* 51 (1981): 49.

Review of an exhibition in which most of the exhibitors are women.

1417 "Greuzen öffnen. 4. Quilt-Biennale in Heidelberg." *Kunst und Handwerk* 91, no. 2 (1991): 35–36, illus.

Text in German. Review of exhibition in which most of the exhibitors were women.

1418 GRONWOLDT, RUTH, and SABINE HESSE. *Art Nouveau: Textil-Dekor um 1900.* Stuttgart: Würtemburgisches Landesmuseum, [c. 1980], 317pp., illus.

Text in German. This survey of Art Nouveau textiles is organised into four countries: Britain, France, Austria and Germany. There is an overview for each followed by short biographies of the designers included. Overall, six women are included: Margarete von Brauchitsch, Lindsay Butterfield, Frida Hansen, Gabrielle Rault, Else Unger and Hermine Winckler.

1419 *Gunta Stölzl: Weberei am Bauhaus und aus eigener Werkstatt.* Berlin in association with Kupfergraben Verlag: Bauhaus-Archiv, 1987, 175pp., illus.

A detailed study of Stölzl's life and work together with detailed biographies of her colleagues and students, who are predominantly female. Each biography includes a bibliography.

1420 HARDINGHAM, MARTIN. "Lausanne." *Crafts* 4 (1973).

Review of the sixth tapestry Biennale at Lausanne that mentions many women.

1421 HAYES, MARSHALL. *British Textile Designers Today.* Leigh-on-Sea: F. Lewis, 1939, 326pp., illus.

After introductory chapters on definitions and techniques, one page of text and some illustrations are devoted to each of some forty designers, of whom a good proportion are women. A more extensive list of textile designers in Britain is given at the end together with their addresses.

1422 HODGE, MAUREEN, and FIONA MATHISON. "Tapestries from Scotland." *Crafts* 30 (1978): 24–29.

A statement of intent from the newly formed Scottish Tapestry Artists' Group.

1423 JARRY, MADELEINE. *La tapissérie: art du XXème siècle.* Fribourg: Office du Livre, 1974, 358pp., illus.

A generously illustrated survey of different aspects of tapestry production this century. There are three main sections: early signs of renewal, renaissance of French tapestry and an international survey of tapestry between 1963 and 1973. There are passages on the most important individuals and countries where production has been particularly significant. There are many women included.

1424 JEFFRIES, JANIS. "Women and Textiles." *Crafts* 67 (1984): 55.

A review of "Women and Textiles: Their Lives and Work," organised by the Women Artists' Slide Library (now the Women's Art Library)

1425 JOSEPH, HELEN. *A Glory of Quilts.* Gateshead: Shipley Art Gallery, 1990, 22pp., illus.

The short text provides an introduction to quilts and includes sections on the Cultra Patchwork collection from the Ulster Folk and Transport Museum, on European quilts as well as the local revival which generated this exhibition. All the exhibitors are women.

1426 KALNIETE, SANDRA, MARTINS HEIMRATS, and VALTS KLEINS. *Latvju tekstilmāksla. Latvian tapestry.* Riga: Liesma, 1989, 279pp., many illus.

Text in Latvian, Russian and English. The introductory essay deals with the strong tradition of textile art in Latvia, which survived the restrictions of Soviet rule which affected the Fine Arts. This is followed by an account of the work of forty contemporary textile designers, the majority of whom are women.

1427 KILLNER, JEANETTE. "Embroidery by the 62 Group." *Crafts* 48 (1981): 51.

Exhibition review.

1428 KONDRATIUK, KRYSTYNA. *L'art de tissu en Pologne de 1962 à 1972.* Paris: Presses artistiques and Manufacture Nationale des Gobelins, 1972, n.p., illus.

After a short essay, the alphabetical catalogue provides brief biographies of the artists and information about their exhibits. The decade covered represents the early phase of the revival of tapestry and its move from the traditional textures and motifs into more experimental fields. All but four of the twenty-six exhibitors are women and include many of the best known individuals in this area, such as Abakanowicz and Butrymowicz.

1429 KONDRATIUK, KRYSTYNA. *Les tissus polonais artistiques contemporains.* Łodz: Museum of Textile History, 1965, 44pp., illus.

Text in French. This exhibition was mounted for part of the International Exhibition of Modern Tapestry. The alphabetical catalogue entries are preceded by an essay on Polish textiles art from 1945. Twenty-four women are featured, with biographical outlines and lists of their exhibitions.

1430 *La tessitura del Bauhaus 1919–33.* Pesaro: Palazzo Ducale, 1985, 95pp., illus.

Text in Italian. Scholarly essays on the role and styles of the textile workshop at the Bauhaus precede the catalogue itself. Of the twenty-seven designers included, all but eight are women.

1431 LOUHIO, ANJA. *Taideryijyjä: Modern Finnish Rugs.* Helsinki: Julkaisija Editors Suomalaisen Kirjallisuuden Kirpaino Oyskk Ltd., 1975, 133pp., mainly illus.

Text in Finnish, with an English summary. Observing that almost all the designers of rugs since the 1950s have been women, the author identifies such outstanding designers as Uhra Simberg-Ehrström, Kirsti Ilvessalo, Airi Snellman-Hänninen and Ritva Puotila. Many examples by these designers are illustrated, together with the works of seventeen other women.

1432 LUTTEMAN, HELENA. *Polen Vaaver Fritt: Polish Textile Art.* Stockholm: National Museum, 1970.

Text in Swedish. Looks at developments in Polish textiles since the first Tapestry Biennale in Lausanne in 1962. All the designers except one are women: Zofia Butrymowicz, Ewa Jaroszynska Pachucka, Maria Laszkiewicz, Jolanta Owidzka, Ewa Stephan and Janina Tworek Pierzgalska.

1433 MARTIN, EDNA, and BEATA SYDHOFF. *Svensk textilkonst: Swedish textile art.* Stockholm: Liber Förlag, 1980, 151pp., illus.

Bilingual text in Swedish and English. A survey of Swedish textile art since 1945, the book examines the materials and subjects of textile art together with the changing forms of commissions and the broadening of the contexts in which textile art was used, including the interiors of public buildings. The majority of artists working in this field are women.

1434 MENDES, VALERIE. *British textiles from 1900–37: The Victoria and Albert Museum's Textiles Collection.* London: Victoria and Albert Museum, 1992, 95pp., 116 pl.

A survey of the subject is followed by a catalogue of the items exhibited and a listing of designers. Seven women are included: Phyllis Barron, Vanessa Bell, Mrs. Archibald Christie, Marion Dorn, Dorothy Larcher, Minnie McLeish and Winifred Kennedy Scott.

1435 *Moderne Hollandsk Tekstilkunst og Glas.* Copenhagen: Kunstindustri-museet, 1979.

Text in Danish, Dutch and English. Introductory essays for each of the sections on glass and textiles precede information on the individual exhibitors. Of the seven textile designers, six are women, while six of the fourteen glass designers are women.

1436 O'MAHONEY, MARIE, and SARAH BRADDOCK (EDS.). *Textiles and New Technology: 2010.* London: Crafts Council, 1994, 96pp., illus.

Collection of critical essays that attempts to analyse the impact of new technologies on textiles. The case studies cited include examples of women from western European countries.

1437 *Out of the Frame: Contemporary and Historical Embroidery and Stitch.* London: Crafts Council, 1992, 32pp., illus.

Consists of a brief history of women and textiles, interviews with four contemporary makers—Loran Moffatt, Susannah Hope, Louise Baldwin and Rozanne Hawksley—and the catalogue itself. Most of the exhibitors are women.

1438 PARKER, ROZSIKA. *The Subversive Stitch. Embroidery and the Making of the Feminine.* London: Women's Press, 1984, 247pp., illus.

An analysis of the ways in which needlework, and in particular embroidery, could be understood as a means not only of conditioning women to their passive, domestic role but also for creating space for women to think. Most of the material relates to the nineteenth century, but the final chapter looks at the way in which contemporary women artists have used fabric to explore issues about femininity and the domestic role.

1439 PARRY, LINDA. *Textiles of the Arts and Crafts movement.* London: Thames and Hudson, 1988, 160pp., illus.

Provides not only essays on the artistic and industrial background, the development of the style and the role of textiles in Arts and Crafts exhibitions, but also gives information about designers, manufacturers and shops where arts and crafts textiles might be purchased. In this last section many women are mentioned but they occur throughout the book.

1440 PARRY, LINDA. *William Morris Textiles.* London: Weidenfeld and Nicolson, 1983, 192pp., illus.

Analyses the production of Morris's workshop by type of textile work. The women associated with the workshop are included, as is his daughter, May (q.v.). There are indices of patterns, sources and collections.

1441 "Queen Bees: Work by a Selection of Contemporary Quiltmakers." *Crafts* 71 (1984): 24–27.

Included are works by Esther Barrett, Pauline Burbidge (q.v.), Lucinda Gane, Iona Heath, Phyllis Ross and Lucy Wallis.

1442 REPEN, MICHAEL. "Embroiderers at Work." *Crafts* 10 (1974): 49.

Review of an exhibition of the 62 Group of embroiderers, most of whom are women.

1443 "Rugs for Churches." *Crafts* 25 (1977): 34–38.

Three of the seven featured designs are by women.

1444 SALICATH, BENT, and ARNE KARLSEN. *Modern Danish Textiles.* Translated by Birtne Andersen. Copenhagen: Danish Society of Arts and Crafts and Industrial Design, 1959, 72pp., illus.

A chapter on the development of Danish textiles for the home from 1930 onward includes Lis Ahlmann, Gerda Henning and Marie Gudme Leth (qq.v.). This is followed by a section on individual designers, each of whom has two pages giving a biographical outline and several paragraphs on the development of their work. The majority of those included are women.

1445 SCHOESER, MARY. *Fabrics and wallpapers. Twentieth century design.* London: Belland Hyman, 1986, 112pp., illus.

A chronological survey with particular emphasis on the period from the late nineteenth century to 1964. A considerable number of women are included in the account, the majority from Britain.

1446 *Stortextil fraan Handarbetets Vaenner.* Stockholm: National Gallery, 1970, n.p., illus.

Text in Swedish with English summary. Exhibition of monumental textiles produced in Sweden in the period 1960–1970. This movement is led by

Edna Martin, who contributes an essay to the catalogue. The work of a number of women is included.

1447 STRAUB, MARIANNE. *Textiles today Selected by Marianne Straub.* Cambridge: Kettle's Yard, 1980, n.p. [27pp.], illus.

An introduction by Straub explains her criteria for this selection of works produced in the late 1970s. An alphabetical section dealing with the sixteen artists, of whom four are men, gives the briefest biographical outline before itemising the exhibits.

1448 SUTTON, ANN. "8th International Tapestry Biennale at Lausanne." *Crafts* 28 (1977): 49–50.

Review of this key event in the textile calendar.

1449 SUTTON, ANN (ED.). *British Craft Textiles.* London: Collins, 1985, 192pp., illus.

Primarily about women, this book is divided into chapters by medium or technique. Each consists of a brief introduction and then a statement by each of a series of selected designers. Works by each are illustrated.

1450 TALLEY, CHARLES. *Contemporary Textile Art: Scandinavia.* [Stockholm?]: Carmina, 1982, 200pp., illus.

After an introductory essay in which female artists from earlier in the century are mentioned, the book is divided into sections by country. Within each of these there is an introduction followed by a focus on six to eight individuals, almost all of whom are women. These in turn are followed by illustrations of the work of additional designers from that country. In all, twenty-four women are included.

1451 *Tapisséries finlandaises.* Paris: Musée d'Art Moderne de la Ville de Paris, 1972, 53pp., illus.

Text in French. The initial short essay examines the tradition of ryijy rugs in Finland and suggests they form the basis for the modern textile artist. All twenty-one artists in this exhibition are women and each is represented by a brief biography and an illustration.

1452 *Textil du nord: culture et industrie.* Paris: Centre Nationale d'Art et de Culture Georges Pompidou, 1984, 85pp., illus.

Text in French. The emphasis is on the textile industry based in Roubaix, near Lille, but a few names of designers emerge. Women mentioned are Jacqueline Régnier, Zofia Rostad and Marianne Kieffer.

1453 TROUPP, LOTTE. *Modern Finnish Textiles.* Helsinki: Otava, 1962, 63pp., illus.

A survey of the different uses to which textiles are put and the chief practitioners of the time. The main chapters cover carpets and ryijy rugs, travelling rugs, furnishing fabrics and fashion. A very high proportion of the designers mentioned are women.

1454 VÖLKER, ANGELA. "Österreichische Textilien des frühen 20. Jahrhunderts." *Alte und Moderne Kunst* 171 (1980): 1–7.
Text in German. Examines textile designs by the Wiener Werkstätte. Four women are mentioned: Lotte Frömel-Fochler, Maria Likarz Strauss (qq.v.), Rosalie Rothansl and Leopoldine Guttmann.

1455 VÖLKER, ANGELA. *Die Stoffe der Wiener Werkstätte, 1910–1932.* Vienna: Christian Brandstätter in association with the Österreichen Museum für angewandte Kunst, Vienna, 1990, 284pp., 415 illus.
Text in German. A detailed examination of the topic, including an alphabetical list of designers. Forty-seven women are included.

1456 "Wall Works." *Crafts Magazine* 73 (1985): 22–27.
Interviews with four women who use mixed media to create works for walls: Helyne Jennings, Susan Kinley, Stephanie Tuckwell and Katherine Virgils.

1457 WALLER, IRENE. "Lausanne Biennale." *Crafts* 16 (1975): 9–10.
Review of the seventh Tapestry Biennale at Lausanne by a practitioner (q.v.).

1458 *Weavers' Worksop: Inaugural Exhibition.* Edinburgh: Weavers' Workshop Gallery, 1971, 30pp., illus.
Opening exhibition on a space dedicated to textile design. Twenty-one women and four men are included in this catalogue. Each is given an outline biography, a selective list of exhibitions and commissions, in addition to details about the work exhibited. The dates of birth of the exhibitors range between 1907 and 1947.

1459 WELTGE, SIGRID WORTMANN. *Bauhaus Textiles: Women Artists and the Weaving Workshop.* London: Thames and Hudson, 1993, 208pp., 220 illus.
A semichronological account of this particular part of the Bauhaus, in which the largest number of women worked. It provides a range of names, works and biographical information for the women she has researched. One chapter addresses the question of the gender issue at the Bauhaus, while the final one looks at their careers in the post-Bauhaus era.

1460 WOLLIN, NILS. *Swedish Textiles 1943–50. Survey of world textiles.* Leigh-on-Sea: Frank Lewis, 1952, 13pp. and 77 illus.
After the very brief introduction are notes on the illustrations. The majority of works are by women designers: Ingrid Skerfe-Nilsson, Edna Martin, Hulda, Frida and Selma Svensson, Ann-Mari Forsberg, Märta Afzelius, Sofia Widén, Alice Lund, Susan Gröndal, Märtha Gahn, Lena Linden, Barbro

Nilsson, Marianne Richter, Astrid Sampe-Hultberg, Tyra Lundgren, Viola Gråsten and Elsa Gullberg.

1461 WOOD, ESTHER. "National Competition of Schools of Art." *Studio* 26 (1902): 286–281.

Despite the title, this is a review of decorative art produced by students. Eighteen works by women are illustrated, and other female designers active in a range of media are mentioned in the text. The strongest fields were textiles and ceramics.

1462 YASINSKAYA, I. *Soviet Textile Design of the Revolutionary Period.* London: Thames and Hudson, 1983, 105pp., many illus.

An introductory essay by John Bowlt discusses women active in the avant-garde groups. This is followed by the author's introduction to textiles in the 1920s and early 1930s. Some of the better known women—Popova, Exter, Stepanova and Mukhina—are mentioned, but it is only with the illustrations, organised by the mills in which the textiles were produced that less familiar names emerge: F. Antonova, O. Fedoseyeva, O. Bogoslovskaya, D. Preobrazhenskaya, R. Matveyeva, M. Anufriyeva, V. Lotonina, M. Nazarevskaya and E. Nikitina.

1463 ZALETOVA, LIDIJA, and FABIO CIOFI. *L'Abito della rivoluzione: tessuti, abiti, costumi nell'Unione Sovietica degli anni 20.* Venice: Cataloghi Marsilio, 1987, 193pp., illus.

Text in Italian. Examines textile design and fashion the years immediately following the revolution, a field in which women were active.

INDIVIDUALS

1464 AAGAARD, GUDRUN STIG (1895–?)

Danish textile designer specialising in printed textiles.

Other Sources

Salicath, Bent, and Arne Karlsen, eds. *Modern Danish Textiles.* Copenhagen: Danish Society of Arts and Crafts and Industrial Design, 1959.

1465 ACKERMANN, SUSE (c. 1905–)

German textile designer.

Other Sources

Gunta Stölzl: Weberei am Bauhaus und aus eigener Werkstatt. Berlin: Bauhaus Archiv in association with Kupfergraben Verlag, 1987. Contains individual bibliographies.

1466 ADLERCREUTZ, MARIA (1936–)
    Swedish textile designer.

Exhibitions

McFadden, David. *Scandinavian Modern Design, 1880–1980.* New York: Abrams in association with the Cooper-Hewitt Museum, 1982.

Other Sources

Byars, Mel. *The Design Encyclopedia.* London: Lawrence King, 1994.
Martin, Edna, and Beata Sydhoff. *Svensk textilkonst. Swedish Textile Art.* Stockholm: Liber Förlag, 1980.

1467 AGÉLII, ELSA
    Swedish designer of textiles.

Other Sources

Martin, Edna, and Beata Sydhoff. *Svensk textilkonst. Swedish Textile Art.* Stockholm: Liber Förlag, 1980.
Talley, Charles. *Contemporary Textile Art: Scandinavia.* Stockholm: Carmina, 1982.

1468 AGGER, MARGRETHE
    Danish designer of textiles.

Other Sources

Talley, Charles. *Contemporary Textile Art: Scandinavia.* Stockholm: Carmina, 1982.

1469 AHLMANN, LIS (1894–1979)
    Danish textile designer.

Main Sources

Møgensen, Thomas. *Lis Ahlmann—Tekstiler.* Copenhagen: Christian Ejlers' Forlag, 1974, 72pp., illus. Text in Danish. One-third of the book is devoted to an essay on her work, while the remainder consists of captioned illustrations.

Exhibitions

Hiesinger, Kathryn, and George Marcus III, eds. *Design since 1945.* Philadelphia: Philadelphia Museum of Art, 1983.

Other Sources

Byars, Mel. *The Design Encyclopedia.* London: Lawrence King, 1994.

Karlsen, Arne. *Møbler tegnet af Børge Mogensen. Furniture Designed by Børge Mogensen.* Copenhagen: Danish Architectural Press, 1968, 138pp., illus.

Naylor, Colin, ed. *Contemporary Designers.* 2nd edition. Chicago and London: St. James Press, 1990.

Salicath, Bent, and Arne Karlsen, eds. *Modern Danish Textiles.* Copenhagen: Danish Society of Arts and Crafts and Industrial Design, 1959.

1470 AHLSTEDT-WILLANDT, MARGARETA (1889–after 1954)
Finnish textile designer.

Other Sources

Mäki, Oili. *Taide ja Työ: Finnish Designers of Today.* Helsinki: Werner Söderström Osakeyhtiö, 1954. Gives an outline biography.

1471 AKERDAHL, ANNA
Swedish-born designer of textiles who worked in Italy.

Other Sources

Fanelli, Giovanni, and Rosalia Fanelli. *Il tessuto art déco e anni trenta: disegno, moda, architettura.* Florence: Cantini, 1986.

1472 ALBERS, ANNI (née ANNELIESE FLEISCHMANN) (1899–1994)
German born textile designer who worked at the Bauhaus and then in America.

Publications

Anni Albers: Pictorial Weavings. Cambridge, Mass: MIT, 1959.

On Designing. New Haven, Connecticut: Pellango Press, 1959. Reprint Middletown, Conn.: Wesleyan University Press, 1962.

On Weaving. Middletown, Conn.: Wesleyan University Press, 1965.

Pre-Columbian Mexican Miniatures. New York: Praeger Press, 1970.

For others see Naylor below.

Main Sources

Margetts, Martina. "Thoroughly Modern Anni." *Crafts* 74 (1985): 14–21. Written on Albers's 86th birthday.

Schoeser. Mary. "Anni Albers." *The Guardian,* 28 May 1994, 43. Obituary.

Exhibitions

Baro, Gene. *Anni Albers.* New York: Brooklyn Museum, 1977, 96pp., mainly illus. Includes an interview with Albers.

Hiesinger, Kathryn, and George Marcus III, eds. *Design since 1945.* Philadelphia: Philadelphia Museum of Art, 1983.

La Tessitura del Bauhaus, 1919–33 nelle collezioni della Repubblica Democratica Tedesca. Venice: Palazzo Ducale and Cataloghi Marsilio, 1985.

Oedekoven-Gerischer, Angela, et al., eds. *Frauen im Design: Berufsbilder und Lebenswege seit 1900. Women in Design: Careers and Life Histories since 1900.* Stuttgart: Design Center, 1989.

Other Sources

Byars, Mel. *The Design Encyclopedia.* London: Lawrence King, 1994.

Constantine, Mildred, and Jack Lenor Larsen. *Beyond Craft: The Art Fabric.* New York: Van Nostrand Reinhold, 1973.

Fanelli, Giovanni, and Rosalia Fanelli. *Il tessuto art déco e anni trenta: disegno, moda, architettura.* Florence: Cantini, 1986.

Gunta Stölzl: Weberei am Bauhaus und aus eigener Werkstatt. Berlin: Bauhaus Archiv in association with Kupfergraben Verlag, 1987.

Naylor, Colin, ed. *Contemporary Designers.* 2nd edition. Chicago and London: St. James Press, 1990. Contains a bibliography.

Weltge, Sigrid Wortmann. *Bauhaus Textiles: Women Artists and the Weaving Workshop.* London: Thames and Hudson, 1993.

1473 ALIFRANGIS, INGE (1937–)
Danish designer of textiles who specialises in weaving.

Exhibitions

16 Plus. Copenhagen: Dansk Kunstindustrimuseet, 1981.

1474 ALMEGARD, ALME
Swedish textile designer.

Other Sources

Jarry, Madeleine. *La tapissérie: art du XXème siècle.* Fribourg: Office du Livre, 1974.

1475 AMOLIŅA, INTA (1952–)
Latvian textile designer.

Other Sources

Kalniete, Sandra. *Latvju tekstilmāksla* [Latvian textile art]. Riga: Liesma, 1989.

1476 ANDERSON, JANET (1946–)
English artist and designer who worked in tapestry until 1980 and who since then has worked in fabric, collage and paint.

Other Sources

Sutton, Ann. *British Craft Textiles.* London: Collins, 1985.

1477 ANDERSSON, MARJA "GRÄSET"
Swedish designer of textiles.

Other Sources

Talley, Charles. *Contemporary Textile Art: Scandinavia.* Stockholm: Carmina, 1982.

1478 ANDRES, MARGARET
Belgian textile designer.

Other Sources

Jarry, Madeleine. *La tapissérie: art du XXème siècle.* Fribourg: Office du Livre, 1974.

1479 ANGUS, CHRISTINE DRUMMOND (Alt. Mrs. WALTER SICKERT) (1877–1921)
English designer and embroiderer of textiles.

Other Sources

Parry, Linda. *Textiles of the Arts and Crafts Movement.* London: Thames and Hudson, 1988.

1480 ANTONOVA, F.
Russian textile designer.

Other Sources

Yasinskaya, I. *Soviet Textile Design of the Revolutionary Period.* London: Thames and Hudson, 1983.

1481 ARNDT, GERTRUD (née HANTSCHK) (1903–)
German photographer and designer of textiles.

Exhibitions

La Tessitura del Bauhaus, 1919–33, nelle collezioni della Repubblica Democratica Tedesca. Venice: Palazzo Ducale and Cataloghi Marsilio, 1985.

Other Sources

Gunta Stölzl: Weberei am Bauhaus und aus eigener Werkstatt. Berlin: Bauhaus Archiv in association with Kupfergraben Verlag, 1987.

Jarry, Madeleine. *La tapissérie: art du XXème siècle.* Fribourg: Office du Livre, 1974.

1482 ATTERBERG, INGRID (1920–)
Swedish designer of glass, ceramics and textiles.

See Glass section.

1483 AURDAL, SYNNØVE ANKER
Norwegian textile designer who represented Norway at the Venice Biennale in 1982.

Exhibitions

Wichstrøm, Anne. *Rooms with a View: Women's Art in Norway, 1880–1990.* Oslo: Royal Ministry of Foreign Affairs, 1989.

Other Sources

Jarry, Madeleine. *La tapissérie: art du XXème siècle.* Fribourg: Office du Livre, 1974.
Talley, Charles. *Contemporary Textile Art: Scandinavia.* Stockholm: Carmina, 1982.

1484 AUSTRIŅA, ILMA (1940–)
Latvian textile designer.

Other Sources

Kalniete, Sandra. *Latvju tekstilmāksla* [Latvian textile art]. Riga: Liesma, 1989.

1485 AUTZINGER, LOUISE
Austrian textile designer who exhibited in the 1960s.

Other Sources

Jarry, Madeleine. *La tapissérie: art du XXème siècle.* Fribourg: Office du Livre, 1974.

1486 BACKHAUS, HANNE (1942–)
Danish textile designer who specialises in printed textiles.

Exhibitions

16 Plus. Copenhagen: Dansk Kunstindustrimuseet, 1981.

1487 BALÁCS, IRÉN (1935–)
Hungarian textile designer.

Exhibitions

9. Fal-Es Tertextyil Biennale [9th National Textile Biennale]. Szombathely: Savaria Museum, 1984.

1488 BALLE, GRETA
Danish textile designer.

Other Sources

Jarry, Madeleine. *La tapissérie: art du XXème siècle.* Fribourg: Office du Livre, 1974.

1489 BANDIERA CERANTOLA, MARISA (1924–)
Italian designer of furniture and textiles.

See Interior Design section.

1490 BARRON, PHYLLIS (1890–1964)
English textile designer who collaborated with Dorothy Larcher (q.v.).

Main Sources

O'Connor, Deryn. "Hand-block printed textiles by Phyllis Barron and Dorothy Larcher." *Crafts* 33 (1978): 51. Review of exhibition.

Exhibitions

Phyllis Barron and Dorothy Larcher: Handblock Printed Textiles. Bath: Craft Study Centre, 1978.
Thirties: British Art and Design before the War. London: Arts Council of Great Britain at the Hayward Gallery, 1979.
Hogben, C. *A Collection in the Making: British Art and Design, 1900–1960.* London: Victoria and Albert Museum, 1983.
Mendes, Valerie. *British Textiles from 1900–1937: The Victoria and Albert Museum's Textile Collection.* London: Victoria and Albert Museum, 1992.

Other Sources

Byars, Mel. *The Design Encyclopedia.* London: Lawrence King, 1994.

1491 BAUMANE, AIJA (1943–)
Latvian textile designer who produces works both in traditional techniques and in three-dimensional experimental forms.

Other Sources

Kalniete, Sandra. *Latvju tekstilmāksla* [Latvian textile art]. Riga: Liesma, 1989.

1492 BAUMGARTNER, ELFREDE
Austrian textile designer.

Other Sources

Jarry, Madeleine. *La tapissérie: art du XXème siècle.* Fribourg: Office du Livre, 1974.

1493 BECHTELER, ELSE
German textile designer.

Other Sources

Jarry, Madeleine. *La tapissérie: art du XXème siècle.* Fribourg: Office du Livre, 1974.

1494 BECKER, KIRSTEN (1915–)
Danish textile designer who worked with her husband John.

Other Sources

Salicath, Bent, and Arne Karlsen, eds. *Modern Danish Textiles.* Copenhagen: Danish Society of Arts and Crafts and Industrial Design, 1959.

1495 BERGER, OTTI (1898–1944)
Designer of textiles who was born in the former Yugoslavia, worked in Germany, the Netherlands and England and died in Auschwitz.

Exhibitions

La Tessitura del Bauhaus, 1919–33, nelle collezioni della Repubblica Democratica Tedesca. Venice: Palazzo Ducale and Cataloghi Marsilio, 1985.

Oedekoven-Gerischer, Angela, et al., eds. *Frauen im Design: Berufsbilder und Lebenswege seit 1900. Women in Design: Careers and Life Histories since 1900.* Stuttgart: Design Center, 1989.

Other Sources

Fanelli, Giovanni, and Rosalia Fanelli. *Il tessuto art déco e anni trenta: disegno, moda, architettura.* Florence: Cantini, 1986.

Gunta Stölzl: Weberei am Bauhaus und aus eigener Werkstatt. Berlin: Bauhaus Archiv in association with Kupfergraben Verlag, 1987. Contains individual bibliographies.

Weltge, Sigrid Wortmann. *Bauhaus Textiles: Women Artists and the Weaving Workshop.* London: Thames and Hudson, 1993.

1496 BERGMAN, STEPHANIE (1946–)
English textile artist and designer.

Main Sources

"Apron Strings." *Crafts* 36 (1979): 32–33. Looks at costume designs for dancers by Bergman.

Other Sources

Parker, Roszika, and Griselda Pollock. *Old Mistresses: Women, Art and Ideology.* London: Routledge, 1982.
Sutton, Ann. *British Craft Textiles.* London: Collins, 1985.

1497 BERGNER, LENA (Alt. HELENE MEYER) (1906–1981)
German designer of textiles who also worked in the USSR and Switzerland.

Exhibitions

La Tessitura del Bauhaus, 1919–33, nelle collezioni della Repubblica Democratica Tedesca. Venice: Palazzo Ducale and Cataloghi Marsilio, 1985.

Other Sources

Byars, Mel. *The Design Encyclopedia.* London: Lawrence King, 1994.
Gunta Stölzl: Weberei am Bauhaus und aus eigener Werkstatt. Berlin: Bauhaus Archiv in association with Kupfergraben Verlag, 1987. Contains individual bibliographies.
Weltge, Sigrid Wortmann. *Bauhaus Textiles: Women Artists and the Weaving Workshop.* London: Thames and Hudson, 1993.

1498 BERGSON, PHILIPPA (c. 1954–)
English textile designer who specialises in quilting.

Other Sources

Sutton, Ann. *British Craft Textiles.* London: Collins, 1985.

1499 BERNHUBER, MARIA VON (c. 1880–?)
Austrian textile designer.

Other Sources

Pirhofer, G., and A. Gmeiner. *Der Österreichische Werkbund.* Vienna: 1985.

1500 BĒRZIŅA, ASTRĪDA (1946–)
Latvian textile designer.

Other Sources

Kalniete, Sandra. *Latvju tekstilmāksla* [Latvian textile art]. Riga: Liesma, 1989.

1501 BEYER, LIS (Alt. VOLGER) (1906–1973)
German designer of textiles.

Exhibitions

La Tessitura del Bauhaus, 1919–33, nelle collezioni della Repubblica Democratica Tedesca. Venice: Palazzo Ducale and Cataloghi Marsilio, 1985.

Other Sources

Fanelli, Giovanni, and Rosalia Fanelli. *Il tessuto art déco e anni trenta: disegno, moda, architettura.* Florence: Cantini, 1986
Gunta Stölzl: Weberei am Bauhaus und aus eigener Werkstatt. Berlin: Bauhaus Archiv in association with Kupfergraben Verlag, 1987. Contains individual bibliographies.
Weltge, Sigrid Wortmann. *Bauhaus Textiles: Women Artists and the Weaving Workshop.* London: Thames and Hudson, 1993.

1502 BIALAS-TERAKOWSKA, MARIA TERESA (1931–)
Polish textile designer.

Exhibitions

Contemporary Polish Weavers. Edinburgh: Weavers' Workshop Gallery, 1972.
Kondratiuk, Krystyna. *L'Art de tissu en Pologne de 1962 à 1972.* Paris: Manufacture Nationale des Gobelins, 1972.

1503 BILGER, MARIA
Austrian textile designer who exhibited in the 1960s.

Other Sources

Jarry, Madeleine. *La tapissérie: art du XXème siècle.* Fribourg: Office du Livre, 1974.

1504 BINNS, POLLY (1950–)
English textile designer whose work explored the soft colours and light qualities on the folded or pleated surfaces of fabrics and paper.

Other Sources

Sutton, Ann. *British Craft Textiles*. London: Collins, 1985.

1505 BLAKSTAD, SIRI
Norwegian textile designer.

Other Sources

Jarry, Madeleine. *La tapissérie: art du XXème siècle*. Fribourg: Office du Livre, 1974.

1506 BLUMATE, IRISA (1948–)
Latvian textile designer.

Other Sources

Kalniete, Sandra. *Latvju tekstilmāksla* [Latvian textile art]. Riga: Liesma, 1989.

1507 BLUMBERGA, RITA (1925–)
Latvian textile designer.

Other Sources

Kalniete, Sandra. *Latvju tekstilmāksla* [Latvian textile art]. Riga: Liesma, 1989.

1508 BOBERG, ANNA KATERINA (1864–1935)
Swedish designer of ceramics, glass and textiles.

See Ceramics section.

1509 BOGOSLOVSKAYA, OLGA VASILIEVNA (1905–)
Russian textile designer.

Other Sources

Byars, Mel. *The Design Encyclopedia*. London: Lawrence King, 1994.
Yasinskaya, I. *Soviet Textile Design of the Revolutionary Period*. London: Thames and Hudson, 1983.

1510 BOGUSTOVA, RUTA (1935–)
Latvian textile designer who produces reliefs using varied materials and techniques.

Other Sources

Kalniete, Sandra. *Latvju tekstilmāksla* [Latvian textile art]. Riga: Liesma, 1989.

1511 BONFANTI, RENATA (1929–)
Italian textile designer.

Exhibitions

Bacci, N. *Il Design delle Donne*. Ravenna: Museo dell'Arredo Contemporaneo, 1991.

Other Sources

Byars, Mel. *The Design Encyclopedia*. London: Lawrence King, 1994.

1512 BORDIER, PRIMEROSE (1929–)
French textile designer.

Other Sources

Byars, Mel. *The Design Encyclopedia*. London: Lawrence King, 1994.

1513 BOSENCE, SUSAN (1913–1996)
English textile printer.

Publications

"Joyce Clissold: Textiles, Collages and Drawings." *Crafts* 72 (1985): 45–46.
Hand Block Printing and Resist Dyeing. Newton Abbot: David and Charles, 1986.

Main Sources

Roscoe, Barley. "Susan Bosence: A Treasury of Textiles." *The Guardian*, 2 March 1996, 28. Obituary.

Exhibitions

Coatts, Margot. *Colour with Cloth*. London: Crafts Council, 1994.

Other Sources

Sutton, Ann. *British Craft Textiles*. London: Collins, 1985.

1514 BOSSCHER, MADELEINE
Dutch textile designer.

Other Sources

Jarry, Madeleine. *La tapissérie: art du XXème siècle*. Fribourg: Office du Livre, 1974.

1515 BÖRNER, HELENE (1870–?)
    German textile designer.

Other Sources

Fanelli, Giovanni, and Rosalia Fanelli. *Il tessuto art déco e anni trenta: disegno, moda, architettura.* Florence: Cantini, 1986.
Gunta Stölzl: Weberei am Bauhaus und aus eigener Werkstatt. Berlin: Bauhaus Archiv in association with Kupfergraben Verlag, 1987. Contains individual bibliographies.

1516 BRENDEL, GERTRUDE (née SELL) (1902–)
    German textile designer.

Other Sources

Gunta Stölzl: Weberei am Bauhaus und aus eigener Werkstatt. Berlin: Bauhaus Archiv in association with Kupfergraben Verlag, 1987. Contains individual bibliographies.

1517 BROCARD, CECILE
    French textile designer specialising in the making of religious objects.

Other Sources

Jarry, Madeleine. *La tapissérie: art du XXème siècle.* Fribourg: Office du Livre, 1974.

1518 BRODSKA, EVA
    Czech textile designer.

Other Sources

Jarry, Madeleine. *La tapissérie: art du XXème siècle.* Fribourg: Office du Livre, 1974.

1519 BROWN, BARBARA (1932–)
    English textile designer.

Main Sources

"Furnishing Fabrics: Heal's Chevron, Complex and Extension." *Design* 233 (May 1968): 42–43.

Exhibitions

Timmers, Margaret. *The Way We Live Now: Designs for Interiors 1950 to the Present Day.* London: Victoria and Albert Museum, 1978.

346

Other Sources

Hiesinger, Kathryn, and George Marcus III, eds. *Design since 1945.* Philadelphia: Philadelphia Museum of Art, 1983.

Other Sources

Byars, Mel. *The Design Encyclopedia.* London: Lawrence King, 1994.
Clark, Charlotte. *Textiles from British Magazines: An Index of Articles.* Manchester: Manchester Metropolitan University Library, 1987.

1520 BRUMMER, EVA (1901–?)
      Finnish textile designer.

Exhibitions

Tapisséries finlandaises. Paris: Musée d'Art Moderne de la Ville de Paris, 1972
Hiesinger, Kathryn, and George Marcus III, eds. *Design since 1945.* Philadelphia: Philadelphia Museum of Art, 1983.

Other Sources

Byars, Mel. *The Design Encyclopedia.* London: Lawrence King, 1994.
Louhio, Anja. *Taideryijyjä Modern Finnish rugs.* Helsinki: Julkaisija Editors Suomalaisen Kirjallisuuden Kirjapaino Oyskk Ltd., 1975. Brummer is included as one of the earlier exponents who used this traditional product in an innovative way.
Mäki, Oili. *Taide ja Työ: Finnish Designers of Today.* Helsinki: Werner Söderström Osakeyhtiö, 1954. Gives an outline biography.

1521 BUCKLE, MARY (active 1888–1906)
      English embroiderer of textiles.

Other Sources

Parry, Linda. *Textiles of the Arts and Crafts Movement.* London: Thames and Hudson, 1988.

1522 BUIC, JAGODA
      Textile designer from the former Yugoslavia.

Exhibitions

Fibres Art '85. Paris: Musée des Arts Décoratifs, 1985.

Other Sources

Jarry, Madeleine. *La tapissérie: art du XXème siècle.* Fribourg: Office du Livre, 1974.

1523 BUJAKOWA, MARIA (1901–)
Polish designer of textiles.

Exhibitions

Kondratiuk, Krystyna. *Les tissus polonais artistiques contemporains.* Translated into French by Gérard Conio. Łodz: Musée de l'Histoire des Textiles, 1965. Contains a short biography and list of exhibitions for each exhibitor.

1524 BUKOWSKA, HELENA (Alt. BUKOWSKA-SZLEKYS)
Polish textile designer.

Exhibitions

Polish Art: Graphic Art, Textiles. London: Victoria and Albert Museum, 1936.

1525 BURBIDGE, PAULINE (1950–)
English textile designer who works in patchwork.

Main Sources

O'Connor, Margarette. "Patchwork quilts by Pauline Burbidge." *Crafts* 39 (1979): 53–54.
Neumark, Victoria. "Quilts." *Crafts* 44 (1980): 22–27.

Exhibitions

A Glory of Quilts. Great Northern Quilt Show III. Gateshead: Shipley Art Gallery, 1990.

Other Sources

Byars, Mel. *The Design Encyclopedia.* London: Lawrence King, 1994.
Sutton, Ann. *British Craft Textiles.* London: Collins, 1985.

1526 BURDEN, BESSIE (née ELIZABETH BURDEN) (1842–1924)
English embroiderer of textiles and sister of Jane, wife of William Morris.

Other Sources

Callen, Anthea. *The Angel in the Studio.* London: Architectural Press, 1979.
Parry, Linda. *Textiles of the Arts and Crafts Movement.* London: Thames and Hudson, 1988.

1527 BUTRYMOWICZ, ZOFIA (1904–)
Polish textile designer.

Exhibitions

Kondratiuk, Krystyna. *Les tissus polonais artistiques contemporains.* Translated into French by Gérard Conio. Łodz: Musée de l'Histoire des Textiles, 1965. Contains a short biography and list of exhibitions for each exhibitor.

Lutteman, Helena. *Polen vaaver fritt. Polish Textile Art.* Stockholm: National Museum, 1970.

Kondratiuk, Krystyna. *L'Art de tissu en Pologne de 1962 à 1972.* Paris: Manufacture Nationale des Gobelins, 1972.

Other Sources

Jarry, Madeleine. *La tapissérie: art du XXème siècle.* Fribourg: Office du Livre, 1974.

1528 CALVI, MARIA RIGOTTI
Italian designer of textiles who worked in the style of the Wiener Werkstätte.

Other Sources

Fanelli, Giovanni, and Rosalia Fanelli. *Il tessuto art déco e anni trenta: disegno, moda, architettura.* Florence: Cantini, 1986.

1529 CAMPBELL, SARAH (1946–)
English textile designer who produces furnishing fabrics with her sister, Susan Collier (q.v.).

Other Sources

Naylor, Colin, ed. *Contemporary Designers.* 2nd edition. Chicago and London: St. James Press, 1990. Contains a bibliography.

1530 CANQUIL-PRINCE, YVONNE
French textile designer specialising in tapestry.

Other Sources

Jarry, Madeleine. *La tapissérie: art du XXème siècle.* Fribourg: Office du Livre, 1974.

1531 CELMA, ANITA (1944–)
Latvian textile designer who subverts the weaving technique to produce open works where the warp and weft become the composition.

Other Sources

Kalniete, Sandra. *Latvju tekstilmāksla* [Latvian textile art]. Riga: Liesma, 1989.

1532   CHETI, FEDE (1905–1978)
Italian textile designer.

Exhibitions

Hiesinger, Kathryn, and George Marcus III, eds. *Design since 1945.* Philadelphia: Philadelphia Museum of Art, 1983.

Other Sources

Alfonsi, Maria Vittoria. *Donna al vertice.* Milan, 1975.
Byars, Mel. *The Design Encyclopedia.* London: Lawrence King, 1994.

1533   CHOJNACKA, MARIA (1931–)
Polish textile designer.

Exhibitions

Contemporary Polish Weavers. Edinburgh: Weavers' Workshop Gallery, 1972.
Kondratiuk, Krystyna. *L'Art de tissu en Pologne de 1962 à 1972.* Paris: Manufacture Nationale des Gobelins, 1972.

Other Sources

Jarry, Madeleine. *La tapissérie: art du XXème siècle.* Fribourg: Office du Livre, 1974.

1534   CHRISTENSEN, RUTH (c. 1929–)
Danish textile designer specialising in printed textiles.

Other Sources

Salicath, Bent, and Arne Karlsen, eds. *Modern Danish Textiles.* Copenhagen: Danish Society of Arts and Crafts and Industrial Design, 1959.

1535   CHRISTIE, GRACE (1872–1938)
English designer of textiles, embroiderer and weaver.

Publications

Embroidery and Tapestry Weaving. London: 1906.
Samplers and Stitches. London: 1920.
English Medieval Embroidery. London: 1938.
Editor of the magazine *Needle and Thread* from 1914.

Exhibitions

Mendes, Valerie. *British Textiles from 1900–1937: The Victoria and Albert Museum's Textile Collection.* London: Victoria and Albert Museum, 1992.

Other Sources

Parry, Linda. *Textiles of the Arts and Crafts Movement.* London: Thames and Hudson, 1988.

1536 CIERNIAK, KRYSTYNA (1938–)
Polish textile designer.

Exhibitions

Kondratiuk, Krystyna. *Les tissus polonais artistiques contemporains.* Translated into French by Gérard Conio. Łodz: Musée de l'Histoire des Textiles, 1965. Contains a short biography and list of exhibitions for each exhibitor.
Contemporary Polish Weavers. Edinburgh: Weavers' Workshop Gallery, 1972.

1537 CLISSOLD, JOYCE (?–1982)
English designer of printed textiles.

Main Sources

Bosence, Susan. "Joyce Clissold: Textiles, Collages and Drawings." *Crafts* 72 (1985): 45–46.

Exhibitions

Seddon, Jill, and Suzette Worden. *Women Designing: Redefining Design Between the Wars.* Brighton: University of Brighton, 1994.

1538 CODINA, MARIA TERESA
Spanish designer of textiles.

Exhibitions

Fibres Art '85. Paris: Musée des Arts Décoratifs, 1985.

1539 COLLIER, SUSAN (1938–)
English textile designer who produces furnishing fabrics with her sister, Sarah Campbell (q.v.).

Publications

See Naylor.

Other Sources

Naylor, Colin, ed. *Contemporary Designers.* 2nd edition. Chicago and London: St. James Press, 1990. Contains a bibliography.

1540 COLLONGES, AIMÉE
     French textile designer who works in Switzerland.

Other Sources

Jarry, Madeleine. *La tapissérie: art du XXème siècle.* Fribourg: Office du Livre, 1974.

1541 CONNOLLY, SYBIL
     Irish designer of textiles and interiors.

See Interior Design section.

1542 COPPEUS, JANINE
     Belgian textile designer.

Other Sources

Jarry, Madeleine. *La tapissérie: art du XXème siècle.* Fribourg: Office du Livre, 1974.

1543 COWERN, JENNY (1943–)
     English painter of large-scale abstract or landscape-related works on fabrics such as felt.

Other Sources

Sutton, Ann. *British Craft Textiles.* London: Collins, 1985.

1544 COWIE, HELEN (1948–)
     English textile designer who produced large-scale fabric designs for interiors, sometimes functioning as curtains or blinds. In the mid-1980s she began to make furniture.

Other Sources

Sutton, Ann. *British Craft Textiles.* London: Collins, 1985.

1545 CURRAN, LYNNE (1954–)
     English textile designer who uses a variety of materials to weave small-scale, often figuratively based pieces.

Main Sources

Silkin, Jon. "Tapestry into landscape." *Crafts* 42 (1980): 36–39.

Other Sources

Sutton, Ann. *British Craft Textiles.* London: Collins, 1985.

1546 CUTTOLI, MARIE
French designer of textiles.

Other Sources

Baron, Stanley. *Sonia Delaunay: The Life of an Artist.* London: Thames and Hudson, 1995.

Byars, Mel. *The Design Encyclopedia.* London: Lawrence King, 1994.

Jarry, Madeleine. *La tapissérie: art du XXème siècle.* Fribourg: Office du Livre, 1974.

1547 CZABOK-LEWEINSKA, ALEXANDRA (1927–)
Polish designer of textiles.

Exhibitions

Kondratiuk, Krystyna. *Les tissus polonais artistiques contemporains.* Translated into French by Gérard Conio. Łodz: Musée de l'Histoire des Textiles, 1965. Contains a short biography and list of exhibitions for each exhibitor.

1548 DABROWSKA-SKRIABIN, HANNA (1933–)
Polish textile designer who produces figurative reliefs in fabric and yarn.

Exhibitions

Contemporary Polish Weavers. Edinburgh: Weavers' Workshop Gallery, 1972.

1549 DAMBLEMONT, MARY
Belgian textile designer specialising in tapestry.

Other Sources

Jarry, Madeleine. *La tapissérie: art du XXème siècle.* Fribourg: Office du Livre, 1974.

1550 DAURO, SOFIA
German textile designer.

Other Sources

Jarry, Madeleine. *La tapissérie: art du XXème siècle.* Fribourg: Office du Livre, 1974.

1551 DAY, LUCIENNE (née CONRADI) (1917–)
     English textile designer.

Main Sources

"Lucienne Day." *Design Quarterly* 36 (1956): 9–10.
Glancy, Jonathan. "Adding Colour to a Material World." *The Guardian,* 24 April 1993, 39.

Exhibitions

Timmers, Margaret. *The Way We Live Now: Designs for Interiors 1950 to the Present Day.* London: Victoria and Albert Museum, 1978.
Hogben, C. *British Art and Design 1900–1960: A Collection in the Making.* London: Victoria and Albert Museum, 1983.
Eidelberg, Martin, ed. *Design 1935–1965: What Modern Was.* New York, Abrams in association with the Musée des Arts Décoratifs, Montreal, 1991.
Lucienne Day: A Career in Design. Manchester: Whitworth Art Gallery, 1993.

Other Sources

Anscombe, Isabelle. *A Woman's Touch: Women in Design from 1860 to the Present Day.* London: Virago Press, 1984.
Byars, Mel. *The Design Encyclopedia.* London: Lawrence King, 1994.
Clark, Charlotte. *Textiles from British Magazines: An Index of Articles.* Manchester: Manchester Metropolitan University Library, 1987.
Hiesinger, Kathryn, and George Marcus III, eds. *Design since 1945.* Philadelphia: Philadelphia Museum of Art, 1983.
Naylor, Colin, ed. *Contemporary Designers.* 2nd edition. Chicago and London: St. James Press, 1990. Contains a bibliography.

1552 DE GOEY, MARIJKE (Alt. DE GOEIJ) (1947–)
     Dutch textile and glass designer who uses fibre or thread with another material, such as paper, and also sometimes adds paint

Exhibitions

Moderne Hollandsk Tekstilkunst og Glas. Copenhagen: Dansk Kunstindustrimuseum, 1979.
Cahen, Judith. *Marijke de Goey.* Breda/Utrecht, 1984.
Broos, Kees. *Beelden in Glass: Glass Sculpture.* Utrecht: Stichting Glas, 1986.

1553 DE LA BAUME DÜRRBACH, JACQUELINE
     French designer of textiles who specialised in tapestry.

Other Sources

Jarry, Madeleine. *La tapissérie: art du XXème siècle.* Fribourg: Office du Livre, 1974.

1554 DEGLAIN, ANNE
Belgian textile designer.

Other Sources

Jarry, Madeleine. *La tapissérie: art du XXème siècle.* Fribourg: Office du Livre, 1974.

1555 DEINHARDT, LIES (Alt. SCHUNKE) (1899–?)
German textile designer and painter.

Other Sources

Gunta Stölzl: Weberei am Bauhaus und aus eigener Werkstätt. Berlin: Bauhaus Archiv in association with Kupfergraben Verlag, 1987. Contains individual bibliographies.

Weltge, Sigrid Wortmann. *Bauhaus Textiles: Women Artists and the Weaving Workshop.* London: Thames and Hudson, 1993.

1556 DELAUNAY, SONIA (1885–1979) (née SOFIA ILINITCHNA STERN TERK from 1890; alt. DELAUNAY-TERK)
Russian-born abstract painter and designer of textiles, fashion, stage designs and costumes who worked in France.

Publications

Compositions, couleurs, idées. Paris: Editions Moreau, 1930.
Tissus et tapis. Paris: Editions Moreau, 1939.
See also Naylor below.

Main Sources

Baron, Stanley. *Sonia Delaunay: The Life of an Artist.* London: Thames and Hudson, 1995, 208pp., illus. Contains a bibliography.

Chadwick, Whitney, and Isabelle De Courtivron, eds. *Significant Others: Creativity and Intimate Partnership.* London: Thames and Hudson, 1993.

Cohen, Arthur. *Sonia Delaunay.* New York: Abrams, 1975.

Damase, Jacques. *Sonia Delaunay: rythmes et couleurs.* Paris: Hermann, 1971.

——. *Sonia Delaunay: Fashion and Fabrics.* London: Thames and Hudson, 1989.

——. *Sonia Delaunay: Mode et Tissus Imprimées.* Paris: Jacques Damase, 1991 and London: Thames and Hudson, 1991, 176pp., mostly illustrations. Looks at her fashion designs, fabrics and simultaneous clothes. Contains a bibliography.

L'Hôte, Andre. *Sonia Delaunay: ses peintures, ses objets, ses tissus simultanés, ses modes.* Paris: Librairie des Arts Décoratifs, 1925.

Marter, Joan. "Three Women Artists Married to Early Modernists." *Arts Magazine* 54 (September 1979): 88–95.

Nemser, Cindy. *Art Talk: Conversations with 12 Women Artists.* New York: Scribner's, 1975.

Rendell, Clare. "Sonia Delaunay and the Expanding Definition of Art." *Women's Art Journal* 4, no. 1 (spring–summer 1983): 35–38.

Exhibitions

Rétrospective Sonia Delaunay. Paris: Centre Nationale d'Art et de Culture Georges Pompidou, 1967.

Sonia et Robert Delaunay. Paris: Bibliothèque Nationale, 1977.

Cinquantenaire de l'Exposition de 1925. Paris: Musée des Arts Décoratifs, 1976. Contains a brief biography.

Abstraction-Création. Paris: Musée d'Art Moderne de la Ville de Paris, 1978.

Russian Women Artists of the Avant-Garde. Cologne: Gallery Gmurzynska, 1979.

Paris-Moscou, 1900–1930. Paris: Centre Nationale d'Art et de Culture Georges Pompidou, 1979.

Paris—Paris: créations en France, 1937–1957. Paris: Centre Nationale d'Art et de Culture Georges Pompidou, 1981.

Robert et Sonia Delaunay, 1885–1985. Paris: Musée d'Art Moderne de la Ville de Paris, 1985.

Dufresne, Jean-Luc, and Olivier Messac, eds. *Femmes créatrices des années vingt.* Granville: Musée Richard Anacréon, 1988. Wide-ranging catalogue with biographical outlines on each woman included.

Other Sources

Brunhammer, Yvonne, and Suzanne Tise. *Les artistes décorateurs, 1900–42.* Paris: Flammarion, 1990.

Dunford, Penny. *A Biographical Dictionary of Women Artists in Europe and America since 1850.* Hemel Hempstead: Harvester Wheatsheaf and Philadelphia: University of Pennsylvania Press, 1990. Contains a bibliography.

Jarry, Madeleine. *La tapissérie: art du XXème siècle.* Fribourg: Office du Livre, 1974.

Naylor, Colin, ed. *Contemporary Designers.* 2nd edition. Chicago and London: St. James Press, 1990. Contains a bibliography.

Spate, Virginia. *Orphism.* Oxford: Clarendon, 1979.

1557 DERKERT, SIRI (Alt. DERHERT)
        Swedish textile designer.

Other Sources

Jarry, Madeleine. *La tapissérie: art du XXème siècle.* Fribourg: Office du Livre, 1974.

Martin, Edna, and Berta Sydhoff. *Svensk Textilkonst. Swedish Textile Art.* Stockholm: Liber Förlag, 1980.

1558 DE RUDDER, HÉLNE (1870–?)

Belgian designer of textiles, best known for her embroidered panels.

Exhibitions

Brunhammer, Yvonne. *Art Nouveau: Belgium-France.* Chicago 1976.

Art Nouveau Belgique. Brussels: Palais des Beaux-Arts, 1980.

Other Sources

Byars, Mel. *The Design Encyclopedia.* London: Lawrence King, 1994.

Fanelli, Giovanni, and Rosalia Fanelli. *Il tessuto Art Nouveau: disegno, moda, architettura.* Florence: Cantini, 1986.

1559 DESSAU, INGRID (née PETERSON) (1923–)

Swedish designer of textiles who specialises in weaving, and winner of the Lunning Prize.

Exhibitions

The Lunning Prize. Stockholm: Nationalmuseum, 1986.

Other Sources

Naylor, Colin, ed. *Contemporary Designers.* 2nd edition. Chicago and London: St. James Press, 1990. Contains a bibliography.

1560 DICKER, FRIEDL (Alt. BRANDEIS) (1898–1944)

Austrian designer of textiles who also worked in Germany. She died in Auschwitz.

Other Sources

Weltge, Sigrid Wortmann. *Bauhaus Textiles: Women Artists and the Weaving Workshop.* London: Thames and Hudson, 1993.

1561 DIRKS, GERTRUD (née PREISWERK) (1902–)

German textile designer.

Other Sources

Gunta Stölzl: Weberei am Bauhaus und aus eigener Werkstatt. Berlin: Bauhaus Archiv in association with Kupfergraben Verlag, 1987. Contains individual bibliographies.

1562 DOBRÁNYI, IDILKÓ
Hungarian textile designer.

Exhibitions

9. Fal-Es Tertextyil Biennale [9th National Textile Biennale]. Szombathely: Savaria Museum, 1984.

1563 DORN, MARION VICTORIA (1899–1964)
American-born textile designer who worked in England between 1924 and 1940, mainly as a designer of furnishing fabrics.

Main Sources

Boydell, Christine. "Women Textile Designers in the 1920s and 1930s: Marion Dorn, a Case Study." In *A View from the Interior: Feminism, Women and Design,* edited by Judy Attfield and Pat Kirkham. London: Women's Press, 1989, pp. 57–70, 4 illus.
Mendes, Valerie. "Marion Dorn: Textile Designer." *Journal of the Decorative Arts Society 1890–1940* 2 (1978): 24–35. A detailed biographical account, especially from the mid-1920s to 1940, when she returned to America.

Exhibitions

Thirties: British Art and Design Before the War. London: Hayward Gallery, 1979.
Bury, Hester. *A Choice of Design, 1850–1980: Fabrics by Warner and Sons Ltd.* Colchester: Minories Gallery, 1981.
Hogben, C. *British Art and Design 1900–1960: A Collection in the Making.* London: Victoria and Albert Museum, 1983.
Mendes, Valerie. *British Textiles from 1900–1937: The Victoria and Albert Museum's Textile Collection.* London: Victoria and Albert Museum, 1992.

Other Sources

Anscombe, Isabelle. *A Woman's Touch: Women in Design from 1860 to the Present Day.* London: Virago Press, 1984.
Byars, Mel. *The Design Encyclopedia.* London: Lawrence King, 1994.

1564 DOSTERT, EDVIGE (née HEDWIG JUNGNIK) (1897–?)
German textile designer.

Other Sources

Gunta Stölzl: Weberei am Bauhaus und aus eigener Werkstatt. Berlin: Bauhaus Archiv in association with Kupfergraben Verlag, 1987. Contains individual bibliographies.

1565 DRNKOVÁ-ZARECKÁ, VERA
Czech textile designer.

Other Sources

Jarry, Madeleine. *La tapissérie: art du XXème siècle.* Fribourg: Office du Livre, 1974.

1566 DROPPA, JUDIT
Hungarian designer of textiles.

Exhibitions

Moderne Ungarische Textilkunst und Keramik aus der Sammlung des Savaria Museum, Szombathely. Linz: Stadtmuseum, 1977.
Fibres Art '85. Paris: Musée des Arts Décoratifs, 1985.
Szot Ösztöndíjasok Kiá·llitá·sa. Budapest: Magyar Nemezeti Galéria, 1986.

1567 DÜLBERG-ARNHEIM, HEDWIG (née ARNHEIM; alt. DÜLBERG-SLUTZKY) (1894–1940/5)
German textile designer who studied at the Bauhaus and died in Auschwitz.

Other Sources

Gunta Stölzl: Weberei am Bauhaus und aus eigener Werkstatt. Berlin: Bauhaus Archiv in association with Kupfergraben Verlag, 1987. Contains individual bibliographies.

1568 DZANGER, MADELEINE
Swedish textile designer.

Other Sources

Jarry, Madeleine. *La tapissérie: art du XXème siècle.* Fribourg: Office du Livre, 1974.

1569 EDENS, GERDA
Dutch textile designer.

Other Sources

Jarry, Madeleine. *La tapissérie: art du XXème siècle.* Fribourg: Office du Livre, 1974.

1570 EDGAR, JANE
English textile designer.

Exhibitions

Hogben, C. *British Art and Design 1900–1960: A Collection in the Making.* London: Victoria and Albert Museum, 1983.

1571 EGGMAN, ROSE-MARIE (1924–)
Swiss designer of textiles, ceramics and sculptor.

Exhibitions

Bourquin-Walford, Cyril, Marie-Lise Disch-Brack, and Claude Frossard, eds. *Tapisséries Suisses: Artistes d'Aujourd'hui.* Lausanne: Genoud, 1977.

1572 EGLITE, SARMA (1943–)
Latvian textile designer who produces both abstract hangings in mixed fibres and figurative works in flatter techniques.

Other Sources

Kalniete, Sandra. *Latvju tekstilmāksla* [Latvian textile art]. Riga: Liesma, 1989.

1573 EHRMANN, MARLI (née MARIE HELENE HEIMANN) (1904–1982)
German designer of textiles who emigrated to America in 1938.

Other Sources

Gunta Stölzl: Weberei am Bauhaus und aus eigener Werkstatt. Berlin: Bauhaus Archiv in association with Kupfergraben Verlag, 1987. Contains individual bibliographies.

Weltge, Sigrid Wortmann. *Bauhaus Textiles: Women Artists and the Weaving Workshop.* London: Thames and Hudson, 1993.

1574 ELTERMANE, ANNA (1929–)
Latvian textile designer.

Other Sources

Kalniete, Sandra. *Latvju tekstilmāksla* [Latvian textile art]. Riga: Liesma, 1989.

1575 ESKOLA, LEA (1923–)
Finnish designer of textiles who specialises in tapestry.

Exhibitions

Tapisséries finlandaises. Paris: Musée d'Art Moderne de la Ville de Paris, 1972.

Other Sources

Louhio, Anja. *Taideryijyjä. Modern Finnish rugs.* Helsinki: Julkaisija Editors Suomalaisen Kirjallisuuden Kirjapaino Oyskk Ltd., 1975. She is included as someone who used the traditional rug in an innovative way.

1576 FALKOWSKA, BARBARA (1931–)
Polish textile designer.

Exhibitions

Kondratiuk, Krystyna. *Les tissus polonais artistiques contemporains.* Translated into French by Gérard Conio. Łodz: Musée de l'Histoire des Textiles, 1965. Contains a short biography and list of exhibitions for each exhibitor.
Contemporary Polish Weavers. Edinburgh: Weavers' Workshop Gallery, 1972.
Kondratiuk, Krystyna. *L'Art de tissu en Pologne de 1962 à 1972.* Paris: Manufacture Nationale des Gobelins, 1972. Contains a brief biography and information about her exhibits.

Other Sources

Jarry, Madeleine. *La tapissérie: art du XXème siècle.* Fribourg: Office du Livre, 1974 (as Kalkowska).

1577 FARMER, MARY
English textile designer.

Main Sources

Peck, Patricia Cleveland. "Tapestry, rugs and carpets by Mary Farmer." *Crafts* 42 (1980): 54.

Exhibitions

Textiles Today: Woven and Embroidered Works Selected by Marianne Straub. Cambridge: Kettle's Yard, 1981.

1578 FEDOSEYEVA, O.
Russian textile designer.

Other Sources

Yasinskaya, I. *Soviet Textile Design of the Revolutionary Period*. London: Thames and Hudson, 1983.

1579 FERENCZY, NOÉMI (1890–1957)
     Hungarian textile designer.

Other Sources

Ferenczy Család Gyujtemény Katalógusa. Szentendre: Ferenczy Múzeum, 1978. Catalogue of the Ferenczy family museum in which the tapestry of Ferenczy is featured together with a short biographical account.

Jarry, Madeleine. *La tapissérie: art du XXème siècle*. Fribourg: Office du Livre, 1974.

1580 FISCHER-TREYDEN, ELSA (1901–after 1989)
     Russian designer of textiles, ceramics and glass who worked in Germany from c. 1925.

Exhibitions

Glass 1959: A Special Exhibition of International Contemporary Glass. Corning, New York: Corning Museum of Glass, 1959.

Oedekoven-Gerischer, Angela, et al., eds. *Frauen im Design: Berufsbilder und Lebenswege seit 1900. Women in Design: Careers and Life Histories since 1900*. Stuttgart: Design Center, 1989.

Mundt, Barbara, Suzanne Netzer, and Innes Hettler. *Interieur + Design in Deutschland, 1945=60*. Berlin: Kunstgewerbemuseum and Dietrich Reimer Verlag, 1994.

Other Sources

Byars, Mel. *The Design Encyclopedia*. London: Lawrence King, 1994.

Hiesinger, Kathryn, and George Marcus III, eds. *Design since 1945*. Philadelphia: Philadelphia Museum of Art, 1983.

1581 FOGHT, HELGA (1902–)
     Danish textile designer specialising in printed textiles.

Other Sources

Salicath, Bent, and Arne Karlsen, eds. *Modern Danish Textiles*. Copenhagen: Danish Society of Arts and Crafts and Industrial Design, 1959.

1582 FORSS-HEINONEN, MAIJA LIISA (1929–)
     Finnish designer of textiles specialising in tapestry.

Exhibitions

Tapisséries finlandaises. Paris: Musée des Arts Décoratifs, 1972.

Other Sources

Louhio, Anja. *Taideryijyjä. Modern Finnish rugs.* Helsinki: Julkaisija Editors Suomalaisen Kirjallisuuden Kirjapaino Oyskk Ltd., 1975. She is included as one of the exponents of the innovative developments of the traditional rug.

1583 FRANCE, GEORGIE EVELYN CAVE (Alt. MRS ARTHUR GASKIN) (1864–1934)
  English painter, illustrator, designer of textiles and embroiderer who worked in Birmingham.

Exhibitions

Crawford, Alan. *By Hammer and Hand: The Arts and Crafts Movement in Birmingham.* Birmingham: City Museum and Art Gallery, 1984.

Other Sources

Callen, Anthea. *The Angel in the Studio: Women Artists of the Arts and Crafts Movement.* London: Architectural Press, 1979.

Marsh, Jan, and Pamela Gerrish Nunn. *Women Artists and the Pre-Raphaelite Movement.* London: Virago, 1989.

Parry, Linda. *Textiles of the Arts and Crafts Movement.* London: Thames and Hudson, 1988.

1584 FRENCH, ANNIE (1872–1965)
  Scottish painter and designer, especially of textiles and embroidery, who trained and then taught at the Glasgow School of Art.

Exhibitions

Burkhauser, Jude, ed. *'Glasgow Girls': Women in Art and Design, 1880–1920.* Edinburgh: Canongate, 1990.

Cumming, Elizabeth. *Glasgow 1900: Art and Design.* Zwolle: Waanders Publishers in association with the Van Gogh Museum, Amsterdam, 1992.

1585 FRÖMEL-FOCHLER, LOTTE (Alt. FRÖMMEL-FOCHLER)
  Austrian designer of textiles who worked first for the Wiener Werkstätte and later in Berlin and Munich.

Other Sources

Fanelli, Giovanni, and Rosalia Fanelli. *Il tessuto art déco e anni trenta: disegno, moda, architettura.* Florence: Cantini, 1986.

Völker, Angela. "Österreichische Textilien des frühen 20. Jahrhunderts." *Alte und Moderne Kunst* 171 (1980): 1–7.

1586 FRUYTIER, WIL (née WILHELMINA) (1915–)

Dutch designer of large-scale textiles who incorporated nontraditional materials such as sisal and, later, artificial fibres into techniques-based on tapestry.

Exhibitions

Moderne Hollandsk Tekstilkunst og Glas. Copenhagen: Dansk Kunst-industrimuseum, 1979.

Fibres Art '85. Paris: Musée des Arts Décoratifs, 1985.

Other Sources

Constantine, Mildred, and Jack Lenor Larsen. *The Art Fabric: Mainstream.* New York: Van Nostrand Reinhold, 1981.

Jarry, Madeleine. *La tapissérie: art du XXème siècle.* Fribourg: Office du Livre, 1974.

1587 FUGLEVAAG, BRIT H.

Norwegian designer of textiles.

Other Sources

Talley, Charles. *Contemporary Textile Art: Scandinavia.* Stockholm: Carmina, 1982.

1588 FUNK, LISSY (1909–)

Swiss designer of textiles.

Exhibitions

Bourquin-Walford, Cyril, Marie-Lise Disch-Brack, and Claude Frossard, eds. *Tapisséries Suisses: Artistes d'Aujourd'hui.* Lausanne: Genoud, 1977.

1589 GALKOWSKA, HELENA (1911–)

Polish textile designer.

Exhibitions

Kondratiuk, Krystyna. *Les tissus polonais artistiques contemporains.* Translated into French by Gérard Conio. Łodz: Musée de l'Histoire des Textiles, 1965. Contains a short biography and list of exhibitions for each exhibitor.

Contemporary Polish Weavers. Edinburgh: Weavers' Workshop Gallery, 1972.

Kondratiuk, Krystyna. *L'Art de tissu en Pologne de 1962 à 1972.* Paris: Manufacture Nationale des Gobelins, 1972.

Other Sources

Jarry, Madeleine. *La tapissérie: art du XXème siècle.* Fribourg: Office du Livre, 1974.

1590 GARNETT, ANNIE (1864–1942)
English designer of textiles, especially weaving, who set up The Spinnery in Windermere and directed local outworkers who produced high-quality fabrics.

Other Sources

Parry, Linda. *Textiles of the Arts and Crafts Movement.* London: Thames and Hudson, 1988.

1591 GASKIN, GEORGIE EVELYN CAVE (1864–1934)
English painter, illustrator, designer of textiles and embroiderer.

See France, Georgie above.

1592 GECSER, LUJZA (1943–)
Hungarian textile designer.

Exhibitions

9. Fal-Es Tertextyil Biennale [9th National Textile Biennale]. Szombathely: Savaria Museum, 1984.

1593 GIAUQUE, ELSI (1900–)
Swiss textile designer who uses tapestry to create abstract compositions.

Exhibitions

Bourquin-Walford, Cyril, Marie-Lise Disch-Brack, and Claude Frossard, eds. *Tapisséries Suisses: Artistes d'Aujourd'hui.* Lausanne: Genoud, 1977. A special introductory essay is devoted to Giauque.

Other Sources

Constantine, Mildred, and Jack Lenor Larsen. *The Art Fabric: Mainstream.* New York: Van Nostrand Reinhold, 1981.
Jarry, Madeleine. *La tapissérie: art du XXème siècle.* Fribourg: Office du Livre, 1974.

1594 GIDASZEWSKA, KAZIMIERA (1924–)
Polish textile designer.

Exhibitions

Contemporary Polish Weavers. Edinburgh: Weavers' Workshop Gallery, 1972.

1595 GINK, JUDIT (1953–)
Hungarian textile designer.

Exhibitions

9. Fal-Es Tertextyil Biennale [9th National Textile Biennale]. Szombathely: Savaria Museum, 1984.

1596 GOECKE, IRMA
German textile designer.

Other Sources

Jarry, Madeleine. *La tapissérie: art du XXème siècle.* Fribourg: Office du Livre, 1974.

1597 GOETZEE, MONIQUE (1959–)
Dutch-born textile designer who came to Britain as a child. She uses resist-dying and hand-painting onto delicate silk fabrics, which are then made into items such as scarves or bed spreads.

Other Sources

Sutton, Ann. *British Craft Textiles.* London: Collins, 1985.

1598 GRASETT, KATIE (active 1898–1916)
English weaver and designer of textiles who founded the London School of Weaving in 1898.

Other Sources

Parry, Linda. *Textiles of the Arts and Crafts Movement.* London: Thames and Hudson, 1988.

1599 GREAVES-LORD, SALLY (1957–)
English designer of textiles for furniture and interiors.

Main Sources

"Esprit de corps." *Crafts* 68 (1984): 16–19.

Exhibitions

Coatts, Margot. *Colour with Cloth.* London: Crafts Council, 1994.

Other Sources

Sutton, Ann. *British Craft Textiles.* London: Collins, 1985.

1600 GRODECKA, JULJA
  Polish textile designer.

Exhibitions

Polish Art: Graphic Art, Textiles. London: Victoria and Albert Museum, 1936.

1601 GRÖNDAL, SUSAN (1901–)
  Swedish textile designer who makes printed textiles.

Exhibitions

Susan Gröndals Verkstad: Tygtryck. Stockholm: National Museum, 1983, 16pp., illus. Text in Swedish. Biographical and other short esays precede the catalogue entries.

1602 GROSSE, GABRIELE
  German textile designer.

Other Sources

Jarry, Madeleine. *La tapissérie: art du XXème siècle.* Fribourg: Office du Livre, 1974.

1603 GROSSEN, FRANÇOISE
  Swiss textile designer.

Other Sources

Jarry, Madeleine. *La tapissérie: art du XXème siècle.* Fribourg: Office du Livre, 1974.

1604 GUERMONPREZ, TRUDE (née JALOWETZ) (1910–1976)
  German designer of textiles who also worked in Scandinavia and the Netherlands before emigrating to America in 1947.

Other Sources

Weltge, Sigrid Wortmann. *Bauhaus Textiles: Women Artists and the Weaving Workshop.* London: Thames and Hudson, 1993.

1605 GULLBERG, ELSA (1886–1984)
Swedish textile designer.

Exhibitions

Lutteman, Helena Dahlbach, ed. *Elsa Gullberg: Textil pionjar.* Stockholm: Nationalmuseum, 1989, 106pp., illus. Contains a very through account of her development as one of the earliest women to work creatively in textiles.

1606 GULYÁS, KATI (1945–)
Hungarian textile designer.

Exhibitions

9. Fal-Es Tertextyil Biennale [9th National Textile Biennale]. Szombathely: Savaria Museum, 1984.
Fibres Art '85. Paris: Musée des Arts Décoratifs, 1985.

1607 HAGER, RITTA (1931–)
Hungarian textile designer.

Exhibitions

9. Fal-Es Tertextyil Biennale [9th National Textile Biennale]. Szombathely: Savaria Museum, 1984.

1608 HAHN, LOTTE (1902–after 1982)
Austrian designer of textiles and graphic art.

Other Sources

Pirhofer, Gottfired, and Astrid Gmeiner. *Der Österreichische Werkbund.* Vienna: 1985.
Schweiger, W. *Weiner Werkstätte: Kunst und Handwerk, 1903–32.* Vienna: Christian Brandstätter Verlag, 1982.

1609 HAIMOLA, NORMA (1938–)
Finnish textile designer specialising in tapestry.

Exhibitions

Tapisséries Finlandaises. Paris: Musée d'Art Moderne de la Ville de Paris, 1972.

Other Sources

Louhio, Anja. *Taideryijyjä. Modern Finnish rugs.* Helsinki: Julkaisija Editors Suomalaisen Kirjallisuuden Kirjapaino Oyskk Ltd., 1975. She is included as someone who used the traditional rug in an innovative way.

1610 HALLEK, MARGARETA
Swedish textile designer.

Other Sources

Jarry, Madeleine. *La tapissérie: art du XXème siècle.* Fribourg: Office du Livre, 1974.

1611 HALLING-KOCH, ANNAGRETE (1947–)
Danish designer of ceramics and textiles.

Other Sources

Byars, Mel. *The Design Encyclopedia.* London: Lawrence King, 1994.

1612 HALLING, ELSE
Norwegian textile designer who founded an atelier linked to the Museum of Decorative Arts in Oslo in the 1940s.

Other Sources

Jarry, Madeleine. *La tapissérie: art du XXème siècle.* Fribourg: Office du Livre, 1974.

1613 HALME, LEENA-KAISA (1940–)
Finnish textile designer specialising in the production of ryijy rugs.

Exhibitions

Tapisséries Finlandaises. Paris: Musée d'Art Moderne de la Ville de Paris, 1972.

Other Sources

Louhio, Anja. *Taideryijyjä. Modern Finnish rugs.* Helsinki: Julkaisija Editors Suomalaisen Kirjallisuuden Kirjapaino Oyskk Ltd., 1975. She is included as someone who used the traditional rug in an innovative way.

1614 HANSEN, FRIDA (1855–1931)
Norwegian textile designer specialising in tapestry.

Exhibitions

Gronwoldt, Ruth, and Sabine Hesse. *Art Nouveau: Textil: Dekor um 1900.* Stuttgart: Würtemburgisches Landesmuseum, [c. 1980].
McFadden, David, ed. *Scandinavian Modern Design, 1880–1980.* New York: Harry Abrams and the Cooper-Hewitt Museum, 1982.
Wichstrøm, Anne. *Rooms with a View: Women's Art in Norway, 1880–1990.* Oslo: Royal Ministry of Foreign Affairs, 1989.

Other Sources

Fanelli, Giovanni, and Rosalia Fanelli. *Il tessuto Art Nouveau: disegno, moda, architettura.* Florence: Cantini, 1986.

Jarry, Madeleine. *La tapissérie: art du XXème siècle.* Fribourg: Office du Livre, 1974.

Talley, Charles. *Contemporary Textile Art: Scandinavia.* Stockholm: Carmina, 1982.

1615 HARRIS, RUTH (c. 1935–)

English textile designer who weaves tapestries in which the contrast between flat and raised surfaces is important.

Other Sources

Sutton, Ann. *British Craft Textiles.* London: Collins, 1985.

1616 HARRISON, DIANA (c. 1959–)

English textile designer who masks cloth, sprays it with dye and then quilts, pleats or tucks it.

Other Sources

Sutton, Ann. *British Craft Textiles.* London: Collins, 1985.

1617 HASSELBERG-OLSSON, ELIZABET

Swedish textile designer.

Other Sources

Jarry, Madeleine. *La tapissérie: art du XXème siècle.* Fribourg: Office du Livre, 1974.

Martin, Edna, and Beata Sydhoff. *Svensk textilkonst. Swedish Textile Art.* Stockholm: Liber Förlag, 1980.

Naylor, Colin, ed. *Contemporary Designers.* 2nd edition. Chicago and London: St. James Press, 1990. Contains a bibliography.

Talley, Charles. *Contemporary Textile Art: Scandinavia.* Stockholm: Carmina, 1982.

1618 HAUSER, BEÁTA (1956–)

Hungarian textile designer.

Exhibitions

9. Fal-Es Tertextyil Biennale [9th National Textile Biennale]. Szombathely: Savaria Museum, 1984.

1619 HEGYI, IBOLYA (1953–)
Hungarian textile designer.

Exhibitions

9. Fal-Es Tertextyil Biennale [9th National Textile Biennale]. Szombathely: Savaria Museum, 1984.

1620 HEIL, INGRID
Austrian textile designer.

Other Sources

Jarry, Madeleine. *La tapissérie: art du XXème siècle*. Fribourg: Office du Livre, 1974.

1621 HEIMRĀTE, LAILA (1955–)
Latvian textile designer.

Other Sources

Kalniete, Sandra. *Latvju tekstilmāksla* [Latvian textile art]. Riga: Liesma, 1989.

1622 HENON, MAUD
Belgian textile designer.

Other Sources

Jarry, Madeleine. *La tapissérie: art du XXème siècle*. Fribourg: Office du Livre, 1974.

1623 HENRI, HÉLÈNE (Alt. HENRY) (1891–1965/8)
French textile designer who developed the use of texture rather than decoration in her furnishing fabrics.

Main Sources

Desliles, B. "Les tissus de Madame Hélène Henry." *Mobilier et Décoration,* April 1929.

Exhibitions

Les Années 25. Paris: Musée des Arts Décoratifs, 1966. Includes examples of her furnishing fabrics.
Cinquantenaire de l'Exposition de 1925. Paris: Musée des Arts Décoratifs, 1976.
Paris-Moscou, 1900–1939. Paris: Centre Nationale d'Art et de Culture Georges Pompidou, 1979.

Dufresne, Jean-Luc, and Olivier Messac, eds. *Femmes créatrices des années vingt.* Granville: Musée Richard Anacréon, 1988. Wide-ranging catalogue with a short biographical account on each woman included.

Les années UAM, 1929–1958. Paris: Musée des Arts Décoratifs, 1988.

Other Sources

Brunhammer, Yvonne. *1925.* Paris: Les Presses de la Connaissance, 1976.

Brunhammer, Yvonne, and Suzanne Tise. *Les artistes décorateurs, 1900–42.* Paris: Flammarion, 1990.

Byars, Mel. *The Design Encyclopedia.* London: Lawrence King, 1994.

Duncan, Alastair. *Art Deco Furniture: The French Designers.* London: Thames and Hudson, 1984.

Fanelli, Giovanni, and Rosalia Fanelli. *Il tessuto art déco e anni trenta: disegno, moda, architettura.* Florence: Cantini, 1986.

1624 HERNMARCK, HELENA MARIA (1941–)

Swedish-born textile designer who worked in Britain for some time producing large tapestries before moving to New York in 1975.

Main Sources

Coleman, M. "Helena Hernmarck." *Crafts* 2 (1973): 36–39.

Exhibitions

McFadden, David, ed. *Scandinavian Modern Design, 1880–1980.* New York: Harry Abrams and the Cooper-Hewitt Museum, 1982.

Other Sources

Byars, Mel. *The Design Encyclopedia.* London: Lawrence King, 1994.

Jarry, Madeleine. *La tapissérie: art du XXème siècle.* Fribourg: Office du Livre, 1974.

Martin, Edna, and Beata Sydhoff. *Svensk textilkonst. Swedish Textile Art.* Stockholm: Liber Förlag, 1980.

Naylor, Colin, ed. *Contemporary Designers.* 2nd edition. Chicago and London: St. James Press, 1990. Contains a bibliography.

1625 HIELLE-VATTER, MARGA (1913–)

German designer of textiles.

Exhibitions

Hiesinger, Kathryn, and George Marcus III, eds. *Design since 1945.* Philadelphia: Philadelphia Museum of Art, 1983.

Other Sources

Byars, Mel. *The Design Encyclopedia.* London: Lawrence King, 1994.

1626 HILDEBRAND, MARGRET (1917–)
German designer of textiles.

Exhibitions

Hiesinger, Kathryn, and George Marcus III, eds. *Design since 1945.* Philadelphia: Philadelphia Museum of Art, 1983.

Mundt, Barbara, Suzanne Netzer, and Innes Hettler. *Interieur + Design in Deutschland, 1945=60.* Berlin: Kunstgewerbemuseum and Dietrich Reimer Verlag, 1994.

Other Sources

Byars, Mel. *The Design Encyclopedia.* London: Lawrence King, 1994.

1627 HILDEBRANDT, LILY UHLMANN (1887–1974)
German painter and designer of textiles.

Other Sources

Weltge, Sigrid Wortmann. *Bauhaus Textiles: Women Artists and the Weaving Workshop.* London: Thames and Hudson, 1993.

1628 HILLFON, MARIA
Swedish designer of textiles.

Other Sources

Martin, Edna, and Beata Sydhoff. *Svensk textilkonst. Swedish Textile Art.* Stockholm: Liber Förlag, 1980.

1629 HIRSCH, HEDDI (1895–1947) (née LEOPOLDINE; alt. HIRSCH-LAN-DESMANN)
Austrian designer, especially of textiles, fashion and graphics.

Exhibitions

Kallir, Jane. *Viennese Design and the Wiener Werkstätte.* New York: Braziller in association with the Galérie St. Etienne, 1986.

Leitgeb, Hildegard, Elizabeth Schmuttermeier, and Angela Völker. *Wiener Werkstätte: atelier viennois, 1903–1932.* Brussels: Galérie CGER, 1987.

Other Sources

Schweiger, W. *Weiner Werkstätte: Kunst und Handwerk, 1903–32.* Vienna: Christian Brandstätter Verlag, 1982.

Völker, Angela. *Wiener Werkstätte: Wiener Mode und Modefotografie. Die Modeabteilung der Wiener Werkstätte, 1922–1932.* Munich and Paris: Schneider-Henn, 1984.

1630 HJELLE, ELIZABETH
Norwegian textile designer.

Other Sources

Jarry, Madeleine. *La tapissérie: art du XXème siècle.* Fribourg: Office du Livre, 1974.

1631 HLADLIKOVÁ, JENNY
Czech textile designer.

Other Sources

Jarry, Madeleine. *La tapissérie: art du XXème siècle.* Fribourg: Office du Livre, 1974.

1632 HOFFMANN-LEDERER, MILA (née LEDERER) (1902–)
German textile designer.

Other Sources

Gunta Stölzl: Weberei am Bauhaus und aus eigener Werkstatt. Berlin: Bauhaus Archiv in association with Kupfergraben Verlag, 1987. Contains individual bibliographies.

1633 HOLLOS, RUTH (Alt. CONSEMÜLLER) (1904–?)
Polish-born designer of textiles, particularly weaving, who worked in Germany.

Exhibitions

La Tessitura del Bauhaus, 1919–33, nelle collezioni della Repubblica Democratica Tedesca. Venice: Palazzo Ducale and Cataloghi Marsilio, 1985.

Other Sources

Gunta Stölzl: Weberei am Bauhaus und aus eigener Werkstatt. Berlin: Bauhaus Archiv in association with Kupfergraben Verlag, 1987. Contains individual bibliographies.

Jarry, Madeleine. *La tapissérie: art du XXème siècle.* Fribourg: Office du Livre, 1974.

Weltge, Sigrid Wortmann. *Bauhaus Textiles: Women Artists and the Weaving Workshop.* London: Thames and Hudson, 1993.

1634 HOPE, POLLY (1933–)
English textile artist who uses quilting, embroidery and other needlework techniques to create figurative images; for some years she divided her time between England and Greece.

Exhibitions

Polly Hope: Soft Art and Drawings, 1971–1982. London: Warwick Arts Trust, 1982, n.p., mainly illus. Contains a statement by Hope on her methods and ideas, a list of exhibitions and an outline biography.

Other Sources

Sutton, Ann. *British Craft Textiles.* London: Collins, 1985.

1635 HØYRUP, MULLE (1913–)
Danish textile designer specialising in printed textiles.

Other Sources

Salicath, Bent, and Arne Karlsen, eds. *Modern Danish Textiles.* Copenhagen: Danish Society of Arts and Crafts and Industrial Design, 1959.

1636 HUGUENIN, SUZANNE.
Swiss designer of textiles.

Exhibitions

Hiesinger, Kathryn, and George Marcus III, eds. *Design since 1945.* Philadelphia: Philadelphia Museum of Art, 1983.

Other Sources

Byars, Mel. *The Design Encyclopedia.* London: Lawrence King, 1994.

1637 HULL, RUTH (1912–)
Danish textile designer specialising in printed textiles.

Other Sources

Salicath, Bent, and Arne Karlsen, eds. *Modern Danish Textiles.* Copenhagen: Danish Society of Arts and Crafts and Industrial Design, 1959.

1638 HUNTER, EILEEN.
English designer of textiles and a writer.

Exhibitions

Thirties: British Art and Design before the War. London: Hayward Gallery, 1979.

1639 IKSE, SANDRA (Alt. IKSE-BERGMAN)
Swedish designer of textiles.

Other Sources

Martin, Edna, and Beata Sydhoff. *Svensk textilkonst. Swedish Textile Art.* Stockholm: Liber Förlag, 1980.
Talley, Charles. *Contemporary Textile Art: Scandinavia.* Stockholm: Carmina, 1982.

1640 ILVESSALO, KIRSTI (1920–)
Finnish textile designer who makes ryijy rugs, and also designs metalwork and silverware.

Exhibitions

Tapisséries Finlandaises. Paris: Musée d'Art Moderne de la Ville de Paris, 1972.

Other Sources

Louhio, Anja. *Taideryijyjä. Modern Finnish Rugs.* Helsinki: Julkaisija Editors Suomalaisen Kirjallisuuden Kirjapaino Oyskk Ltd., 1975. Many examples by this designer are included as she is classed by the author as one of the outstanding exponents of this form of art/design.
Mäki, Oili. *Taide ja Työ: Finnish Designers of Today.* Helsinki: Werner Söderström Osakeyhtiö, 1954. Gives an outline biography.

1641 JACOBI, RITZI
German textile designer who works with her husband, Peter.

Other Sources

Jarry, Madeleine. *La tapissérie: art du XXème siècle.* Fribourg: Office du Livre, 1974.

1642 JACOBSEN, ELSE MARIE
Norwegian textile designer.

Other Sources

Jarry, Madeleine. *La tapissérie: art du XXème siècle.* Fribourg: Office du Livre, 1974.

1643 JAKOBI, INESE (1949–)
Latvian textile designer who creates three-dimensional forms that resemble reliefs or sculpture.

Other Sources

Kalniete, Sandra. *Latvju tekstilmāksla* [Latvian textile art]. Riga: Liesma, 1989.

1644 JANSONE, VIDA (1941–)
Latvian textile designer who uses braiding to create open-work hangings.

Other Sources

Kalniete, Sandra. *Latvju tekstilmāksla* [Latvian textile art]. Riga: Liesma, 1989.

1645 JANSSEN, DANIELLE (1948–)
Dutch textile designer who has since the 1980s worked in partnership with the ceramicist Marja Hooft (q.v.).

Exhibitions

Duits, Thimo Te. *Keramiek '90. Moderne Keramiek in Nederland.* The Hague: SDU Uitgevrerij, 1990.

1646 JAROSZYNSKA, EWA (1936–)
Polish textile designer.

Exhibitions

Lutteman, Helena. *Polen vaaver fritt. Polish Textile Art.* Stockholm: National Museum, 1970.

1647 JASTRZEBOVSKY, WANDA
Polish designer of textiles who tried to revive tapestry in Poland after World War I.

Other Sources

Jarry, Madeleine. *La tapissérie: art du XXème siècle.* Fribourg: Office du Livre, 1974.

1648 JERSILD, ANNETTE
Danish textile designer.

Other Sources

Jarry, Madeleine. *La tapissérie: art du XXème siècle.* Fribourg: Office du Livre, 1974.

1649 JESSEN, GRO
Norwegian designer of textiles.

Other Sources

Talley, Charles. *Contemporary Textile Art: Scandinavia*. Stockholm: Carmina, 1982.

1650 JOHNSEN, ELI MARIE
Norwegian textile designer who specialised in hangings and the use of mixed techniques; she won the Lunning Prize.

Exhibitions

The Lunning Prize. Stockholm: Nationalmuseum, 1986.

Other Sources

Jarry, Madeleine. *La tapissérie: art du XXème siècle*. Fribourg: Office du Livre, 1974.

1651 JUEL, ANNETTE (1934–)
Danish textile designer specialising in weaving.

Other Sources

Jarry, Madeleine. *La tapissérie: art du XXème siècle*. Fribourg: Office du Livre, 1974.
Salicath, Bent, and Arne Karlsen, eds. *Modern Danish Textiles*. Copenhagen: Danish Society of Arts and Crafts and Industrial Design, 1959.
Talley, Charles. *Contemporary Textile Art: Scandinavia*. Stockholm: Carmina, 1982.

1652 JUNG, DORA (1906–1980)
Finnish textile designer.

Exhibitions

McFadden, David, ed. *Scandinavian Modern Design, 1880–1980*. New York: Harry Abrams and the Cooper-Hewitt Museum, 1982.

Other Sources

Byars, Mel. *The Design Encyclopedia*. London: Lawrence King, 1994.
Mäki, Oili. *Taide ja Työ: Finnish Designers of Today*. Helsinki: Werner Söderström Osakeyhtiö, 1954. Includes an outline biography.
Talley, Charles. *Contemporary Textile Art: Scandinavia*. Stockholm: Carmina, 1982.

1653 KADOW, ELISABETH (née JÄGER) (1906–1979)
German textile designer.

Other Sources

Gunta Stölzl: Weberei am Bauhaus und aus eigener Werkstatt. Berlin: Bauhaus Archiv in association with Kupfergraben Verlag, 1987. Contains individual bibliographies.

Jarry, Madeleine. *La tapissérie: art du XXème siècle.* Fribourg: Office du Livre, 1974.

1654 KALCHER, KATHARINA
German textile designer.

Other Sources

Jarry, Madeleine. *La tapissérie: art du XXème siècle.* Fribourg: Office du Livre, 1974.

1655 KALSO, ALICE
Danish textile designer.

Other Sources

Jarry, Madeleine. *La tapissérie: art du XXème siècle.* Fribourg: Office du Livre, 1974.

1656 KANAGINIS, NIKI
Greek designer of textiles who worked in tapestry from 1960.

Other Sources

Jarry, Madeleine. *La tapissérie: art du XXème siècle.* Fribourg: Office du Livre, 1974.

1657 KARTTUNEN, LAILA (1895–after 1954)
Finnish textile designer.

Other Sources

Mäki, Oili. *Taide ja Työ: Finnish Designers of Today.* Helsinki: Werner Söderström Osakeyhtiö, 1954. Gives an outline biography.

1658 KASS, ESZTER (1959–)
Hungarian textile designer.

Exhibitions

9. Fal-Es Tertextyil Biennale [9th National Textile Biennale]. Szombathely: Savaria Museum, 1984.

1659 KÅSTRUP-OLSEN, HELLE
Danish designer of textiles.

Other Sources

Talley, Charles. *Contemporary Textile Art: Scandinavia.* Stockholm: Carmina, 1982.

1660 KAUGURE, LAIMA (1952–)
Latvian textile designer whose abstract works often include decorative themes found in folk art.

Other Sources

Kalniete, Sandra. *Latvju tekstilmāksla* [Latvian textile art]. Riga: Liesma, 1989.

1661 KECSKÉS, ÁGNES (1942–)
Hungarian textile designer.

Exhibitions

9. Fal-Es Tertextyil Biennale [9th National Textile Biennale]. Szombathely: Savaria Museum, 1984.

1662 KELECSÉNYI, CSILLA (1953–)
Hungarian textile designer.

Exhibitions

9. Fal-Es Tertextyil Biennale [9th National Textile Biennale]. Szombathely: Savaria Museum, 1984.

1663 KELEMEN, KATA (1952–)
Hungarian textile designer.

Exhibitions

9. Fal-Es Tertextyil Biennale [9th National Textile Biennale]. Szombathely: Savaria Museum, 1984.

1664 KIRK, VALERIE (1957–)
Scottish textile designer using woven tapestry.

Other Sources

Sutton, Ann. *British Craft Textiles.* London: Collins, 1985.

1665 KLINT, VIBEKE (1927–)
   Danish textile designer specialising in weaving.

Exhibitions

16 Plus. Copenhagen: Dansk Kunstindustrimuseet, 1981.
McFadden, David, ed. *Scandinavian Modern Design, 1880–1980.* New York:
Harry Abrams and the Cooper-Hewitt Museum, 1982.

Other Sources

Salicath, Bent, and Arne Karlsen, eds. *Modern Danish Textiles.* Copenhagen:
Danish Society of Arts and Crafts and Industrial Design, 1959.

1666 KOCH, EA (1905–)
   Danish textile designer, especially known for her rugs.

Other Sources

Salicath, Bent, and Arne Karlsen, eds. *Modern Danish Textiles.* Copenhagen:
Danish Society of Arts and Crafts and Industrial Design, 1959.

1667 KOLLIN, LILLI (1924–)
   Finnish designer of textiles specialising in tapestry.

Other Sources

Tapisséries Finlandaises. Paris: Musée d'Art Moderne de la Ville de Paris,
1972.

1668 KOLSI-MÄKELÄ, MAIJA
   Finnish textile designer specialising in tapestry.

Exhibitions

Tapisséries Finlandaises. Paris: Musée d'Art Moderne de la Ville de Paris,
1972.

Other Sources

Louhio, Anja. *Taideryijyjä. Modern Finnish rugs.* Helsinki: Julkaisija Editors
Suomalaisen Kirjallisuuden Kirjapaino Oyskk Ltd., 1975. She is included as someone who used the traditional rug in an innovative way.

1669 KOMISSAR, ANNE MARIE
   Norwegian designer of textiles.

Other Sources

Talley, Charles. *Contemporary Textile Art: Scandinavia.* Stockholm: Carmina, 1982.

1670 KORNERUP, ANNE MARIE
Danish textile designer.

Other Sources

Jarry, Madeleine. *La tapissérie: art du XXème siècle.* Fribourg: Office du Livre, 1974.

1671 KOROMA, ALLI (1907–)
Finnish textile designer.

Other Sources

Mäki, Oili. *Taide ja Työ: Finnish Designers of Today.* Helsinki: Werner Söderström Osakeyhtiö, 1954. Gives an outline biography.

1672 KÖHLER, MARGARETE (née BITTKOW) (1895–1965)
German textile designer.

Other Sources

Gunta Stölzl: Weberei am Bauhaus und aus eigener Werkstatt. Berlin: Bauhaus Archiv in association with Kupfergraben Verlag, 1987. Contains individual bibliographies.

1673 KÖHLER, MELA (née MELANIE LEOPOLDINA; alt. KÖHLER-BRO-MAN) (1885–1960)
Austrian designer of graphics, textiles and other media.

Main Sources

Schweiger, Werner. *Bilderbögen der Wiener Werkstätte.* Vienna: Christian Brandstätter, 1983, 6pp. and 18pp. of illus. One of two women included in this booklet.

Exhibitions

Kallir, Jane. *Viennese Design and the Wiener Werkstätte.* New York: Braziller in association with the Galérie St. Etienne, 1986.

Oedekoven-Gerischer, Angela, et al., eds. *Frauen im Design: Berufsbilder und Lebenswege seit 1900. Women in Design: Careers and Life Histories since 1900.* Stuttgart: Design Center, 1989.

Other Sources

Fanelli, Giovanni, and Rosalia Fanelli. *Il tessuto art déco e anni trenta: disegno, moda, architettura.* Florence: Cantini, 1986.

Pirhofer, G., and A. Gmeiner. *Der Österreichische Werkbund.* Vienna: 1985.

Schweiger, W. *Weiner Werkstätte: Kunst und Handwerk, 1903–32.* Vienna: Christian Brandstätter Verlag, 1982.

Völker, Angela. *Wiener Werkstätte: Wiener Mode und Modefotografie. Die Modeabteilung der Wiener Werkstätte, 1922–1932.* Munich and Paris: Schneider-Henn, 1984.

1674 KRAZKIEWICZ, MARIE
Polish textile designer.

Other Sources

Jarry, Madeleine. *La tapissérie: art du XXème siècle.* Fribourg: Office du Livre, 1974.

1675 KRIEBEL, GERTRUD
Austrian textile designer.

Other Sources

Jarry, Madeleine. *La tapissérie: art du XXème siècle.* Fribourg: Office du Livre, 1974.

1676 KUCHAROVÁ, ALICE
Czech textile designer.

Other Sources

Jarry, Madeleine. *La tapissérie: art du XXème siècle.* Fribourg: Office du Livre, 1974.

1677 KUKKASJÄRVI, IRMA ANNELI (née HILSKA) (1941–)
Finnish textile designer.

Other Sources

Naylor, Colin, ed. *Contemporary Designers.* 2nd edition. Chicago and London: St. James Press, 1990. Contains a bibliography.

Talley, Charles. *Contemporary Textile Art: Scandinavia.* Stockholm: Carmina, 1982.

1678 LAHTINEN, RAIJA (1941–)
Finnish textile designer specialising in tapestry.

Exhibitions

Tapisséries Finlandaises. Paris: Musée d'Art Moderne de la Ville de Paris, 1972.

Other Sources

Louhio, Anja. *Taideryijyjä. Modern Finnish rugs.* Helsinki: Julkaisija Editors Suomalaisen Kirjallisuuden Kirjapaino Oyskk Ltd., 1975. She is included as someone who used the traditional rug in an innovative way.

1679 LALIQUE, SUZANNE (1899–?)
French designer of textiles, ceramics and painter; daughter of René Lalique.

Exhibitions

Les Années 25. Paris: Musée des Arts Décoratifs, 1966. Includes some of her work which had been shown in the 1925 International Exposition.

Dufresne, Jean-Luc, and Olivier Messac, eds. *Femmes créatrices des années vingt.* Granville: Musée Richard Anacréon, 1988. Wide-ranging catalogue with a short biographical account on each woman included.

1680 LAMBRECHT, BERNADETTE
Belgian textile designer.

Other Sources

Jarry, Madeleine. *La tapissérie: art du XXème siècle.* Fribourg: Office du Livre, 1974.

1681 LARCHER, DOROTHY (1884–1952)
English textile designer who collaborated with Phyllis Barron (q.v.).

Main Sources

O'Connor, Deryn. "Hand-block printed textiles by Phyllis Barron and Dorothy Larcher." *Crafts* 33 (1978): 51. Review of exhibition.

Exhibitions

Phyllis Barron and Dorothy Larcher: Handblock Printed Textiles. Bath: Craft Study Centre, 1978.

Thirties: British Art and Design Before the War. London: Hayward Gallery, 1979.

Hogben, C. *A Collection in the Making: British Art and Design, 1900–1960.* London: Victoria and Albert Museum, 1983.

Mendes, Valerie. *British Textiles from 1900–1937: The Victoria and Albert Museum's Textiles Collection.* London: Victoria and Albert Museum, 1992.

Other Sources

Anscombe, Isabelle. *A Woman's Touch: Women in Design from 1860 to the Present Day*. London: Virago Press, 1984.

Byars, Mel. *The Design Encyclopedia*. London: Lawrence King, 1994.

1682 LASZKIEWICZ, MARIA (1891/2–?)
Polish textile designer.

Exhibitions

Kondratiuk, Krystyna. *Les tissus polonais artistiques contemporains*. Translated into French by Gérard Conio. Łodz: Musée de l'Histoire des Textiles, 1965. Contains a short biography and list of exhibitions for each exhibitor.

Lutteman, Helena. *Polen vaaver fritt. Polish Textile Art*. Stockholm: National Museum, 1970.

Contemporary Polish Weavers. Edinburgh: Weavers' Workshop Gallery, 1972.

Kondratiuk, Krystyna. *L'Art de tissu en Pologne de 1962 à 1972*. Paris: Manufacture Nationale des Gobelins, 1972.

Other Sources

Jarry, Madeleine. *La tapissérie: art du XXème siècle*. Fribourg: Office du Livre, 1974.

1683 LAURELL, ISABELLA
Italian designer of textiles specialising in tapestry.

Other Sources

Jarry, Madeleine. *La tapissérie: art du XXème siècle*. Fribourg: Office du Livre, 1974.

1684 LAURENCIN, MARIE (1885–1956)
French painter and designer of textiles, wallpapers, stage sets and costumes.

See Painting section, volume 2.

1685 LAVONEN, MAIJA (1931–)
Finnish textile designer.

Publications

See Naylor below.

Exhibitions

McFadden, David. *Scandinavian Modern Design, 1880–1980*. New York: Harry Abrams and the Cooper-Hewitt Museum, 1982.

Other Sources

Byars, Mel. *The Design Encyclopedia*. London: Lawrence King, 1994.

Naylor, Colin, ed. *Contemporary Designers*. 2nd edition. Chicago and London: St. James Press, 1990. Contains a bibliography.

Talley, Charles. *Contemporary Textile Art: Scandinavia*. Stockholm: Carmina, 1982.

1686 LEISCHNER, MARGARET (1907–1970)

German designer of textiles who emigrated to England in 1938.

Other Sources

Byars, Mel. *The Design Encyclopedia*. London: Lawrence King, 1994.

Gunta Stölzl: Weberei am Bauhaus und aus eigener Werkstatt. Berlin: Bauhaus Archiv in association with Kupfergraben Verlag, 1987. Contains individual bibliographies.

Weltge, Sigrid Wortmann. *Bauhaus Textiles: Women Artists and the Weaving Workshop*. London: Thames and Hudson, 1993.

1687 LERCHE, URIKKE

Danish textile designer.

Other Sources

Jarry, Madeleine. *La tapissérie: art du XXème siècle*. Fribourg: Office du Livre, 1974.

1688 LETH, MARIA GUDME (alt. GUDME-LETH) (1895–?)

Danish textile designer specialising in printed textiles.

Exhibitions

McFadden, David, ed. *Scandinavian Modern Design, 1880–1980*. New York: Harry Abrams and the Cooper-Hewitt Museum, 1982.

Other Sources

Byars, Mel. *The Design Encyclopedia*. London: Lawrence King, 1994.

Salicath, Bent, and Arne Karlsen, eds. *Modern Danish Textiles*. Copenhagen: Danish Society of Arts and Crafts and Industrial Design, 1959.

1689 LJUNG, AGNETA

Swedish designer of textiles.

Other Sources

Martin, Edna, and Beata Sydhoff. *Svensk textilkonst. Swedish Textile Art*. Stockholm: Liber Förlag, 1980.

1690 LÖNNING, SUNNIVA
Norwegian textile designer.

Other Sources

Jarry, Madeleine. *La tapissérie: art du XXème siècle.* Fribourg: Office du Livre, 1974.

1691 MÅÅS-FJETTERSTRÖM, MÄRTA (1873–1941)
Swedish textile designer.

Exhibitions

McFadden, David, ed. *Scandinavian Modern Design, 1880–1980.* New York: Harry Abrams and the Cooper-Hewitt Museum, 1982.

Other Sources

Byars, Mel. *The Design Encyclopedia.* London: Lawrence King, 1994.
Jarry, Madeleine. *La tapissérie: art du XXème siècle.* Fribourg: Office du Livre, 1974.
Martin, Edna, and Beata Sydhoff. *Svensk textilkonst. Swedish Textile Art.* Stockholm: Liber Forlag, 1980.

1692 MACBETH, ANN (1875–1948)
Scottish designer, especially of textiles and embroidery.

Main Sources

Newbery, Francis. "An Appreciation of Ann Macbeth." *Studio* 27 (1903): 40–49.

Exhibitions

Burkhauser, Jude, ed. *'Glasgow Girls': Women in Art and Design, 1880–1920.* Edinburgh: Canongate, 1990.
Cumming, Elizabeth. *Glasgow 1900: Art and Design.* Zwolle: Waanders Publishers in association with the Van Gogh Museum, Amsterdam, 1992.

Other Sources

Callen, Anthea. *Angel in the Studio: Women in the Arts and Crafts Movement, 1870–1914.* London: Architectural Press, 1979.
Parry, Linda. *Textiles of the Arts and Crafts Movement.* London: Thames and Hudson, 1988.

1693 McFARLANE, KATHLEEN (1922–)
English textile designer who moved from weaving to paint and textured reliefs. At this point she encountered the Polish school of textile art represented by Abakanowicz (q.v.).

Other Sources

Sutton, Ann. *British Craft Textiles.* London: Collins, 1985.

1694 MAIRET, ETHEL (née PARTRIDGE) (1872–1952)
    English textile designer.

Publications

A Book on Vegetable Dyes. London: Hampshire House Press, 1916.
Mairet, Ethel, and Philip Mairet. *An essay on Crafts and Obedience.* Ditchling Press, 1918.
Hand-Weaving Today: Traditions and Changes. London: Faber & Faber, 1939.
Handweaving and education. London: Faber and Faber, 1942.
Handweaving: Notes for Teachers. London: Faber and Faber, 1949.
See also Byars and Coatts below.

Main Sources

Crawford, Alan. "A Weaver's Life: Ethel Mairet." *Crafts* 68 (1984): 46. Exhibition review.

Exhibitions

Thirties: British Art and Design before the War. London: Hayward Gallery, 1979.
Coatts, Margot. *A Weaver's Life: Ethel Mairet, 1972–1952.* London: Crafts Council, 1984, 136pp., illus. Contains a full bibliography.

Other Sources

Anscombe, Isabelle. *A Woman's Touch: Women in Design from 1860 to the Present Day.* London: Virago Press, 1984.
Byars, Mel. *The Design Encyclopedia.* London: Lawrence King, 1994. Gives a list of her extensive publications.

1695 MÁLIK, IRÉN (1945–)
    Hungarian textile designer.

Exhibitions

9. Fal-Es Tertextyil Biennale [9th National Textile Biennale]. Szombathely: Savaria Museum, 1984.

1696 MALINOVSKI, RUTH
    Danish designer of textiles.

Other Sources

Talley, Charles. *Contemporary Textile Art: Scandinavia.* Stockholm: Carmina, 1982.

1697 MALINOWSKI, RUTH (1928–)
Austrian textile designer who worked in Denmark and Sweden.

Exhibitions

McFadden, David. *Scandinavian Modern Design, 1880–1980.* New York: Harry Abrams in association with the Cooper-Hewitt Museum, 1982.

Other Sources

Byars, Mel. *The Design Encyclopedia.* London: Lawrence King, 1994.

1698 MANN, KATHLEEN (Alt. CRAWFORD) (c. 1905–)
English designer of textiles who was Head of Embroidery at the Glasgow School of Art; later in life she turned to painting and illustration.

Exhibitions

Burkhauser, Jude, ed. *'Glasgow Girls': Women in Art and Design, 1880–1920.* Edinburgh: Canongate, 1990.

1699 MARTIN, EDNA
Swedish designer of textiles who was a key figure in working with leading artists on schemes in tapestry. She was also Director of the Handarbetets Vanner for over twenty years.

Publications

Martin, Edna, and Beata Sydhoff. *Svensk textilkonst. Swedish Textile Art.* Stockholm: Liber Förlag, 1980.

Other Sources

Jarry, Madeleine. *La tapissérie: art du XXème siècle.* Fribourg: Office du Livre, 1974.
Talley, Charles. *Contemporary Textile Art: Scandinavia.* Stockholm: Carmina, 1982.

1700 MARX, ENID CRYSTAL DOROTHY (1902–1993)
English graphic artist and textile designer.

Publications

"Pattern Papers." *Penrose Annual* 44 (1950): 51–53, plus illustrations.

Lambert, Margaret, and Enid Marx. *English Popular and Traditional Art.* London: Batsford, 1946.

For other publications see Naylor.

Main Sources

Herald, Jacqueline. "A Portrait of Enid Marx." *Crafts* 40 (1979): 17–21.

Exhibitions

Sutton, Ann, et al. *Enid Marx: A retrospective Exhibition.* London: Camden Arts Centre, 1979.

Thirties: British Art and Design before the War. London: Hayward Gallery, 1979.

Hiesinger, Kathryn, and George Marcus III, eds. *Design since 1945.* Philadelphia: Philadelphia Museum of Art, 1983.

Seddon, Jill, and Suzette Worden, eds. *Women designing: Redefining Design in Britain between the Wars.* Brighton: University of Brighton, 1994.

Other Sources

Anscombe, Isabelle. *A Woman's Touch: Women in Design from 1860 to the Present Day.* London: Virago Press, 1984.

Byars, Mel. *The Design Encyclopedia.* London: Lawrence King, 1994.

Naylor, Colin, ed. *Contemporary Designers.* 2nd edition. Chicago and London: St. James Press, 1990. Contains a bibliography.

1701 MATHISON, FIONA (1947–)
Scottish textile designer who makes figurative tapestries.

Exhibitions

Textiles Today: Woven and Embroidered Works Selected by Marianne Straub. Cambridge: Kettle's Yard, 1981.

Other Sources

Sutton, Ann. *British Craft Textiles.* London: Collins, 1985.

1702 MATHOVÁ, MARIE (1942–)
Czech designer of textiles who produces open, lacy work interpersed with bobbin work for large-scale pieces.

Exhibitions

Marie Mathová; Bohdan Mrazek—tapiserie. Brno: Moravská Galéria, 1972. Includes a biography with a summary in English.

1703 MATVEYEVA, R.
Russian textile designer.

Other Sources

Yasinskaya, I. *Soviet Textile Design of the Revolutionary Period.* London: Thames and Hudson, 1983.

1704 MEIER-MICHEL, JOHANNA (c. 1880–?)
Czech-born designer of textiles and other decorative objects who worked in Austria.

Other Sources

Pirhofer, G., and A. Gmeiner. *Der Österreichische Werkbund.* Vienna: 1985.

1705 METSOVAARA, MARJETTA (1928–)
Finnish textile designer.

Exhibitions

Hiesinger, Kathryn, and George Marcus III, eds. *Design since 1945.* Philadelphia: Philadelphia Museum of Art, 1983.

Other Sources

Byars, Mel. *The Design Encyclopedia.* London: Lawrence King, 1994.
Naylor, Colin, ed. *Contemporary Designers.* 2nd edition. Chicago and London: St. James Press, 1990. Contains a bibliography.

1706 MIKKOLA, IRJA
Finnish designer of textiles.

Other Sources

Louhio, Anja. *Taideryijyjä. Modern Finnish rugs.* Helsinki: Julkaisija Editors Suomalaisen Kirjallisuuden Kirjapaino Oyskk Ltd., 1975. She is included as someone who used the traditional rug in an innovative way.
Talley, Charles. *Contemporary Textile Art: Scandinavia.* Stockholm: Carmina, 1982.

1707 MILLS, ELERI, (1955–)
Welsh designer of figurative works, often landscapes, on fabric using spray paint and hand-stitching.

Main Sources

Taylor, A. R. "Painted and stitched by Eleri Mills." *Crafts* 44 (1980): 49.

Other Sources

Sutton, Ann. *British Craft Textiles.* London: Collins, 1985.

1708 MITSCHERLICH, IMMEKE (née ALEXANDRA SCWOLLMANN) (1899–1985)
   German textile designer.

Other Sources

Gunta Stölzl: Weberei am Bauhaus und aus eigener Werkstatt. Berlin: Bauhaus Archiv in association with Kupfergraben Verlag, 1987. Contains individual bibliographies.

1709 MOLIN, BRITA
   Swedish designer of textiles.

Other Sources

Martin, Edna, and Beata Sydhoff. *Svensk textilkonst. Swedish Textile Art.* Stockholm: Liber Förlag, 1980.

1710 MONACI, MARIA GALLENGA
   Italian designer of textiles.

Other Sources

Fanelli, Giovanni, and Rosalia Fanelli. *Il tessuto art déco e anni trenta: disegno, moda, architettura.* Florence: Cantini, 1986.

1711 MOORMAN, THEO (1907–1990)
   English textile designer and weaver.

Main Sources

Clough, Paul. "Theo Moorman." *Crafts* 17 (1975): 29–30.
Norrie, Jane. "Theo Moorman." *Crafts* 88 (1987): 40–41. On Moorman's eightieth birthday.

Exhibitions

Thirties: British Art and Design Before the War. London: Hayward Gallery, 1979.
Bury, Hester. *A Choice of Design, 1850–1980.* Colchester: Minories Gallery, 1983.
Seddon Jill, and Suzette Worden, eds. *Women designing: Redefining Design in Britain between the Wars.* Brighton: University of Brighton, 1994.

Other Sources

Byars, Mel. *The Design Encyclopedia.* London: Lawrence King, 1994.
Day, Michael. *Modern Art in Church: A Gazetteer.* London, 1982.
Sutton, Ann. *British Craft Textiles.* London: Collins, 1985.

1712 MOREAU, SUZANNE
       French textile designer.

Other Sources

Jarry, Madeleine. *La tapissérie: art du XXème siècle.* Fribourg: Office du Livre, 1974.

1713 MORRELL, ANNE (1938–)
       English textile designer working in embroidery. She was instrumental in the growth of the School of Embroidery at Manchester Metropolitan University.

Publications

"Constance Howard." *Crafts* 55 (1982): 32–34.

Other Sources

Sutton, Ann. *British Craft Textiles.* London: Collins, 1985.

1714 MORRIS, JANE (née BURDEN) (1839–1914)
       English embroiderer of textiles and wife of William Morris.

Main Sources

Callen, Anthea. *The Angel in the Studio.* London: Astragal Books, 1979.
Marsh, Jan. *Jane and May Morris: A Biographical Story, 1839–1928.* London: Pandora, 1986.

Other Sources

Parry, Linda. *William Morris Textiles.* London: Weidenfeld & Nicolson, 1983.
———. *Textiles of the Arts and Crafts Movement.* London: Thames and Hudson, 1988.

1715 MORRIS, MAY (1862–1938)
       English designer of textiles, wallpaper and jewellery who took over the embroidery workshop from her father, William.

Main Sources

Coatts, Margot. "May Morris 1862–1938." *Crafts* 99 (1989): 52. Review of exhibition cited below.

Exhibitions

May Morris, 1862–1938. Waltham Forest: William Morris Gallery, 1989, 22pp., illus. Contains a bibliography and includes references to her publications. There are detailed notes on the exhibits.

Other Sources

Callen, Anthea. *The Angel in the Studio.* London: Architectural Press, 1979.
Parry, Linda. *William Morris Textiles.* London: Weidenfeld & Nicolson, 1983.
———. *Textiles of the Arts and Crafts Movement.* London: Thames and Hudson, 1988.

1716 MOULINIER, MARIE
French textile designer specialising in tapestry.

Other Sources

Jarry, Madeleine. *La tapissérie: art du XXème siècle.* Fribourg: Office du Livre, 1974.

1717 MÖGELINE, ELSE (Alt. MÖGELIN) (1887–1982)
German painter and designer of textiles and ceramics who worked at the Bauhaus.

Exhibitions

La Tessitura del Bauhaus, 1919–33, nelle collezioni della Repubblica Democratica Tedesca. Venice: Palazzo Ducale and Cataloghi Marsilio, 1985.
Weber, Klaus, ed. *Keramik und Bauhaus.* Berlin: Bauhaus-Archiv, 1989.

Other Sources

Gunta Stölzl: Weberei am Bauhaus und aus eigener Werkstatt. Berlin: Bauhaus Archiv in association with Kupfergraben Verlag, 1987. Contains individual bibliographies.
Weltge, Sigrid Wortmann. *Bauhaus Textiles: Women Artists and the Weaving Workshop.* London: Thames and Hudson, 1993.

1718 MÖSCHL, GABI (Alt. GABRIELE MARIA MÖSCHL-LAGUS) (1887–after 1939)
Austrian designer, especially of textiles and fashion.

Other Sources

Schweiger, W. *Weiner Werkstätte: Kunst und Handwerk, 1903–32.* Vienna: Christian Brandstätter Verlag, 1982.

1719 MUNSTERS, CARLA (1939–)
      Dutch textile designer.

Exhibitions

Moderne Hollandsk Tekstilkunst og Glas. Copenhagen: Dansk Kunstindustri-museum, 1979.

Other Sources

Jarry, Madeleine. *La tapissérie: art du XXème siècle.* Fribourg: Office du Livre, 1974.

1720 MUÑOZ, AURELIA
      Spanish designer of textiles who specialised in tapestry.

Other Sources

Jarry, Madeleine. *La tapissérie: art du XXème siècle.* Fribourg: Office du Livre, 1974.

1721 MUSTAKALLIO-SUOMINEN, KAIJA (1916–)
      Finnish designer of textiles who specialised in ryijy rugs.

Other Sources

Mäki, Oili. *Taide ja Työ: Finnish Designers of Today.* Helsinki: Werner Söderström Osakeyhtiö, 1954. Gives an outline biography.

1722 MUSZYNSKA, TERESA (1938–)
      Polish textile designer.

Exhibitions

Contemporary Polish Weavers. Edinburgh: Weavers' Workshop Gallery, 1972.
      Kondratiuk, Krystyna. *L'Art de tissu en Pologne de 1962 à 1972.* Paris: Manufacture Nationale des Gobelins, 1972.

Other Sources

Jarry, Madeleine. *La tapissérie: art du XXème siècle.* Fribourg: Office du Livre, 1974.

1723 MUZE, AINA (1943–)
      Latvian textile designer whose tapestries deal with historical themes and with the sea.

Other Sources

Kalniete, Sandra. *Latvju tekstilmāksla* [Latvian textile art]. Riga: Liesma, 1989.

1724 MÜLLER-HELLWIG, ALEN (1902–?)
German designer of textiles, especially embroidery.

Other Sources

Weltge, Sigrid Wortmann. *Bauhaus Textiles: Women Artists and the Weaving Workshop*. London: Thames and Hudson, 1993.

1725 NAGY, JUDIT (1954–)
Hungarian textile designer.

Exhibitions

9. Fal-Es Tertextyil Biennale [9th National Textile Biennale]. Szombathely: Savaria Museum, 1984.

1726 NAZAREVSKAYA, M.
Russian textile designer.

Other Sources

Yasinskaya, I. *Soviet Textile Design of the Revolutionary Period*. London: Thames and Hudson, 1983.

1727 NETER-KÄHLER, GRETEN (née KÄHLER) (1906–1986)
German designer of textiles, especially weaving, who worked in the Netherlands from 1932.

Other Sources

Gunta Stölzl: Weberei am Bauhaus und aus eigener Werkstatt. Berlin: Bauhaus Archiv in association with Kupfergraben Verlag, 1987. Contains individual bibliographies.

Weltge, Sigrid Wortmann. *Bauhaus Textiles: Women Artists and the Weaving Workshop*. London: Thames and Hudson, 1993.

1728 NEWBERY, JESSIE (née ROWAT) (1864–1948)
Scottish designer of textiles, especially embroidery, and fashion who taught at the Glasgow School of Art; she also designed metalwork.

Exhibitions

A Centenary Exhibition to Celebrate the Founding of the Glasgow Society of Lady Artists in 1882. Glasgow: Collins Gallery, 1982.

Burkhauser, Jude, ed. *'Glasgow Girls': Women in Art and Design, 1880–1920*. Edinburgh: Canongate, 1990.

Cumming, Elizabeth. *Glasgow 1900: Art and Design*. Zwolle: Waanders Publishers in association with the Van Gogh Museum, Amsterdam, 1992.

Other Sources

Callen, Anthea. *Angel in the Studio: Women in the Arts and Crafts Movement, 1870–1914*. London: Architectural Press, 1979.

Parry, Linda. *Textiles of the Arts and Crafts Movement*. London: Thames and Hudson, 1988.

1729 NIELSON, DORIS (1903–)
Danish textile designer.

Other Sources

Salicath, Bent, and Arne Karlsen, eds. *Modern Danish Textiles*. Copenhagen: Danish Society of Arts and Crafts and Industrial Design, 1959.

1730 NILSSON, BARBRO (née LUNDBERG) (1899–?)
Swedish textile designer.

Main Sources

Møller, Viggo Sten. *En bok om Barbro Nilsson*. Stockholm: Höganäs, 1977.

Exhibitions

McFadden, David, ed. *Scandinavian Modern Design, 1880–1980*. New York: Harry Abrams and the Cooper-Hewitt Museum, 1982.

Other Sources

Byars, Mel. *The Design Encyclopedia*. London: Lawrence King, 1994.

Martin, Edna, and Beata Sydhoff. *Svensk textilkonst. Swedish Textile Art*. Stockholm: Liber Förlag, 1980.

Naylor, Colin, ed. *Contemporary Designers*. 2nd edition. Chicago and London: St. James Press, 1990. Contains a bibliography.

1731 NISSEN, NANNA
Danish textile designer.

Other Sources

Jarry, Madeleine. *La tapissérie: art du XXème siècle*. Fribourg: Office du Livre, 1974.

1732 NONNE-SCHMIDT, HÉLÈNE (1891–1976)
German designer of textiles.

Other Sources

Byars, Mel. *The Design Encyclopedia.* London: Lawrence King, 1994.

Fanelli, Giovanni, and Rosalia Fanelli. *Il tessuto art déco e anni trenta: disegno, moda, architettura.* Florence: Cantini, 1986.

Gunta Stölzl: Weberei am Bauhaus und aus eigener Werkstatt. Berlin: Bauhaus Archiv in association with Kupfergraben Verlag, 1987. Contains individual bibliographies.

Weltge, Sigrid Wortmann. *Bauhaus Textiles: Women Artists and the Weaving Workshop.* London: Thames and Hudson, 1993.

1733 NOWOTNY, AMALIA (1893–?)
Austrian designer of textiles and other media.

Other Sources

Pirhofer, G., and A. Gmeiner. *Der Österreichische Werkbund.* Vienna: 1985.

1734 OESTREICHER, LISBETH (Alt. BIRMAN) (1902–1989)
German designer of textiles and fashion who worked in the Netherlands from 1930.

Other Sources

Gunta Stölzl: Weberei am Bauhaus und aus eigener Werkstatt. Berlin: Bauhaus Archiv in association with Kupfergraben Verlag, 1987. Contains individual bibliographies.

Weltge, Sigrid Wortmann. *Bauhaus Textiles: Women Artists and the Weaving Workshop.* London: Thames and Hudson, 1993.

1735 OHNDORF-RÖSIGER, UTA
German textile designer.

Other Sources

Jarry, Madeleine. *La tapissérie: art du XXème siècle.* Fribourg: Office du Livre, 1974.

1736 ORTLOFF, EDITH MÜLLER
German textile designer.

Other Sources

Jarry, Madeleine. *La tapissérie: art du XXème siècle.* Fribourg: Office du Livre, 1974.

1737 ORTVED, KIRSTEN
  Danish textile designer.

Other Sources

Jarry, Madeleine. *La tapissérie: art du XXème siècle.* Fribourg: Office du Livre, 1974.

1738 OSELE, ERNA (1915–)
  Latvian textile designer whose wall hangings derive from traditional Latvian textiles and folk lore.

Other Sources

Kalniete, Sandra. *Latvju tekstilmāksla* [Latvian textile art]. Riga: Liesma, 1989.

1739 OTTE, BENITA (Alt. KOCH, OTTE-KOCH) (1892–1976)
  German designer of textiles.

Exhibitions

La Tessitura del Bauhaus, 1919–33, nelle collezioni della Repubblica Democratica Tedesca. Venice: Palazzo Ducale and Cataloghi Marsilio, 1985.

Other Sources

Byars, Mel. *The Design Encyclopedia.* London: Lawrence King, 1994.
Gunta Stölzl: Weberei am Bauhaus und aus eigener Werkstatt. Berlin: Bauhaus Archiv in association with Kupfergraben Verlag, 1987. Contains individual bibliographies.
Weltge, Sigrid Wortmann. *Bauhaus Textiles: Women Artists and the Weaving Workshop.* London: Thames and Hudson, 1993.

1740 OWIDSKA, JANINA (1927–)
  Polish textile designer specialising in tapestry.

Exhibitions

Kondratiuk, Krystyna. *Les tissus polonais artistiques contemporains.* Translated into French by Gérard Conio. Łodz: Musée de l'Histoire des Textiles, 1965. Contains a short biography and list of exhibitions for each exhibitor.
Lutteman, Helena. *Polen vaaver fritt. Polish Textile Art.* Stockholm: National Museum, 1970.

Other Sources

Jarry, Madeleine. *La tapissérie: art du XXème siècle.* Fribourg: Office du Livre, 1974.

1741 PAULI, ANNA (1944–)
Hungarian designer of textiles.

Exhibitions

Fibres Art '85. Paris: Musée des Arts Décoratifs, 1985.
Szot Ösztöndíjasok Kiállitása. Budapest: Magyar Nemezeti Galéria, 1986.

1742 PAXTON BROWN, HELEN (1876–1956)
Scottish designer of textiles, especially embroidery.

Exhibitions

A Centenary Exhibition to Celebrate the Founding of the Glasgow Society of Lady Artists in 1882. Glasgow: Collins Gallery, 1982.
Burkhauser, Jude, ed. *'Glasgow Girls': Women in Art and Design, 1880–1920.* Edinburgh: Canongate, 1990.

1743 PEACOCK, ELIZABETH (1880–1969)
English designer of textiles who specialised in weaving.

Exhibitions

Thirties: British Art and Design before the War. London: Arts Council of Great Britain at the Hayward Gallery, 1979.
Hogben, C. *A Collection in the Making: British Art and Design, 1900–1960.* London: Victoria and Albert Museum, 1983.

1744 PERELLI, ZSUZSA
Hungarian designer of textiles.

Exhibitions

Moderne Ungarische Textilkunst und Keramik aus der Sammlung des Savaria Museum, Szombathely. Linz: Stadtmuseum, 1977.

1745 PESEL, LOUISA (1870–1947)
English designer and teacher of textiles, particularly embroidery. At one time director of the Royal Hellenic Schools of Needlework, she later became an Inspector of Art Needlework and the first president of the Embroiderers' Guild.

Other Sources

Parry, Linda. *Textiles of the Arts and Crafts Movement.* London: Thames and Hudson, 1988.

1746 PETTER-ZEIS, VALERI (1881–1963)
Austrian designer in several media, including textiles.

Other Sources

Pirhofer, G., and A. Gmeiner. *Der Österreichische Werkbund.* Vienna: 1985.
Schweiger, W. *Weiner Werkstätte: Kunst und Handwerk, 1903–32.* Vienna:
Christian Brandstätter Verlag, 1982.

1747 PITTONI, ANITA
Italian painter, writer and designer of textiles.

Other Sources

Fanelli, Giovanni, and Rosalia Fanelli. *Il tessuto art déco e anni trenta: disegno, moda, architettura.* Florence: Cantini, 1986.

1748 PLACHKY, MARIA
Austrian textile designer who exhibited in the 1960s.

Other Sources

Jarry, Madeleine. *La tapissérie: art du XXème siècle.* Fribourg: Office du
Livre, 1974.

1749 PLEWKA-SCHMIDT, URSZULA (1939–)
Polish textile designer.

Exhibitions

Contemporary Polish Weavers. Copenhagen: Weavers' Workshop Gallery,
1972.

1750 PLUM, LISE
Danish textile designer specialising in weaving.

Other Sources

Salicath, Bent, and Arne Karlsen, eds. *Modern Danish Textiles.* Copenhagen:
Danish Society of Arts and Crafts and Industrial Design, 1959.

1751 PLUTYNSKA, ELEONORA (1886–?)
Polish textile designer who was active from the 1930s.

Exhibitions

Kondratiuk, Krystyna. *Les tissus polonais artistiques contemporains.*
Translated into French by Gérard Conio. Łodz: Musée de l'Histoire des Textiles,
1965. Contains a short biography and list of exhibitions for each exhibitor.

Other Sources

Jarry, Madeleine. *La tapissérie: art du XXème siècle.* Fribourg: Office du Livre, 1974.

1752 POHJANHEIMO, KREETA
Finnish designer of textiles.

Other Sources

Mäki, Oili. *Taide ja Työ: Finnish Designers of Today.* Helsinki: Werner Söderström Osakeyhtiö, 1954. Gives an outline biography.

1753 POLENOVA, ELENA
Russian designer of textiles.

Other Sources

Fanelli, Giovanni, and Rosalia Fanelli. *Il tessuto Art Nouveau: disegno, moda, architettura.* Florence: Cantini, 1986.

1754 POLGÁR, RÓZSA (1936–)
Hungarian textile designer.

Exhibitions

9. Fal-Es Tertextyil Biennale [9th National Textile Biennale]. Szombathely: Savaria Museum, 1984.

1755 POSTAŽA, LILITA (1941–)
Latvian textile designer who produces figurative tapestries based on folklore.

Other Sources

Kalniete, Sandra. *Latvju tekstilmāksla* [Latvian textile art]. Riga: Liesma, 1989.

1756 PREOBRAZHENSKAYA, DARIA NIKOLAEVNA (1908–1972)
Russian textile designer.

Other Sources

Byars, Mel. *The Design Encyclopedia.* London: Lawrence King, 1994.
Yasinskaya, I. *Soviet Textile Design of the Revolutionary Period.* London: Thames and Hudson, 1983.

1757 PUOTILA, RITVA (née RITVA SOILIKKI SAIRANEN) (1935–)
Finnish designer of textiles and glass.

Other Sources

Louhio, Anja. *Taideryijyjä. Modern Finnish rugs.* Helsinki: Julkaisija Editors Suomalaisen Kirjallisuuden Kirjapaino Oyskk Ltd., 1975. Many examples by this designer are included as she is classed by the author as one of the outstanding exponents of this form of art/design.

Naylor, Colin, ed. *Contemporary Designers.* 2nd edition. Chicago and London: St. James Press, 1990. Contains a bibliography.

1758 PUTRAMA, ZAIGA (1956–)
Latvian textile designer who works with rags to construct works reminiscent of traditional rugs and fabrics.

Other Sources

Kalniete, Sandra. *Latvju tekstilmāksla* [Latvian textile art]. Riga: Liesma, 1989.

1759 RAASCHOU, DORTE (c. 1930–)
Danish textile designer specialising in printed textiles.

Other Sources

Salicath, Bent, and Arne Karlsen, eds. *Modern Danish Textiles.* Copenhagen: Danish Society of Arts and Crafts and Industrial Design, 1959.

1760 RADO, CLAIRE
French textile designer specialising in tapestry.

Other Sources

Jarry, Madeleine. *La tapissérie: art du XXème siècle.* Fribourg: Office du Livre, 1974.

1761 RAGE, LIJA (1948–)
Latvian textile designer whose tapestries use both traditional and innovative techniques and materials.

Other Sources

Kalniete, Sandra. *Latvju tekstilmāksla* [Latvian textile art]. Riga: Liesma, 1989.

1762 RAGNO, FRANÇOISE
Swiss designer of textiles.

Other Sources

Jarry, Madeleine. *La tapissérie: art du XXème siècle.* Fribourg: Office du Livre, 1974.

1763 RANTANEN, KIRSTI
Finnish designer of textiles.

Other Sources

Louhio, Anja. *Taideryijyjä. Modern Finnish rugs.* Helsinki: Julkaisija Editors Suomalaisen Kirjallisuuden Kirjapaino Oyskk Ltd., 1975. She is included as someone who used the traditional rug in an innovative way.

Talley, Charles. *Contemporary Textile Art: Scandinavia.* Stockholm: Carmina, 1982.

1764 RASMUSSEN, FRANKA
Danish textile designer.

Other Sources

Jarry, Madeleine. *La tapissérie: art du XXème siècle.* Fribourg: Office du Livre, 1974.

Salicath, Bent, and Arne Karlsen, eds. *Modern Danish Textiles.* Copenhagen: Danish Society of Arts and Crafts and Industrial Design, 1959.

1765 REICHARDT, GRETE (née MARGARETE; alt. WAGNER) (1907–1984)
German textile designer.

Other Sources

Byars, Mel. *The Design Encyclopedia.* London: Lawrence King, 1994.

Gunta Stölzl: Weberei am Bauhaus und aus eigener Werkstatt. Berlin: Bauhaus Archiv in association with Kupfergraben Verlag, 1987. Contains individual bibliographies.

Weltge, Sigrid Wortmann. *Bauhaus Textiles: Women Artists and the Weaving Workshop.* London: Thames and Hudson, 1993.

1766 REINDL, HILDE (Alt. CIELUSZEK) (1909–)
German textile designer.

Other Sources

Byars, Mel. *The Design Encyclopedia.* London: Lawrence King, 1994.

Gunta Stölzl: Weberei am Bauhaus und aus eigener Werkstatt. Berlin: Bauhaus Archiv in association with Kupfergraben Verlag, 1987. Contains individual bibliographies.

1767 RENÉ, DENISE
French designer of textiles.

Other Sources

Jarry, Madeleine. *La tapissérie: art du XXème siècle*. Fribourg: Office du Livre, 1974.

1768 REPKOVA, SILVA (1928–)
Czech designer of textiles who uses experiemental techniques for wall-hangings.

Exhibitions

Silva Repková: tkané tapiserie 1971–2. Brno: Moravská Galéria, 1972.

1769 RESTIAUX, MARY (c. 1946–)
English textile designer who weaves narrow cloths in fine silk and brilliant colours.

Main Sources

Frayling, Christopher. "From Itten to Ikat." *Crafts* 92 (1988): 38–41.

Exhibitions

Textiles Today: Woven and Embroidered Works Selected by Marianne Straub. Cambridge: Kettle's Yard, 1981.

Other Sources

Sutton, Ann. *British Craft Textiles*. London: Collins, 1985.

1770 RIBBENTROP-LEUDESDORFF, LORE (Alt. ENGSTFELD)
German textile designer and pioneer film animator.

Other Sources

Gunta Stölzl: Weberei am Bauhaus und aus eigener Werkstatt. Berlin: Bauhaus Archiv in association with Kupfergraben Verlag, 1987. Contains individual bibliographies.

1771 RIEGLER, MAGGIE (1944–)
Scottish textile designer who makes tapestries and hangings from unconventional materials and techniques.

Other Sources

Sutton, Ann. *British Craft Textiles*. London: Collins, 1985.

1772 RILEY, CATHERINE
English designer and sculptor with textiles.

Main Sources

"Fun and frisson." *Crafts* 25 (1977): 30–33.

Other Sources

Sutton, Ann. *British Craft Textiles.* London: Collins, 1985.

1773 RING, LOTTA
Finnish textile designer who weaves tapestries.

Other Sources

Mäki, Oili. *Taide ja Työ: Finnish Designers of Today.* Helsinki: Werner Söderström Osakeyhtiö, 1954. Gives an outline biography.

1774 RIX, FELICE (1893–1967)
Austrian designer of textiles and fashion who worked in Japan from 1935; sister of Kitty Rix (q.v.).

Other Sources

Byars, Mel. *The Design Encyclopedia.* London: Lawrence King, 1994.

1775 ROBERTSON, EVA
Swedish textile designer.

Other Sources

Jarry, Madeleine. *La tapissérie: art du XXème siècle.* Fribourg: Office du Livre, 1974.

1776 ROBERTS, PATRICIA (c. 1942–)
English designer of handknitted garments. She produces both ready-made collections and kits for people to make up her designs themselves.

Other Sources

Sutton, Ann. *British Craft Textiles.* London: Collins, 1985.

1777 ROGHE, AGNES EMMA ADELE (1901–1927)
German textile designer.

Other Sources

Fanelli, Giovanni, and Rosalia Fanelli. *Il tessuto art déco e anni trenta: disegno, moda, architettura.* Florence: Cantini, 1986.
Gunta Stölzl: Weberei am Bauhaus und aus eigener Werkstatt. Berlin: Bauhaus Archiv in association with Kupfergraben Verlag, 1987. Contains individual bibliographies.

Weltge, Sigrid Wortmann. *Bauhaus Textiles: Women Artists and the Weaving Workshop.* London: Thames and Hudson, 1993.

1778 ROGINSKAYA, F.
Russian textile designer.

Other Sources

Yasinskaya, I. *Soviet Textile Design of the Revolutionary Period.* London: Thames and Hudson, 1983.

1779 ROGOYSKA, MARTA (1950–)
Textile designer who works in England.

Main Sources

Johnson, Pamela. "The Narrative Voice." *Crafts* 101 (1989): 22–29. A discussion with Rogoyska about an exhibition which she organised.
Starsmore, Ian. "Theatre of images." *Crafts* 63 (1983): 20–25. Interview with Rogoyska.

Other Sources

Sutton, Ann. *British Craft Textiles.* London: Collins, 1985.

1780 ROLF, MARGOT (1940–)
Dutch textile designer.

Exhibitions

Moderne Hollandsk Tekstilkunst og Glas. Copenhagen: Dansk Kunstindustrimuseum, 1979.

Other Sources

Weltge, Sigrid Wortmann. *Bauhaus Textiles: Women Artists and the Weaving Workshop.* London: Thames and Hudson, 1993.

1781 RÓNAI, ÉVA (1931–)
Hungarian textile designer.

Exhibitions

9. Fal-Es Tertextyil Biennale [9th National Textile Biennale]. Szombathely: Savaria Museum, 1984.

1782 ROSE, KATJA (née SCHMIDT) (1905–)
German textile designer.

Other Sources

Byars, Mel. *The Design Encyclopedia.* London: Lawrence King, 1994.

1783 ROSS, PHYLLIS (1934–)

New Zealand-born and trained, Ross has exhibited her quilted pieces in the technique of Italian quilting in England since 1980.

Exhibitions

Textiles Today: Woven and Embroidered Works Selected by Marianne Straub. Cambridge: Kettle's Yard, 1981.

Other Sources

Sutton, Ann. *British Craft Textiles.* London: Collins, 1985.

1784 RUSZCZYNSKA-SZAFRANSKA, AGNIESKA (1929–)

Polish textile designer.

Exhibitions

Contemporary Polish Weavers. Edinburgh: Weavers' Workshop Gallery, 1972.

Kondratiuk, Krystyna. *L'Art de tissu en Pologne de 1962 à 1972.* Paris: Manufacture Nationale des Gobelins, 1972.

1785 RUUSUVAARA, LIISA

Finnish designer of textiles specialising in rugs.

Other Sources

Louhio, Anja. *Taideryijyjä. Modern Finnish rugs.* Helsinki: Julkaisija Editors Suomalaisen Kirjallisuuden Kirjapaino Oyskk Ltd., 1975. She is included as some-one who used the traditional rug in an innovative way.

1786 RYGGEN, HANNAH (1894–1970)

Swedish-born textile designer who worked in Norway.

Exhibitions

Cinq artistes norvégiens. Paris: Petit Palais, 1954.

McFadden, David, ed. *Scandinavian Modern Design, 1880–1980.* New York: Harry Abrams and the Cooper-Hewitt Museum, 1982.

Wichstrøm, Anne. *Rooms with a View: Women's Art in Norway, 1880–1990.* Oslo: Royal Ministry of Foreign Affairs, 1989.

Other Sources

Byars, Mel. *The Design Encyclopedia.* London: Lawrence King, 1994.

Jarry, Madeleine. *La tapissérie: art du XXème siècle.* Fribourg: Office du Livre, 1974.

Martin, Edna, and Beata Sydhoff. *Svensk textilkonst. Swedish Textile Art.* Stockholm: Liber Förlag, 1980.

Talley, Charles. *Contemporary Textile Art: Scandinavia.* Stockholm: Carmina, 1982.

1787 SALZMAN, MARTINE.
  French textile designer.

Exhibitions

Fibres Art '85. Paris: Musée des Arts Décoratifs, 1985.

1788 SAMPE, ASTRID (Alt. SAMPE-HULTBERG) (1909–)
  Swedish textile designer.

Exhibitions

McFadden, David, ed. *Scandinavian Modern Design, 1880–1980.* New York: Harry Abrams and the Cooper-Hewitt Museum, 1982.

Hiesinger, Kathryn, and George Marcus III, eds. *Design since 1945.* Philadelphia: Philadelphia Museum of Art, 1983.

Other Sources

Byars, Mel. *The Design Encyclopedia.* London: Lawrence King, 1994.

Fanelli, Giovanni, and Rosalia Fanelli. *Il tessuto art déco e anni trenta: disegno, moda, architettura.* Florence: Cantini, 1986.

1789 SCHIDIO, JOHANNA
  Austrian textile designer who exhibited in the 1960s.

Other Sources

Jarry, Madeleine. *La tapissérie: art du XXème siècle.* Fribourg: Office du Livre, 1974.

1790 SCHIELE, MOIK (1938–)
  Swiss designer of textiles.

Exhibitions

Bourquin-Walford, Cyril, Marie-Lise Disch-Brack, and Claude Frossard, eds. *Tapisséries Suisses: Artistes d'Aujourd'hui.* Lausanne: Genoud, 1977.

1791 SCHOLTEN-VAN DE RIVIÈRE, DESIRÉE (Alt. SCHOLTEN; VAN DE RIVIÈRE) (1920–)
Dutch textile designer.

Exhibitions

Moderne Hollandsk Tekstilkunst og Glas. Copenhagen: Dansk Kunst-industrimuseum, 1979.
Fibres Art '85. Paris: Musée des Arts Décoratifs, 1985.

Other Sources

Jarry, Madeleine. *La tapissérie: art du XXème siècle.* Fribourg: Office du Livre, 1974.

1792 SCHREYER, MARGARETE (c. 1904–?)
German textile designer.

Other Sources

Gunta Stölzl: Weberei am Bauhaus und aus eigener Werkstatt. Berlin: Bauhaus Archiv in association with Kupfergraben Verlag, 1987. Contains individual bibliographies.

1793 SEIDL-REITER, EDDA
Austrian textile designer who exhibited in the 1960s.

Other Sources

Jarry, Madeleine. *La tapissérie: art du XXème siècle.* Fribourg: Office du Livre, 1974.

1794 SHARIFI, PURY (1952–)
Textile designer who works in England and uses subtly coloured textured yarns which may be woven or knitted into garments.

Other Sources

Sutton, Ann. *British Craft Textiles.* London: Collins, 1985.

1795 SHORT, EIRIAN (1924–)
Welsh textile designer who works in embroidery.

Other Sources

Sutton, Ann. *British Craft Textiles.* London: Collins, 1985.

1796 SICHER, ANNE
French-born textile painter who has worked in England since 1973.

Other Sources

Sutton, Ann. *British Craft Textiles.* London: Collins, 1985.

1797 SIEGFRIED, LISELOTTE. (1935–)
Swiss designer of textiles.

Exhibitions

Bourquin-Walford, Cyril, Marie-Lise Disch-Brack, and Claude Frossard, eds. *Tapisséries Suisses: Artistes d'Aujourd'hui.* Lausanne: Genoud, 1977.

1798 SIENKIEWICZ, DANUTA (1923–)
Polish textile designer.

Exhibitions

Kondratiuk, Krystyna. *Les tissus polonais artistiques contemporains.* Translated into French by Gérard Conio. Lodz: Musée de l'Histoire des Textiles, 1965. Contains a short biography and list of exhibitions for each exhibitor. *Contemporary Polish Weavers.* Edinburgh: Weavers' Workshop Gallery, 1972.
Kondratiuk, Krystyna. *L'Art de tissu en Pologne de 1962 à 1972.* Paris: Manufacture Nationale des Gobelins, 1972.

1799 SIGSGÅRD, DORTHE (1943–)
Danish textile designer who specialises in tapestry.

Exhibitions

Vaev + Raku. Copenhagen: Dansk Kunstindustrimuseet, 1981.

1800 SIMBERG-EHRSTRÖM, UHRA-BEATA (1914–)
Finnish textile designer who produces tapestries and ryijy rugs where colour is the main focus of the work.

Exhibitions

Tapisséries Finlandaises. Paris: Musée d'Art Moderne de la Ville de Paris, 1972.

Other Sources

Louhio, Anja. *Taideryijyjä. Modern Finnish rugs.* Helsinki: Julkaisija Editors Suomalaisen Kirjallisuuden Kirjapaino Oyskk Ltd., 1975. Many examples by this designer are included as she is classed by the author as one of the outstanding exponents of this form of art/design.
Mäki, Oili. *Taide ja Työ: Finnish Designers of Today.* Helsinki: Werner Söderström Osakeyhtiö, 1954. Gives an outline biography.

1801 SIMEON, MARGARET (c. 1903–?)
    English textile designer.

Exhibitions

Thirties: British Art and Design before the War. London: Hayward Gallery, 1979.
    Bury, Hester. *A Choice of Design, 1850–1980: Fabrics by Warner and Sons Ltd.* Colchester: Minories Gallery, 1981.

1802 SIODLOWSKA-WISNIEWSKA, ALICE (alt. ALICYA) (1921–)
    Polish textile designer.

Exhibitions

Contemporary Polish Weavers. Edinburgh: Weavers' Workshop Gallery, 1972.

Other Sources

Jarry, Madeleine. *La tapissérie: art du XXème siècle.* Fribourg: Office du Livre, 1974.

1803 SITTER-LIVER, BEATRIX (1938–)
    Swiss textile designer.

Exhibitions

Bourquin-Walford, Cyril, Marie-Lise Disch-Brack, and Claude Frossard, eds. *Tapisséries Suisses: Artistes d'Aujourd'hui.* Lausanne: Genoud, 1977.

Other Sources

Jarry, Madeleine. *La tapissérie: art du XXème siècle.* Fribourg: Office du Livre, 1974.

1804 SKICZMASZEWKA, HELENA
    Polish textile designer.

Exhibitions

Polish Art: Graphic Art, Textiles. London: Victoria and Albert Museum, 1936.

1805 SKOGHOLT, INGUNN (1952–)
    Norwegian-born textile designer who has worked in England since 1977. She produces tapestries in which colour is a primary concern.

Main Sources

Roberts, Francesca Temple. "Unsentimental education." *Crafts* 45 (1980): 34–37.

Exhibitions

Textiles Today: Woven and Embroidered Works Selected by Marianne Straub. Cambridge: Kettle's Yard, 1981.

Other Sources

Sutton, Ann. *British Craft Textiles.* London: Collins, 1985.

1806 SKOGSTER-LEHTINEN, GRETA (1900–)
     Finnish textile designer.

Exhibitions

Tapisséries Finlandaises. Paris: Musée d'Art Moderne de la Ville de Paris, 1972.

Other Sources

Byars, Mel. *The Design Encyclopedia.* London: Lawrence King, 1994.
Mäki, Oili. *Taide ja Työ: Finnish Designers of Today.* Helsinki: Werner Söderström Osakeyhtiö, 1954. Gives an outline biography.

1807 SLEDZIEWSKA, ANNA (1900/5–)
     Polish textile designer.

Exhibitions

Kondratiuk, Krystyna. *Les tissus polonais artistiques contemporains.* Translated into French by Gérard Conio. Lodz: Musée de l'Histoire des Textiles, 1965. Contains a short biography and list of exhibitions for each exhibitor.
Kondratiuk, Krystyna. *L'Art de tissu en Pologne de 1962 à 1972.* Paris: Manufacture Nationale des Gobelins, 1972.
Contemporary Polish Weavers. Edinburgh: Weavers' Workshop Gallery, 1972.

1808 SNELLMAN-HÄNNINEN, AIRI
     Finnish designer of textiles who specialises in producing rugs.

Other Sources

Louhio, Anja. *Taideryijyjä. Modern Finnish rugs.* Helsinki: Julkaisija Editors Suomalaisen Kirjallisuuden Kirjapaino Oyskk Ltd., 1975. Many examples by this designer are included as she is classed by the author as one of the outstanding exponents of this form of art/design.

1809 SNICKARS, SHEILA
  Swedish textile designer active in the 1970s.

Other Sources

Jarry, Madeleine. *La tapissérie: art du XXème siècle.* Fribourg: Office du Livre, 1974.

1810 SOVRÁDI, VALÉRIA (1950–)
  Hungarian textile designer.

Exhibitions

9. Fal-Es Tertextyil Biennale [9th National Textile Biennale]. Szombathely: Savaria Museum, 1984.

1811 STAEHELIN, MARLISE (1927–)
  Swiss textile designer.

Exhibitions

Bourquin-Walford, Cyril, Marie-Lise Disch-Brack, and Claude Frossard, eds. *Tapisséries Suisses: Artistes d'Aujourd'hui.* Lausanne: Genoud, 1977.

Other Sources

Jarry, Madeleine. *La tapissérie: art du XXème siècle.* Fribourg: Office du Livre, 1974.

1812 STARSAKOWNA, NORMA (1945–)
  Textile designer who works in batik, at times on a large scale and at others producing three-dimensional forms.

Other Sources

Sutton, Ann. *British Craft Textiles.* London: Collins, 1985.

1813 STEPHAN, EWA (1943–)
  Polish textile designer.

Exhibitions

Lutteman, Helena. *Polen vaaver fritt. Polish Textile Art.* Stockholm: National Museum, 1970.

1814 STÖLZL, GUNTA (née ADELGUNDE. From 1929 SHARON-STÖLZL; from 1942 STADLER-STÖLZL) (1897–1983)
German textile designer.

Main Sources

Gunta Stölzl: Weberei am Bauhaus und aus eigener Werkstatt. Berlin: Bauhaus Archiv in association with Kupfergraben Verlag, 1987.

Weltge, Sigrid Wortmann. *Bauhaus Textiles: Women Artists and the Weaving Workshop.* London: Thames and Hudson, 1993.

Exhibitions

La Tessitura del Bauhaus, 1919–33, nelle collezioni della Repubblica Democratica Tedesca. Venice: Palazzo Ducale and Cataloghi Marsilio, 1985.

Oedekoven-Gerischer, Angela, et al, eds. *Frauen im Design: Berufsbilder und Lebenswege seit 1900. Women in Design: Careers and Life Histories since 1900.* Stuttgart: Design Center, 1989.

Other Sources

Byars, Mel. *The Design Encyclopedia.* London: Lawrence King, 1994.

Droste, Magdalena. *Bauhaus: 1919–1933.* Berlin: Bauhaus Archiv Museum and Benedict Taschen Verlag GmbH & Co KG, 1990.

Fanelli, Giovanni, and Rosalia Fanelli. *Il tessuto art déco e anni trenta: disegno, moda, architettura.* Florence: Cantini, 1986.

Jarry, Madeleine. *La tapissérie: art du XXème siècle.* Fribourg: Office du Livre, 1974.

1815 STRAUB, MARIANNE (1909–1994)
Swiss-born textile designer who came to England in the early 1930s. She designed fabrics for Helios, Warner & Sons and others; she played an important role in education and was made a Royal Designer for Industry in 1972.

Publications

Handweaving and Cloth Design. London: Pelham Books, 1976.

Textiles Today Selected by Marianne Straub. Cambridge: Kettle's Yard. 1980.

Main Sources

Coleman, Marigold. "A weaver's life." *Crafts* 32 (1978): 39–43. Interview with Straub.

Frost, Abigail. "Marianne Straub by Mary Schoeser." *Crafts* 72 (1985): 40–41.

Harrod, Tanya. "Sources of Inspiration." *Crafts* 96 (1989): 32–33.

Howes, Justin. "Broad Cloth of Life: Marianne Straub." *The Guardian* 22 (November 1994): 17. Obituary.

Exhibitions

Timmers, Margaret. *The Way We Live Now: Designs for Interiors 1950 to the Present Day.* London: Victoria and Albert Museum, 1978.
Thirties: British Art and Design Before the War. London: Hayward Gallery, 1979.
Bury, Hester. *A Choice of Design, 1850–1980: Fabrics by Warner and Sons Ltd.* Colchester: Minories Gallery, 1981.
Hiesinger, Kathryn, and George Marcus III, eds. *Design since 1945.* Philadelphia: Philadelphia Museum of Art, 1983.
Hogben, C. *British Art and Design 1900–1960: A Collection in the Making.* Victoria and Albert Museum, London, 1983.
Schoeser, Mary. *Marianne Straub R.D.I.* London 1985.
Eidelberg, Martin, ed. *Design 1935–1965: What Modern Was.* New York: Abrams in association with the Musée des Arts Décoratifs, Montreal, 1991.

Other Sources

Byars, Mel. *The Design Encyclopedia.* London: Lawrence King, 1994.
Sutton, Ann. *British Craft Textiles.* London: Collins, 1985.

1816 STRYJENSKA, ZOFIA
Polish designer of textiles who tried to revive tapestry in Poland after World War I.

Other Sources

Jarry, Madeleine. *La tapissérie: art du XXème siècle.* Fribourg: Office du Livre, 1974.

1817 SUNDBYE, KARIN
Norwegian textile designer.

Other Sources

Jarry, Madeleine. *La tapissérie: art du XXème siècle.* Fribourg: Office du Livre, 1974.

1818 SUTTON, ANN (c. 1933–)
English textile designer and writer.

Publications

Tablet Weaving. London: Batsford, 1973.
"Eight International Tapestry Biennale, Lausanne." *Crafts* 28 (1977): 49–50.

"Weaving for Fun and Profit." *Crafts* 35 (1978): 38–43.
The Craft of the Weaver. London: BBC Publications, 1980.
The Structure of Weaving. London: Hutchinson, 1982.
Tartans. London: Bellew, 1984.
Colour and Weave. London: Bellew, 1984.
British Craft Textiles. London: Collins, 1985.
"Who's afraid of computers?" *Crafts* 85 (1987): 14–15.

Main Sources

Morgan, Fay, and Roger Oates. "Ann Sutton." *Crafts* 24 (1977): 46.

Other Sources

Sutton, Ann. *British Craft Textiles.* London: Collins, 1985.

1819 SVENSSON, INEX GUDRUN LINNEA (1932–)
      Swedish designer of textiles and ceramics.

Exhibitions

McFadden, David. *Scandinavian Modern Design, 1880–1980.* New York: Harry Abrams and the Cooper-Hewitt Museum, 1982.

Other Sources

Martin, Edna, and Beata Sydhoff. *Svensk textilkonst. Swedish Textile Art.* Stockholm: Liber Forlag, 1980.
      Naylor, Colin, ed. *Contemporary Designers.* 2nd edition. Chicago and London: St. James Press, 1990. Contains a bibliography.

1820 SZABÓ, MARGIT E. (1945–)
      Hungarian designer of textiles.

Exhibitions

Szot Ösztöndíjasok Kiállitása. Budapest: Magyar Nemezeti Galéria, 1986.

1821 SZABÓ, VERENA
      Hungarian designer of textiles.

Exhibitions

Moderne Ungarische Textilkunst und Keramik aus der Sammlung des Savaria Museum, Szombathely. Linz: Stadtmuseum, 1977.

1822 SZÉKELYI, KATI (1952–)
      Hungarian textile designer.

Exhibitions

9. Fal-Es Tertextyil Biennale [9th National Textile Biennale]. Szombathely: Savaria Museum, 1984.

1823 SZENES, ZSUZSA (1931–)
Hungarian textile designer.

Exhibitions

Moderne Ungarische Textilkunst und Keramik aus der Sammlung des Savaria Museum, Szombathely. Linz: Stadtmuseum, 1977.
9.Fal-Es Tertextyil Biennale [9th National Textile Biennale]. Szombathely: Savaria Museum, 1984.
Fibres Art '85. Paris: Musée des Arts Décoratifs, 1985.

1824 SZILVITZKY, MARGIT
Hungarian designer of textiles.

Exhibitions

Moderne Ungarische Textilkunst und Keramik aus der Sammlung des Savaria Museum, Szombathely. Linz: Stadtmuseum, 1977.
Fibres Art '85. Paris: Musée des Arts Décoratifs, 1985.

1825 SZYMANSKA-PLESKOWSKA, ROMANA (1934–)
Polish textile designer.

Exhibitions

Contemporary Polish Weavers. Edinburgh: Weavers' Workshop Gallery, 1972.

1826 TAIPALE, MARTTA (1893–after 1954)
Finnish textile designer.

Other Sources

Mäki, Oili. *Taide ja Työ: Finnish Designers of Today.* Helsinki: Werner Söderström Osakeyhtiö, 1954. Gives an outline biography.

1827 TEINITSEROVA, MARIE (1879–1960)
Czech textile designer.

Other Sources

Byars, Mel. *The Design Encyclopedia.* London: Lawrence King, 1994.

1828 THOMMESEN, ANNA (1908–)
Danish textile designer specialising in weaving.

Other Sources

Salicath, Bent, and Arne Karlsen, eds. *Modern Danish Textiles.* Copenhagen: Danish Society of Arts and Crafts and Industrial Design, 1959.

1829 TILLERS, SONJA
Austrian textile designer.

Other Sources

Jarry, Madeleine. *La tapissérie: art du XXème siècle.* Fribourg: Office du Livre, 1974.

1830 TORMA, ANNA (1953–)
Hungarian textile designer.

Exhibitions

9. Fal-Es Tertextyil Biennale [9th National Textile Biennale]. Szombathely: Savaria Museum, 1984.

1831 TOW, ENG (c. 1950–)
Textile print designer who turned to making reliefs in textiles which are then coloured by paint or embroidery.

Other Sources

Sutton, Ann. *British Craft Textiles.* London: Collins, 1985.

1832 TOWNLEY, MARJORIE BERTHA (née TEMPLER) (1898–1993)
English painter and textile designer.

Publications

Townley, Marjorie, and Frank Scarlett. *Arts décoratifs 1925—a Personal Recollection of the Paris Exhibition*, 1975.

Main Sources

Heaword, R. "Marjorie Townley." *The Independent* 20 (February 1993): 32. Obituary.

1833 TRILLER, MARIA
Swedish designer of textiles.

Other Sources

Martin, Edna, and Beata Sydhoff. *Svensk textilkonst. Swedish Textile Art.* Stockholm: Liber Forlag, 1980.

Talley, Charles. *Contemporary Textile Art: Scandinavia.* Stockholm: Carmina, 1982.

1834 TROCK, PAULA (1889–1979)
Danish textile designer specialising in weaving.

Exhibitions

Hiesinger, Kathryn, and George Marcus III, eds. *Design since 1945.* Philadelphia: Philadelphia Museum of Art, 1983.

Other Sources

Byars, Mel. *The Design Encyclopedia.* London: Lawrence King, 1994.
Salicath, Bent, and Arne Karlsen, eds. *Modern Danish Textiles.* Copenhagen: Danish Society of Arts and Crafts and Industrial Design, 1959.

1835 TUSCHNEROVA, INEZ (1932–)
Czech designer of textiles.

Exhibitions

Inez Tuschnerová: netkany textil v architekture [Unwoven textiles in architecture]. Brno: Moravská Galérie, 1975, n.p., illus. Text in Czech with a supplementary pamphlet giving translations of the text and biographical information in Russian, English and German.

1836 TWOREK-PIERZGALSKA, JANINA (1933–)
Polish textile designer.

Exhibitions

Lutteman, Helena. *Polen vaaver fritt. Polish Textile Art.* Stockholm: National Museum, 1970.
Contemporary Polish Weavers. Edinburgh: Weavers' Workshop Gallery, 1972.
Kondratiuk, Krystyna. *L'Art de tissu en Pologne de 1962 à 1972.* Paris: Manufacture Nationale des Gobelins, 1972.

1837 UNGER ELSE (Alt. HOLZINGER) (1873–c. 1930)
Austrian designer of furniture, metalwork, textiles, bookbindings and other decorative items.

See Interior Design section.

1838 UNSELD, VRONY (1927–)
Swiss designer of textiles.

Exhibitions

Bourquin-Walford, Cyril, Marie-Lise Disch-Brack, and Claude Frossard, eds. *Tapisséries Suisses: Artistes d'Aujourd'hui.* Lausanne: Genoud, 1977.

1839 URBANOWICZ-KROWACKA, ANNA (1938–)
   Polish textile designer.

Exhibitions

Contemporary Polish Weavers. Edinburgh: Weavers' Workshop Gallery, 1972.
   Kondratiuk, Krystyna. *L'Art de tissu en Pologne de 1962 à 1972.* Paris: Manufacture Nationale des Gobelins, 1972.

1840 VAHLE, INGE
   German textile designer.

Other Sources

Jarry, Madeleine. *La tapissérie: art du XXème siècle.* Fribourg: Office du Livre, 1974.

1841 VALENTIN, RUTH (Alt. VALLENTIN; also CITROEN, CIDOR) (1906–?)
   German textile designer.

Other Sources

Fanelli, Giovanni, and Rosalia Fanelli. *Il tessuto art déco e anni trenta: disegno, moda, architettura.* Florence: Cantini, 1986.
   Gunta Stölzl: Weberei am Bauhaus und aus eigener Werkstatt. Berlin: Bauhaus Archiv in association with Kupfergraben Verlag, 1987. Contains individual bibliographies.
   Weltge, Sigrid Wortmann. *Bauhaus Textiles: Women Artists and the Weaving Workshop.* London: Thames and Hudson, 1993.

1842 VAN DER GRACHT, GISELE
   Dutch textile designer.

Other Sources

Jarry, Madeleine. *La tapissérie: art du XXème siècle.* Fribourg: Office du Livre, 1974.

1843 VAN DER MIJLL DEKKER, KITTY (Alt. FISCHER) (1908–?)
   Dutch textile designer.

Other Sources

Gunta Stölzl: Weberei am Bauhaus und aus eigener Werkstatt. Berlin: Bauhaus Archiv in association with Kupfergraben Verlag, 1987. Contains individual bibliographies.

Weltge, Sigrid Wortmann. *Bauhaus Textiles: Women Artists and the Weaving Workshop.* London: Thames and Hudson, 1993.

1844 VAN EYCK, RIA (1938–)
Dutch textile designer.

Exhibitions

Moderne Hollandsk Tekstilkunst og Glas. Copenhagen: Dansk Kunstindustrimuseum, 1979.

Other Sources

Jarry, Madeleine. *La tapissérie: art du XXème siècle.* Fribourg: Office du Livre, 1974.

1845 VAN OELE VAN GORP, MARIE
Dutch textile designer.

Other Sources

Jarry, Madeleine. *La tapissérie: art du XXème siècle.* Fribourg: Office du Livre, 1974.

1846 VÁRAI, ILONA (1923–)
Hungarian textile designer.

Exhibitions

9. Fal-Es Tertextyil Biennale [9th National Textile Biennale]. Szombathely: Savaria Museum, 1984.

1847 VEHMANEN-TENNBERG, LEA
Finnish textile designer specialising in tapestry.

Other Sources

Mäki, Oili. *Taide ja Työ: Finnish Designers of Today.* Helsinki: Werner Söderström Osakeyhtiö, 1954. Gives an outline biography.

1848 VERSCHUURE, ANNA (1935–1980)
Dutch textile designer.

Exhibitions

Fibres Art '85. Paris: Musée des Arts Décoratifs, 1985.

1849 VESIMAA, EILA-ANNIKI
Finnish textile designer who produced tapestries.

Other Sources

Mäki, Oili. *Taide ja Työ: Finnish Designers of Today.* Helsinki: Werner Söderström Osakeyhtiö, 1954. Gives an outline biography.

1850 VIDUKA, VERA (1916–)
Latvian textile designer whose works contain mostly geometrical areas of flat colour in thick textures.

Other Sources

Kalniete, Sandra. *Latvju tekstilmāksla* [Latvian textile art]. Riga: Liesma, 1989.

1851 VĪGNERE, EDITE (1939–)
Latvian textile designer whose work ranges from tapestry to sculptural formations in threads.

Other Sources

Kalniete, Sandra. *Latvju tekstilmāksla* [Latvian textile art]. Riga: Liesma, 1989.

1852 VIRGILS, KATHERINE (1954–)
American-born textile artist/designer who works in England at the boundaries of painting and textiles. She produces works which resemble paintings in format but which are made up from layers, often of silk and paper, which are worked into patinated surfaces.

Other Sources

Sutton, Ann. *British Craft Textiles.* London: Collins, 1985.

1853 VOGEL, GUDRUN
Austrian textile designer.

Other Sources

Jarry, Madeleine. *La tapissérie: art du XXème siècle.* Fribourg: Office du Livre, 1974.

1854 VOIRET, VERENA (1939–)
    Swiss designer of textiles.

Exhibitions

Bourquin-Walford, Cyril, Marie-Lise Disch-Brack, and Claude Frossard, eds. *Tapisséries Suisses: Artistes d'Aujourd'hui.* Lausanne: Genoud, 1977.

1855 VOÎTA (née DENISE VOÎTA) (1928–)
    Swiss textile designer, painter and engraver.

Exhibitions

Bourquin-Walford, Cyril, Marie-Lise Disch-Brack, and Claude Frossard, eds. *Tapisséries Suisses: Artistes d'Aujourd'hui.* Lausanne: Genoud, 1977.

Other Sources

Jarry, Madeleine. *La tapissérie: art du XXème siècle.* Fribourg: Office du Livre, 1974.

1856 VON BRAUCHITSCH, MARGARETHA
    German designer of textiles.

Exhibitions

Grönwoldt, Ruth, and Sabine Hesse. *Art Nouveau: Textil: Dekor um 1900.* Stuttgart: Wurtemburgisches Landesmuseum, 1980.
Hiesinger, Kathryn, ed. *Art Nouveau in Munich: Masters of Jugenstil from the Stadtmuseum, Munich and Other Collections.* Munich Prestel in association with the Philadelphia Museum of Art, 1988. Von Brauchitsch is one of only two women included.

Other Sources

Byars, Mel. *The Design Encyclopedia.* London: Lawrence King, 1994.
Fanelli, Giovanni, and Rosalia Fanelli. *Il tessuto Art Nouveau: disegno, moda, architettura.* Florence: Cantini, 1986.

1857 WALDMANN-HEBEISEN, BARBARA (1947–)
    Swiss designer of textiles.

Exhibitions

Bourquin-Walford, Cyril, Marie-Lise Disch-Brack, and Claude Frossard, eds. *Tapisséries Suisses: Artistes d'Aujourd'hui.* Lausanne: Genoud, 1977.

1858 WALKER, AUDREY (1928–)
    English textile designer and educator.

Publications

"Embroidered and painted wall panels and quilts by Kate Hobson." *Crafts* 46 (1980): 55.

Other Sources

Sutton, Ann. *British Craft Textiles.* London: Collins, 1985.

1859 WALLER, IRENE
   English textile designer.

Publications

"Lausanne Biennale." *Crafts* 16 (1975): Review of the 7th Tapestry Biennale which includes Abakanowicz and Buic.
"Kathleen McFarlane." *Crafts* 20 (1976): 48–49.
"Textiles and Jewellery." *Crafts* 25 (1977): 49. Review of exhibition in which the majority of exhibitors are women.

1860 WARSINSKI, BRIT FUGLEVAAG
   Norwegian textile designer.

Other Sources

Jarry, Madeleine. *La tapissérie: art du XXème siècle.* Fribourg: Office du Livre, 1974.

1861 WEDEKIND, HERTA OTTOLENCHI
   Italian sculptor and, later, designer of textiles.

Other Sources

Fanelli, Giovanni, and Rosalia Fanelli. *Il tessuto art déco e anni trenta: disegno, moda, architettura.* Florence: Cantini, 1986.

1862 WEFRING, TUSTA (1925–)
   Danish textile designer specialising in printed textiles.

Other Sources

Salicath, Bent, and Arne Karlsen, eds. *Modern Danish Textiles.* Copenhagen: Danish Society of Arts and Crafts and Industrial Design, 1959.

1863 WEGERIF-GRAVENSTEIN, AGATHA
   Dutch designer of textiles, specialising in batik, who exhibited at the Universal Exposition in Paris in 1900 and at Turin in 1902.

Other Sources

Fanelli, Giovanni, and Rosalia Fanelli. *Il tessuto Art Nouveau: disegno, moda, architettura.* Florence: Cantini, 1986.

1864 WIERUSZ-KOWALSKI, TAPTA
    Polish-born textile designer who works in Belgium.

Other Sources

Jarry, Madeleine. *La tapissérie: art du XXème siècle.* Fribourg: Office du Livre, 1974.

1865 WILLERS, MARGARETE (1883–1977)
    German textile designer.

Other Sources

Byars, Mel. *The Design Encyclopedia.* London: Lawrence King, 1994.
Gunta Stölzl: Weberei am Bauhaus und aus eigener Werkstatt. Berlin: Bauhaus Archiv in association with Kupfergraben Verlag, 1987. Contains individual bibliographies.
Weltge, Sigrid Wortmann. *Bauhaus Textiles: Women Artists and the Weaving Workshop.* London: Thames and Hudson, 1993.

1866 WOJTYNA-DROUET, KRYSTYNA (1926–)
    Polish designer of textiles.

Exhibitions

Kondratiuk, Krystyna. *Les tissus polonais artistiques contemporains.* Translated into French by Gérard Conio. Łodz: Musée de l'Histoire des Textiles, 1965. Contains a short biography and list of exhibitions for each exhibitor.

1867 WRIGHT, ELLEN MARY (active from c. 1890)
    English designer of textiles, particularly embroidery.

Other Sources

Parry, Linda. *Textiles of the Arts and Crafts Movement.* London: Thames and Hudson, 1988.

1868 ZOVETTI, AMINTA
    Italian designer of textiles.

Other Sources

Fanelli, Giovanni, and Rosalia Fanelli. *Il tessuto art déco e anni trenta: disegno, moda, architettura.* Florence: Cantini, 1986.

1869 ZWANN, FREP
    Dutch textile designer.

Exhibitions

Fibres Art '85. Paris: Musée des Arts Décoratifs, 1985.
La Matière Pensée: art textile. Le Havre: Musée des Beaux-Arts, 1986.